Secondary
School
Administration

SECONDARY SCHOOL ADMINISTRATION

JAMES J. JONES
Professor and Chairman,
Department of Educational Administration
Temple University

C. JACKSON SALISBURY
Professor of Educational Administration and
Director, Educational Service Bureau
Temple University

RALPH L. SPENCER
Associate Professor of Educational Administration
Associate Dean of the Graduate School
Temple University

McGRAW–HILL BOOK COMPANY
New York   St. Louis   San Francisco
Toronto   London   Sydney

PREFACE

The basic purpose of this book is to provide an overview of the field of secondary school administration. It is intended to fill the gap between those textbooks which represent the practical handbook approach and ones which present a theoretical approach. This book emphasizes both theory and practice. Its central focus is for graduate students who are beginning the study of administration and who intend to specialize in secondary school administration. It is intended also to be useful to practicing principals who want to study their jobs and to attempt professional improvement.

There are several recurring themes woven throughout the book. One of the most significant is the theme of adaptability. This idea portrays rather vividly that one of the dominant facts of modern life is that today's (and tomorrow's) students must be taught to live in a world characterized by change. This book emphasizes change in its approach to the educational program and also in its treatment of the idea of the continually adjusting secondary school.

A second recurring theme is the primacy of the instructional program in relation to administration. The reader is constantly reminded that administration is an important process in which the measure of success is always indicated by its contribution to the basic purpose of schools, that is, the teaching–learning process. All school administration is justified and judged by this criterion.

A third significant theme is the attention devoted to the actual performance of the secondary administrator. Leadership is treated as furnishing conceptual tools for better role performance. Throughout the book it is recognized that the principal works through others and becomes effective to the extent that he organizes and inspires others to perform their respective roles better. The principal is envisioned as the one who knows about all phases of administering the school and establishes procedures and a working environment that make it possible for others to carry out the work of the school.

Likewise, it is recognized that most secondary schools are members of an entire school district and therefore that the principal is a member of a larger administrative team.

A special feature of the book is its comprehensiveness and emphasis on the importance of the principal's position. Each chapter presents two different classes of information. First, each presents purposes, backgrounds, philosophy, theory, and research appropriate to that topic. Second, each chapter provides recommended procedures drawn from the theories and research presented. The chapters provide a wealth of conceptual material and follow with supporting recommended practices.

The authors are indebted to their colleagues, both past and present, as well as to the many graduate students who have assisted them.

To our wives, Doris, Helen, and Marion, and our children we extend our grateful thanks for their patience, interest, and understanding.

Finally, we offer a special thanks to Mrs. Clarice Smith for typing the manuscript.

James J. Jones
C. Jackson Salisbury
Ralph L. Spencer

CONTENTS

SECTION II

LEADERSHIP FOR SECONDARY SCHOOLS

SEC-TION 1

the setting for administering schools

INTRODUCTION   There is great need today—in the face of rapid demographic, sociological, and technological change—for school administrators who are equipped to face new problems. It is not possible today to give all the answers to all of tomorrow's problems. But it is possible to assist people to develop competency in applying theory, research, and experimental methods to the school and community setting. Persons with the proper professional training and with the requisite personal qualifications can guide, tutor, lead, manage, and maneuver the human, physical, and social resources of the community toward the solution of problems. Of importance in reaching solutions is the *manner* in which they are reached. The leaders of the educational enterprise in the community must ensure that planning, using democratic processes, will:

1. Lead to solution of community problems
2. Facilitate the establishment of a community and school environment dedicated to maximum human development
3. Elicit citizen participation and contribution in school and community affairs
4. Maximize interpersonal and intra-personal relationships [1]

A recent yearbook of the American Association of School Administrators points out that typical problems and issues confronting schools and school systems make two things clear: (1) Schools and school administrators must operate in a community setting, and (2) The problems and issues involved arise from changes in the social structure which are recent or of past origin.[2]

It would be desirable if every citizen were cognizant of the total cultural heritage, but it is unlikely that this can ever be the case. However, it is essential that those educators who will teach, supervise, and administer in our schools have an understanding of our society and of the total culture in which we are both inheritors and builders.[3] To be able to assess the need for education in our present society, we must also hold an accurate concept of the American economic and governmental systems and of the place of the individual under our democratic form of government.

The educator must know the purposes for which society has created its institutions, so that the decisions which he is called upon to make regarding education are made within a realistic framework.

SOCIETY AND CULTURE

The sociologist defines *society* as a group of people who hold common ways of doing, valuing, believing, etc., and who think of themselves as members of a distinct group. The mores of a social group are said to make up its *culture*. Culture includes all "that complex whole which includes knowledge, beliefs, art, morals, laws, custom and other capabilities acquired by man as a member of society." [4] Culture can be said to consist of the communicative arts, the industrial arts, the social arts, the aesthetic arts, and the intellectual arts, which man has cherished and transmitted to his inheritors.[5] The relationship of these arts to each other and to society will vary from time to time within one society and from

[1] Community Development Institute, Southern Illinois University Brochure, Carbondale, Ill., 1961, 2 pp.
[2] *Educational Administration in a Changing Community*, Thirty-Seventh Yearbook, The American Association of School Administrators, Washington, D.C., 1959, p. 54.
[3] Ralph L. Pounds and James R. Bryner, *The School in American Society*, The Macmillan Company, New York, 1959, p. 4.
[4] Edward Tylor, *Primitive Culture*, 7th ed., Brentano, 1924, as quoted in Harry M. Johnson, *Sociology: A Systematic Introduction*, Harcourt, Brace & World, Inc., New York, 1960.
[5] Arthur B. Moehlman, *School Administration*, Houghton Mifflin Company, Boston, 1951, p. 4.

one society to another. The varied ways in which they are related give differing cultural patterns.

The longer man remains on this earth, the more he inherits from other times and other societies. Transportation and communications improvements and technological advancements are themselves cultural additions. However, they also bring in items from hitherto remote locations of other societies to be added to man's total cultural stockpile. Much tends to be added to the stockpile by invention and discovery. Man has, therefore, created agencies for the operation and maintenance of the cultural patterns—institutions.

Institutions

Institutions provide generally accepted ways of achieving important social goals. The three major institutions which have evolved, according to Kirkpatrick, take the forms of the family, religion, and government.[6]

The family institution consists of the provisions in a particular culture for "sex expression, reproduction, child rearing, and the inter-relationships of age, sex, and kinship groups."[7]

Moehlman and Van Zwoll summarize the development of religious forms in the following manner:

Man's innate desire to solve the riddles of natural phenomena and to discover his own place in the universe has led to the growth of reverence, fear, magic, mysticism, symbolism, and a ritualism which readily lends itself to the substitution of form for substance. These results of man's attempts to understand the universe are reflected in part in the magic and religion of the simply organized society and in the sciences and the church of the more highly organized and complex society.[8]

An *institution* as defined by Everett Cherrington Hughes is "one of those features of social life which outlast biological generations or survive drastic changes that might have been expected to bring them to an end."[9] Thus man transmits to future generations his acquired ways of behaving and his knowledge about how the institution grew up, and justifies them to posterity. Society has developed many institutions besides those for education purposes. Herbert Spencer classified social institutions as domestic, ceremonial, political, ecclesiastical, professional, and industrial. Spencer, writing at the turn of the twentieth century, did not specifically

[6] Clifford Kirkpatrick, *The Family as Process and Institution*, The Ronald Press Company, New York, p. 13.

[7] *Ibid.*, pp. 13–14.

[8] Arthur B. Moehlman and James A. Van Zwoll, *School Public Relations*, Appleton-Century-Crofts, Inc., New York, 1957, p. 5.

[9] Everett Cherrington Hughes, "Institutions Defined," in Alfred M. Lee (ed.), *Principles of Sociology*, College Outline Series, Barnes & Noble, Inc., New York, p. 225.

name education. However, current sociologists have added social welfare and educational institutions to Spencer's list.

Government was devised to provide security for each individual as a member of the group. Organization for larger group control and protection has developed into the various governmental forms found today. To gain group security, the individual must give up a degree of his individual freedom. Governments differ in the degree of sacrifice of freedom demanded as the price of security, in the economic system which regulates the production and distribution of wealth, and in the purpose for the existence of that system of government. Basically speaking, two divergent views exist.

1. The *totalitarian* concept holds that the state (national state) is supreme and that the individual exists only to perpetuate the state. The state is an end in itself. Soviet Russia is the prime example.

2. The *democratic* concept is that each individual contributes to the sovereignty of the government through voluntary association. Government exists only to serve the people individually and collectively. By serving the individual, society is also served and the nation strengthened. The United States government is the prime example.

In a democracy man has given up his individual freedom to a lesser degree. He has retained the right to differ with his government and to try by peaceful and legal means to bring public policies more in line with his own beliefs. People in a democracy possess the power to change or to eliminate entirely their social institutions.[10]

It is on education as an institution and on its relationships with other social institutions and with the cultural patterns, that attention is now directed.

[10] Moehlman and Van Zwoll, *op. cit.*, p. 23.

CHAPTER 1

THE SOCIAL AND CULTURAL SETTING FOR AMERICAN SECONDARY SCHOOLS

THE NEED FOR EDUCATION

Basically speaking, every society must provide for the education of its members. This is true in a simple society as well as in the more complex, interdependent societies. It is as true for the totalitarian state as for the democratic or pluralistic society.

In a simple, less interdependent society, the school is perhaps the total community, and, by like reasoning, the community is the school. The young are apprenticed to the main occupation of the community—obtaining food to stay alive. So the young boys work with their fathers in the hunting, fishing, gathering, or farming necessary to gain their livelihood. The girls work with the women gathering nuts, fruits, herbs, etc., and learning how to make pottery, tan hides, sew, weave, cook, bake, tend the young, and care for the sick and the aged. This is actual life in the community, and the young are a real part of it. The only dropouts from this schooling are given burial.

As better control of the food supply becomes possible, more time can be given to the development of specialized crafts and skills. In time, the specialized craft artisans may no longer engage in the actual food-securing

5

activities of the community. The artisans supply the arrows, tools, pottery, etc., for the community in return for food raised and even prepared by others. Thus, as the interdependence of society becomes greater and more complex, it is no longer possible for everybody to do everything connected with the economy of the community. The children of those who specialize in certain crafts can no longer learn certain skills from their parents, or perhaps even from their entire family. Because society to survive must teach its young how to secure their food, the education of the children of the artisans may be entrusted to others. The artisans, in turn, may teach the children of others the skills of their crafts. Thus, a new specialization develops—that of the community teachers.

With the development of symbolization and the ability to record knowledge, the need for the new specialization grows. As simple crafts give way to industry and as more people earn their livelihood in newer and different pursuits removed from the home, a specialized institution, the school, is needed to train the young. The home or the entire community is no longer the school. The school has become a formalized institution of society. Schools may become so formalized that they grow aloof from the community and its problems, and pupils, seeing no connection between their life needs and school offerings, may drop out of school.

Continuity of Society

Man perpetuates the human race by biological reproduction and bequeaths to his children their inherited physical characteristics. The arrangements for biological continuity were provided by nature, but man himself must make the arrangements for transmitting the cultural patterns from generation to generation. "This transmission of the cultural heritage, or social reproduction, has been called education." [1] Education as an institution of society therefore becomes a part of the culture which it is called upon to transmit.

In order to fulfill its task of transmitting man's culture. education must become custodian of the cultural heritage. That which is to be transmitted must be preserved and guarded so that it will be available when the time comes for transmission. Because the culture is continually changing, and changing at a rapid rate for the complex technological society, education must communicate these cultural changes throughout the society. Opinions may differ as to the extent to which education should become a means for striving to improve the culture. However, there seems to be general agreement that in a democracy education has certain responsibilities to help the individual adjust to his changing culture and

---

[1] Arthur B. Moehlman, *School Administration*, Houghton Mifflin Company, Boston, 1951, p. 3.

grow to the extent of his abilities. Education has become an arm of the government to help maximize opportunities for the individual and to perform other social tasks.

Society then has a need for education to perform certain functions—preservation or conservation of the cultural heritage, transmission of the culture, and adjustment and growth of the individual so that he can keep abreast of cultural change.

Demands of the Times

This description of the need for education is made at a critical period in the history of our nation and the world. Conflict, interpersonal and intrapersonal as well as international, is ever with us during these times. Another characteristic of this period is change. Our culture has undergone many changes in the last 50 years. The most significant factor about these cultural changes in the past 20 years has been the increasing rate of their occurrence.

Technological advancement alone has given us, in nuclear energy, a new source of power which could lead either to man's deliverance or to his destruction. Many people now earn their living in a different section of the country from where they were born and reared, and at jobs which did not exist as little as 25 years ago. It is possible that 75 percent of the industrial work force 10 years from now will be making products not yet invented or discovered.

Man has entered space, orbited the earth, performed increasingly complex missions, and returned safely. His space vehicles, yet unmanned, have crashed on or have passed close to other planets. Preparations are under way to place a man on the moon by 1970.

Transportation and communication in today's world are swift and convenient, so that people and news of events travel freely. What happens in one corner of the earth may have instant effect on another section of the world half a globe away.[2] The problems which we face are outlined in more detail in the following section.

Man has been confronted basically with three choices in his struggle for survival. He could adjust to his environment, attempt to adjust the environment to himself, or perish. Because the choices are not mutually exclusive, man as an individual has done all three at some time. Mankind has continued to survive even though certain societies and their civilizations have perished. However, as man continues to make strides to adjust his environment to himself, he creates concomitant demands upon himself to adjust to the new environment.

[2] C. Jackson Salisbury, *Needs for the Improvement of Virginia Education*, Virginia State Chamber of Commerce, Richmond, Va., 1959, p. 12.

SOCIAL FACTORS AFFECTING THE CURRENT SCENE

Population Growth

Man's control of his environment has been increased steadily by advancements in the fields of medicine, health, and food production, as well as in others. The conquering of infectious diseases such as bubonic plague, cholera, smallpox, tuberculosis, venereal diseases, typhus, typhoid, and infantile paralysis, has tended to lengthen the expected life-span of the individual. Medical discoveries of recent years, while not yet conquering all man's afflictions, promise breakthroughs in the areas of heart diseases, cancer, and nervous disorders, to name but a few.

The scourge of disease as an important check on population increase has had an able ally in the shortage of food. However, man's discoveries through the development of better seeds, fertilizers, and agricultural processes have increased the productivity of land. Research into soil conditioners, the conversion of salt water for irrigation, hormone effects on plant growth, and hydroponic farms promise even greater productivity and new sources of food.

The elimination of the effects of disease and famine on population growth has helped cause a population explosion. Another contributing factor to this boom, of course, has been the increased birthrate both in this country and in the world. In the United States today the population is not only growing in numbers, but is changing in composition. There is an increased proportion of the population under fourteen years of age, and another proportional increase in the population segment over sixty-five years of age. The former will probably be a temporary proportional change. The figures in the decade 1957–1967 indicate that there has been a waning in the live birthrate in the United States.

Population Mobility

During the period of World War II and after, the people of the United States moved from one section of the country to another with astonishing rapidity. Figures from the 1960 census show that one out of four persons in the United States was living in a state other than where he had been born. Many of these moved into sections of the country hundreds and even thousands of miles from their birthplaces. This high rate of mobility continues, and little reason exists for expecting it to diminish. Much of this mobility of population is connected with what can be called industrial expansion.[3] Many who moved into areas of industrial concentration tended to come from rural areas. This tendency to move from the rural

---

[3] Ralph L. Pounds and James R. Bryner, *The School in American Society*, The Macmillan Company, New York, 1959, p. 310.

areas to the cities is termed *urbanization*. Whereas in 1800, 95 percent of our people were farmers, in 1965 only 7 percent of the population raised the food and fiber for the rest of the country. According to the 1960 census, about 70 percent of the population in the United States is classified as urban. Thirty-nine of the fifty states had over half of their population living in urban areas. Urbanization is expected to increase to the extent that by the year 2000, 80 percent of the expected 400 million Americans will live in cities. These cities will probably be vast megalopolises or "strip cities" extending hundreds of miles along so-called metropolitan corridors.

Family Life

The complexity of the factors of modern life mentioned above has had a tremendous impact on family life in the United States. While still functioning as the social unit for reproduction and care of the young, the pattern of family life is affected by other cultural changes. The family is not a producing unit in the economy, but rather is a consuming one. The number of activities which were related to producing and which could be shared by family members has thereby been reduced.[4]

The movement of primary family units—parents and young children —to other states often reduces the kinship ties and their corresponding social control. The greater age of senior citizens often brings conflict between generations in a time of smaller dwellings and larger families. The older family members may tend to resist the faster changes, apply standards of values of a previous age to a changing cultural scene, and want to enjoy the pleasures of grandchildren without the corresponding responsibilities.

Some students of family life are most pessimistic about its future in our society. They point to divorce and separation as indications that the family is moving toward virtual disintegration. If, as many psychologists point out, the home is where the child learns the behavior patterns which he will exhibit toward others, family life continues to be of great importance in society.

Fortunately, many other sociologists hold a more optimistic viewpoint regarding the future of the family. Burgess, writing in the late 1940s, stated that the apparent disintegration of the modern family was really the result of a major institution's changing from a form adapted to a stable culture to a form more in keeping with the demands of a rapidly changing culture.[5]

[4] B. Othanel Smith, William O. Stanley, and J. Harlan Shores, *Fundamentals of Curriculum Development*, rev. ed., Harcourt, Brace & World, Inc., New York, 1957, pp. 45–47.
[5] Ernest W. Burgess, "The Family in a Changing Society," *American Journal of Sociology*, vol. 53, pp. 417–422, May, 1948.

Pounds and Bryner agree on the side of optimism:

Such an interpretation is in harmony with the entire tempo of modern American life and education, where adaptability is becoming more essential to success in most fields than is stability. Adaptability as a major personality characteristic of the members of the family may well become the most important single factor in the success of marriage and family life.[6]

Family life is also affected by the number of working wives and mothers. Many women, having finished childbearing by the age of thirty, are seeking gainful employment outside the home. This is being done not only as a means of securing additional income for an increase in the family standard of living, but as a means of finding the emotional self-reassurance of their worth as individuals.

Family life is, of course, affected by the mother's absence from the home. Juvenile delinquency has been partially attributed to this by some.

Community Life

The American community of an earlier age can be characterized as containing inhabitants who were in basic agreement about the values, beliefs, and mores of their society. A knowledge about each other and a closely knit relationship were fostered by kinship and friendship. The effect of local opinions and traditions shaped the behavior of each member. Social control was evident and felt personally by the individual.[7] Family members knew the same people on a face-to-face basis because most of them had lived in the community all their lives. Many were of families that had lived in the community for several generations.

Today, however, the modern city with its size and complexity tends to isolate the family among strangers. There may be very little overlap in the number of acquaintances held in common by family members. The only close friends which the father may have may be found among his business associates. Mother's coterie of friends may not be residents of the immediate neighborhood but may come from different sections surrounding the city whose social, cultural, or religious interests have brought them together. Children of different ages are probably in different schools and have contact with different family groups from their parents or siblings. Thus, the unifying force of the closely knit community, as well as its social control, is lacking in our highly urbanized areas. "With the growth of urbanism, the life of the individual becomes less and less shaped by the total community and more and more molded by his occupation and other specialized activities."[8]

6 Pounds and Bryner, *op. cit.*, p. 202.
7 *Ibid.*, p. 206.
8 Smith, Stanley, and Shores, *op. cit.*, p. 31.

SCIENTIFIC AND TECHNOLOGICAL ADVANCEMENTS

It has been said that science has advanced more in the last 25 years than in all the previous years of man's existence. The discoveries in the realm of pure science have seemed almost fantastic, but the application of scientific findings to new products and processes has had more visible effect on the average citizen. The substitution of atomic power to create electricity, drive ships and submarines, and create radioactive isotopes for various human physical disorders has created new opportunities and challenges.

Entire new industries have been created to market the products derived from electronic, chemical, and mechanical discoveries. Plastic devices have supplanted many commonplace household items which were formerly made of metal and wood and have made possible new techniques and products because of their lightweight strength and nonconductivity.

Power and Transportation

Jet propulsion applied to aircraft has reduced the time of a cross-continental flight to the point that a mother traveling with a small baby is reported to have characterized her jet flight from New York to Los Angeles as "a one-bottle flight." It now may take longer to get from the airport into the city than to make the flight itself.

Rocket power has been applied to experimental aircraft of advanced design to put within reach even more rapid transportation from one spot on the earth to another.

The more dramatic effect of rocket power has been the placing of man-made satellites in orbit around the earth. The Russian *Sputnik* which blasted into orbit in October, 1957, also blasted American complacency and started a race for space. Developments since that time have enabled men to ride these craft into space and return safely to earth. The space rivalry of the U.S.S.R. and the United States has increased in intensity. The variety and range of space missions already accomplished, as well as those proposed, stagger the imagination.

Such awesome power in man's hands can have other uses than the probing of space, however. War between nations using nuclear warheads on ballistic missiles could cause the destruction of civilization as we know it.

Communications

Research projects in space exploration have also contributed to many advancements in communications. The use of transistors instead of tubes, printed circuits instead of complex wiring in radios, computers, and other electronic devices has made it possible to miniaturize the instruments sent into space. These smaller components have made it possible to gain more information for a given payload weight.

One of the many satellites put into orbit from the United States was *Telstar*. The United States government provided the rocketry at cost, and the American Telephone and Telegraph Company provided a communications relay satellite. *Telstar* made it possible to beam television broadcasts between North America and Europe at times when the satellite was in proper position. The placing of a series of these satellites in space has now made it possible to have continuous TV communications between continents.

The mass media of communications themselves have been sophisticated, refined, and extended. Radios, recorders, and television sets have been made smaller, more efficient, and more easily portable.

Television reaches into most United States homes. Color television sets, while still expensive as compared with black-and-white television sets, are becoming more widespread as improved production techniques reduce the cost.

Automation

The use of computers and the electronic control of the flow of components in a manufactured item have revolutionized whole industries. Complex machinery with automated controls has drastically reduced the number of workers needed. A Labor Department official, addressing a national conference on school finance, stated that with automated machinery already installed eight men could make all the light bulbs needed in the United States.

Obviously these eight men must do more than push a broom or lift boxes! As Russell put it in his well-publicized lecture at the National War College, "In American society, a person who has only his energy to sell is coming to have nothing to sell: we cannot use him at all." [9] This points out the need for scientifically and technically educated operators for modern industry.

ECONOMIC FACTORS AFFECTING THE CURRENT AMERICAN SCENE

Interdependence of Society

The economics of present-day industrial production is characterized by specialization. This specialization brings with it conditions in which even large geographic areas are not self-sufficient. Generally speaking, people

[9] James E. Russell, *American Education and the National Interest*, National School Boards Association, Evanston, Ill., April, 1960, p. 7.

in a local area consume only a small part of the goods which they produce. They must exchange these locally produced goods for those of other regions of the country or of the world. Thus, the increasing complexity of the material culture has made man more interdependent than ever before.[10] The exchanging of locally produced goods which may be components of more complex products indicates the need for other specialized activities—communications and transportation.

The advances made in the various scientific and technical fields have made life easier for most Americans. In keeping with a long cherished American ideal, the economy is producing a rising standard of living for all people. Our economy, based on the free enterprise concept, strives to produce goods and services to satisfy consumer demands. As new processes lead to new and better products, they are demonstrated, advertised, and placed on the market. Mass media advertising is a means to educate the consumer to the new choices of products available.

Many laborsaving devices have reduced the work time for the homemaker and have also made the lot of the man of the house less of a chore.

The constant striving to produce better products through research, experimentation, and development is a characteristic of business in our economy. The cost of producing an item is not as vital to business as the degree of consumer satisfaction generated.[11] If the good produced commands healthy consumer demand, the price will tend to take care of itself. This follows the time-honored law of supply and demand.

The time which the average American must work in order to secure the basic necessities has reduced in almost each generation. Put another way, the amount paid to an American for a given unit of output has continued to increase. Thus, there are earnings over and above the amount required to subsist. This margin of earnings over basic need performs more than one function. It enables the consumer to satisfy his want for better things if he chooses, and it contributes to the savings and investment base available for further economic expansion.

New Occupations

In order that business and industry can supply the new goods and services which our technology makes available and which our rising standard of living demands, a properly trained work force is needed.

The new plastics, electronics, and space-related industries have come into prominence just in the last 15 to 25 years. New technical skills are in great demand. It is estimated that approximately 75 percent of the work-

[10] Charles S. Benson, *The Economics of Public Education*, Houghton Mifflin Company, Boston, 1961, p. 216.
[11] Roe L. Johns and Edgar L. Morphet, *Financing the Public Schools*, Prentice-Hall, Inc., Englewood Cliffs, N.J., 1960, p. 94.

ing population in one Connecticut town earns its living at jobs and professions which did not exist 25 years ago. Examination of a standard book of occupational titles supports this estimate.

Displacement of Workers

As has been noted before, the effect of automation and other technological developments has been to reduce the number of men needed to produce even more goods and services. The men displaced by machines will probably find it difficult to find a job of the same kind and at an equal wage, e.g., new sources of power have reduced the need for coal. Those sections of the country formerly devoted to coal mining have become economically depressed. This can take place at a time when other industries are critically short of trained manpower. The coal miners have skills which are obsolescent. "When an industry is completely eliminated, when a new process of making a product is employed, or when engineering achievements replace old machines, the worker who is thereby displaced is called upon to develop new skills if he is to find employment." [12]

In addition to the acquiring of new skills, the displaced worker may be forced to move to another section of the country to find employment. Schools must teach these economic facts of life if our people are to adjust to ever-changing conditions. It has been estimated that our most recent graduates will need to be retrained three or four times during their lifespan if they are to continue to be productive members of society.

CONFLICT: A FACTOR IN MODERN LIFE

In the foregoing section, an attempt was made to identify some of the major areas of cultural change currently affecting the American and world scene. Each change has usually been accompanied or followed by social dislocations or conflict of some kind.

International Tension

After World War II, the victorious Allies established the United Nations organization as a means of preventing future global conflagration and of bettering the lot of human beings the world over. Having created this organization, the major powers separated into two camps: the Western powers of Britain, France, Italy, Canada, the United States, etc., on the one hand, and the Soviet bloc nations headed by Russia, on the other. The formation of a third group, the neutrals or nonaligned powers, has not altered the tension significantly. The zeal of the Communist bloc to foment trouble, unrest, and revolution has kept the world in a turmoil. The cold war has become warm and even hot at times, but so far has been

---

[12] Smith, Stanley, and Shores, *op. cit.*, p. 52.

of a limited nature. The "main eventers" have not yet faced each other in the arena directly. Threats, counterthreats, "brinkmanship," and rocket rattling have been the order of the day. Yet the United Nations remains the hope of the world that peace, law, and progress will eventually win out. In the meantime, the United States and its allies have attempted through regional organizations to pool their economic, military, and political resources to guard against Communist aggression.

The former Russian premier threatened that "we will surpass you" and that "your [American] grandchildren will live under Communism." We must, therefore, make no mistake. There is no doubt that "all Americans must recognize that we are today engaged in a competition for survival imposed upon us by a nation of vast resources, whose leaders, through education offered to people with a boundless zeal for self-improvement, are determined to cast the shadow of Communism over the entire world." [13]

New and Emerging Nations

The newly independent nations which have recently thrown off colonial status are striving for world recognition, opportunity for a better life, and a voice in international affairs.[14] Whether freed peacefully by agreement, world opinion, or through revolutionary means, these new nations are important because many of them have been dumped into nationhood without proper preparation. Other nations have been independent for years but have not made the social, political, and economic advances of the modern industrialized countries. These developing countries also want to achieve full modernization.

Many of these striving nations, whether new or old, have such tremendous problems as:

a dearth of experienced leaders in modern fields of endeavor;
a lack of familiarity with democratic self-government under law;
a social structure which excludes a majority of the people from educational and economic opportunities, land, and home ownership;
economic weaknesses stemming from lack of investment capital and runaway inflation, and over-dependence on one or two export items;
insufficient food supply and inadequate housing, educational, and health programs.[15]

All are being wooed to embrace communism. The Soviet bloc salesmen of slavery and subversion are busy throughout the world.

The United States through its international development and cultural

[13] Commission on Public Education, *Virginia Schools in the Atomic Age*, Commonwealth of Virginia, Department of Purchases and Supply, Richmond, Va., 1960, p. 11.
[14] The Advertising Council, Inc., p. 7.
[15] *Ibid.*, p. 7.

exchange programs, the Peace Corps, and other economic, educational, and military aid missions is trying to help the peoples of the emerging nations to help themselves. We have the better product but we need to do a better job of letting the peoples of the world see what it can do.

Interpersonal Conflict

There have always been groups with conflicting interests in the American culture. There are groups of Americans who differ from each other in the areas of socioeconomic status, race, religion, national origin, and regional background.[16]

Americans like to think that theirs is a classless society, when actually this is a myth. Despite the relative ease of moving from one class to another (vertical mobility), large numbers of Americans suffer discrimination because of the social strata to which they are relegated.[17] The American Negro is restricted even further because he is born into a caste from which for most there is little likelihood of escaping. Studies of American class structure have been made by the Lynds, W. Lloyd Warner, and other sociologists. The number of classes into which these researchers divide our society are not always in agreement, but in one respect they do agree. There is a norm or middle class made up primarily of a white Anglo-Saxon Protestant majority. The person who differs in one or more of these characteristics will probably encounter certain prejudices of the norm group.

The American Negro is the center of the greatest controversy or inter-group conflict in the United States today. He is discriminated against in education, housing, economic opportunity, and social acceptance. The Negro displaced from agriculture in the South has moved to the large cities of the North where he can live only in already overcrowded slums. His plight is described very thoroughly in Conant's *Slums and Suburbs*.[18] The Negro, although he has won telling legal victories in securing equal job opportunities and desegregated schools, still has many handicaps to overcome before obtaining total social acceptance. The full results of civil rights legislation and militant protests to overcome these handicaps cannot yet be determined. It well may be that violence and rioting stemming from protests will cause a reaction which will slow needed reforms.

Discrimination against the American Indian and the Oriental races has declined on a national scale. In fact, it is now fashionable to boast of Indian blood in one's ancestry. Yet not too long ago the only good Indian was a dead one, and "squaw-man" and "half-breed" were terms of contempt.

[16] Pounds and Bryner, *op. cit.*, p. 323.
[17] *Ibid.*, p. 324.
[18] James B. Conant, *Slums and Suburbs*, McGraw-Hill Book Company, New York, 1961.

According to Pounds and Bryner, discrimination against Americans by Americans because of religious differences is on a long-term decline.[19] Anti-Semitism is still found, but to a lessening degree with the passing of time. Reasons for this are many, but can probably be laid to sympathy with Jews for their sufferings under Hitler's Germany, the success of the new Jewish nation of Israel on many fronts including the military rout of numerically superior Arab forces, the large numbers of Jews who no longer cling to the strict clannishness of orthodoxy, their dedication to education, their very low crime rate, and their success in professional and academic pursuits.

Anti-Catholicism has reached such a low that in 1960, John F. Kennedy was elected the first Catholic president of the United States.

Discrimination against persons because of national origin has been reduced because of the comparatively small trickle of new immigrants and because the assimilation of such groups is accomplished more rapidly. New legislation has replaced the old national origins quota so that new-comers may soon come in considerable numbers from countries which formerly furnished very few of our immigrants.

American citizens of the Southwest and Puerto Rico whose Spanish language and culture set them apart have had to face the most recent discrimination. These make up a great number of the culturally deprived found in the slum areas of many of our major cities, as do refugees from Cuba.

Wherever the currents of population mobility bring in numbers of people who have characteristics of some sort which distinguish them from the majority already there, prejudice is likely to result. Prejudice based on ignorance and fear will cause severe strains on intergroup relations.

SUMMARY

The foregoing sections of this chapter have touched upon some of the changes arising out of man's progress in the natural sciences and tech-nology. But man has found that his achievement in the social sciences has not kept pace, and consequently, conflict in human relationships has in-creased. Man, armed with the weapons of advanced scientific technology but lacking a commensurate social, moral, and spiritual comprehension, can well bring about his own demise. It is only through gaining a balance between his achievement in the natural sciences and the social sciences that man can prevent his own destruction. This is *the social and cultural framework* within which the school, a social institution, must do its job.

[19] *Ibid.*, p. 330.

SUGGESTED EXERCISES

1.   List five recent areas of conflict in the national and world scene, and relate them to the task of the schools.

2.   Study the most recent sociological studies dealing with the status of the family in American life. What is the prognosis regarding the future of the family?

3.   Have there been any recent additions to the list of man's institutions? Does your concept of an institution agree with that advanced in this chapter?

4.   What is meant by the term "transmit the cultural heritage"? What responsibilities does the secondary school principal have in such transmission?

5.   What does recent research show about population growth and composition in the United States and in the world?

6.   What did an English clergyman named Malthus have to say about the relationship of population and food supply in the world?

SELECTED REFERENCES

AYER, P. F., "Poverty and Reeducation," *Educational Leadership,* vol. 22, no. 27, May, 1965.

DOWNEY, LAWRENCE W., AND FREDERICK ENNS (eds.), *The Social Sciences and Educational Administration,* The Division of Educational Administration, The University of Alberta, Edmonton, Alberta, 1963.

HOEBEL, E. ADAMSON, *Anthropology: The Study of Man,* 3d ed., McGraw-Hill Book Company, New York, 1966.

"New Jobs with a Big Future," *Changing Times, The Kiplinger Magazine,* November, 1967, pp. 6–10.

"Oh, How Your Life Has Changed," *Changing Times, The Kiplinger Magazine,* November, 1967, pp. 6–14.

PARKER, FRANKLIN, "Current Forces Shaping U.S. Education: The New Guard Emerges," *Changing Education,* Winter, 1967.

SOWELL, THOMAS, "The Need for More Education," *AAUP Bulletin,* vol. 52, no. 4, December, 1966.

CHAPTER | 2

AN ANALYSIS OF THE PRESENT-DAY SECONDARY SCHOOL

WHAT IS A SECONDARY SCHOOL?

It would be quite simple just to assume that everyone knows what a secondary school is and then go ahead and analyze it. But in the interest of clarity the authors state that a secondary school is one that comes after an elementary school.

The secondary school may be called a junior high school, a senior high school, or a junior-senior high school. Recently, the term "junior high school" has been replaced in some places by the terms "middle school" and "intermediate school." Certain patterns of grade organization are covered in more detail in Chapter 5.

ORIGIN AND DEVELOPMENT

Old World Influences

Writings on the evolution of secondary education in the United States seem to be content to ignore the historical antecedents, to connect it only with the English grammar schools, or to hint that it sprang full-grown from the heads of the Puritan theocrats.

While it is true that the Thirteen Colonies on the Atlantic seaboard of the North American continent were ruled by the British and that most of the colonists were of British ancestry, there were sizable numbers of Dutch, Swedes, French, and Germans who were here quite early. Thus the influences of the Old World on the American system of education did not come from the British Isles *only*. One group of British Puritans emigrated first to Holland before journeying on to New England. Whatever their reasons for leaving, these people all came with the mark of Europe stamped on them.

Other continental influences can be shown, e.g., Johann Sturm of Strasbourg has been credited by some as the first great secondary school administrator,[1] and his *Gymnasium* established in 1534 was a model for the great private and state schools of Germany, France, and the public (private) schools of England. In 1538 Sturm wrote a treatise, *The Right Mode of Instituting Schools,* which had great influence on school systems throughout Europe. Sturm was admired and imitated in England, where his friend Roger Ascham disseminated his ideas.

Actually Sturm modeled his own school on that of the school he had attended in Liège conducted by the Brethren of the Common Life. These early schools often contained as many as two thousand students who were admitted at age six and could remain for a 10-year course. Research will reveal even earlier examples of continental secondary schools. Johann Sturm popularized and perfected for the needs of the generation under his charge that which already existed before he came along. The point of view of the authors is that American secondary education is no more unique in origin than was Sturm's Strasbourg *Gymnasium*. The uniqueness of American secondary education arises from adapting what has gone before and adding new elements to meet the ever-changing needs of the New World.

New World Needs

As has been pointed out in the preceding section, the American colonists brought with them a heritage of educational thought and experience from Europe. Quite naturally the colonists modeled their schools after those they had known in Europe. Because schools reflect the society which they serve, it is not surprising that those established had to be able to adapt to the unique colonial social, economic, and governmental environment or be replaced by those which did. In fact the first 250 years of secondary education was spent largely in establishing schools and devel-

---

[1] Paul B. Jacobson, William C. Reavis, and James D. Logsdon, *The Effective School Principal*, 2d ed., Prentice-Hall, Inc., Englewood Cliffs, N.J., 1963, p. 492.

oping the types that would give the programs suited to the needs of the new nation.[2]

The Latin grammar school is considered the forerunner of the modern secondary school. Its chief functions were to prepare young persons (boys) for college entrance and eventually for the ministry and government leadership.[3] Thus in the age group served, it is an acknowledged predecessor. However, it was a school for an elite few, and the narrowness of its curriculum did not meet the purposes of the growing and powerful commercial middle class in the New England and Middle Colonies. Americans soon rejected the Old World idea that only the children of the upper class should receive a substantial education. New economic and social conditions demanded a liberalizing of the offerings at the secondary level. Thus arose the tuition academies, the first of which Benjamin Franklin is given credit for founding.[4]

Franklin's proposals for a more utilitarian curriculum were only partially successful, and although the academy curriculum was broader than that of the Latin grammar school, it did not encompass all that Franklin envisioned. It served a larger proportion of youth, admitted girls to secondary education for the first time, and reflected a growing belief in education for use.[5]

"By 1850 there were about 6,085 academies enrolling approximately 260,000 students." [6] These schools were not free schools but depended upon tuition payments by students and donations from private benefactors.

The public high school was the result of a struggle to secure free public education for their children by the small business men and skilled artisans of the larger cities. The first one, the English Classical School, was opened in Boston in 1821. From this time on:

> The trend, however, was unmistakable. The forces of democracy, industrialism, humanitarianism, secularism, and an expanding population all pointed to the establishment of something new under the sun, a free public school system dedicated to the proposition that equality of educational opportunity is essential for the achievement of a truly democratic society.[7]

The idea of common schools taught in English, to which all people might send their children, spread slowly but inexorably. Only one insti-

---

[2] Lester W. Anderson and Lauren A. Van Dyke, *Secondary School Administration*, Houghton Mifflin Company, Boston, 1963, p. 47.

[3] Chris A. De Young and Richard Wynn, *American Education*, 5th ed., McGraw-Hill Book Company, New York, 1964, pp. 170–171.

[4] *Ibid.*, p. 171.

[5] Anderson and Van Dyke, *op. cit.*, p. 52.

[6] *Ibid.*, p. 53.

[7] R. Freeman Butts, *A Cultural History of Education*, McGraw-Hill Book Company, New York, 1947, p. 485.

tution in a free society could serve everyone on an equal basis and could be controlled by everyone—the government. These schools to be acceptable to everyone had also to be nonsectarian in religious outlook.[8]

Colonial Attitudes toward Schools

To understand certain regional differences in attitudes toward schools which exist even today, it is necessary to examine those of earlier times. This section cannot go into all the details of the major social, economic, political, and religious influences on schools but will endeavor to summarize the major influences in the development of schools by geographic regions.

New England Colonies   According to Meyer, the Massachusetts Bay Colony leaders were themselves bearers of a high-grade schooling (at least for those times) and were concerned that learned men should develop to carry on the church and government.[9] However, they were concerned not only with the education of future leaders but also with literacy for all their people. Literacy was essential so that every Puritan could read Holy Scripture for his soul's salvation. In fact, the Massachusetts Colony has been called the "Bible State." [10]

Regardless of the devotion to only two R's—reading and religion—found in Massachusetts, education flourished there, and the legislation passed to ensure its establishment set the pattern for the surrounding colonies and in fact for the entire country as time went on. Because no differences of opinion were allowed from the party line of Puritanism and because great importance was placed on education, the people of the Bible State remained Puritans. One either remained a Puritan and followed prescribed patterns or was banished. Surrounding areas were settled by many who either got out or were driven out.

Tax support of schools, compulsory education, the first college, and the first successful secondary school are all educational milestones which can be credited to this colony.

While the Massachusetts colonists firmly supported literacy for all, this was not at first true for secondary education. Puritanism was built on recognition of a classed society. The leaders of the church-government were at the top of the hierarchy; artisans, servants, hired hands, and unskilled laborers followed in that order. As time went on, a new group, the successful merchant class, came to share in the top power and influence which their new wealth secured for them.[11] Social position established both the order on class rolls at Harvard and Yale and the location of one's

[8] R. Freeman Butts, "Search for Freedom," *NEA Journal*, March, 1960, p. 38.
[9] Adolphe E. Meyer, *Educational History of the American People*, McGraw-Hill Book Company, New York, 1957.
[10] *Ibid.*, p. 20.
[11] *Ibid.*, p. 22.

church pew. The Puritans were no different from most others of their time: They were intolerant of the religious and political views of others and believed in a divinely ordered arrangement of social classes. Their need was to secure some diversity out of their perverse unity.

The Middle Colonies   The colonies of the Atlantic seaboard from New England to Maryland are grouped together and called the Middle Colonies. Comprising the present-day states of New York, New Jersey, Delaware, and Pennsylvania, the area was settled by people of diverse religious groups, nationalities, and tongues. The liberal policies of the Dutch West India Company made it possible for people of many lands and religions to settle in New Netherland. Except for one or two brief relapses, religious freedom in the Dutch colony was much in advance of its time. In fact the religious toleration and prosperity in the home country made it difficult for the Dutch government to get many of its own people to go to New Netherland. When New Netherland was seized by the British, its population was not even a third of that of Massachusetts. In 1664 New Netherland became the British colony of New York.

New Jersey and Pennsylvania, by the nature of their charters and the men who held them, also attracted various religious and social groups. The diversity of religious groups meant that each sought to develop its own denominational schools.[12]

Political authority of the state over education was established in these Middle Colonies because the church and private schools operated under specific grant from crown, proprietor, or legislature.

The task of these colonies was to secure more unity from their diversity before the experiment could begin.

Free enterprise entered the market for schooling, particularly in New York and Pennsylvania, to supply the growing demand for useful subjects in the curriculum by the growing commercial class. The academy arose because of this insistence on useful knowledge.[13]

The Southern Colonies   These colonies were founded by Englishmen who were not dissenters either politically or religiously, but supporters of the established monarchy and Anglican Church. These conservative fortune hunters came to an area whose economy was to be dominated for generations by its climate, geography, and one-crop agriculture. These political, religious, and economic determinants molded the colonies' attitude toward education.

The sparse population in the South because of the plantation system meant there were few towns of any size. The large holdings of land and the nature of the crops planted thereon necessitated a large force of un-

[12] B. J. Chandler, *Education and the Teacher*, Dodd, Mead & Company, Inc., New York, 1961, p. 27.
[13] Meyer, *op. cit.*, p. 89.

skilled labor. Although inducements such as indenture to pay passage were offered, free labor could not meet the demand.

Kidnapping, shanghaiing, importation of prisoners, and the like, were all tried as a means of increasing the labor supply.[14] By the early 1700s the stranglehold of certain European nations on the traffic in Negro slavery was broken, and the Southern colonies were able to satisfy their demand for cheap labor. The competition of goods produced by slave labor forced many of the small planters to move on to other areas of the developing country or to become tenant farmers for the large planters. The planter aristocracy, the working classes, and slaves were the elements in a system that was almost feudal in nature. This class and caste system together with its economic conditions tended to prevent the rise of a strong middle class.[15] Because the middle class is that group which has tended to strive for a system of free public schools, Virginia and the other Southern states were to suffer long delay in establishing a system of public education.

Another factor affecting the attitude toward schools found in the South was the viewpoint of the official church, the Church of England, or Anglican Church. Education for the sake of literacy for each person's salvation was not considered necessary. The church in the South was charged with educating paupers and young apprentices at public expense, and did so to a certain extent.

The attitude toward public education held by Virginia's Royal Governor Berkeley during his 36-year regime (1642–1677) rather sharply reflects the general attitude of the colony.[16] Berkeley wrote:

> I thank God there are no free schools or printing presses and I hope we shall not have them this hundred years: for learning has brought disobedience and heresy, and sects into the world and printing has divulged them and libels against the best of governments. God keep us from both.[17]

His wish regarding free schools seems to have been heard because it was not until the middle of the nineteenth century that a public system of free schools can be said to have been established in Virginia. Establishment of public schools in the South had to await major changes in the social and economic structure of the region.

That the small bands of colonists who had to struggle to earn a living in the New World, to make their peace with their God, and to strive to give their children a better life had time to establish public education is miraculous. But during the colonial period, they did establish it even

---

[14] *Ibid.*, p. 45.
[15] Chandler, *op. cit.*, p. 28.
[16] J. L. Blair Buck, *The Development of Public Schools in Virginia: 1607–1952*, Commonwealth of Virginia, Richmond, Va., 1952, p. 3.
[17] Henry W. Elson, *History of the United States*, The Macmillan Company, New York, 1915, p. 66.

if only in broad outline. It was to be subjected to many buffets and blows and was to be affected by various political, social, and economic forces. If present and future school administrators are to understand the effects of certain cultural forces on education, they can learn much from a study of the past.

Post-revolutionary War Period

The thirteen British colonies hung precariously on the East Coast of the New World. Most of them had been established for various secondary reasons, but the prime reason was economic. It took capital to outfit the colonizing expeditions and to keep them going. Persons willing to risk capital in such enterprises usually do so with the expectation of substantial returns on their investment. Investors of the colonial period were no different from those of today. Because the official British government policy toward the colonies during much of the period preceding the Revolution was one of exploitation, friction arose between the colonies and the mother country.

Great Britain, during this period, had many problems throughout the world and was affected by major currents running through Europe. The Industrial Revolution caused by the application of power to machines was a current of cataclysmic proportions. Thousands of Europeans thrown out of work by power-driven machinery came to America. Thus, Europe's loss ultimately became America's gain. For although the descent of thousands of lower-class immigrants brought dislocations, including the arrest of the drive toward universal education, it brought human resources which enabled the new nation to sweep across the continent in a relatively short time. Such a sequence of events has happened since, and is happening again today. A model of this circular effect is shown in Figure 2-1.

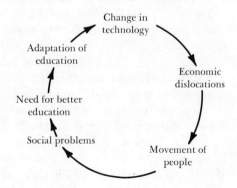

Fig. 2-1. A Model of the Relationship between and among Economic and Social Forces, and Education.

The friction between Great Britain and her American colonies became part of a worldwide conflagration. Britain was fighting for survival all over the globe and was, therefore, hard-pressed to put down the rebellious colonies. Certainly no serious student of history could make the mistake of thinking that the American colonies single-handedly defeated the mighty British Empire to secure their independence. But the same student can readily see the effect which the prelude to war, war, and postwar periods have on education. Especially in those areas through which armies march, countermarch, and battle, education tends to be neglected during such periods because the struggle for survival is paramount.

Although the period from 1770 to 1800 was not one of great activity in the educational sphere, some progress was made.

As has already been related earlier in this chapter, the academy came into being in 1751 and spread rapidly after the end of the Revolutionary War. During the establishment of the new nation, the new states, and their governments, constitutional provisions were made that were to affect profoundly the growth of American education. Because the Constitution of the United States did not mention education directly as a function of the United States government, it became a state and local function. This was through the operation of the Tenth Amendment, which states that: "the powers not delegated to the United States by the Constitution, or prohibited by it to the States, are reserved to the States respectively, or to the people." By 1800, sixteen of the states had placed provisions for schools in their constitutions, and new states seeking admission to the Union were required by Congress to make such provisions before being admitted.

The Period 1800–1860

The philosophy of the new government expressed belief in the political, social, and economic rights of the common man. To bring this ideal to fruition, it was essential that the common man be freed from ignorance and that educational opportunity not be limited by social or economic status. Thus, the concept of free, universal education at public expense came into being. It has been supported and encouraged by the masses of people in the nation ever since. True to the spirit of American democracy, groups of people who did not support this concept, and even challenged it, were free to do so. They also might send their children to private schools if they desired and could afford to do so. This is also true today.

The 50 years or so prior to the outbreak of the Civil War has often been referred by educational historians as the "state school period." For this was the period in which such great architects of American educational structure as Horace Mann and Henry Barnard did their great work.

The influence of these two men, who worked in three New England states (Mann in Massachusetts and Barnard in Connecticut and Rhode Island), was to spread throughout the country. A look into original documents of this period or into detailed histories will show that theirs was not an easy task. Formidable opposition arose to "the policy of taxing the property of all people to provide free schooling for all children." [18] While most New England states did not find this difficult to accept, different ideas of the relationship of the individual to his government existed in Pennsylvania, Rhode Island, and the Southern states.[19] The fight for public free schools in these states was long and bitter.

The influx of immigrants to the cities brought masses of people together where their growing political power soon overcame opposition to free schools. The confidence which Americans came to have in their public schools as an instrument for social and economic betterment has remained basically unshaken.

It was during this period that the American high school was instituted as the answer to the demand for vocational preparation. Although various writers give different dates for the opening of this first high school in Boston, it did open in May, 1821. For the first three years of its existence, it was called the English Classical School, but in 1824, it came to be called the English High School. The term "English" in its title was to distinguish it from the Latin Grammar School and Harvard College.[20] The term "high" was borrowed from a description of certain European schools written by John Griscom in his *A Year in Europe* published in 1819.

The idea of the free public high school spread slowly at first. By 1840, there were about eighty in the country, of which half were in Massachusetts alone. After 1850, there was a rapid rise in the number of public high schools, and by 1860, there were several hundred—many replacing private academies. Although progress in this respect was delayed by the Civil War, it picked up momentum afterward and carried into all the states.

The Dismal Decade (1860–1870)

In 1860, the American nation stood poised on the brink of the bloodiest fratricidal conflict in man's history. As is always the case in war, much that is good and beautiful is lost, and society's progress is halted for a time. Thus it was that the Civil War, with its 4 years of constant fighting and its fearful aftermath of reprisals, reconstruction, and crushing debt, comprised a period in which all schools at best only marked time. In some areas of the country all schools were disbanded.

[18] Frederick Eby, *The Development of Modern Education*, 2d ed., Prentice-Hall, Inc., Englewood Cliffs, N.J., 1960, p. 560.
[19] *Ibid.*
[20] *Ibid.*, p. 563.

Contrary to popular opinion, there were some public-supported primary schools in most of the Southern states before the Civil War. The proceeds of the literary fund in Virginia had been used for the support of such schools. The Virginia Convention of 1861, which voted the Ordinance of Secession, also shifted these proceeds of the literary fund to the military defense of the state. As a result, the primary schools were suspended.[21] Most of the academies and what few endowed free high schools there were in the South went out of existence also.

The Search for Direction (1870–1920)

Picking up the pieces of the educational structure after the Civil War and Reconstruction took some doing, especially in those areas which had been the battlefield. Man continued to struggle amidst adversity so that progress might begin again. Slowly at first, but with ever-increasing momentum, the wounded nation began to heal.

The court decision in the Kalamazoo case was a milestone in the development of secondary education. Handed down in 1874, the decision established the legality of tax-supported public schools at all levels and paved the way for the phenomenal growth in this new instrument of democracy.[22] The public educational ladder now reached from kindergarten to the university.

The high schools of the earlier periods had been planned neither to follow the grammar grades, nor to feed into colleges and universities. There was much overlap in ages taught. The original purpose of the high school had been to furnish a terminal program for boys who would enter business and commerce. Like the early academies whose original purpose had been similar, the new public high schools would change to reflect current needs. Unlike the academies whose concept of needs became more narrowly conceived, the public high schools have come to provide educational programs on a broad front. They now provide both vocational and college-preparatory courses.

By the late 1880s public schools had increased so rapidly that they numbered about twenty-five hundred. Here was the beginning of the great diversity in course offerings, scope, sequence, and standards for promotion and graduation. In the search for order from this confusing diversity, many new European educational ideas were imported, scrutinized, and even adopted in some cases.

The Pestalozzian and Herbartian influences were especially strong and gave impetus to the profession to seek a scientific methodology based on newer theories of learning. Educational theory and practice were also influenced by Americans such as G. Stanley Hall, John Dewey, Charles H.

[21] Buck, *op. cit.*
[22] De Young and Wynn, *op. cit.*, p. 172.

Judd, Francis W. Parker, and many others. Pragmatism, a philosophy based upon seeking answers through experimental testing of theories and hypotheses, grew up in America.

John Dewey, Will James, and C. S. Peirce are credited with originating the new philosophy. This philosophy mandates the use of the scientific method in problem solving. The work of these pioneers was to be developed further at a later period when it came to have a profound effect on educational programs.[23]

Many critics of modern-day schools blame Dewey and the Progressive Education Association for ills both real and imagined. The truth of the matter is that many of these critics have never read Dewey's writings to know just what he did advocate. The authors know of an editor of a metropolitan daily newspaper who wrote an editorial condemning "Dewey's theories" but who admitted later that he hadn't read Dewey. In effect he adopted the bias of someone else, which is very easy to do. This amounts to intellectual dishonesty and points out a pitfall that school administrators must themselves avoid.

The Committee of Ten was appointed by the National Education Association in 1892 and published its controversial report in 1893. Although stating that the secondary schools of the country did not exist for the purpose of college preparation, the report devoted considerable space to outlining four courses of study, the satisfactory completion of any one of which "should admit to corresponding courses in colleges and scientific schools." [24] Whatever the intentions of the committee members, they stirred up a hornet's nest of controversy for years to come and did cause a move toward uniformity in curricula by promoting the modern academic subjects.[25] The new influx of immigration and other social and economic changes of the first half of the twentieth century made the committee's recommendations impractical.[26] Conditions became such that the high schools faced demands for more practical subjects, preparation for citizenship, and comprehensiveness of offerings.

The work of the Committee on College-entrance Requirements of the NEA was begun in 1895. This committee was composed of moderate revisionists who did not want to see students' programs differentiated on the basis of their educational and vocational goals. They did not subscribe to an unlimited election but did seek to give status to the modern academic studies as opposed to the classical tradition.[27] Like the Commit-

---

[23] Anderson and Van Dyke, op. cit., p. 53.
[24] National Education Association, *Report of the Committee of Ten on Secondary School Studies*, American Book Company, New York, 1894, p. 53.
[25] Edward A. Krug, *The Shaping of the American High School*, Harper & Row, Publishers, Incorporated, New York, 1964, p. 89.
[26] Anderson and Van Dyke, op. cit., p. 54.
[27] Krug, op. cit., p. 141.

tee of Ten, these men saw preparation for life as synonymous with preparation for college. For some reason, although its report followed many of the same recommendations made by the Committee of Ten, the Committee on College-entrance Requirements did not engender the same high degree of controversy or interest. The important outcomes of this latter committee came not from the work it did but from the work which some thought they should have done but didn't do.

These outcomes were (1) the establishment of a means for admission to college by examination, the college entrance examination and (2) a form of certification of schools through inspection by accrediting agencies.[28]

Although both of these will be discussed in more detail later in the text, they are mentioned here to show how long some of the influences on the current educational scene have been around.

The search for direction was greatly aided by the report of the Commission on the Reorganization of Secondary Education of the NEA in 1918. This report included the work of committees in all subject fields then taught in the high school. Some of the committees actually antedated the commission, which was appointed in 1913. The general report of the commission, known as the *Cardinal Principles of Secondary Education,* was published by the then U.S. Bureau of Education. It presented little that was new but owes its fame to a "masterly summary of doctrines current at that time, and it worked them out in a somewhat original combination." [29]

The report opened with a statement that is of historical significance. It stated that: "Secondary education should be determined by the needs of society to be served, the character of the individuals to be educated, and the knowledge of educational theory and practice." [30] Pointing to certain changes in American life, to increasing numbers of youth in the secondary schools, and to certain changes in educational theory, the commission went on to establish the goal of education in a democracy and its main objectives, or the Seven Cardinal Principles of Secondary Education. They are (1) health, (2) command of fundamental processes, (3) worthy home membership, (4) vocational efficiency, (5) civic participation, (6) worthy use of leisure time, and (7) ethical character. Krug writes that the commission evidently had no particular order of priorities in mind.[31] The order of the objectives was probably not as important as how and when they would be achieved. The report clearly advocated a composite (comprehensive) high school which would bring unity out of the diverse

[28] *Ibid.,* p. 146
[29] *Ibid.,* p. 386.
[30] Commission on the Reorganization of Secondary Education, *Cardinal Principles of Secondary Education,* U.S. Bureau of Education, Bulletin 35, 1918.
[31] Krug, *op. cit.,* p. 388.

elements in the United States and sounded the call for education "so reorganized that every normal boy and girl will be encouraged to remain in school to the age of eighteen, on full time, if possible, otherwise on part time." [32] The ideal of universal secondary education was thus put into the record for all to see. So much has been written about the seven cardinal principles that many people have not read the rest of the report, which has much significance for secondary education even today.

It is from the past that the present-day secondary school has come; little is new at any one time, for we strive to catch up with what we already know. Over the long haul, progress is evident, but because life is short and because we must contribute to that progress, we must find ways to exploit our strengths, to overcome our shortcomings, and to adapt our educational offerings to changing conditions.

SHORTCOMINGS OF PRESENT–DAY SECONDARY SCHOOLS

The foregoing section of this chapter delved somewhat into the origin and development of the present-day secondary school. It was the thesis of that section that the secondary school administrator of today must have an understanding of the forces which have impinged on secondary schools. The problems of today may have arisen in the past. Their answers may be found in the application of the distillation of old knowledge, filtered through today's conditions, with additives of new knowledge and skills.

If the secondary school of tomorrow is to overcome educational lag, we must discover the shortcomings of today. The practicing secondary school administrator needs to assess his own school to find its shortcomings, using all the resources he can find in this endeavor.

In this section of the chapter an attempt will be made to outline a few of the shortcomings found in some of today's secondary schools that prevent a desirable climate for learning.

Curricular Shortcomings

Some researchers into so-called discipline cases and into cases of students who drop out of school are convinced that the majority are caused by the school program and/or by school personnel.

What kinds of programs exist for youth in your schools? Are there the kinds of programs to meet their needs now and to help them develop adaptability so that they can meet the problems in an ever-changing world of the future?

One of the factors which hampers proper curriculum planning is the lack of specified people to be constantly reviewing, reaffirming, revising, or replacing the content and/or the organization of programs to which

[32] Commission on the Reorganization of Secondary Education, *op. cit.*, pp. 29–30.

the school systems commit themselves.[33] Curriculums cannot be inflexible for there are adaptive differences at the level of the different districts and individual schools according to local needs. At the present time there is little regard given to the necessity of curriculum planning in the light of dominant pupil, teacher, and neighborhood characteristics.[34] Some large cities have a single curriculum plan which does not take into consideration that what might be effective and adaptable in one socioeconomic neighborhood might be inappropriate for another.[35]

Deductive learning should prevail in our secondary schools. Consequently, curriculums must be based on the *why's* of the subject matter. Subject content often, in our present curriculums, does not permit a child to discover for himself. Rather, it is teacher-oriented, with the teacher bluntly telling the class that *this is so*. This area of curriculum development must be improved so that a child can function independently in his society.[36]

The capacity of children and youth to learn difficult material has been grievously underestimated. Curriculums must include a new emphasis on greater rigor, higher standards, and broader goals that will make possible the survival of the nation and the expansion and further development of the culture.[37]

Several of the present curriculums do not allow or encourage the below-average student to achieve a desirable balance in his general, specialized, and extraclass educational programs. Schools of today stress academic achievement and plan their curriculum accordingly. Not enough emphasis is put on commercial and technical curriculums.[38]

A short time ago, one of the authors asked the principal of a large high school about follow-up studies of graduates. The author was promptly told by the principal and the guidance counselors that 61 percent of the graduates had gone to college and that three-fourths of those had done passing work in their first year of college. However, these school officials admitted that they didn't know what happened to those graduates who had not gone to college, nor did they know from either group what was most valuable or least valuable in the graduates' opinion about the educational programs or what was lacking from the programs and services of the school.

In some of the small high schools in any state, youth still have to take a college-preparatory course whether they are going to college or not. This is so that from the graduating class of twenty-three or twenty-four

[33] William R. Odell, *Educational Survey Report for the Philadelphia Board of Public Education*, Board of Education, School District of Philadelphia, 1965, p. 265.
[34] *Ibid.*
[35] *Ibid.*, p. 266.
[36] *Ibid.*
[37] Robert W. Heath, *New Curricula*, Harper & Row, Publishers, Incorporated, New York, 1964, p. 7.
[38] *Ibid.*, p. 14.

(or smaller), the two or three going to college will get there. Is there any wonder that when compulsory attendance laws force youth to be in school and the instructional fare has no relationship to their life goals, little climate exists for learning?

Personnel Shortcomings

If students are products of the society, teachers are also. If some of the problems existing in a school are caused by the mobility of student population, they are certainly affected by a lack of permanence in the staff of a school. If there is little continuity in a faculty, it is difficult for any standards of behavior to become widely accepted.

Many of today's teachers are in the business for a salary only, and some young female teachers especially are just marking time until somebody pops the question. The business of teaching is done—or attempted— by too many with part-time commitment to education—if indeed it can be called commitment at all.

Others who man our classrooms are crippled personalities who have disastrous effects on the climate for learning in our schools. These are the ones who cause most of their own discipline problems because of ignorance, stupidity, or plain laziness. Counselors and principals can cite case after case of clashes between students and teachers which can be traced to nothing more than lack of preparation for class on the part of the teacher. These teachers may be the ones who ridicule young people and pin them to the wall for not having completed five pages of unimaginative and boring homework, but who have not done their own homework in planning to make the best climate for learning or in trying to find out how learning takes place.

But all the blame cannot be put on the teachers for their shortcomings. Indeed many of them don't know of their shortcomings or, even if these have been pointed out, have had no help in overcoming them. Some principals and other administrators feel that as long as there are not many parental complaints and everything seems to be under control, there is no cause to evaluate the school and its programs. Teachers with inadequate preparation or who are teaching out of their fields are found in many schools.

Guidance Shortcomings

Guidance services are set up to assist young people to see the alternatives from which they may choose in reaching any decision. Guidance personnel need certain knowledge and skills if they are to do their job well. They must be able to diagnose educational problems and attempt to bring about improvement in student achievement and/or attitude. This diagnosing should provide excellent feedback by which the faculty gets information about program weaknesses, scheduling difficulties, inter- and intrapersonal conflicts, etc. A good guidance person is worth his weight in gold.

The brutal fact is that too many guidance people are not adequately prepared to do their jobs. Even those that are capable are faced with the almost insurmountable obstacles of heavy teaching loads, high counselor-student ratio, inadequate clerical help, and lack of proper physical facilities.

The changing school population, the high mobility of families, and the increasing number of disorganized families with job shortages have all combined to increase the complexities and difficulties confronting that part of the school program which has as its primary responsibility the maintenance of a focus upon the individual and his needs.[39] Specialists in the field of guidance have an almost impossible load to carry. When the need arises for individual attention, often this is not given or not enough guidance is offered. More personnel in the area of guidance are needed. But these personnel should be screened before being hired, for certain members of this staff have been shown to be lacking in the proper background to perform an adequate job. The guidance staff requires constant observation and evaluation in order to improve or perfect a personnel situation.[40]

The working relationships among pupil personnel, counseling services, special education programs, and psychologists need to be reexamined and the roles of each aligned in a more comprehensive team enterprise.[41] A functional guidance program should permeate the entire school. The teaching staff should work with the guidance personnel, not as a separate link.[42]

The guidance program in many high schools is organized mainly to deal with the maladjusted. This implies poor organization. The guidance service should be continuous and serve all youth, not merely the maladjusted, in ways which will help foster their best growth.[43] Currently, a great deal of counseling is administered after serious problems arise. If guidance could be arranged so that it deals not only with the serious problems but also with causes of such problems in order to prevent them from arising or to prepare better for their solution, perhaps then a program concerned with improving pupil self-knowledge and self-direction could be achieved.[44]

[39] David B. Austin, Will French, and J. Dan Hull, *American High School Administration*, Holt, Rinehart and Winston, Inc., New York, 1962, p. 422.
[40] Paul E. Elicker, *The Administration of Junior and Senior High Schools*, Prentice-Hall, Inc., Englewood Cliffs, N.J., 1964, p. 48.
[41] *Ibid.*, p. 44.
[42] *Ibid.*, p. 49.
[43] *Ibid.*
[44] *Ibid.*

Inadequate Facilities

Before World War II, few new school buildings and other school facilities had been built for many years. Declining birthrates of the early 1940s seemed to indicate little need for expansion. Some replacement or renovation was done as a part of Public Works Administration projects during the Depression, but this was a drop in the bucket compared with the need to replace obsolete structures. During World War II, new school buildings were limited to those needed in urban areas where defense plants brought in hordes of workers. After World War II, there was a drastic rise in the birthrate in this country. Communities have struggled to build schools to keep abreast of the wave of population and at the same time replace obsolete and uneconomical structures. But in fast developing communities and especially in suburban systems on the metropolitan fringe, there seems to be no letup in the need for school facilities.

New schools opened in September are soon filled to overflowing. In some rapidly growing systems, new schools open every month. To put them into operation and relieve crowding in other schools causes a disruption to students and teachers—and indeed the whole community.

Overcrowding can, of course, be an obstacle to a good climate for learning. If buildings are old and in disrepair as well, there is no pride in the school and again the climate for learning suffers.

Buildings that are overheated can soon cause tempers to overheat also. Yet, we find the purse-string holders—who may work in air-conditioned offices—extolling the virtues of working under adverse conditions. (It's good for building guts and determination!) A hopeful sign to alleviate this is found in the increased demand for summer school programs, because this suddenly makes air-conditioned schools defensible.

Poor planning of new buildings may not provide for the best climate either. In fact, we may build in such things as traffic control problems and dangers to health and safety. These will be considered more fully in Chapter 20.

Parental Disengagement

The loss of social control is evident in many of our highly urbanized areas and is alarming because it is frequently loss of control over children *and* parents. The lack of association between parents of students in our schools prevents communication about mutual parental problems.

Some teen-agers get their way at home by saying the old, familiar, "but Mom, all the other kids do." Where do most of the parents turn in such a case? They probably turn in retreat!

In most communities, the kids are able to get things their way not because they have better organization, but because the parents and other adults don't have any. In other words, a true community does not exist. Thus there is a need for communication and consultation.

In many schools, students come from diverse social and economic backgrounds. The school is expected to provide equal opportunity for all children irrespective of socioeconomic or minority status.[45] This goal has not been achieved because of the diverse demands of the community on the school. Each distinct group demands that its values and beliefs be taught within the school. Consequently, what is presently found is groups battling each other for domination of what is to be taught in the school.[46]

On the other hand, parental apathy is a basic problem in many secondary schools of the present day. Parents show little concern about the performance of their children and fail to obtain outside help. They seem to look distastefully at parent-teacher conferences or parent-guidance meetings.

Community members seem to protest *total* school planning but put forth no effort to cooperate with the *single* child's problems or difficulties. They yell loudly about racial and social questions but neglect their individual family members' work skills.

Some community members want school improvement, but they refuse to accept the fact that past educational programs and financial support levels are not adequate to meet the accumulated tasks of the local public schools. Adequate funds from parents and governmental levels have not been forthcoming.

SUMMARY

American secondary education developed into what it is today because of its heritage from early Old World models and because of the influences of our changing society and developing government. The first $2\frac{1}{2}$ centuries were spent in developing schools that could adapt to changing needs.

Free public schools threw off the stigma of being pauper schools in some sections of the country, overcame resistance to taxing all people to educate the children of the community, and carried out the education tasks assigned to them.

The schools have had to assume considerable responsibility in adapting to meet the changes wrought by technological advancements, economic dislocations, demographic movements, and the resultant social problems.

While our schools have improved significantly over the years, we still must find ways to overcome our shortcomings, and to utilize better what we already know.

[45] Grace Graham, *The Public School in the American Community*, Harper & Row, Publishers, Incorporated, New York, 1963, p. 346.
[46] *Ibid.*

SUGGESTED EXERCISES

1. How has the purpose of the academy changed over the years? Does it perform the same function which Benjamin Franklin conceived for it?

2. Draw up your own list of educational milestones in the development of schools in your own country. What distinguishes this list from one which might be compiled for some other country?

3. Go to the library in your own community, and see whether you can find facts about the educational history of your town, city, township, parish, or county. Read that history and identify bench marks to social change. If there isn't any such record easily identifiable, then suggest this as a project for social studies classes in your school.

4. Go to a person of advanced years, and have him describe the changes in schools which he has seen in his lifetime.

5. Examine the Seven Cardinal Principles of Secondary Education, and see how many are still worthy objectives for schools today. Add others which you think are necessary because of the many changes since 1918.

6. Analyze your own secondary school, and see whether any of the shortcomings identified in this chapter are to be found. What is being done about the shortcomings you found?

SELECTED REFERENCES

AUSTIN, DAVID B., WILL FRENCH, AND J. DAN HULL, *American High School Administration*, 3d ed., Holt, Rinehart and Winston, Inc., New York, 1962, 590 pp., chap. 3.

BUTTS, R. FREEMAN, *A Cultural History of Western Education*, 2d ed., McGraw-Hill Book Company, New York, 1955, 726 pp., part II.

COX, PHILIP W. L., AND BLAINE E. MERCER, *Education in Democracy*, McGraw-Hill Book Company, New York, 1961, 570 pp.

DE YOUNG, CHRIS A., AND RICHARD WYNN, *American Education*, 5th ed., McGraw-Hill Book Company, New York, 1964, 557 pp., chap. 2.

KRUG, EDWARD A., *The Shaping of the American High School*, Harper & Row, Publishers, Incorporated, New York, 1964, 486 pp.

MEYER, ADOLPHE E., *Educational History of the American People*, McGraw-Hill Book Company, New York, 1957, 444 pp.

National Committee on Secondary Education, "Background for Choice-Making in Secondary Education," *NASSP Bulletin*, vol. 50, no. 313, pp. 1–49, November, 1966.

POUNDS, RALPH L., AND JAMES R. BRYNER, *The School in American Society*, The Macmillan Company, New York, 1959, 518 pp., chaps. 3 and 4.

CHAPTER 3

THE
"NEW LOOK"
IN
SECONDARY
SCHOOLS Some secondary schools have already assessed
their needs and resources and are moving toward new programs, new
services, new staffing patterns, new media, and new administrative and
instructional organizations. These "new-look" schools may hold the key
to future directions for secondary education. Certainly those schools that
are not moving to meet society's needs will be under certain pressures
to catch up.

CHARACTERISTICS OF NEW–LOOK SCHOOLS

Schools of today are what they are because somebody has made some
decisions in the past. Schools for the future will assume a certain form,
provide certain programs and services, and follow certain procedures
because of decisions made today. The very act of selecting certain goals
for schools over others is itself decision making. Such decisions are influenced, of course, by the forces which impinge on our society. Sometimes
social trends and forces ignore for a time what we know about how learning takes place and about new advances in the organization of knowledge.

Even knowledge about man and how he is affected by the interrelated forces in his culture is sometimes ignored. In the communities in which good schools are found, however, good leadership also exists. These leaders keep their communities well informed so that the new knowledge about man and his world is considered in public policy decisions. Wherever good schools are found, there is also strong community moral and financial support for the public schools.

Increased Size

Modern secondary schools are larger. Two parallel movements have contributed to making the secondary schools of today larger than ever before. The movement of people toward the cities (urbanization) and the movement of people from the cities into surrounding suburban areas have caused large concentrations of school-age youth within comparatively small areas. Schools serving these areas, therefore, have had large numbers for whom to provide. The other movement contributing to the increased size of secondary schools has been the consolidation of small, inefficient, and uneconomical schools into centrally located schools housed in modern facilities. The trend is toward secondary schools of one thousand or more students, and it is not uncommon to find high schools with over two thousand and up to forty-five hundred in enrollment.

Of course, size in itself does not make a school a good one. But larger schools do make it possible to offer broader programs and services at a more reasonable cost per pupil. Junior high schools or intermediate schools are also increasing in size.

Consolidated Schools Much of the growth in size of the modern secondary school in rural and urban areas has been planned. That is, small, inefficient, and uneconomical schools have been consolidated into centrally located schools housed in modern facilities. These new schools are able to offer broader programs and services at a reduced cost per pupil. Better roads and other factors affecting improved transportation have helped make consolidation more feasible. That consolidation efforts have always been successful is, of course, not true. It takes a concerted leadership effort to overcome local pride, apathy, and vested interests. The need for consolidation can best be made apparent by comparing the limited offerings at high cost per pupil in the small high school with the broader offerings at more reasonable cost in the larger school resulting from consolidation.

One of the factors in recent years which has given impetus to this consolidation has been Conant's *The American High School Today*. In this report of his study of secondary schools of the United States, Conant indicated that one of the criteria for ensuring an adequate educational program in a school has to do with the size of the graduating class. He stated that the school must be of such a size as to graduate at least 100 students each year. While, of course, the size of the graduating class is not the only criterion of a good school, it does indicate whether or not the school is large enough to present the comprehensive program essential to meet the needs of today's youth.

Even if the school board and school administration are convinced of the value of consolidating, it may take many years to bring about. It sometimes takes that long to overcome entrenched vested interests and those who feel that "what was good enough for grandpa, pa, and me is good enough for these kids today." Then, of course, there is the jealousy that sometimes occurs over the location of the new schools.

Another reason that schools have become larger is just by the natural increase in population which has forced several additions to buildings. These schools are like Topsy—"they just growed." Some that waited found themselves bigger schools in spite of themselves.

These newer and larger schools are striving for ways to utilize the advantages of their larger size and at the same time devising ways to prevent the individual student from being lost in a mass. Chapter 5 explores some of these experiments.

Diversity of Offerings

As was pointed out in the preceding section, one reason for moving toward larger high schools was to ensure broader offerings for students. The need for broader offerings becomes evident when one examines America's intention that all youth shall have opportunity for a meaningful secondary school education.[1] This movement toward universality of secondary education for all of America's youth is a product of the present century. The Commission on the Reorganization of Secondary Education proposed in its report in 1918 that the comprehensive high school should become the standard type of secondary school. Since that time many groups and individuals have supported that proposal, also seeing the comprehensive high school as the best means to provide the educational programs for youth of varying abilities and interests. Perhaps the best known advocate of the comprehensive high school is James B. Conant. Conant, although his *The American High School Today* published in 1958 is the better known repository for his faith in and strong advocacy of the comprehensive high school, as early as 1952 stated his position in favor of the American comprehensive high school.[2] He followed with another look at *The Comprehensive High School* in 1967.[3]

The comprehensive high school is one with several courses of study:

[1] *The High School in a Changing World,* Thirty-sixth Yearbook, The American Association of School Administrators, Washington, D.C., 1958.
[2] James B. Conant, *Education and Liberty,* Harvard University Press, Cambridge, Mass., 1953, p. 57.
[3] James B. Conant, *The Comprehensive High School,* McGraw-Hill Book Company, New York, 1967.

the college preparatory; the commercial; the vocational, with several programs from which to choose; and the general, for those who may not have yet determined on their ultimate goal. This school is designed for two purposes. One is to provide for children from all social and economic levels. The second is to provide a diversity of subjects to meet the general needs and vocational interests of students.[4]

Austin, French, and Hull say that "the comprehensive high school is the typical secondary school in the United States today."[5] This type of school is designed to provide experiences which will prepare students to understand others in our society. It is claimed, however, that perhaps the major limitation of our comprehensive high schools has been their close attachment to academic emphasis. One cause of this is the provision made in some states that vocational schools be supported separately from other educational institutions.

While the comprehensive high school has become the general model toward which many communities continue to strive, there continue to be a number of specialized schools usually found in the big cities. These schools may specialize in the vocational fields, in science and mathematics, or in general academic fields. Others specialize not just in a specific course of study, but in the kinds of students served, e.g., culturally deprived, returned dropouts, and continuation schools. These specialized schools have a tendency to deprive comprehensive schools of students interested in specialized fields and thereby limit the comprehensiveness possible.

While some cities of medium size have recently opened technical high schools, it is interesting to note that there is a resistance on the part of some parents to enrolling their children in them. In effect, they feel that there is a stigma attached to having their children in such a school. This may be the result of using these schools as a dumping ground for a troublesome element or misfits, or it may be simply that the democratic sense of parents is offended by having their children segregated from their age-mates. This also might be considered evidence of a demand for even more extended educational opportunities. In other words, American parents are saying, "We want our children to go on to college or other post-high school programs. Therefore, they must take academic courses in high school so that they will be admitted."

Writers in the field seem to disagree about the number of truly comprehensive high schools in the country. Conant talked of the degree of "comprehensiveness" of the high school, but he also stated: "The comprehensive high school is characteristic of our society and further that it has come into being because of our economic history and our devotion to

[4] James B. Conant, *The American High School Today*, McGraw-Hill Book Company, New York, 1959, p. 22.

[5] David B. Austin, Will French, and J. Dan Hull, *American High School Administration*, Holt, Rinehart and Winston, Inc., New York, 1962, p. 103.

the ideals of equality of opportunity and equality of status." [6] Whatever the reasons why such a school has come into being, and whatever "true" comprehensiveness means, most public and many private high schools in the United States lean more toward the comprehensive side of the scale than toward the specialized side.[7]

Quality Programs

Americans seem to believe with Conant that the comprehensive high school can furnish as good a quality of education for those with specialized abilities and interests as any school set up for a single specialty.[8] A comparison of the test and achievement records of college students who came from public comprehensive high schools with records of those who came from either public or private specialized academic schools reveals that the academic training received by the public comprehensive high school graduate is as good as (and in many cases better than) that in a specialized academic high school.

The new-look schools are providing quality programs of great diversity. They are also demanding greater overall proficiency from students of all ability levels. Obviously the level of proficiency demanded must be relative to the ability of the individual and the quality of learning experiences provided. The demand for academic excellence from those going on to college is a part of the emphasis of our society. New organization of subject matter, newer media of instruction, the explosion of knowledge, new understandings about people and how they learn—all have their impact on quality educational programs. In those communities where quality is demanded from their schools, there is also a commitment to good education on the part of the people.[9]

Flexibility of Programs and Schedules

If the job of the secondary school is to provide for the education of all children and youth through programs that are adjusted to varying abilities, interests, and needs, if new knowledge is added to the stockpile with such rapidity that it is doubled in a decade, and if occupational patterns are modified at a similar rate, then there is a need for greater flexibility in organizing educational experiences, staff, and space. To get flexibility, we need to have alternatives. Alternatives are developed only after they are recognized. Therefore, the first requirement for flexibility is the removal of the limitations imposed by traditional concepts. This removal

[6] Conant, *The American High School Today*, p. 8.
[7] Chris A. De Young and Richard Wynn, *American Education*, 5th ed., McGraw-Hill Book Company, New York, 1964, pp. 182–183.
[8] *Ibid.*, pp. 81–82.
[9] National Education Association, *Schools for the Sixties*, McGraw-Hill Book Company, New York, 1963.

must be engineered by leaders who have a dedication to overcome obstacles which impede progress.

Such leaders possess the skills and characteristics described at some length in Section II of this book. These are educators who are not afraid to rock the boat with embarrassing questions asked in high places as well as right at home.

These questions might include the following:

1. Do all youth learn in the same way?
2. Do all youth require the same amount of time to learn?
3. Do all youth in the same grade come to school with the same cultural background?
4. Do all youth have the same academic abilities?
5. Are some youth more capable than some of their teachers?
6. How do we know that educational television gives better results for the youth in our school?
7. Why can't we abolish Carnegie units?
8. Why must our high school be accredited by the regional accrediting association?
9. Do all classes have to meet for equal periods of time each day?
10. Why can't we teach about sex, race, and other closed areas?

The answers to these questions may raise other questions. Demands of staff and community for realistic programs and services for youth will call for new departures from traditional ways. If permission must be obtained from the state department of education to engage in a new departure from traditional procedures, such necessary requests should not be considered a block. Cogent supporting reasons for wanting to experiment and the advantages to be derived from such are presented. With the increasing emphasis on research and development in government and industry, the increasing awareness of newer programs, media, and techniques on the part of the public, and the growing respect for the competence and training of the administrators of the complex modern high school, little difficulty is encountered in most cases. The commissioner of education in New York State has fostered experimentation leading to instructional improvement. He has had published *The Commissioner's Catalog of Educational Change,* and *Organizing for Educational Change.* Other states are also encouraging constructive experimentation.

While the authors would not want to encourage anyone to engage in unethical practices by neglecting to secure necessary permission or to go ahead anyhow if permission has been denied, it should be pointed out that the educator may need to tell the story better and to secure support from others. In other words, if an educator finds inflexibility in others, he should increase his own flexibility and attack again from another position and with supporting forces.

It may seem that considerable space has been given to overcoming obstacles which may never exist. This may be true because many if not most of the changes needed to bring about flexibility can be made by the principal and his staff. But principals should not allow necessary changes in programs and schedules to be blocked by arbitrary regulations, rigid interpretations, apathy on the part of the public or staff without judicious protest. He may need to resort to the right of any minority—to disagree and to try to convince others of the soundness of his position.

Earlier in this section, it was stated that the first step in securing flexibility of programs and schedules was to remove the limitations. The next step is to realize that technical means now exist to organize along lines sufficiently flexible to meet the general requirements of all students and the individual needs of all.[10] As Bush and Allen state, "The possibility of developing a flexible high school schedule to serve educational needs of pupils has become a reality with the advent of electronic data processing procedures and high-speed computers." [11]

The report of the NEA Project on Instruction, *Schools for the Sixties,* contained several recommendations related to the need for decision making about what to teach and how. Recommendations for cooperative endeavor among local schools, state departments of education, and universities for initiating innovation and conducting experimentation and research leading to improved instructional programs were also made.[12] Those schools that are on the frontier of educational innovation have prepared for changes, have made changes, and are preparing for new changes. For even as school staffs are taking steps to meet current needs, the rules of the game are changing. Only by the continuing efforts of educational and community leaders can our schools be responsive to the needs of society and each individual in it.[13]

Appropriate Facilities

New programs require facilities which will maximize their contribution to the education of youth. The desire for flexible programs may be partially thwarted if school plants and facilities act as straitjackets. Flexible programs demand a functional but flexible environment for learning. Secondary schools which have been planned to house new-look programs are a radical departure from the little red schoolhouse of yesteryear.

[10] Robert N. Bush and Dwight W. Allen, *A New Design for High School Education,* McGraw-Hill Book Company, New York, 1964, p. vii.
[11] *Ibid.,* p. 5.
[12] National Education Association, *op. cit.,* pp. 124–125.
[13] *Ibid.,* p. 25.

Recent schools have been designed for efficiency, variety, and aesthetic effect. New materials and new techniques have been employed. These school buildings are efficient because they provide the functional space for current programs requiring spaces of varying size; they have powered retractable partitions which give immediate flexibility to move from small group instruction to large group instruction and back again. Study spaces for individuals, seminar groups, and teachers are found in several of the newer schools.

School buildings have been designed so that they can be expanded easily without interrupting the educational program during new construction. Service facilities in these schools are designed to handle the additional loads to be placed on them by future expansions.

Forward-looking communities recognize that these new facilities will be used into the next century, and they have therefore provided for convertibility. As programs of tomorrow come into being, the interiors of such schools can be rearranged easily because of nonbearing interior walls and modular construction.

Newer schools are not only using new materials in construction, they are using them to deinstitutionalize the atmosphere thus created. Some new schools are carpeting classrooms, replacing venetian blinds with attractive draperies (if indeed they have windows at all) in an attempt to soften, humanize, and make the school more attractive and homelike. Furniture in these new schools is not only functional, but attractive and comfortable as well. Research in the campus high school at the University of Chicago indicates that classroom carpeting not only deadens sound but seems to cause an improvement in student behavior.

The effects of new programs and new environments on the learner are reflected in changes in his attitude and behavior. As more and more responsibility is placed on the individual for his own learning and as he reacts with increasing maturity, he is given more freedom of movement within the school. Flexibility of scheduling for the more responsible students relieves them of having to jump at the ringing of a bell to run to the next class.[14]

A number of schools have been built not only to provide for easily controlled and rearranged space, but to provide facilities for incorporating the best and most current items of "teaching hardware." Facilities are provided for flexible use of films, filmstrips, tapes, recordings, educational television, programmed materials, etc. The "instructional materials and resources center is the production, supply and nerve center of the school."[15] Throughout these schools, there are outlets for plugging in to

[14] *The Cost of a Schoolhouse*, Educational Facilities Laboratories, Inc., New York, 1960, pp. 133–134.
[15] *Planning and Organizing for Teaching*, A Report of the Project on Instruction, The National Education Association, Washington, D.C., 1963, p. 134.

programs of all kinds furnished by a variety of electronic aids. Computers, automatic data processing equipment, and trained programmers are available to assist with any number of administrative and instructional problems.

The facilities described above are not the crystal ball predictions of architects but are found in American schools today. They were not, in many cases, any more costly than those being built today by yesterday's designs. "The environment for learning can be built into every modern school structure and at a cost that will provide even more school facilities in return for the taxpayers' dollar." [16] The school building more than any other building broadcasts the intention of the community toward meeting tomorrow's problems. Winston Churchill once said, "We shape our buildings; thereafter, they shape us."

Responsibility for Broader Community Services

The better schools of the future will recognize their responsibility for providing those community services not offered by other community agencies. If services are already being offered efficiently by either private or public agencies or a combination of both, then the schools do not become involved. If the services needed are educational in nature, then the schools should offer them.

Adult Education   It has been mentioned that present graduates of our high schools may have to be retrained three or four times during their life-span if they are to continue to make a contribution to society. These adults will need educational programs to provide the training so they can upgrade their skills.

Another part of the responsibility for the educational development of adults involves literacy and Americanization. While an illiterate may need to start at the elementary level, he is an adult. The better secondary schools for the seventies, or any other time, will accept the responsibility not only for providing night classes but for providing training for citizenship as well.

More and more of the communities that have better schools look to them for opportunities for cultural enrichment and for help in activities related to the economic activities of the community. Thus, an adult evening education program might have a class in music or art appreciation, photography, upholstering, or a class in conversational Spanish for those who hire Mexican nationals as farm or ranch labor.

Many school districts throughout the United States provide extension activities for the adult community by furnishing evening classes for those interested in basic education, secondary education, and post-high school

---

[16] *Environment for Learning*, National Lumber Manufacturers Association, Washington, D.C., p. 1.

interests—general, vocational, and recreational. Normally, tuition for adults is merely nominal. Textbooks are often loaned without cost if they are used in day school. Many school districts go as far as providing nursery services for those with small children.[17]

Junior College While it may be that local patterns place the responsibility for junior college education on a separate organization, in many localities the high school furnishes the facilities and many of the teachers. This may be true only in the organizational stage, or it may continue as the accepted pattern. In some states, such as Virginia, the so-called community or junior college is conducted under the auspices of one of the public institutions of higher education in the state. In other states, the junior college is a joint operation of several school districts or divisions, or it is the function of the local school system.

Disaster Preparedness In many communities, the school is the rallying center for preparation in disaster preparedness or civil defense. The science teachers may train members of radiological teams, and school nurses and physical education teachers may give training in Red Cross lifesaving or first aid. The schools in such communities provide fallout shelter areas for civil defense, store disaster supplies and provisions, and become the center for housing evacuees during natural disasters.

In the Commonwealth of Virginia, the operational survival plan of civil defense designates the division superintendent of schools as chief of the warden service. Other school personnel can expect assignments of a nature commensurate with their special skills and/or leadership responsibilities.

Recreation Center While it may be argued that the school should handle only educational matters, it is sometimes difficult to separate educational activities from recreational ones. Summer and after-school recreation programs may include instruction in any number of skills and crafts as well as in sports of all kinds.

Communities have large investments in their school facilities. If the facilities are not needed for regular school activities, why not utilize them to a greater extent in the community recreation program? The school system of the city of Chesapeake, Virginia, is charged with the responsibility for carrying out the recreational program. The city provides a separate recreational budget for this purpose. When new high schools and stadiums are planned, the total community utilization of such facilities is considered and provided for.

In Lynchburg, Virginia, the auditorium of the E. C. Glass High School was designed to provide for total community auditorium needs. This prevented needless duplication of community facilities at considerable

[17] Philadelphia Board of Education, *Bulletin of School Extension Activities*, School District of Philadelphia, Philadelphia, 1966.

cost. Such schools are looked upon as natural community centers. Not just parents but the other citizens as well come and go in these schools.

Health Services   Modern secondary schools provide many services to their students using the justification that if they did not do so, then their educational program would not be effective. In these schools, adequate clinic space is found in which school nurses can supervise and isolate those who become ill at school, handle emergency accident cases, and advise about what other health and medical services are needed. Some school systems retain physicians and dentists to give health examinations and render diagnostic services. Local public health departments may provide all or part of such services.

Liaison with other governmental and private agencies will be a characteristic of the schools of the seventies.

Careful Articulation with Other Levels

The secondary school may be an intermediate, junior high, or senior high school. Those schools which would be selected as the better ones pay careful attention to articulation with the school below and the school above. The better junior highs work closely with their feeder elementary schools and the senior high or highs into which they feed. Such work includes conducting guidance orientation sessions for those in the lower levels to select programs and to become acquainted. The senior high school works closely with colleges, technical institutes, and universities in articulating the educational offerings to ensure that graduates can meet admission requirements. The principal as the instructional leader in his school leads teachers in the various subject fields to study the curricula so that there is careful attention to the sequence and scope of offerings.

Joint subject field study groups composed of teachers of all grades and in all schools from kindergarten through the twelfth grade evaluate and develop the curriculum so that children and youth are assured of continuity in their education.

Advancement in tomorrow's schools will be determined by professional decision. Each student's readiness to move and mental and emotional maturity will be determined, as well as his capacity for receiving organized instruction.

Years and grades as such will be dropped by curriculum makers, and unregimented steps will replace them. Each step will depend upon the student's past achievements and his capacity to take the next step.

Levels themselves will not be distinct, for individuals will progress differently in diverse subjects, skills, and at different ages. Progressively, it is safe to assume that students will, as they grow older, have more time for specialized studies according to their own interests and aptitudes.

Guidance

The guidance program of the better secondary school has well-trained and experienced guidance personnel. All such personnel have at least a master's degree in guidance and such personal attributes as to make them attractive to youth. Guidance committees are composed of the counselors, teacher representatives, the assistant principals, and the principal. The primary purpose of this committee is the planning and coordinating of guidance services. Occupational and educational needs of students are systematically evaluated. On the basis of these evaluations, additional information is secured as needed to enable adjustment of services. Guidance suites are arranged to give privacy for personal conferences and easy access to the necessary records.

The testing program in the better schools is designed for educational diagnostic and prognostic purposes in order to feed back information needed to improve curricular offerings, assist in course elections, guide in the grouping and placement of students, and to help students know themselves better. Follow-up studies are made of graduates and dropouts alike. These schools know about all students—not just the graduates who went to college. Vocational placement services are coordinated with the state employment service, and assistance in finding summer and part-time employment is provided.

NEW MEDIA FOR LEARNING

The secondary schools which are providing the best in education are utilizing an ever-increasing number of teaching techniques, devices, and instructional materials to meet the varied needs, interests, and abilities of their students. Their professional personnel have evaluated new media of instruction in the light of the schools' goals and their own convictions. They resist fad chasing and pressures to keep up with the Joneses, but they engage in well-designed experimentation and through their own study decide which of the media and techniques to adopt, modify, or reject.

Teaching Machines and Programmed Instruction

Although called "new media for learning," it is interesting to note that all of the media are not new. Teaching machines were in an incipient stage in the 1920s through the efforts of Professor S. L. Pressey at Ohio State University. However, relatively little was done with them until about 1954, when B. F. Skinner, disgusted with the way his daughter was being taught mathematics, decided to do something about it. Professor

Skinner developed a program to do the job he felt was not being done in his daughter's school.

Many people use the terms "teaching machines" and "programmed instruction" synonymously. Actually, teaching machines may be defined as "devices that house, display and present instructional programs," [18] while programmed instruction is the *use* of programmed materials in achieving objectives of education.

Programmed instruction has had an impact on conventional instruction in at least five areas: student knowledge of results, explicit educational objectives, appropriate student practice, concern for individual student differences, responsibility for learning and curriculum content.

The first principle, which is being incorporated into conventional teaching, states that the student should learn quickly the correctness of his responses. Teachers who have a knowledge of programmed instruction can easily adopt this principle of knowledge of results into their regular classroom procedures.

It is in the area of explicit educational objectives that programmed instruction perhaps has had its most significant impact. Student behavior is generally specified in the instructional objectives of programmers, but this is not the case with classroom teachers. Now school personnel are recognizing the advantages of stating specific objectives and are beginning to stress their value in preservice and in-service training classes.

Due to the impact of the third principle, teachers are making greater efforts to relate more meaningfully the activities of students to the desired goals. In the past, learning activities for students were only peripherally relevant to these goals.

The fourth area of impact which programmed instruction has had on conventional instruction is quite different from the first three. Few teachers have really tried to implement the principle of individual student differences. However, teachers cannot hear the frequently given accounts of how superior students are finishing whole year courses in half the time without giving thought to the fact that such allowances are rarely made in the conventional classroom for individual differences. At least, with respect to individualized instruction, many conventional teachers are beginning to have guilt feelings. In the future, this will be manifested in greater emphasis on self-pacing in traditional classrooms.

Regarding the fifth area of impact that programmed instruction has made on conventional teaching, it can be stated that the responsibility for the quality of instruction has shifted from the teacher to the programmer. In W. James Popham's words: "Many conventional teachers are impressed with the fact that programmers are willing to accept this burden

---

[18] William F. Ryan, "Utilization Patterns in Programmed Instruction," *Educational Communications Convention Proceedings*, The State Education Department, Albany, 1964, p. 171.

of proof and put their instructional effectiveness on the line by testing a program's quality in terms of student behavior."[19] Many teachers are now beginning to view poor achievement of objectives as caused by their own teaching inadequacies instead of "inattentive students."

Teaching machines may use such displays as printed sheets, printed cards, printed roller sheets, 35 mm slides, filmstrips, microfilm, 8/16 mm motion-picture film magnetic tape (audio), television (audio-video). The learner may respond by any one of the following methods: pushing a multiple-choice button, writing complete answers, filling in missing words or letters, typing an answer, pulling tabs, marking with special ink, erasing overlays, plugging an electric probe into a contact, talking into a microphone, or thinking a response. Indicators of correct responses could be any of the following: colored lights flash, a new question appears, an electric typewriter types a reply, a visual display on a screen shows the learner the correct answer, an audio recording states that the response is correct, or the learner compares his answer with the correct answer.

Should the displays, learner responses, and indicators of responses in the preceding paragraph be combined in every possible arrangement, the reader would get some idea of the number of teaching machines being tested or actually out on the market.

At the present time, teaching machines have not really found wide acceptance in the public schools. Programmed materials (such as scrambled textbooks) have been tested more frequently in secondary schools because of their availability and lower cost compared with teaching machines. Teaching machines are presently being used in a small number of colleges and universities and in the armed services to a small extent. Therefore, it can be stated that the prospect of using teaching machines and/or programmed materials in the public schools is dim for the present. As stated by Finn and Perrin:

> Field testing is going on here and there in the country. The Center for Programmed Instruction of New York City has several such tests underway, as has Encyclopaedia Britannica Films and the Institute for Communication Research of Stanford University. The research side of the state of the art of teaching machines and programmed learning is, however, in flux. It will be some time before the ultimate questions are answered.[20]

Because of the lack of initiative on the part of public schools, prohibitive costs, and the state of flux which is now in evidence, the government

---

[19] "The Impact of Programmed Instruction on Conventional Instruction," G. D. Ofiesh and W. C. Meierhenry (eds.), *Trends in Programmed Instruction*, National Education Association, Washington, D.C., 1964, p. 67.
[20] James D. Finn and D. G. Perrin, "Teaching Machines and Programmed Learning, 1962: A Survey of the Industry," *Technological Development Project of the NEA*, National Education Association, Washington, D.C., 1962, p. 2.

or industry will probably take the lead in introducing teaching machines and programmed materials to the public.

Educational Television In the better schools there has been a reevaluation of the role of television in the instructional program. As better-trained teachers are secured, as in-service programs improve those already in the ranks, and as individualization of instruction increases, there is less need for all students in a subject watching the same live telecast by a television teacher. Instead a teaching segment is placed on video tape, catalogued and made available in closed-circuit television on screens in an individual classroom, or on a viewer in an I. M. center study carrel just by dialing the proper code. Historical events and other programs are video-taped from either commercial, educational, or closed-circuit television and handled in the same way. The better schools have outstripped the technology at times and have forced new developments from the electronics industry.

If video-tape cameras are not available, the better schools because of their flexibility of programs and schedules have little difficulty in reconciling broadcast times of regional ETV with instructional schedules or in providing feedback from classrooms to television teachers. Educational television is recognized as another instructional aid or tool for teachers to use—just as are educational films. Like films, educational television needs the direction and selection of the goal and purpose by a teacher.

Educational TV, like teaching machines and programmed instruction, is undergoing a thorough examination to determine its value as an educational aid for instruction. The evidence has been and still is conflicting.

Opposition to television has centered upon the lack of feedback or discussion. However, according to some writers, this is due to failure to use television properly. Many see television as a teaching adjunct instead of a substitute for good live teaching.

Some of the advantages of television and some of the areas where it is having its greatest impact are the following: (1) One of the greatest contributions is its distribution factor. (2) Close-up views which live demonstrations cannot supply are another big advantage. (3) Organized teaching programs have proved to be successful in many instances (the opposite has been true when informal, free-choice programming is used). (4) Closed-circuit television makes possible magnification and telecasts from any room in a building. (5) Television imposes a sharper discipline on teaching methods.

The main reason why there is not widespread adoption of television for educational purposes is the cost. It has been found that when 200 or more students are taught simultaneously in a course, television costs less than conventional teaching for the same number of students. Sources of income for teaching via television may be private groups, industry, and the government.

Language Laboratory Foreign language teachers who give imaginative and competent instruction have learned to use the language laboratory as an aid to instruction. In a language laboratory, the student participates actively and as an individual moving forward at his own speed and according to his own need. This is in contrast to the traditional lock-step, passive method so often found. Foreign language teachers in the better schools have been instructed in the best techniques in using language laboratories by attending colleges and universities where the best of such equipment is to be found. Local funds are provided to subsidize this in-service education of teachers.

The purposes of foreign language teaching are to develop the ability to speak the language, oral comprehension, and the ability to read and write it.[21] Foreign languages, as in other subjects, require a great deal of drill and repetition. This is the heart of the audio-lingual program. The language laboratory, supplied with a stimulating array of tapes, can facilitate the student's overlearning of the material while still holding his interest.

There is still controversy concerning what a language laboratory actually is. Many types of equipment are in existence and are being used in numerous ways. The laboratory had its beginnings in the use of phonograph records in the classroom. The first time an actual laboratory was used was for the Army Specialized Training Program.

The main purpose of the language laboratory is to help students to listen, to distinguish different sounds and sound patterns, and to imitate what they hear. The advantages of a machine over a teacher in accomplishing these objectives is simple; the machine can offer sustained repetition. This process would most often cause extreme fatigue in a living person. Responses can also be recorded and replayed for the critical evaluation of both teachers and students.

The main components of the laboratory usually consist of tape recorders, earphones, and microphones. At times, provisions are made for visual materials. The basic processes are that a student listens to a master voice, repeats what is said, and records his response for analysis. Language laboratories can only be as good as the material they present and the quality of the integration of this material in the classroom.

Because learning a language is based primarily on listening and speaking, the audio advantages of the laboratory receive the greatest stress. However, visual materials can evoke a great deal of learning in foreign languages. There are many proponents of the introduction of visual ma-

[21] Theodore Huebner, *How to Teach Foreign Languages Effectively*, New York University Press, New York, 1959, p. 9.

terials into the labs. These materials range from the simplest pictures and objects to motion pictures.

At higher levels of language learning, the laboratory can provide enriching experiences for the student in the form of hearing literary selections, musical compositions, speeches, and the like. Laboratories can also offer a unique means of testing and evaluating student achievement.

When the installation of a language laboratory is being considered, the decision-making element of the school is faced with several problems. The administrators of the school working in conjunction with the language experts must make decisions with regard to equipment, installation, maintenance and operational costs, scheduling, supervision, and programs. Of prime importance to the administration are the usual matters of budget, salary, and purchase expenditures.[22] The decision of selecting one piece of equipment rather than another, the locating and designing of the laboratory installation, and the scheduling and supervision of lab periods are some of the tasks which must be faced jointly by the administration and teaching force.

There is a need for further research in the area of foreign language learning and instruction, especially in the use of language laboratories. What is being studied and the nature of language learning must clearly be defined. Recognizing the shortage of trained teachers in the language area, it seems evident that the laboratory, or some similar instructional device is needed if successful language learning is to be accomplished.[23]

Recent studies show that the foreign language laboratory is making a positive contribution to language teaching and learning. Reports show that the labs are doing exactly what was expected of them.[24] However, since there is a relatively low frequency of laboratory use, a lack of widely accepted standardized tests, a lag in the reeducation of language teachers, and an unsettled problem of what actually constitutes maximum laboratory use, further research into this expanding field is greatly needed.[25]

Instructional Materials Center and Learning Resource Center

The instructional resources of the school are brought together in the instructional materials center and/or in the learning resource center.

J. Lloyd Trump and Dorsey Baynham suggest that the schools of tomorrow will have included in their architectural designs, provisions for learning resource centers. They propose that schools should contain an instructional materials center for teachers as well as a learning resource

[22] Nelson Brooks, *Language and Language Learning*, Harcourt, Brace & World, Inc., New York, 1960, p. 148.
[23] John J. Porter and Sally F. Porter, "A Critique of the Keating Report," *MLA Journal*, vol. 48, p. 195, April, 1964.
[24] Edward M. Stack, "The Keating Report," *MLA Journal*, vol. 48, p. 194, April, 1964.
[25] Frank Grittner, "The Shortcomings of Language Laboratory Findings in the IAR Bulletin," *MLA Journal*, vol. 48, p. 210, April, 1964.

center for students. School facilities will provide for an expanse of audio-visual materials housed in a central area.[26] Automated and programmed instructional devices will be available in laboratories and available for use by large groups or independent study projects. Correlated with students' study areas will be an instructional materials center housing instructional devices. This center would include rooms of various sizes, from individual cubicles to rooms for large-group instruction to facilitate the use of such devices.

Most views relating to learning resource centers tend to see the library as the central place for storing, circulating, and using the audio-visual materials. The librarian must understand the curriculum of the school and be ready to aid the school's educational program with the many devices included in the library. The physical setting of the library must be planned in accordance with the use of this equipment. The ease with which these services and materials are used reflects the effectiveness of the center.[27]

Thus the school library becomes much more than books and magazines. The center secures, produces, distributes, and instructs in the use of supplementary aids such as films, filmstrips, recordings, tapes, maps, microfilms, globes, charts, and realia, as well as books and magazines. In order to efficiently utilize these aids, the center is also responsible for accounting, distribution, and instruction in the use of the equipment.

Librarians, audio-visual experts, graphic arts specialists, and instructional aides and clerks are the personnel found in instructional materials and learning resource centers in the new-look schools.

NEW PROGRAMS

The terms "acceleration," "enrichment," and "in-depth study" are often found in present-day educational literature. It should also be noted that these terms are being used interchangeably by many educators. This is due to the fact that in most instances each program is dependent upon the others. Many schools today are using a form of at least one of the programs.

Acceleration and Advanced Placement

By *acceleration* we mean a program designed for the gifted student that enables him either to move ahead and finish school in a shorter period of time or to complete a greater body of knowledge within the usual 12-year program.

Starting on the junior high level are various programs of acceleration

[26] Lloyd J. Trump and Dorsey Baynham, *Guide to Better Schools*, Rand McNally & Company, Chicago, 1961, pp. 35–38.
[27] Austin, French, and Hull, *op. cit.*, p. 324.

such as a regular 3-year course completed in 2 years, skipping grades, and subject acceleration without skipping. Although various authorities have different opinions on the matter, it seems that grade acceleration is not considered an acceptable present-day procedure. Rather than permit students to leave their peer groups and omit a grade level, it is more desirable and effective to have subject acceleration. Courses are added to the curriculum which accelerate and enrich the various disciplines.

The accelerated programs started on the junior high school level or before must continue into the high school if they are to be worthwhile to the student. A current use of acceleration is found in the advanced placement program of high schools and colleges. The program, begun in 1955 with the cooperation of the Fund for the Advancement of Education, the College Entrance Examination Board, and the Educational Testing Service, has expanded very rapidly. This philosophy of acceleration goes along with that being practiced by most junior highs in that it does not push the student into college before he finishes his 12 years.

Both the high school and the college share the responsibility for providing an enriched and challenging program for the gifted student. The high schools teach the courses while the colleges place the students and credit them with the work. The College Entrance Examination Board coordinates the program. It helps prepare criteria and syllabi for the courses and makeup examinations to be given for placement. Their exams are given in English, American history, European history, French, German, Latin, Spanish, mathematics, biology, chemistry, and physics. These examinations estimate the level at which the student should begin his college study. The acceleration made by the student may mean that he takes one or more courses on the sophomore level although he enters college as a freshman.

The advanced placement program has increased from 12 institutions originally participating to over 400 colleges and universities. In 1955–1956, 1,229 students from 104 high schools took 2,199 examinations and entered 130 colleges. In 1959–1960, 10,531 students from 890 schools took 14,158 examinations and entered 567 colleges. In 1963–1964, 28,874 students took the advanced placement examinations.

Many questions still need to be answered as to whether accelerated programs of any type are beneficial and if so what is the best program to follow. It stands to reason that since some children develop more rapidly than others and differ from each other in varied ways, failure to develop their potential involves danger. They are more likely to develop behavior and personality problems. It also seems that those opposing acceleration of one kind or another have not supported their disapproval with enough facts, nor have they come up with any better programs to justify abandoning the presently practiced accelerated programs.

Enrichment

The purpose of enrichment is to widen and deepen the understanding of the child. It is virtually impossible to have an accelerated program without enrichment, but this does not mean that an enrichment program is useful only for the advanced student. Enrichment programs can be valuable to students of all levels of ability.

Before examining the enrichment program, it should be pointed out that in order for it to be considered enrichment, it must be integrated with the general curriculum. It should not be assumed to result from casual trips, unsystematic collections of various kinds, periodic use of television for various events, and the like. It must not be merely busy-work. A good enrichment program demands cooperation from the administration, thorough planning in the curriculum, and an imaginative and understanding teacher.[28]

Enrichment of the educational experiences of the gifted is recognized by most schools as a necessity if the needs of the student are to be met adequately.

Enrichment can be used or implemented in many different ways. We find programmed instruction for the slow learner and all along the line for the gifted learner. The use of television and summer school sessions also provides for enrichment. Summer school has many advantages, some of which include:

1. Absence of the tie-up of laboratory facilities that might exist during the regular school year
2. Less conflict with course preparation on the part of the teacher
3. Greater flexibility in scheduling
4. Less demand on audio-visual and other equipment
5. Greater ease for the student

Individualized Instruction

In recent years there has been a tremendous drive in secondary schools to provide the student with more individualized instruction. This concept has been implemented through various new media of learning and through the use of teaching techniques geared to the individual.

By means of differentiated assignments, job contracts, and the use of individual study and research, the student can have more meaningful learning experiences. In the new-look schools we are finally acknowledging the fact that individual differences do exist.

[28] Wallace J. Howell, "Influence of Curriculum Enrichment in a High School Honors Group on College Board Examination Scores," *The Journal of Educational Research*, vol. 59, pp. 113–114, November, 1965.

Salvage Programs

The dropout problem in our educational system is as old as schooling itself. However, it has reached such staggering proportions that one out of every three ninth-grade students will leave high school before graduation. This means that approximately 7.5 million youths will have dropped out of school during the 1960–1970 decade. Many salvage programs have developed in recent years to cope with the dropout problem. Some of these salvage programs are as follows:

1. *Complete Special Service Programs* These increase or introduce special services such as guidance and counseling, speech therapy, remedial programs, testing, psychological assistance, and health services. At the present time, these aids are not being offered early enough and completely enough, particularly at the elementary level. With the initiation of these programs in the elementary schools, the potential dropouts are being found. These new programs help to correct the problems associated with dropouts and convince potential dropouts to stay in school to develop goals compatible with their talents. They should commence when the child begins school and be carried through the high school level.

2. *High School Projects* These include developing various areas in the high school curriculum to cope with potential dropouts. These new programs include such projects as Job Preparation and Guidance, and Exploratory Occupational Skill Units.

3. *Realistic Curriculum for the Predicted Dropout* Many secondary schools have adopted programs in occupational training for all who require it, particularly for the potential dropout. Even before the passage of the Vocational Education Act of 1963, a number of school systems began to offer new programs such as in custodial services, barbering, shoe repair, duplicating services, decorating and furniture refinishing, lawn and garden care, cosmetology, laundering, family services, food preparation, and for nurse's aides. The U.S. Department of Labor is providing leadership in regional programs to ensure that curricular changes are in accordance with manpower needs.

4. *Work-study Programs* These offer much promise in salvaging potential dropouts. In New York City students alternate weekly between school and paid positions in the city's civil service agencies. San Francisco has a similar program. In a state-sponsored experimental program called STEP, seven cities in New York pay potential dropouts 70 cents an hour for working in

the various public buildings. The students attend school for only part of the day.

5. *PTA Programs* Parents want to see their children get ahead, and some PTAs have taken the initiative to create programs to help potential dropouts and to provide them with much needed leadership. The PTAs throughout our country are recognizing that the dropout problem is not simply a school problem, but it is a community problem—one that every PTA can use its resources to help resolve.

6. *Operation Return Program* Currently being utilized in New York City and in Seattle this program features a joint effort by the schools and other community agencies and organizations to strengthen the educational background and employability of those who dropped out of school.

7. *Higher Horizons Program* This program begins in the elementary school (third grade) and extends through the junior high schools. It focuses on the socioeconomic conditions of the dropout and combines both classroom activities and a cultural enrichment program. It is being utilized in Philadelphia, as well as other places, and gives indications of being successful.

8. *Adult Evening School* A greater emphasis is being placed on evening schools where the high school dropout can continue his education and earn a diploma. The programs are being updated, special services are being offered, and new courses are being offered to students to enhance their marketable skills.

9. *Youth Opportunity Centers* These centers are being established throughout our country and give employment service to the young, with attention to dropouts and others unsuited for competition in the present-day labor market. Centers are set up in metropolitan areas, with mobile units for rural areas and small communities. Contact is kept with community action programs set up under the Economic Opportunity Act.

10. *Neighborhood Youth Corps* This program came about through a provision of the Economic Opportunity Act. The corps functions under the Department of Labor. Title I-B is the work-training provision for the 16 to 22 age group. The U.S. Employment Service helps the local sponsors with their corps projects. Currently the program seeks out the poor and disadvantaged and selects those who need work and training. The corps encourages students who feel like quitting school to stay and complete their courses.

11. *Manpower Development and Training Act Program* This experimental project involves young male high school dropouts.

This program consists of training in business labs, in mechanics, in electrical work, and in machine shop work and includes visits to local firms to determine the kinds of occupations and qualifications employers are seeking. It was found that the dropouts in this program were careless in speech, had disadvantaged backgrounds, and had an inability to understand just where their place was in society.

The social consequences of unemployment in relation to dropouts, where one out of every four will not find employment, has been a cause for much concern. We can only hope that these programs will help alleviate this concern.

USE OF SPECIALISTS

Many new ideas are quietly changing the high school. The typical high school of 1955 was not basically different from the high school of 1925; in fact, a student, were he to find himself transported in time from the one school to the other, would scarcely be able to tell the difference. His period of adjustment would seem short-lived and painless.

One of the prime reasons for the vast changes currently taking place throughout many secondary schools is the recognition by educators of the need for specialization in many major areas. A quick look at some new terms recently added to the educator's vocabulary will show how the need for specialists has increased. When high school educators talk shop these days they discuss such topics as video-tape recording, teleprojection, programmed instruction, team teaching, the spiral curriculum, learning laboratories, materials resource centers, language laboratories, flexible scheduling, BSCS biology, PSSC physics, SMSG mathematics, and various specialized areas of administration. All the new terms indicate the need for specialists. Some of the new and varied types of specialists currently establishing the new look in secondary schools are described below.

Teachers

The teaching team is gradually replacing the individual teacher as the basic organizational unit of the school, and in some schools, departments representing narrow, unrealistic compartments of knowledge are giving way to broader educational units.

There is one team-teaching high school in Waylan, Massachusetts, which has only four departments—the physical sciences, languages, social sciences, and the arts. Such an organizational plan encourages teachers to communicate with one another across the traditional subject-matter lines so that knowledge can be more easily related, correlated, and integrated.

Effective team teaching to a large extent then will depend on a successful analysis of three major factors: (1) the instructional task, (2) the respective talents of the participating staff members, and (3) the physical facilities, technological aids, and educational materials available.

The organizational plan of the use of teachers for a team teaching approach should revolve around large-group instruction, seminars, programmed learning laboratories, and independent study with students progressing at their own rate through a series of units and through a sequence of courses. In all instances, provisions must be made for variation of content, depth study, and interest-centered activities. The growing need for the use of varied types of supplementary instructional devices has brought into existence the audio-visual specialist. He is usually a person who has knowledge about a wide assortment of materials such as the stereoscope, opaque projector, slide projector, microprojector, filmstrip projector, motion-picture projector, and tape recorders. The audiovisual expert in education is or has been a teacher who has had some interest in electronics or elementary mechanics and is currently involved in the new media of learning mentioned in other sections of this book.

In addition to the traditional and current kinds of audio-visual materials and equipment known to the specialist, the expert of tomorrow will have to understand today the direction of educational trends in the development of technology and new media.

The teacher in the nongraded secondary school will have to change his concepts and techniques in teaching to correspond to a new kind of learning. In this kind of program, as in team teaching, the teacher must work with the rate of learning and accomplishment of each student.

The high schools of the new look emphasize the professional role of the educator. Teachers are called on to use their professional knowledge and skill to direct intellectual inquiry and to motivate and guide learning. Ability to marshal total learning resources receives increased emphasis. New roles, such as *team leader* and *master teacher,* reflect individual differences among teachers and will provide new directions for advancement along an instructional route.

Administrators

As the new look in secondary school administration is considered, there are indications that changes in instructional patterns and emphases have created major shifts in program and personnel policies in school districts. Personnel administration has become much better organized, and a clearer delineation of the responsibilities of principals, central-office personnel, and superintendents has developed. Systemwide written policies and regulations have become more common, and increased time and effort has gone into development of policies designed to strengthen educational programs. Principals assume major responsibilities for improvement of school instructional programs. Decentralization in school districts leads increasingly to the addition to secondary school staffs of competent professionals who assist principals with instructional leadership.

Some of the job-description titles which are becoming more and more prevalent with respect to administrative positions are director of programs, coordinator of adult education, director of pupil services, director of staff personnel, coordinator of transportation, coordinator of cafeteria, business administrator, director of research, director of business affairs, coordinator of guidance, instructional supervisor and/or consultant, and coordinator of secondary education.

Special Professional Service Personnel

The services of specialists in the area of programs for emotionally and socially maladjusted students have been in extreme demand. The recognition by both educators and laymen of the great need for specialized instruction for this kind of student has gained wide acceptance. A well-organized and successful approach to this problem has been the use of the special services team which ideally consists of a psychologist, social workers, remedial instructors, a psychiatrist, a diagnostic reading and disability specialist, a neurologist, a speech and hearing specialist, a guidance person, and a coordinator of the special services team. Each specialist works independently with a specific student or may work in cooperation with other members of the team when necessary.

Working in close cooperation with the student personnel and health departments within the schools, this kind of special services team tries to accomplish the following:

1. Identify students with serious problems that are interfering with expected school progress
2. Study and diagnose the problem
3. Plan a program of remediation and rehabilitation
4. Make recommendations consistent with the total program needed by the individual student
5. Implement the recommendations of the team
6. Make a follow-up study of each student to be evaluated by all specialists within the team

The professional team concept calls for group action and interaction, cooperative planning, and the pooling of professional knowledge toward a single focal point, namely, the child and his problems.

The Professional Librarian The librarian should be an extremely important and integral part of the teaching team in each school. On the secondary level, the need for efficiency and effectiveness is great since all specialized programs within a school are usually reflected in library materials. The librarian's responsibility is no longer limited to books, magazines, charts, pictures, and "fugitive" materials, but he is now responsible for the library as an instructional and learning resources center, where teachers as well as students can turn for materials to enrich the program of instruction beyond the textbook.

The Health Services Staff   The health services available in any secondary school is in large measure determined by school size, availability of funds, local health standards, and services offered. If a special services team such as described above is available, a nurse and a physician may be the only staff requirements. Without the team, however, the health services staff would probably be expanded. In many school systems, the health staff has an integral part to play in the health education of youth. This would naturally be in addition to health care and emergency duties which exist from day to day.

The health staff of today is usually composed of fully and legally qualified members according to accepted health and medical standards.

Teacher Aides   Teacher aides in the past decade have been employed in a number of school systems throughout the country. The function of the teacher aide is to relieve teachers of custodial, clerical, and police functions which can be performed by assistants, clerks, and machines. Teachers can then use their professional knowledge and skill to direct intellectual inquiry and to motivate and guide learning. Many teacher training institutions are developing curriculums to train teacher aides and other paraprofessionals.

There can be little doubt that in the future, education will rely on the services of more educational specialists. The success of this innovation in education will depend largely on the cooperation of all those engaged in educating our youth of tomorrow.

SUMMARY

Today's secondary schools are characterized by an increase in size, a diversity of offerings, and flexibility in programs and schedules. The comprehensive high school has received great support from many leading educators as the best way of providing for the needs of all youth. Regional high schools for vocational and technical training are increasing in number.

Appropriate facilities and staff must be provided to enable the secondary school to carry out its responsibility for broader community services, salvage programs, new media for learning, enrichment, individualized instruction, advanced placement, and other services.

New media and concepts of learning make the learner more than just a passive receptor of knowledge: It makes him increasingly responsible for independent study and research. Teaching machines and programmed instruction, educational television, instructional materials or learning resource centers combined with belief in individualized instruction have placed computerized learning within the realm of possibility.

Attempts to free the teacher for the things he does best and to better utilize his time and talents have led to providing him with the services of various supportive specialists.

The modern secondary school accepts its role of careful articulation of programs and services with other schools and agencies. The secondary school concentrates a considerable amount of attention on the guidance of the youth with which it is entrusted.

The leadership of the entire enterprise is the responsibility of the principal.

SUGGESTED EXERCISES

1. List the new programs and services inaugurated in your own secondary schools in the last 5 years.

2. What new media and new instructional organization are you evaluating in your school at this time? If you are not doing so, give defensible reasons for not doing so.

3. Would you characterize your secondary school as thoroughly modern and a new-look school? If so, why? If not, why not?

4. Is yours really just a new-look school on the surface, or is there a real commitment to new concepts of learning and to individualizing instruction?

5. Obtain a copy of the *Evaluative Criteria* from your regional accrediting association, and see in what ways your school surpasses the criteria.

6. Is time devoted at faculty meetings at your school to discussion of new media and strategies for change?

7. Read a journal from a foreign country, and list new ideas which might be considered for your school. Lead in discussing them with others.

SELECTED REFERENCES

BAILEY, THOMAS D., "The Dynamic Future," *NASSP Bulletin,* vol. 48, no. 290, March, 1964.

BECKER, JAMES W., "It Can't Replace the Teacher—Yet," *Phi Delta Kappan,* vol. 48, no. 5, January, 1967.

BROWNELL, S. M., "Education and Urbanization," *The Journal of Teacher Education,* vol. 13, no. 2, pp. 203–207, June, 1962.

CLOWARD, ROBERT D., "The Nonprofessional in Education," *Educational Leadership,* vol. 24, no. 7, pp. 604–606, April, 1967.

CONANT, JAMES B., "Are Schools Getting Better?" *U.S. News and World Report,* vol. 62, no. 17, pp. 102–106, October 23, 1967.

——, *The American High School Today,* McGraw-Hill Book Company, New York, 1959, 140 pp.

——, *The Comprehensive High School,* McGraw-Hill Book Company, New York, 1967, 95 pp.

LEVINE, DANIEL U., "Whatever Happened to the Ideal of the Comprehensive School?" *Phi Delta Kappan,* vol. 48, no. 2, October, 1966.

SHOBEN, EDWARD J., "Education in Megalopolis," *The Educational Forum,* vol. 31, no. 4, pp. 431–439, May, 1967.

TORKELSON, GERALD M., AND EMILY A. TORKELSON, "How Mechanized Should the Classroom Be?" *NEA Journal,* vol. 56, no. 3, March, 1967.

VREDEVOE, LAWRENCE E., "Secondary Education in the Next Decade," *NASSP Bulletin,* vol. 46, no. 275, September, 1962.

CHAPTER 4

DEMANDS
ON
SECONDARY
SCHOOLS One of the stern realities facing the principal and
his secondary school is that many demands are made on his time and
attention and on that of his faculty. While these demands may vary in
different areas of the country, most of them are similar for all schools.
A principal whose school is located in a disadvantaged area of one of
our large urban centers will necessarily face problems that are different
from those of a principal of a school in a wealthy suburban school
system. Wherever he may be located, however, there will be many demands on him and the school. The future will probably bring many
more.

Demands and pressures made on the schools may arise because certain
individuals or groups want the schools to do certain things. Causes for
demands and pressures are varied. There may be a desire on the part of
some to (1) maintain the status quo, (2) obtain a better or different service for themselves or their children, (3) secure favorable treatment for
themselves or their children, and (4) seek changes in administrative decisions respecting programs and services offered.

CONFLICTING DEMANDS FOR CHANGES

One of the dismaying facts which the principal on the firing line soon grasps is that many of the demands are in conflict with each other. Thus if the principal were to give in to the demand of one individual or group, he would alienate someone else. It is a real challenge for the principal and his faculty to be able to evaluate these varied demands and to make an intelligent selection of the alternative courses of action available or urged on them.

This chapter will examine some of the demands (1) for changes in the curriculum, (2) for meeting pressing social and economic needs, (3) on teachers' time and talents, and (4) on the time, energy, and funds of students.

Back to the Good Old Days

Some adults like to look back into the past and to see former ways of doing things as producing results better than those being produced today. Persons who indulge in this type of thinking do not recognize that the halo effect of the years has blotted out the unpleasant and left only the positive. To such people the frequent answer for present-day problems is to go back to the good old days.

Certain critics of the present-day secondary school claim that today's high school graduates can't read, figure, or spell. Such statements often go unchallenged even though good research evidence proves the contrary. Merely citing such research evidence may not be nearly as effective as demonstrating the competencies of your students.

One of the authors, while principal of a junior high school a few years ago, challenged the statement of a leading citizen that "the kids nowadays can't spell worth a ——!" The statement was made at a luncheon meeting of one of the local service clubs. The challenge was for the person making the statement to choose a team from the membership of the service club and meet an eighth-grade team from the local junior high school in a spelling bee. As you might expect, the team of leading community citizens went down to defeat before the eighth graders. This scotched such statements made openly for a time.

In his article "Graduates of the Good Old Days," Shannon confessed that, with twenty-nine boys out of a graduating class of sixty-two, it was not difficult to keep track of most of the 1914 male classmates of Garfield High School in Indiana. The fractional distribution of successes and failures was almost even. One-fourth have been successful, one-fourth tragic failures, one-fourth just so-so, and one-fourth out of touch with him. In his opinion, the fractional relationships were disproportionate, for the boys should have made a better showing since they went to school back in the good old days. His concern is with the one-fourth that included three who went insane and one who committed suicide. The failure, Shannon contended, cannot be based on the survival of the fittest; nor on a cause-and-effect relationship between "the program of studies, the organization and administration of the school, and the personnel and methods of teaching, on the one hand, and the high incidence of future failure of the other; nor that the school was atypical." Excessive participation in extracurricular activities cannot be blamed. Boys who became successes and failures took part in school activities. That the 1914 graduating class at Garfield was stigmatized by a large number of failures in the good old days indicates that the memories of those nostalgic years may really be blurred episodes in the minds of dreamers.[1]

Principals must expect, however, that from time to time there will be claims for the efficacy of methods and curriculums of the good old days. Persons making such claims will demand a return to such methods and curriculums. The principal and faculty of each school, together with central office personnel, must examine all alternative courses of action regardless of where they come from.

Be More Responsive to Current Needs

Among the groups of persons demanding changes in the curriculum are some who claim that the problems facing today's youth are considerably different from those of even a few years ago.

Thoughtful leaders of the past considered the adolescent's four most pressing problems to be self-realization, sex channelization, social reformation, and search for God or cosmic meaning.[2] What remains of these problems, according to certain students of teen-age behavior, is the need to make a vocational choice, the need to adapt to changing trends, and a concern for social control of overt manifestations of sex interest.[3]

If the secondary schools are to make genuine contributions to the maturation, mental health, and social productivity of youth, they must examine the curriculum in the light of the pressing problems of our day. Otherwise, the curriculum will remain an isolated entity, not vitally associated with the life and times of the student. Certain critics have charged that the curriculum is antiquated.[4]

Another group believes that the three *real* problems of teen-agers today are conformity, insecurity, and apathy.[5] Their prescription to deal

[1] J. R. Shannon, "Graduates of the Good Old Days," *The Clearing House*, vol. 34, pp. 462–464, April, 1960.
[2] Solomon Simonson, "A New Curriculum for Teen Agers," *The Clearing House*, vol. 40, no. 1, September, 1965, p. 14.
[3] *Ibid.*, p. 15.
[4] *Ibid.*, p. 14.
[5] *Ibid.*, pp. 15–16.

with these ills includes three new subjects to be placed in the curriculum. These are: (1) Applied Logic: An educational program can guard against the most serious of all conformities, the conformity of thought, by recognizing and encouraging the sovereignty of reason. Inductive thinking can be cultivated in any subject field. (2) Applied Ethics: Reason alone is not enough to take the sting out of emotional insecurity. A reexamination of our value system and an appraisal of the rights and obligations we have in human relations are indispensable to the healthy maturation of youth. There is no greater protection from insecurity than a conscious commitment to value systems. (3) Applied Rhetoric: Teachers of communication can fortify the student against the glibness of persuaders and propagandists. "The most formidable way to exorcise apathy from our teen-agers is to fortify them against propaganda." [6]

It must be emphasized that the authors are not espousing any of the positions expressed in the above section but merely reporting them as examples of demands for changes in the secondary curriculum.

Higher Academic Standards for All

Many laymen and educators interested in improving the schools feel that the best way to do so is to raise the academic standards for all. Their position is that we do not demand enough from the students in our schools today and that if we expect more from students, they will produce. In certain cases this could be true, but we should be aware that such a position carried to extremes would result in impossible demands on students.

One of the authors, while engaged recently in the comprehensive survey of a school system in a city of about one hundred thousand people, discovered that one of the senior high schools required all students to *pass* one year of algebra in order to graduate. Such an arbitrary requirement disregarded the differences in program, ability, or aspirations of the students. As one might expect, the dropout rate was extremely high. In fact the faculty of the school referred to it as a "kickout" rate rather than dropout rate.

Emphasize Science and Mathematics

Following the advent in 1957 of the first Russian *Sputnik* satellite around the earth, many Americans turned on their schools in wrath and dismay. To many people, including some educators, this loss of American world prestige was caused because our curriculum did not concentrate heavily enough on science and mathematics. These critics were composed of at least two groups: one group which still believed in faculty psychology or that tough subjects supposedly toughen the mind, and another group

[6] *Ibid.*, p. 18.

which believed that we were not giving our students enough math and science to enable us to keep up with the Russians in the applications of science and technology. No one seemed willing to admit that we could have been first if certain decisions made by our elected officials had been made differently and that these decisions were not relative to the amount of science and mathematics education in our schools compared with that in the Russian schools. Our error was one of political science—not mathematics and science.

Whatever the reasoning behind the public's concern over its schools because of the Russian satellite, in the long run the schools have benefited. The public's apathy about its schools was dispelled, and the complaisance of educators shaken badly. The National Defense Education Act of 1958 made funds available for the improvement of facilities and of the teaching of mathematics, the sciences, and foreign languages, and the expansion of proper guidance of youth. The act establishing the National Science Foundation epitomized congressional efforts to upgrade these critical areas in the curriculum. A nationally subsidized foundation to stimulate the humanities and the arts had to wait for several years before its turn arrived. By this time the American people were concerned about education as a whole—not just some of its parts. But it should be borne in mind that demands affecting particular phases of the curriculum will come and go, and educators should be prepared for those of the future.

Educate Only the Academically Talented

The viewpoint that only the elite should be educated is not a new one, nor is it completely without advocates today. The definition of who should constitute the elite will vary with time and place. In certain Western European nations today the elite are those of superior academic talent regardless of family, wealth, or position, whereas formerly the elite were those of certain select families holding great wealth and powerful positions.

Whether one uses the terms "intellectually elite," "academically talented," or "the gifted," he is referring to a comparatively small percentage of the total population of a country.

In the United States today, there are those who believe that we cannot afford to educate all our citizens and that we should therefore educate only those who will be the leaders. By their definition the leaders are those who are academically talented, and so schooling to any significant degree should be provided only for them.

Prepare Youth for the World of Work

Conflicting with the views of those who want to restrict society's efforts to education for the academically talented are persons who want the curriculum work-oriented. Their position is that all persons must work; therefore, all the school's endeavors should be directed toward preparing youth to enter the world of work. Under such an emphasis the curriculum should provide work-study experiences for young people. It should not be thought that this concept is restricted to labor and industrial leaders. Surprising or not, such leaders usually have a more balanced view of the offerings schools should make available.

Abolish Fads and Frills in Schools

In recent years schools have been urged to eliminate the "fads and frills." [7] Whether one could obtain a consensus on what constitutes a fad or a frill is debatable. To some people a fad is something followed for a time with exaggerated ardor and then dropped for something else. It is a temporary phenomenon. A frill is something that is considered non-essential to the basic purpose of a school or of anything else. It should be pointed out, however, that what is considered a fad or a frill by one person may be considered a hard-core subject by someone else. The following subjects have at some time, by some persons, been considered fads or frills: Latin, Euclidean geometry, and grammar. All three are still around after a considerable period of time in the high school curriculum, with good prospects for long life.

Programs for Exceptional Youth

In the past, little provision was made for educating exceptional children beyond the elementary level. Today, however, in attempting to provide a free secondary education for all who can learn, the public is demanding provisions for educating the physically and mentally handicapped as well as providing a challenging and stimulating education for those with superior ability.

One extremely important milestone has been the recognition of those who are "exceptional." By definition these are students who have educational needs beyond those of the average student. These needs may be physical, intellectual, or social and emotional. In this chapter the exceptional youth is "one who deviates from the average in mental, physical, social, or emotional characteristics to such an extent that he is unable to profit adequately from the regular high school curriculum alone; and

[7] Albert J. Taylor, "Frills and Fads," *The Clearing House*, vol. 38, no. 3, November, 1963, p. 182.

requires special educational services in order to have educational opportunity equal to that provided the usual pupil." [8]

Generally there are ten recognized groups of exceptionality. These are the blind, the partially seeing, the deaf, the hard of hearing, the speech handicapped, the physically handicapped, those with special health problems, the mentally retarded, the gifted, and the socially or emotionally maladjusted. Each group has its own peculiar needs.

Until a few years ago children and youth with many of the above named handicaps were either hidden away at home or institutionalized. But parents and educators have prevailed on Congress and the state legislatures to recognize the responsibility of the schools to provide programs for the exceptional child. The demands on school principals and faculty will be over how best to provide the programs for such youth—different groups will espouse different means.

Closed Areas in Society

Many areas of cultural and social life are beset with controversy. Therefore many schools avoid taking any responsibility for teaching about religion, sex, or other local taboos. This avoidance, however, does not protect the schools from the demands of one group advocating action and another demanding continuation of no action.

The school which wants to do something about the problems facing youth in the area of religion may run into obstacles as a result of local prejudices.

Some persons advocate leaving sex education to parents. Others point out that the results of recent studies show it is not being handled adequately by parents.

Surveys have indicated that only one person in fourteen receives information regarding sex before receiving it from other teen-agers. It has been reported that one-third of the brides of high school age are pregnant prior to marriage. Further, reported cases of syphilis among teen-agers have tripled in the past 10 years, and only one person in twenty-two learns about venereal diseases from his parents.[9]

If this information is accepted as being valid, it is obvious that parents, the logical transmitters of sex information, are not fulfilling the needs of youth and that a universal, effective means of conveying facts and accepted values must be established.[10]

Dr. Mary Calderone, the executive director of the Sex Information and Education Council, speaking before the American Association of School

[8] Lloyd M. Dunn, "Exceptional Youth in the American High Schools," *NASSP Bulletin*, January, 1955, pp. 5–11.

[9] Leonard Gross, "Education Comes of Age," *Look*, March 8, 1966, p. 22.

[10] F. B. Gannon, "Sex Education: Where, Why and How?" *NASSP Bulletin*, vol. 45, p. 109, September, 1961.

Administrators, stated, "Schools must play a major role in dispensing the knowledge which has been criminally and deliberately withheld about the one greatest universal experience." By the age of ten, Dr. Calderone asserted, every child should have "mastery of the factual aspects of animal and human reproductivity."

Sex education restricted to hygiene or biology courses in high school does not appear to be meeting the demands of today's society. It must be done earlier. In a recent survey of senior high school teachers it was found that "the treatment of sex in some modern novels is the most serious problem involved in their teaching of modern works." [11] It must be realized that sex is an important motif not only in today's novel but also in everyday advertising.

The need for sex education has been recognized by the American Lutheran Church, which has prepared a program of sex education for all ages for its 2½ million members.[12] What about the other millions of Americans? Should educators let nature take its course, or should a well-directed program of sex education be developed and conveyed through means of the public schools in cooperation with parents and community agencies?

DEMANDS TO MEET PRESSING SOCIAL AND ECONOMIC NEEDS

Because of the great faith which the American people have in education they turn to the schools for assistance to meet many pressing social and economic needs. It is not difficult to understand that the War on Poverty provided for educational programs to help raise the skill level of those living in poverty, many of whom dropped out of school before high school graduation. Nor is it surprising that schools are faced with demands to help with other social and economic problems.

Unemployment among Dropouts

Generally speaking, the unskilled high school student who leaves school before graduation to take a job will not hold that job long. Recent figures indicate that an alarmingly high percentage of the people out of work were teen-agers who had an incomplete educational record. Today about 35 percent of the children enrolling in high schools will become dropouts, and one-fifth of out-of-school youths under twenty-one are unemployed.[13] The outlook for these people is bleak. They will drift from

---

[11] Harry E. Hand, "Sex in the Modern Novel: A Teaching Problem," *The English Journal*, vol. 48, p. 473, November, 1959.
[12] *The New York Times*, April 13, 1966, p. 31, col. 3.
[13] Grant Venn, *Man: Education and Work*, American Council on Education, Washington, D.C., 1965, p. 2.

job to job and may become part of the statistics of crime, violence, and welfare which mar the record of excellence in the United States.

Perhaps part of the reason for the failure of many of our youth in school can be attributed to our overemphasis on the college-oriented programs. Eighty percent of our youth do not graduate from college!

Need for More Education in a Competitive World

If one were to try to characterize the last half century in the world of work in one word, he would probably select the word "change." The list by Borow below indicates some of those changes:

1. The changing length of working life
2. The changing composition of the work force
3. The changing industrial structure
4. The changing occupational standings
5. The changing geography of American industry
6. The changing productivity of the American worker
7. The changing educational and training prerequisites for employment.[14]

The last of the above-noted changes is the one which best explains the predicament in which many of our youth find themselves. Over the last 50 years the situation in our country has changed from one in which one out of ten persons was an unskilled laborer, and one in twenty was a professional person, to a situation in which one in ten is a professional, and one in twenty is an unskilled laborer.

Need for Retraining

Whether a person is college-trained, trained in a technical institute, or has learned the skills of a trade, he can never say his education is complete. The rate of change in all areas of professional, business, and industrial life is so rapid that any person expecting to keep even abreast of his field must expect to undergo retraining several times during his productive years. Obviously those desiring promotions and/or job changes must expect to improve their knowledge and skills.

The schools must help our citizens meet the demands made on them. This will require adjustments in our educational systems. The schools must provide varied programs and current curriculums and must encourage our citizens, young and middle-aged, to take advantage of every avenue of education. Only by such provisions can the schools meet the demands for the requisite programs to keep our people productive in an increasingly competitive world.

[14] Henry Borow, *Man in a World at Work*, Houghton Mifflin Company, Boston, 1964, p. 1.

Longer Life and More Leisure Time

The worthy use of leisure time was listed as one of the Seven Cardinal Principles of Secondary Education, yet it has been shown that many students do not pursue leisure activities which the schools stress as being important. Students cease serious reading and seldom listen to the "best" music. It presents the schools with a challenge—even more than ever as life expectancy increases.

Leisure time use is greatly influenced by the amount of schooling a person has had. Students who do not have a full secondary education are less likely to pursue "interest studies" or to belong to clubs and organizations of any sort. They are also less likely to read books and magazines. Even the range of interests of the high school graduate is much less than that of his counterpart—the college-educated man.[15] There is a demand on the principal and his staff that they do all they can to overcome such shortcomings. For additional information see Chapter 14.

One purpose of the curriculum should include developing a well-rounded citizen and a society of free-minded citizens. Leisure time used well will also advance the individual's freedom and his sense of responsibility.

The principal and the faculty should ensure that the entire curriculum promotes the wise use of leisure time both directly and indirectly.

Juvenile Delinquency

Because juvenile delinquency has become widespread, the schools have faced increasing demands to combat it. Delinquency is not limited to any special group of young people and may occur in any school. It becomes a function of the school to do all it can to try to prevent delinquency and, if needed, to meet and suppress the problem whenever it arises. The principal and his staff must start by learning what roles they have in recognizing a delinquent, determining what his needs and real problems are, and planning whatever action is necessary to fulfill the role determined by the school and other social agencies. The principal and/or certain members of his staff in some schools may have to spend considerable time in court. Some such appearances may be to assist school youth in trouble, and in other cases school personnel may be called as witnesses in hearings before a judicial decision is rendered. If the judge places the young person on probation with regular school attendance as part of the stipulations, the school is automatically involved. This relationship is another demand on the time and energy of school personnel. Guidance personnel by the very nature of their work will be called upon for their assistance as will

---

[15] Chester W. Harris (ed.), *Encyclopedia of Educational Research*, 3d., The Macmillan Company, New York, 1960, p. 1292.

the principal and other members of the school staff. Youth who are guilty of delinquent behavior whether in the school itself or outside seem to demand a disproportionate amount of staff time. Because this is so, preventive measures need to be taken by the principal and his staff.

One of the first steps is to see whether the potential delinquent can be discovered before he gets into trouble.

Dr. Eleanor Guleck, a Harvard researcher, has developed a battery of tests which it is claimed can predict with an 82 percent probability those who will and will not turn out delinquent. The testing involves measuring personality traits and family life factors. These important factors in the tests are (1) innate destructfulness of the child, (2) the submissiveness of the child to parental authority, (3) the mother's supervision of the boy, (4) the mother's discipline of the boy, and (5) the cohesiveness of the family life.

Special personnel and services can be put to work on diagnosing the needs of the delinquent. The guidance office should be the center of the focus on prevention. The principal should urge his staff to use their experience and service. If community clinics are available, they provide another excellent source of service which the school should utilize.

The school curriculum can be of tremendous help if it is flexible and under constant revision. Research shows an extremely high correlation between delinquency problems and reading problems. Success in reading may generate success in other phases of school life and in life in general.

The principal should know his personnel well and, after careful deliberation, assign his teachers best qualified in delinquency prevention to the appropriate trouble spots.

In summary, it can be said that the problem of juvenile delinquency can be met and reduced greatly. Psychological testing and professional inspection of delinquent trends among students should be encouraged by the administrator. Community clinics, special programs, special personnel, and the careful selection of teaching assignments will help serve the delinquent's needs and, in time, eradicate his undesirable behavior.

Desegregation

A demand made on administrators, teachers, and students alike has been in the area of changing national policy regarding the education of Negroes. Segregation of the Negro for educational purposes has not been limited to the South. Whether segregation is *de jure* or *de facto*, it has existed in both North and South. Changing public policy as a result of an awakening public conscience has decreed by judicial decisions and legislative enactment that public schools must be open to all on an equal basis. Plans for the desegregation of schools, and even the integration of schools, have been required if certain public funds are to be available to school systems.

Thus many secondary schools have seen an evolution in terms of the kinds of students to be educated. Such changes have placed demands of tolerance, forbearance, tact, diplomacy, and intestinal fortitude on all involved. Parents, teachers, students, administrators, and law enforcement officials have been tried in the crucible of dramatic social change. Except in a few cases, American schools and their communities have proved that the United States of America continues to be a self-repairing state which can bring vast and far-reaching changes by legal and evolutionary means. The problems are not all solved by any stretch of the imagination. In each community, relations between the races will change and evolve as the economic, political, and social status of the minority race changes. In such instances it places grave responsibility on all persons to see that no one is denied opportunity for the best education possible. On school personnel the responsibility is doubly grave because they must face such change in their own daily professional lives.

DEMANDS ON TEACHERS

The two foregoing sections of this chapter have presented certain demands which may be made on the secondary school. Some of these demands were concerned with changes in the curriculum, and others with meeting a variety of social and economic needs of society. While these demands may be said to be made on the school, they are really demands on people. Teachers, administrators, and even students will be the ones who must eventually implement any decisions made to meet the demands of society through school programs.

This section of the chapter will attempt to identify some of the other major demands affecting teachers as they attempt to do their jobs.

Facilitator of Learning

Most educators would probably agree that a teacher's primary role is as a facilitator of learning. In this role the teacher must organize the learning situation, guide group learning activities, help individual learners, and plan and work for improved instruction.[16]

Organizing the learning situation requires organization of facilities, materials, equipment, time, and students. The modern classroom should have a variety of instructional materials which must be selected and obtained by the teacher. Materials must be easily available to students. A variety of learning experiences must be arranged, and the class organ-

[16] W. M. Alexander and P. M. Halverson, *Effective Teaching in Secondary Schools*, Holt, Rinehart and Winston, Inc., New York, 1956, pp. 19–23.

ized for large-group, small-group, or individual instruction. Supplemental learning experiences must be available for those not involved with the teacher at the moment. Sociometric data and mental ability must be considered in making assignment to groups. Interests and abilities must be considered in directing children to certain learning experiences.

Organizing for learning also means developing attitudes and responsibilities, establishing ground rules for class operation, and assigning duties. The class should participate in making these plans. The teacher must therefore not only know what has to be done but must also be skilled in leading group planning.

Guiding group learning experiences also requires skillful leadership of groups and individuals. Good class discussion does not usually occur spontaneously. Lecturing can be effective if planned carefully and considered from the student's point of view. The educational value of field trips should be planned carefully and the students prepared to seek specific information. Small-group instruction must be similarly well organized, planned, and led. Students probably have little skill at group problem solving, debating, panel discussion, or role playing, and therefore need to be taught these skills.

To help individual learners, the teacher must know each student's abilities and weaknesses. Different ways of approaching topics must be planned. Realistic goals for slow- and fast-learning students must be established. Challenging work must be offered the gifted child to make his education interesting and meaningful. The teacher must also be alert to recognize need for special help. Specially trained teachers may be needed for very slow students. Psychological help or medical assistance may be required for children with emotional, social, or physical problems. Community resource people may be able to challenge a gifted student in an area beyond the teacher's ability. In a world where continuing education is essential, helping individual learners develop good study and work habits may be more important than learning subject matter.

In planning and improving instruction, the teacher feels the demands of modern education most clearly. Here the teacher realizes his lack of knowledge of his learners and how they learn. Here he feels the need to know more about new curriculums, organizations, materials, and methods. Here he struggles to plan stimulating work for gifted students and seeks ways to open the doors to slow learners. Here he realizes his inability to stimulate reluctant learners and underachievers.

Be a Counselor

Although most high schools have one or more professional guidance counselors today, counseling students remains a major role of the classroom teacher. Nearly 10 percent of all metropolitan teachers counsel students on a regular schedule.[17] There are still too few guidance counselors in most schools to guide and counsel all the students. Even if not a scheduled duty, counseling is a role which teachers fill daily. The more intimate association of pupils with teachers and the interest most teachers have in their students will always result in a counseling relationship. It is a function that most teachers feel is very important, and they will often delay or fail to do other duties to talk and listen to students who need personal help.

Teachers know that a child with problems he cannot solve alone is not receptive to learning. Most teachers also know that not all objectives of education are attained through formal education. Many things can be learned better if related to personal problems in counseling situations. In fact, it is sometimes difficult to distinguish between individual instruction and counseling.

Teachers' responsibilities have also increased because of the greater number of children with physical and mental handicaps and emotional problems attending school. These children need help in learning to live with their problems and adjust to their environments. Similarly, our greater concern with dropouts, culturally deprived children, poverty, and integration has added to the counseling burden on teachers.[18]

Parents also need counseling to understand the potentialities of their children and to develop realistic expectations and goals for them. Parents must also understand the school's objectives and programs and support the teacher's efforts. Few parents can do these things without help, and the teacher must plan to give such help as needed.

Performer of School Duties

Each teacher must accept certain other responsibilities in the school such as supervising student areas, sponsoring student activities, working on faculty committees, and performing administrative functions. Twenty percent of the average teacher's 46-hour week is spent in this way.[19]

Faculty committees should be an important part of every school. These committees should develop uniform policies on discipline, homework, grading, and similar matters which concern every teacher. There should also be agreement on educational philosophy and objectives. Students should not be confused by different philosophies or policies in their several classes. While these committees demand a great deal of the teacher's time, they are essential to a good school.

Teachers should also accept responsibilities for improving school-community relations. They should willingly attend and support the PTA.

[17] "Profile of the Metropolitan Teacher," *NEA Research Bulletin*, October, 1962, pp. 69–74.
[18] Gene F. Ackerman, "Pressures on Teachers," *Educational Leadership*, vol. 22, no. 3, p. 159, December, 1964.
[19] "Time Devoted to School Duties," *NEA Research Bulletin*, October, 1962, p. 87.

They should cooperate with the press. In any such duties, teachers should honestly represent the aims and policies of the school.

Many of the other demands come into focus in the teacher's role as mediator of the culture. He cannot make good decisions as a director of learning or counsel students wisely or contribute effectively to faculty committees unless he perceives cultural requirements and interprets them correctly.

Unfortunately, the many other, more immediate demands on a teacher's time and energy make it particularly difficult for him to meet these pervasive cultural demands effectively. He needs broad education and experiences, time to read widely, and social contacts to meet and discuss with persons in other fields. He needs to be informed on events, conditions, and trends in business, economics, government, science and technology, and many other fields.

Community Worker

Teachers have always been informal links with the community. Just by living in the community and talking with other citizens, teachers act as representatives of the school.

Today many teachers are asked to perform more formal duties as agents of the school's community relations program (see Chapter 21). Schools recognize the need for a continual flow of information to the public. Teachers may serve on community relations committees or coordinate a school's relations with the press or interpret their work through the mass media. Each of these duties requires new skills and information that the teacher must learn.

The traditional links of personal contacts must also be expanded and made more effective. Teachers must know the community power structure and the structure through which information is disseminated and decisions made. They should know which persons are influential in opinion forming. Above all, they should be sure that they have accurate, factual information to provide and that they understand school policies and programs.[20]

Professional Contributor

Each teacher has professional responsibilities and receives benefits as a member of the profession. In addition to giving his best efforts to his professional duties, he should belong to the appropriate professional organizations and support them with his time and talents. He should take pride in his profession and strive to improve it. He should encourage

---

[20] G. McCloskey, *Education and Public Understanding*, Harper & Row, Publishers, Incorporated, New York, 1959, pp. 289–334.

interested and qualified young people to enter the profession and should honestly explain its advantages and disadvantages to them.

Any member of a profession should contribute to the knowledge of that profession through research and writing. Education needs all the knowledge it can gain, and teachers should engage in research and testing of ideas whenever possible.

A profession also has responsibilities to the public which places its trust in that profession. Teachers should explain honestly education's needs to the public and help people understand these needs. They should also honestly admit education's shortcomings without violating their professional ethics. When necessary, they must take strong action to protect the public from malpractices and misrepresentations.

The welfare of the members of the profession must also concern each teacher. He should work for those benefits and policies that improve the security, living standards, and dignity of teachers. These benefit not just his colleagues and himself but the profession and therefore the children who attend the schools of the nation.

Other Demands

Teachers are also subjected to other demands on their time and energy. Communities often have high expectations for teachers to participate in many community services and activities. The teacher's family also has a rightful demand upon his time. These demands must be considered as part of the total pressure felt by the modern teacher.

Of metropolitan teachers 63.9 percent were active in one or more religious, civic, charitable, or political organizations, and 27.3 percent were active in three or more such groups. In smaller communities 84.7 percent were active in one or more organizations, and 43.9 percent were active in three or more.[21] The record of community service of teachers is a good one; the reasons for this are probably the same as those which caused them to select teaching as a career. Because they often have knowledge that others lack, teachers probably carry a larger burden in these groups than others, and the time invested is probably large.

The same survey showed that 83 percent of all men teachers and 75 percent of all women teachers were married. The families of married men teachers average 1.9 children, and those of married women teachers average 1.4 children.[22] Families and homes require attention. Children especially require a parent's time, attention, and patience, and the duties of a parent are probably taken seriously by most teachers.

Economic demands are felt by most teachers. Communities expect their teachers to reflect a desirable middle-class status, even if they do not pro-

21 "Teachers in the Public Schools," *NEA Research Bulletin*, February, 1963, p. 26.
22 *Ibid.*

vide comparable salaries. Teachers themselves feel a need to maintain a standard of living that evokes the respect of their students and the community and enhances their own dignity. Professional requirements of membership in associations, additional education, broad reference libraries, and cultural enrichment add up to sizable expenditures of money. Salaries of teachers in most communities do not enable a teacher to meet these demands. Therefore, 60 percent of all men teachers and 12 percent of all women teachers supplement their income through summer employment, and 47.4 percent of the men and 7.6 percent of the women hold part-time jobs during the school year. Men teachers average 14.1 percent of their income from other jobs and women average 4.2 percent of their income from outside jobs.[23]

DEMANDS ON YOUTH

Every individual must expect that a certain number of demands will be made on him. Because life is demanding, the way in which individuals meet the necessities of life determines the individual's mental and emotional health. Adolescence is a period of intense pressure, mainly because it is a transition period between childhood and adulthood. The secondary school student is faced with numerous academic and nonacademic demands, which become increasingly characteristic of those which will be made on him when he reaches adulthood.

Developmental Tasks

According to Havighurst, each individual has to complete certain "developmental tasks" before he can progress to those of a more difficult nature characteristic to a certain age level. "The term development is significant. The tasks, or the skills, attitudes and understanding essential to the task, must be learned at the appropriate time." [24] These tasks and attitudes, which are developed gradually, are inculcated in the adolescent by means of the school, church, and home.

Necessarily, the achievement of developmental abilities and attitudes entails a certain amount of pressure. In secondary school, students are faced with the need for mastering certain basic tasks.

The developmental tasks which are so important throughout life may be classified according to their relation to the physical, mental, and emotional health of the student. The secondary student is faced most directly with the problem of growing up physically, emotionally, and mentally. Biological development differs among individuals; however, certain generalized abilities and attitudes should be achieved by the time

[23] *Ibid.*, p. 25.
[24] *The High School in a Changing World,* Thirty-sixth Yearbook, The American Association of School Administrators, Washington, D.C., 1958, p. 42.

a child reaches high school age. The mastery of certain social skills determines whether he is accepted or rejected by a peer group. The development of the physical ability to participate in sports as well as to dance properly is often an outstanding achievement for the young person because it shows not only his physical capability but his emotional and mental maturity by indicating that he is able to cope with the problems presented by his peers.

The student is expected to have understood successfully and accepted his proper sex role. Improper sex identification can become a psychological problem which intensifies the already existing pressures on the young person. He is often rejected by his friends, parents, and teachers. Too often psychiatric help is not given until the individual is older.

Another demand facing the student as he matures is his need to achieve independence, while, at the same time, he wishes security. The individual must learn to be responsible for his own acts. "Rebellion against parents is sometimes transformed into rebellion against teachers." [25] The struggle for independence is ambivalent and too often misunderstood by parents and teachers as well as the young person himself. Outbreaks of deviant behavior can be expected as manifestations of adolescent rebellion against economic and social demands in almost any era.

Along with the individual's achievement of independence, it is necessary for him to consider seriously his occupational future. This consideration is perhaps the greatest cause for pressure upon the student today. Our society demands that everyone be somewhat productive; therefore, the preparation for a vocation is a major concern to the youth of today. The school should help guide and train the young person into an area of study to which he feels suited. A rather pressing concern is to choose an occupation which will be useful in our changing society. For this reason, higher and more specialized training is desirable today. More high school students are feeling the need to go to college or to seek some other form of education beyond the high school.

"Anxiety seems to come from a personal sense of not being able to meet the future." [26] The increased attention upon training for the future will continue. The middle-class American ideal of long-range preparation has gradually penetrated all classes within the United States due to the influence of mass media. The expectations placed upon boys remains greater than upon girls. However, the increased number of women in the work world has intensified pressure upon the young woman to obtain a good education to prepare her for her occupation also.

As well as learning to cope with the future occupationally and socially,

[25] Robert Havighurst, *Human Development and Education*, David McKay Company, Inc., New York, 1953, p. 124.
[26] *Growing Up in an Anxious Age*, 1952 Yearbook, Association for Supervision and Curriculum Development, Washington, D.C., 1952, p. 25.

the student must acquire "self-confidence and a system of values." [27] Each high school student is in the midst of trying out his values, changing them, or incorporating them into a new value system. A stable philosophy of life is necessary before a person can meet the everyday tensions present in today's adult world. Churches and school play an important part in educating the child so that he is able to maintain a secure system of values; however, home background takes precedence. "The school is now the primary supplement to the home." [28] The family may fail to provide the much needed help a young person needs, thus creating a poor frame of reference from which the young person can base his life. This failure may hinder the individual for the rest of his life, for inadequate development of ethical and moral attitudes are detrimental to the individual's philosophy of life in his attitude toward discrimination and prejudice. Today, this is a major consideration. Although most prejudices are ingrained by the family, fair and democratic treatment of all students within a school will tend to lessen pressure upon those who are discriminated against and upon those who are the discriminators.

Demand to Succeed

Ambitions, fears, and needs are the basic motivations for many of the demands upon the student. Success depends on motivation. Each student is either motivated or not to take part in the academic and nonacademic life around him. Stimulation of motivation is the most important factor in helping a young person develop his potential. "Many problems of behavior and low achievement in school can be solved by reassuring boys and girls that they are normal even if their pattern of development is not that of the average person." [29]

Most parents and teachers help motivate the student toward the middle-class ideal of success. They set the standards of achievement to which the young person must strive. Each individual is basically self-centered and thus sets his goals accordingly. Frequently, there may be conflict between the objectives of the parent, the teacher, and the student.

The "success motive" is a rather vague term; however, most Americans will agree to some of its basic components. The ideal of getting ahead, economically and socially, is a somewhat long-range objective to which most Americans subscribe. Getting ahead denotes the need for a degree of aggressiveness on the part of the individual, which can only be motivated by a confidence achieved first through success in social and academic areas in school and later through financial capability. The strong emphasis on the power of the dollar in our country and the ability to obtain it

[27] *The High School in a Changing World*, p. 43.
[28] James Hymes, Jr., *Effective Home-School Relations*, Prentice-Hall, Inc., Englewood Cliffs, N.J., 1953, p. 1.
[29] Havighurst, *op. cit.*, p. 122.

puts pressure upon the young person in his early attempts to achieve prestige academically and socially. Often, he feels that early achievement will ensure future success.

"When an individual fails to acquire the skills required to meet the demands of society, various unfortunate reactions take place." [30] Failure as the alternative to success in school may put the student in an embarrassing light before his peers, teachers, and parents. Often, he feels frustrated and defeated. For this reason, extra pressure is placed upon the student to maintain high standards of achievement in all fields, whether football or algebra. Overparticipation and fear of failure sometimes result in the inability of the student to accomplish the necessities of high school academic life.

Today there is a renewed stress on the academic side of education. The young person frequently feels that he must obtain a high school diploma, and further that he must pursue a college degree. Too often many students who are unable to achieve excellence are neglected by schools. "Excellence, too, has come to be judged against a public, rather than a personal criterion." [31] Public recognition of excellence may be valuable at times; however, it often results in disturbing those who failed or those who were unable to participate as well as frequently leading the achiever to becoming a "swelled head."

Everyone needs to succeed. Our society and especially our schools are based upon the success motive to an overwhelming degree. We must provide for those who wish to succeed but who, perhaps through some inefficiency in our educational system, are unable to do so. Nothing motivates one to succeed like success.

SUMMARY

The secondary school as an agent for change has many conflicting demands made on its students and staff. Some persons want decisions made regarding the curriculum which they claim will reinstate conditions which existed in some ideal time in the past. Others want educators to stop pampering students and demand rigorous academic standards for all students. Still others feel that we should educate only an academically talented elite and put the others to work.

For almost every demand made, there may be someone else demanding just the opposite course of action. As an example of this phenomenon the authors point out the area of sex education. With an increasing rate of venereal disease and unwed mothers among teen-agers, it seems evident that something needs to be done of an educational nature. Some advocate

[30] *The High School in a Changing World*, p. 61.
[31] O. L. Davis, Jr., "Pressure on Pupils in the Schools," *Educational Leadership, Journal of the Association for Supervision and Curriculum Development*, vol. 21, p. 426, April, 1964.

that the schools must assume some of the responsibility for solving these problems, while others don't even want the word sex uttered in schools.

The advances made in the technology of educational resources, new knowledge of all kinds, new organizational patterns for instruction, and the increasing number of research and developmental projects are all part of the pressures to which the school staff is exposed.

The young people in our schools are also constantly being subjected to demands.

One of the developmental tasks assigned to youth is to succeed. The pressures to succeed academically, socially, and economically are acute. The great American dream of getting ahead and making something of oneself emphasizes academic success as a means to social and economic success. Those whose gifts are in fields other than the academic ones must also be given opportunities to know success.

The secondary school administrator must know about the demands made on schools because he must understand that this is part of the setting within which schools operate. An understanding of this setting is essential if he is to exercise wise leadership.

SUGGESTED EXERCISES

1. Keep a log for a week of the requests made on the time and talents of students and staff. On whom do most of them fall?

2. List the changes made in programs and services over the last year, and see whether you can discover where the demands came for them.

3. Plan the speech you will make to the local Kiwanis Club to refute the statement that today's high school graduates can't read, spell, or figure. Use research results to support your position.

4. Outline the presentation you will make to the school board in support of a proposal to establish work experience programs in cooperation with local business and industry.

5. Debate with a colleague the pros and cons of the separate vocational/technical school versus vocational and technical provisions within the comprehensive high school. You debate the position opposite from that in which you believe.

6. Poll your teachers about their feeling of security or lack of it in teaching about local issues of sex education, politics, crime, business practices, religion, race, etc.

7. Find out whether your board of education has a stated policy (or rigid practice) which requires preference to local vendors, suppliers, contractors, and salesmen.

8. Ask each teacher in your secondary schools to keep a time log of the time spent at school and in performing work connected with school.

9. How many of your colleagues teach or have other responsibilities in rela-tion to a Sunday school? How many work in scouting or similar organizations not directly connected with the schools but having to do with children and/or youth? Does the community expect this participation?

10. Does your secondary school limit the participation of students in school-related activities? Do you think a similar limitation ought to be established to protect teachers?

SELECTED REFERENCES

ACKERMAN, GENE F., "Pressures on Teachers," *Educational Leadership,* vol. 22, no. 3, December, 1964.

ANDERSON, ROBERT H., *Teaching in a World of Change,* Harcourt, Brace & World, Inc., New York, 1966.

BROUDY, HARRY S., B. OTHANEL SMITH, AND JOE R. BURNETT, *Democracy and Excellence in American Secondary Education,* Rand McNally & Company, Chicago, 1964, 302 pp., chap. 2.

COULSON, JOHN E., "Automation, Electronic Computers, and Education," *Phi Delta Kappan,* vol. 47, no. 7, March, 1966.

DAVIS, O. L., JR., "Pressures on Pupils in the School," *Educational Leadership,* vol. 21, no. 7, April, 1964.

McCLEARY, LLOYD E., AND STEPHEN P. HENCLEY, *Secondary School Administration,* Dodd, Mead & Company, Inc., New York, 1965, 399 pp., chap. 3.

CHAPTER 5

ORGANIZING
SECONDARY
SCHOOLS
FOR
ADAPTABILITY

EDUCATION FOR ADAPTABILITY

Adaptability is not new to Americans. It is a part of our heritage from the Old World influenced by our revolutionary and liberal experiment in government. Through the years, social and legal standards were scrutinized and modified to fit into the emerging American concept of democracy or, if found unacceptable, were discarded. Even homegrown traditions and practices were rejected when they offended the changing pattern of what the new nation thought was desirable. In this "conceptual design," as Hamilton and Mort call it,[1] new ideas were tried and evaluated and, if acceptable, became a part of the emerging pattern for a time but would face reevaluation if they became suspect.

The schools of the present should reflect the needs of society at this time and attempt to prepare the citizens of the future. This seems like an Herculean task—to preserve and transmit the social and cultural heritage, while at the same time trying to improve society and attempting to aid the individual to adjust to his environment and to develop to the

[1] Robert Hamilton and Paul R. Mort, *The Law and Public Education*, Foundation Press, Chicago, 1947.

utmost of his abilities. As educators, we have concentrated our efforts on the preservation and transmission of an idealized version of the heritage. Our teacher training institutions and other colleges and universities have perpetuated this emphasis. But, if this is all that schools teach, who teaches young people about the changes in our society, the nature of the alternatives in our developing society, and how to make judgments in the selection of alternatives?

Never has man acquired knowledge at the present pace "nor on so broad a technological area. . . . It has been suggested that the sum total of all man's knowledge may very likely double in the next decade. . . . There are amazing new tools at hand for exploration and for problem solving." [2] Such a staggering amount of knowledge means that no person can be expected to learn it all, and certainly that learning cannot just be limited to the elementary, secondary, and college experiences in a person's life-span. Two implications for education arise from that statement. First, we have an obligation to teach the basic skills of communication and computation upon which to build further knowledge. But further, and perhaps more important, we must teach citizens of all ages "to locate, verify, interpret, and apply knowledge." [3]

This knowledge, the tools for acquiring it, and the beliefs about man and his relation to man and to the physical world are also changing. In such a dynamic situation the individual must be prepared to examine new discoveries and hypotheses, test them, and if found useful, adopt or adapt; or if found wanting, reject them. Older facts, concepts, and values must be held up to the same light and tested against new conditions.[4]

Second, it must not be considered that a person's education is ever finished. A story is told of the obituary notices of a bygone age. The notice might say that the deceased "finished his education at Podunk College." If he reached the age of seventy-five and had truly finished with education at twenty-two, he had been dead for many years and didn't know it.[5]

With so much to learn, people must be made aware that progress cannot wait for a new generation with new skills. A person may have to be retrained three or four times during his lifetime if he is to continue productive contributions to society. This can mean but one thing: An educational system must be developed which is geared for people of all ages, preparing them for problems which cannot be foreseen adequately.

[2] Commission on Public Education, *Virginia in the Space Age*, Report of the Commission to the Governor and the General Assembly of Virginia, Commonwealth of Virginia, Department of Purchases and Supply, Richmond, Va., 1961, p. 8.
[3] Ralph L. Pounds and James R. Bryner, *The School in American Society*, The Macmillan Company, New York, 1959, p. 495.
[4] *Ibid.*
[5] M. Dale Baughman, *Teacher's Treasury of Stories for Every Occasion*, Prentice-Hall, Inc., Englewood Cliffs, N.J., 1958, p. 72.

One purpose of this book is to provide a starting place for those who will be the administrators in the secondary schools of tomorrow. The educational task confronting them will be a continuing challenge. To meet that challenge, schools must have administrators who are constant evaluators of social and cultural changes. They must know how to relate these changes to the problems facing citizens today, and they must teach methods for solving problems which have not yet been imagined. Administrators are needed who never lose sight of the fact that they must always be learners themselves. They must be learning continually about the needs of society, about new knowledges and skills still in process of development, and particularly about their own role in the educative process. The competent school administrator first of all must be a social scientist!

ADMINISTRATIVE ORGANIZATION

Just as the teacher needs to know the characteristics of the child at all ages, so must those studying to become competent school administrators know the characteristics of all types of schools to be found and the governmental framework within which the schools operate.

One definition of the term "organization" is "a systematic preparation for action." If action is considered here to mean education, then whatever society does to prepare for education should be included in a study of organization. The institution developed by society to handle its business is government. Therefore, study of the history of organization must include examination of the development of government's role in education at the various levels.

A National System of Education

A national system of education in this country does not exist in the same sense that there is a French, a British, or a Peruvian system of education. Consequently, we have fifty different state school systems and many differences between local school systems in the same state. Each state has developed its own plan of organization in keeping with its sovereign rights. The differences between state systems are more in the details than in the fundamentals. As was pointed out in the first section of this book, the nature of education in the early colonies was affected by certain major influences which helped shape and control the setting of educational policy. The major influences were similar in each of the colonies. Therefore, the state systems of education now have somewhat similar forms of organization, means of administration, types of curriculum, means of financial support, requirements for certification, and so forth.

The differences which exist among state systems of education in the United States arose because of the unique traditions affecting the development of educational policy in the early colonies. When the colonies became states in the United States after the Revolutionary War, the Constitution of 1787 made no mention of education. The distrust of our founding forefathers of a highly centralized government caused them to limit carefully the powers of the federal government. This is underscored by the Tenth Amendment to the Constitution of the United States, which states: "The powers not delegated to the United States by the Constitution, nor prohibited by it to the States, are reserved to the States respectively, or to the people." On the basis of the above, education in the United States is generally considered to be a *state* function.

The complexities of modern life demand well-educated citizens. They must be educated for living with and advancing further our knowledge and technology for surviving in a competitive world, for cooperating because of increased interdependence on each other, and for protecting our way of life. Thus education has become a *national concern,* and the provision of financial aid from the federal level of government reflects that concern.

State Organization for Education

The organization for education in a state is provided for in the constitution of that state and in the statutes enacted by its legislature. All state constitutions provide that a system of public education must be established, maintained, and continued by the legislature. Most state legislatures have established state boards of education to implement school legislation. These state boards of education are responsible for determining statewide policies and promulgating rules and regulations pertaining to the operation of schools.[6]

All states in the United States have established a position for a chief state school officer called, variously, state superintendent of public instruction, state superintendent of schools, state commissioner of education, and so forth. Although the exact relationship of this officer to the state board of education varies, state by state, he usually acts as executive officer for the board. He carries out the policy for the board and directs the overall activities of a professional staff. Together with his staff, the chief state school officer is responsible for the coordination and administration of certain services.[7]

[6] Edgar L. Morphet, Roe L. Johns, and Theodore L. Reller, *Educational Administration,* Prentice-Hall, Inc., Englewood Cliffs, N.J., 1959, p. 14.
[7] Lee M. Thurston and William H. Roe, *State School Administration,* Harper & Row, Publishers, Incorporated, New York, 1957, pp. 79–82.

Functions of State Departments of Education

Although many lists of the functions of state departments of education have been made three general functions should suffice:

(1) Regulation—those activities which ensure that constitutional and legislative enactments, and state board regulations are complied with.
(2) Administration of special services—such as, schools and services for the handicapped, financial services, informational services, and film library and teaching materials distribution.
(3) Leadership—mobilizing and coordinating the resources of the state for improvement of education.[8]

Planning, research, public relations, coordination, and so forth, can readily be placed under one or more of the three main functions listed above.

As the level of leadership at the local level increases, the need for the strict regulatory function decreases. The state superintendent and his staff can then exert their energies leading to the development of better programs and services in the local school systems.

Within their variously defined roles, state departments share in the responsibility for program improvement. At the least, they attempt to bring up low-standard districts, and at the optimum level, they challenge even the best districts to seek additional improvements. In general, state departments attempt to set minimum standards below which no district is permitted to sink.

As important shapers of educational policy, strong state departments of education are advocated by James B. Conant. In his book *Shaping Educational Policy,* he states: "What is needed are strong state boards of education, a first-class chief state school officer, a well-organized state staff, and good support from the legislature." [9]

Public law 89-10, The Elementary and Secondary Education Act of 1965, included provisions for strengthening state departments of education. Title V of the act authorized the United States Commissioner to issue grants "to stimulate and assist States in strengthening the leadership resources of their State educational agencies, and to assist those agencies in the establishment and improvement of programs to identify and meet the educational needs of States."

Local School Systems

The local school district is the operational unit in American public education. As pointed out in the preceding section, education has traditionally been considered a state function. However, the states have placed

[8] *Ibid.*
[9] James B. Conant, *Shaping Educational Policy,* McGraw-Hill Book Company, New York, 1964, p. 31.

the responsibility for carrying out this function upon the local school division. Thus, education is said to be a *local* responsibility. The locality discharges this responsibility through a local school board. The local school board members may be elected by the people in some states, such as Indiana, California, and Pennsylvania, or appointed by circuit court judges, county boards of supervisors, city councils, or even by another board especially appointed for that purpose. It has been estimated that in the United States over 75 percent of the school population is found in districts which have elected boards.

Whether elected or appointed, the school board is legally an agent of the state government, even though it also represents local interests. The school board member is thus a state officer.

The school board's functions are those of: (1) establishing policy (sometimes called legislating) and (2) appraising or evaluating. Some experts in the field insist that the appointment of the superintendent is an executive function and is the most important single task any board may be called upon to perform. These experts will insist that the executive function of the board should end at that point. From there on the administration should be done by the superintendent, who is the board's chief executive. As has been pointed out several times in this book, the level of leadership provided by a school system's administrators determines to a large degree the caliber of its schools.

Certainly it is within the prerogative of local administrators to recommend to their school board the plan of organization which to them seems to facilitate best the programs and services offered to the children and youth of the district. Just as certain is the fact that it is within the authority of the school board to decide which pattern of organization shall be adopted. As long as the educational program and supporting services are the basis for organizational changes, no one should argue. But to change the organizational structure without improving educational opportunities is to cause unnecessary upheaval, demands for adaptation, and considerable expense. Better educational opportunities for the district's children and youth should be the deciding factor.

Purpose of Any Plan of Organization

The purpose of any plan of organization whether in a school system, in industry, in the church, or in the Armed Forces is the same. That purpose is to maximize the utilization of the resources available to accomplish the tasks assigned. Administrators strive through organization to bring the human, physical, and social resources to bear on the job to be done.

School administration has only one purpose: That purpose is to facilitate the total educational program of the community. While this can be stated as a simple fact, it is in operation a very complex process. The complexity arises from the number of programs and services offered to the community, multiplied by the number of pupils, teachers, other school personnel, buildings, busses, equipment, supplies, and so forth, involved.

Patterns of School Organization

School organization is the means by which students in a school system are arranged into groups or divisions. This is done so that administration can facilitate more effectively the instructional program. Administration acts through organization. The grade levels in our American public schools rise like a ladder from kindergarten to grade 12. In some systems nursery education and grades 13 and 14 have become a part of the public educational offering. Therefore, a plan of school organization is referred to as a vertical plan. Several possible vertical plans of school organization are shown in Figure 5-1 (pp. 96–97).

In Figure 5-1, certain organizational plans are shown. *A* shows the 6-6 plan often found in sparsely populated rural areas. In this plan the elementary school contains the first six grades while the last six grades are lumped together as a junior–senior high school.

B in Figure 5-1 shows the traditional Virginia 7-5 plan, in which pupils in grades 1 through 7 are gathered into an elementary school, and pupils in grades 8 through 12 into a high school. A few other states, mostly Eastern or Southern, have used this plan.

C shows the 6-3-3 plan which consists of a 6-year elementary school, a 3-year junior high school, and a 3-year senior high school. This is the predominant pattern for large and middle-sized school systems in the United States.

In the 6-2-4 plan shown in *D* of Figure 5-1, a 6-year elementary school, a 2-year junior high, and a 4-year senior high school are found.

The ladder marked *E* shows the 5-3-4 plan which provides for a primary or elementary school containing grades 1 through 5, an intermediate, or middle school of grades 6 through 8, and a four-year high school grades 9 through 12.

The plan shown in *G* is now found in only a few places in the United States, but seems to be growing in popularity in some cities in certain sections of the country. In such an arrangement the primary grades, grades 1, 2, and 3 are organized and housed in a building separate from older children. This enables the establishment of neighborhood schools for the smaller children and lends itself nicely to an ungraded primary instructional program. In areas where public kindergartens are maintained, they are an integral part of the primary school, the natural starting place for the educational experiences of children. The other groupings of grades are similar to the other plans.

In plan *H* grades 1 through 4 are housed separately from older children (this plan can also include kindergartens). Grades 5 through 8 are housed in what is called a middle or intermediate school, and grades 9 through 12 comprise the senior high school.

It is difficult to say that one plan or organization is better than another regardless of the situation. The most important thing to keep in mind is the kind of instructional program that is wanted in our schools. As will probably always be the case, the teacher is the most important and most direct influence upon the education of the individual child or youth. A *good* teacher is the first requisite of a good education *if* proper equipment, materials, services, and other school facilities are provided. Bringing all the factors facilitating the instructional classroom program to the aid of the teacher is the task of the administrators of the school system.

Because this book is concerned primarily with the secondary school, no attempt will be made to describe the organization, programs, and services of the elementary school, except as the need for discussing articulation among the various levels of schools arises.

The Junior High or Middle Schools

While most persons reading this book may be familiar with junior and senior high schools from their own experiences, some may not. If a person's total knowledge of something is limited to his own experience, however, then he may fail to benefit from the knowledge of others. Therefore, it seems wise to review briefly what administrators should know about those schools lumped together under the heading of "secondary schools."

It should be remembered that until 1896 there were only two levels of schools in most states—the elementary school of eight grades, and the high school of four grades. In 1896 the city of Richmond, Indiana, placed its seventh and eighth grades in a separate building and developed a modified curriculum. The curriculum provided changes in the areas of English, mathematics, and social studies and added a foreign language and a practical arts course.[10] Grades 7 and 8 in this city, and in other schools opening in other cities, tended to be considered as part of the secondary school rather than of the elementary school. Departmentalized teaching and promotion by subjects were characteristics of these early seventh- and eighth-grade schools. Later on the ninth grade was added in many systems which gave a 6-3-3 pattern of organization. Other systems put their seventh and eighth grades in with grades 9 through 12 and thus established a 6-6

[10] Roland C. Faunce and Morrel J. Clute, *Teaching and Learning in the Junior High School*, Wadsworth Publishing Co., Belmont, Calif., 1963, p. 6.

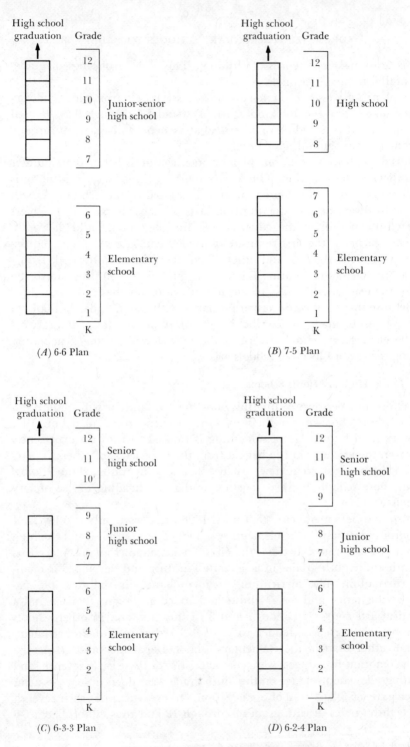

High school
graduation   Grade

| 12 |
| 11 |
| 10 | Junior-senior
| 9 | high school
| 8 |
| 7 |

| 6 |
| 5 |
| 4 | Elementary
| 3 | school
| 2 |
| 1 |
| K |

(A) 6-6 Plan

High school
graduation   Grade

| 12 |
| 11 |
| 10 | High school
| 9 |
| 8 |

| 7 |
| 6 |
| 5 |
| 4 | Elementary
| 3 | school
| 2 |
| 1 |
| K |

(B) 7-5 Plan

High school
graduation   Grade

| 12 |
| 11 | Senior
| 10 | high school

| 9 |
| 8 | Junior
| 7 | high school

| 6 |
| 5 |
| 4 | Elementary
| 3 | school
| 2 |
| 1 |
| K |

(C) 6-3-3 Plan

High school
graduation   Grade

| 12 |
| 11 | Senior
| 10 | high school
| 9 |

| 8 | Junior
| 7 | high school

| 6 |
| 5 |
| 4 | Elementary
| 3 | school
| 2 |
| 1 |
| K |

(D) 6-2-4 Plan

Fig. 5-1. Selected Patterns of School Organization.

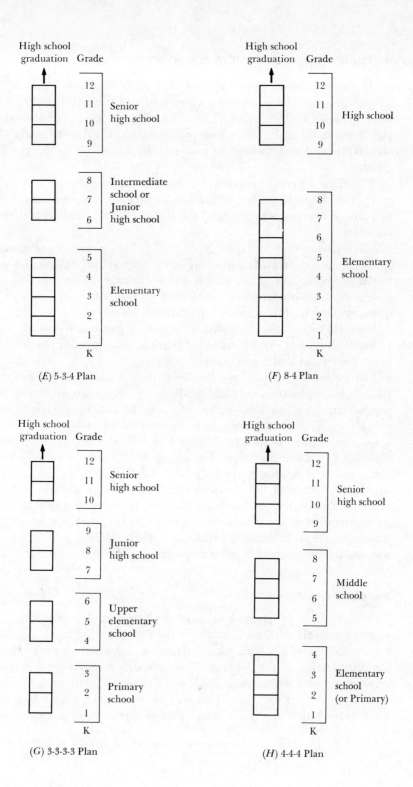

High school graduation | Grade

| 12 |
| 11 | Senior high school
| 10 |
| 9 |

| 8 | Intermediate school or Junior high school
| 7 |
| 6 |

| 5 |
| 4 |
| 3 | Elementary school
| 2 |
| 1 |
| K |

(E) 5-3-4 Plan

High school graduation | Grade

| 12 |
| 11 | High school
| 10 |
| 9 |

| 8 |
| 7 |
| 6 |
| 5 | Elementary school
| 4 |
| 3 |
| 2 |
| 1 |
| K |

(F) 8-4 Plan

High school graduation | Grade

| 12 |
| 11 | Senior high school
| 10 |

| 9 |
| 8 | Junior high school
| 7 |

| 6 |
| 5 | Upper elementary school
| 4 |

| 3 |
| 2 | Primary school
| 1 |
| K |

(G) 3-3-3-3 Plan

High school graduation | Grade

| 12 |
| 11 | Senior high school
| 10 |
| 9 |

| 8 |
| 7 | Middle school
| 6 |
| 5 |

| 4 |
| 3 | Elementary school (or Primary)
| 2 |
| 1 |
| K |

(H) 4-4-4 Plan

grade pattern. Some New England and some Southern states left the seventh grade in the elementary school and put the eighth grade in with the high school which resulted in a 7-5 plan. In Virginia there was no eighth grade for many years, and pupils who finished seven years of elementary school and wanted to go on to high school entered the ninth grade.

The plans of vertical organization tried in this country are very diverse, and junior highs of grades 7-10, 6-8, and 5-8 can be found. In the latter two cases the school may be called the *intermediate school,* or perhaps the *middle school.*

While earlier in this chapter it was stated that the most valid reason for changing to a different plan of organization was to improve the educational program, this is not always the prevailing reason for change. In fact, it is rather obvious that many changes result from enrollment pressures, existing buildings, state laws, limited resources, etc.[11]

After surveying the diversity of school organization found for the junior high years, Conant concluded that the placement of the grades was not as important as the program provided.[12]

The junior high school was initiated to give early adolescents opportunities for exploration in wider fields, to put an age group facing similar psychological and physiological changes in the care of specialists, and to provide guidance and adjustment opportunities for boys and girls. Yet, a so-called junior high school with fine facilities might not really be fulfilling the above functions. The reason for this might be a sterile program and a lack of services to youth. Sterile programs in schools are usually a result of a lack of competent professional leadership. For the principal to say that his hands are tied by the superintendent or for the superintendent to say that his board won't let him do the kinds of things he wants to do is to evade the real issue. The real issue is whether or not security in the position is more important to the administrator than his professional integrity.

The Senior High School

The types of programs and services to be found in the senior high school are dealt with in later chapters. The organization of the senior high school years has been the determining influence, in many cases, on the organization of the lower grades. Although recent available research shows the 3-year senior high school as the predominant plan in cities of medium and large size, other plans are found. In fact the authors of this book believe they discern a trend in the direction of a return to the

---

[11] James B. Conant, *Education in the Junior High School Years,* Educational Testing Service, Princeton, N.J., 1960, p. 10.
[12] *Ibid.,* p. 2.

4-year high school. One cause for such a trend is likely to be the increasing number and proportion of high school graduates going on for higher education. Thus the ninth grade becomes of great importance because subjects taken and grades achieved are "for the record." It is increasingly evident that colleges and universities (or at least the segment of society ambitious to send their children to higher education) are influencing not only the curriculum but the organization as well.

The patterns of school organization presented earlier in this chapter dealt only with school systems which end at twelfth-grade high school graduation. It should be noted that some senior high schools are found in school systems in which junior or community colleges serve as extensions of the public school system. In such organizations the 2-year senior high school may be a part of a senior division which also includes grades 13 and 14. It would be possible then to find such patterns as K-6-3-5, K-6-2-6, and K-6-4-4.

The Junior or Community College

The original purpose of the junior college was to offer 2-year terminal programs for vocational preparation. This purpose has been modified over the years since World War II, so that today most junior colleges are multifunctional. That is, they offer terminal programs but also offer general education programs that enable students after 2 years to enter the junior year of a 4-year college. Among many educators it is believed that general education should continue through the thirteenth and fourteenth year as a part of public secondary education. The vast system of public-supported junior colleges in California is the prime example of this belief translated into actuality.

Other states such as Illinois, Florida, Texas, and Pennsylvania have inaugurated systems of junior or community colleges also supported in the main with public funds, but organized on different plans. However junior colleges are supported and administered, whether as part of a special junior college district, as part of a regular school district, or as a colony of an established municipal or state 4-year college or university, it is evident that the demand will continue to grow.

Elicker indicates that communities must prepare to increase the rate of growth of junior or community colleges by three or four times during the next decade to keep pace with the demands for higher education.[13]

The advantages of the junior or community college in terms of reducing the costs to the individual seeking higher education and to state governments seeking to cope with the waves of citizens seeking to enter

___

[13] Paul E. Elicker, *The Administration of Junior and Senior High Schools,* Prentice-Hall, Inc., Englewood Cliffs, N.J., 1965, pp. 237–238, 260, 250–256.

the established state institutions of higher learning can easily be perceived.

Articulation with Other Levels

Regardless of the level of school he is assigned to administer—middle school, junior high, senior high, or junior college—the secondary school administrator will have responsibility for articulation with the levels above and below. He must organize in harmony with his peers to see that this responsibility is carried out efficiently. Many articulation problems arise from the fact that elementary and secondary schools are often operating with contradictory functions and purposes and, in some states, even under different superintendents and boards of education.

Among recent organizational plans for improving articulation are such arrangements as educational parks, K-12 schools, K-12 curriculum committees, administrative councils, and integrated administrative organizations. In addition to providing for physical proximity, the educational park system provides for integration of teaching and learning at various levels. It is claimed that K-12 organizational plans unify the functions and purposes of all levels and provide for cooperative program implementation.

INSTRUCTIONAL ORGANIZATION

Primacy of Instruction and Human Dignity

Although administrative organization of the schools was discussed earlier in this chapter, it should not be concluded that it is more important than instruction. In fact a recurring theme in this book is that organization and administration exist *only* to facilitate the instructional program carried on in the schools. This means that the first and foremost idea, thought, responsibility, endeavor, or whatever of the secondary principal and his staff must be to provide the best climate for learning possible within the limitations of the personnel and resources available.

The prime criterion upon which every issue should be decided is how does it affect people and/or the instructional program? This means that the administrator in allotting his time must place the importance of the instructional program, pupils, and staff ahead of counting the lunch money and other routine clerical tasks which he should not do or be expected to do.

It has been said that people get done those things they think are important. The principal who spends his time counting the lunch room money, overseeing the lining of the football field, or attending the league coaches meeting to the detriment of the instructional program has cast his vote for what he thinks is important. Such a person has no business in the position which should be synonymous with educational leader.

Organize to Accomplish Purposes

It is, of course, in the individual school that the teaching-learning function is performed. That function is performed by teachers for and with students who are assigned to them. Programming youth of varying abilities, interests, goals, etc., into preferred patterns of educational experiences with teachers who also have varying abilities, interests, and goals taxes the administrator's competency.

It is in the individual school that the principal, together with his staff, must organize resources maximally in order to accomplish the purposes of the school. Strategies to study and accomplish change must be developed cooperatively. When staff members are inadequately prepared to aid in such development, a retooling of skills and an acquisition of new knowledge by those persons is essential.

John Stuart Mill said, "No great improvements in the lot of mankind are possible, until a great change takes place in the fundamental constitution of their modes of thought." The continuing education of all members of the faculty is necessary and is a valid concern of any principal. The principal, however, who is concerned that his teachers and staff associates be able to adapt to needed innovations and changes must do something about it. Their very modes of thought must be changed as Mill has suggested. These changes in thought and the development of adaptability should become a goal of the districtwide and individual school in-service program. This is not to say that the in-service program be limited in scope for this purpose only. McCleary and Hencley proposed that the objective of the in-service program should be to provide opportunity for growth on a broad front rather than to concentrate efforts in any single problem area.[14]

Staff Utilization

The shortage of trained teachers, inadequate school facilities, the emergence of new instructional programs based on research findings pose serious problems in the effective utilization of secondary school personnel.

In 1956, J. Lloyd Trump was commissioned by the National Association of Secondary School Principals to undertake a study leading to the development of improved techniques in staff utilization. This movement placed in sharp focus the need for breaking the lock step and for looking for more effective methods to implement modern educational theory. Through experimentation and innovation much has been learned which

[14] Lloyd E. McCleary and Stephen P. Hencley, *Secondary School Administration*, Dodd, Mead & Company, Inc., New York, 1965, p. 290.

can be utilized to increase the effectiveness of instruction. Some of these methods are summarized briefly in the following sections.

Team Teaching Of all the ideas to come out of the recent experiments in organizing the school for good teaching, one of those capturing the most attention is team teaching. There is no one definition of team teaching because it lends itself so well to local conditions, needs, and teacher talents. Team teaching is more than just cooperation among a group of teachers; it is a method of teaching which utilizes teacher talents and school space and equipment to their utmost. The heart of the team idea seems to be that members of the team plan together, communicate, and collaborate without restraint. It also preserves the interrelatedness of subjects and learning. Even a small team has a leader. The plan as used in some school systems has a hierarchy of team leader, master teachers, regular teacher, intern teacher, and nonprofessionals such as instructional and clerical aides. Teams may work either at all grade levels in a single subject or at one grade level. Bush and Allen recommend that teams be organized by each department for its own unique purposes because different purposes may not be served by identical patterns.[15]

At the high school level teams usually work in one subject area. Thus, a team of four English teachers might teach freshman English to 150 or more students. One member could be researching and preparing to make a superior presentation of the work to be taken up the next week or the week following, while his team colleagues are providing the students with high-level instruction for the current work. Some days the group may be divided up into smaller groups for practice, discussion, remedial or advanced work, makeup, testing, etc.[16]

The school which does not have rooms large enough for large-group instruction can use smaller teams or rotate groups.

Since team teaching emphasizes the professional role of the teacher, it is important that there are a sufficient number of general aides, clerks, and instructional assistants. Other assistance should also come from special consultants in the central office and the community at large.

If the team presents ordinary lectures, then no matter how different the physical setting there will be no improvement. A variety of teaching aids and technical aids should be used. An overhead projector, other projectors, television, recorders, and a flannel board should be available. All students must be able to hear and see well. There should be well-equipped independent study workrooms with projection and recording devices. Books, printed materials, programmed instruction devices, and specialized tools of the subject should be brought to hand easily.

[15] Robert N. Bush and Dwight W. Allen, *A New Design for High School Education*, McGraw-Hill Book Company, New York, 1964, p. 49.
[16] J. Lloyd Trump, "What Is Team Teaching?" *Education*, vol. 85, p. 327, February, 1965.

Good team teaching requires careful planning. Because some staff members may have reservations about their expected role as team members, there should be a full orientation program for all those taking part in the program. There should be sufficient time for planning the organizational patterns to be used. Planning time must be part of the program, and there should be continuous evaluation of the program in progress.

Planning determines who will do what. The best teaching the team can provide is presented in large-group sessions. This instruction aims to motivate students, to bring them knowledge not readily available elsewhere, and to indicate what students are to do during independent study and research periods.

Independent study is conducted on either an individual or a group basis. Students cover the essential knowledge and skills of the course and hopefully go on to further creative and depth studies, each according to his own motivations and talents. Groups for remedial work or advanced study are organized as needed. Team teachers plan, prepare, and help assemble a variety of materials for students to use in various resource centers. Small-group discussions develop communication skills, teach problem solving and critical thinking, and encourage better interpersonal relations.

Another requirement for good team teaching is flexible scheduling. Control over time is given to the team for daily or weekly changes. Students also need the privilege of changing the amounts of time and the locale of their independent study.

Team evaluation of individual progress is another ingredient of team teaching. Team members report on changes in pupil behavior as observed in small groups. Anecdotal reports are received and interpreted by each team member who bears responsibility for the portion of the team's students assigned to him.

Team teaching is not limited to the academically talented, and schools that have gone into this program have involved all of the school population.

At this point, the jury is still out on team teaching; although most evaluation reports are tentative, they are basically optimistic. Any new program takes time, and when people change their way of doing things, there must be a period of adjustment.

The best team teaching would probably be in a building which has flexibility of space, so that groups of varying size could be accommodated. Such buildings have been built and are being built at approximately the same cost as the traditional school building. But a school system need not wait for such a building to inaugurate team teaching. All that is needed is the understanding and acceptance of the idea by the teachers who will make up a team and the support of the administration and community.

Use of Noncertified Personnel   One of the relatively new ways to use the teaching staff in a more efficient way is to use noncertified personnel to do many of the tasks which the certified staff now does, permitting the professional person to use his talents to their greatest advantage. This could lead to an ultimate staff of the future somewhat like the following, which is suggested by Trump in his report on the staff utilization studies.[17]

1. Professional teachers
2. Instruction assistants
3. Clerks
4. General aides
5. Community consultants
6. Staff specialists

Such a staff would make the best use of all the types of talent available in a faculty. Each level of the staff would require a different type and length of training, and because some people could begin working with very little training, this could help alleviate the teacher shortage.

While Trump suggested such a staff for the school of the future, certain aspects of it are already in use. Many schools have inaugurated types of systems which use instruction assistants, the most common example of this being the use of *lay readers*. The use of lay readers involves people who are well-educated, although not specifically trained for teaching. These people work with English teachers or science teachers, and they mark the many papers required of students in such areas. The teacher and the lay reader who reads for him then sit down together and discuss some of the shortcomings of the papers and perhaps even what sort of grade should be given.

The lay reader program has proved to be generally successful in providing teachers with more time for other required activities, and it has made possible more student writing. One major obstacle seems to be a legal one; many schools are not permitted to pay noncertified instructional personnel from board funds. Changes in such laws are proceeding in some states, but much more needs to be done. Clerks can be used to provide more teaching time for teachers by monitoring study halls, taking and checking attendance, preparing A-V materials, preparing library resource materials, assisting on the playground, and clerking in the library.[18]

It should not prove difficult to recruit such people, for parents are often willing to help, and in some instances the parents will volunteer their labor. In a "Time to Teach" report it was discovered that parents were typing, filling out records, supervising in the library, helping in the

[17] J. Lloyd Trump, *Images of the Future*, Commission on Experimental Study of the Utilization of Staff in the Secondary Schools, Urbana, Ill., 1959, p. 15.
[18] William Hard, "Fourteen Ways to Use Non-teachers," *Nations Schools*, vol. 76, no. 42, pp. 43–44, December, 1965.

classrooms, typing stencils, and watching over the cafeteria.[19] In all these cases, the parents volunteered a few hours a week to the school, and no money was needed to pay them.

As pointed out then, Trump's "staff of the future" is already being tried in our schools. Because most of these experimental projects have had many positive results, one would expect to see a growing use of such programs. The problems that have already been faced will help provide answers to those attempting such programs at a later date, and soon such programs may be widely and successfully used.

In Boston, Massachusetts, there is an experiment going on in partnership teaching.[20] This idea has been developed by the Women's Educational and Industrial Union, and it involves the use of two people to do the work of one. There are many women today who would like to work but cannot give enough time for a full-time job; there are also many shortages in the teaching profession, particularly in the elementary schools. This experiment plans to find women who can give at least enough time for a half day of school; two such women will be matched, each teaching one-half of a regular teacher's day. In this way, one class would have two teachers for the year rather than one. While it seems to present many extra problems (imagine, for instance, the increased size of faculty alone), it will solve the important problem of the lack of teachers for many of the classes.

A similar experiment is being tried in New York City, where women are being hired on a part-time basis. Each woman will work as many hours a day as she can, releasing the regular teacher for some other duty; enough such women and the work load which can be carried by the faculty will be increased greatly. This, like the one in Massachusetts, is strictly in the experimental stage, and many problems will have to be solved before it can be used widely.

All these attempts at a solution to a problem are attempts to merely alleviate a problem, namely, a shortage of qualified teachers. Unfortunately, none attack the central issue, which is the recruitment of more and more qualified teachers. While these attempts are all worthy and noble, they should be considered only as stopgap measures, as something which will make living possible until the situation is rectified. The final solution must be made in the area of teacher recruitment.

The Nongraded High School

The nongraded high school is an attack on what some educators consider to be the most limiting aspect of our schools today, namely, the inflexibility and the inadequacy of chronological-age education. It is an

[19] John Lloyd, "Parents Provide 'Time to Teach,' " *Scholastic Teaching*, vol. 35, no. 16, pp. 5–6, March 25, 1966.
[20] "Partnership Teaching," *Saturday Review*, March 17, 1966, p. 16.

attempt at educational organization that is both imaginative and dynamic. Central to the concept is the need to provide different programs for different levels of ability. Progress has been made in identifying these different levels of achievement, but relatively little has been done in devising programs of instruction appropriate to the various levels identified.

Thus, a nongraded school is an educational design planned around an individual's readiness for learning. It is a sweeping reform in which the structure for learning is completely revamped. The reorganization is based on the individual. Students are classified on the basis of achievement rather than chronological age. While the conventional school groups students by age, the nongraded school groups together those students who are at approximately the same level of learning.

The grade is seen as a barrier, an administrative device of convenience. One of the major purposes of education is held to be that each student should progress at his own best rate of learning. The nongraded school is proposed as a means to that end. It is a program where the number of years in school, the rate of progress, and the subjects covered are determined by the capacities of the individual student rather than the collective capacity of the class.[21]

Therefore, a nongraded plan must provide for the accurate classification of students of near-equal achievement and also provide for frequent reclassification so that students can move forward on an individual basis as rapidly as they are able.[22] Students are accelerated through subject matter on a continuing rather than a yearly basis.

Not only are the pupils grouped differently, the actual instruction takes a different form.[23] The self-contained classroom of approximately thirty students is no more. Large- and small-group instruction together with individual study replaces the traditional concept.[24] Students spend about 10 percent of their time in large lectures, 45 percent of their time in small discussion groups, and 45 percent of their time in individual study. This aspect of the plan is based on belief in the team teaching approach. Thus, presentations are made to large groups, discussions take place in small groups, and ample time is provided for individual study and research.

The concept of independent study is, perhaps, the greatest innovation in the nongraded plan. The idea that high school students are capable of this degree of dedication is not readily accepted. However, to advocates

[21] B. Frank Brown, *The Nongraded High School*, Prentice-Hall, Inc., Englewood Cliffs, N.J., 1965, p. 44.
[22] B. Frank Brown, "The Nongraded School," *NASSP Bulletin*, vol. 47, no. 283, p. 65, May, 1963.
[23] Laurence Niblett, "No Bells Ring for Dr. Trump," *NASSP Bulletin*, vol. 46, no. 272, p. 88, March, 1962.
[24] J. Lloyd Trump and Dorsey Baynham, *Focus on Change: Guide to Better Schools*, Rand McNally & Company, Chicago, 1961, p. 32.

of the plan, the gifted, the talented, and the creative are best challenged in this way, and any student who has a genuine interest and curiosity in a particular area can profit from this type of study activity. It is an extremely effective component of the learning process and fills a need often not met by conventional methods.

The nongraded school is still an innovation. Those who have had the courage to depart from the conventional, report in glowing terms of its success. Perhaps B. Frank Brown is its leading advocate. His Melbourne High School, Melbourne, Florida, is by far the best known example of the theory put into practice. However, Setauket, New York, and Middletown, Rhode Island, as well as other schools in California, are experimenting with the idea. It may well be the prototype of the schools of tomorrow.

Schools-within-a-School

The schools-within-a-school concept has been developing since at least 1919 as a means of accommodating increasing numbers of secondary school pupils while continuing to emphasize individual attention. They are known variously as houses, divisions, little schools, and units; but "schools-within-a-school" is the most descriptive term. Basically, it is an organizational plan that divides a large secondary school into several smaller units. Each small school has its own pupils, administration, and guidance personnel. Some faculty and some building space are assigned to each school, while some teachers and facilities are shared by all the small schools. Of course, there is a central administration head for the entire school.[25]

The organization of such a school must be determined by a principal and his staff according to their purposes and after giving careful thought to specific questions. Decentralization cannot be considered without first determining what purposes it would serve. Usually this is a desire to retain the close interpersonal relationship of a small school while also enjoying the broad curriculum and specialized facilities of a large school.

It must be decided what plan of pupil organization will be adopted. In general, two plans are in common use, but a school is only limited by its imagination. Some students from each grade can be assigned to a school so that each little school is a miniature of the larger school. This is known as *vertical organization*.[26] Its advantages lie in equal-sized little schools, pupils mingle with others of a different maturity level, and teachers remain with groups for more than one year.

The horizontal organization separates the school by grade level. This

[25] Karl R. Plath, *Schools within Schools: A Study of High School Organization*, Secondary School Administration Series, ed. David B. Austin, Bureau of Publications, Teachers College, Columbia University, New York, 1965, p. 1.
[26] *Ibid.*, p. 4.

facilitates curriculum integration at each grade level, but any increase in enrollment in any grade will result in uneven-sized little schools. Combinations and variations are possible. Two grades in each little school give a 2-2 or a 2-2-2 organization and enable the little school to focus on 2 years of the curriculum.

The program offerings within each little school must be determined. Of course, as many classes as possible should be scheduled within the little school to retain the personal relationships.[27] However, ability grouping and the numerous elective choices make this more difficult as a pupil progresses through school. Administration is contained within the unit, and guidance services are almost without exception a function within the scope of the little school.

A necessary decision concerning school organization is the enrollment limits.[28] This decision will have some effect on each of the foregoing decisions and varies, in general, according to the size of the total school. The range may be as few as 125 and as large as 1,100 pupils in each unit. Most schools operate with units in the 400- to 600-pupil range.

Older schools which adopt the schools-within-a-school plan designate an area of the building for each unit. However, new institutions which are built to accommodate the plan usually have a separate building for each little school.[29] The facilities which are needed include classrooms and a workroom for unit teachers, offices for administration and counseling, a large-group instruction area, and a place for small conferences.

The primary advantages of the plan are found in the close interpersonal relationship and in the improvement of counseling services.[30] A second area of advantage lies in the development of ideas concerning program, techniques of instruction, administration, and school operation which accrue from the closeness of the little school faculty working together. Other advantages are: (1) subject-matter integration and continuity are improved; (2) an increased student activity program results; (3) there is an improved feeling of belonging; (4) the principal is relieved of administration routine, and improved supervision is possible; (5) more effective student control is realized; (6) teacher orientation improves; (7) faculty morale improves; and (8) greater adaptability of the program results because of a willingness to experiment within a little school.

The principal and his staff must realize that a plan of organization will not guarantee improved education. If schools-within-a-school are organized, it must be a result of careful consideration and a desire to meet individual needs. The success of any organizational plan rests on valid

[27] *Ibid.*, p. 24.
[28] *Ibid.*, p. 28.
[29] *Ibid.*, p. 63.
[30] Nelson C. Price, "An Evaluation of the 'School-Within-a-School' Plan of Secondary School Organization," *NASSP Bulletin*, vol. 46, no. 275, p. 186, September, 1962.

purposes for the organization, sound principles embodied in its structure, and periodic evaluation. If the decision is reached to use the little-school plan, then careful study should precede its adoption. Practices at other schools should be studied, but only with the realization that they may be a guide. Each school organization must be a product of its own needs and the needs of the students it serves. It would seem that no school could attempt to strengthen its focus on the individual, however, without at least examining the schools-within-a-school concept.

SUMMARY

One of the tasks assigned to the school has been to assist the individual to develop to the extent of his abilities. Because the development of an individual must extend over his lifetime and because the conditions which face the individual change over his lifetime, the individual must be able to adapt to new conditions. The most important job of the school may well be the development of adaptability in our young people.

The individual public secondary school is part of a local school district which in turn is part of a state system of education. How the local school district is organized may be determined by many factors, but the determining factor should be the instructional program provided for children and youth. All levels of government now have an impact on education, and, therefore, the principal needs to have concern for the way in which educational policy making takes place. He must know how the framework of three branches of government at three levels affects schools.

The individual school, the school district, and the state system of education must all be adaptable if they are to facilitate the development of adaptability in the citizens of the future. The utilization of staff and plant resources is one of the biggest challenges facing the principal and his staff. Flexible scheduling, team teaching, use of noncertificated personnel, nongrading, schools-within-a-school, etc. are possible means of organizing the programs to meet the needs of our youth. The selection among various alternatives of action is the responsibility of the principal and his staff. The organization developed must be that which provides the best conditions for fulfilling the purposes of the school.

SUGGESTED EXERCISES

1. Divide into class committees, and have each committee then undertake to define *adaptability* in terms of the behavior expected of persons who are adaptable. Then compare the various committee findings.

2. Assume that you are program chairman for the next annual convention of the National Association of Secondary School Principals. The convention theme is to be "Educating for Adaptability." Develop plans for the convention in terms

of related topics for group discusion, and assemble a list of speakers and panel members to deal with the topics.

3. Develop a checklist of items which you think would indicate whether or not a secondary school is organized for preparing young people to adapt to changing conditions. Apply the checklist as an evaluative instrument in a real school situation.

4. Find out how many and the extent of reorganizations which have taken place in the state department of education of your state and a nearby one in the last 20 years.

5. Discover any new patterns of vertical school organization which are not listed in this chapter. What are the stated reasons for such new patterns of organization?

SELECTED REFERENCES

BROWN, B. FRANK, *The Nongraded High School,* Prentice-Hall, Inc., Englewood Cliffs, N.J., 1963, 223 pp.

CREMIN, LAWRENCE A., *The Genius of American Education,* Vintage Books, Random House, Inc., New York, 1965, 116 pp.

DRUCKER, PETER F., *Landmarks of Tomorrow,* Harper & Row, Publishers, Incorporated, New York, 1965, 270 pp.

GLINES, DON, "Changing a School," *Phi Delta Kappan,* vol. 48, no. 4, December, 1966.

JENNINGS, FRANK G., "Education Reform 1957–1967: It Didn't Start With Sputnik," *Saturday Review,* September 16, 1967, pp. 77–79, 95–97.

TRUMP, J. LLOYD, *Images of the Future,* Commission on the Experimental Study of the Utilization of the Staff in the Secondary School, National Association of Secondary-School Principals, Urbana, Ill., 1959, 116 pp.

———, "Junior High versus Middle School," *NASSP Bulletin,* vol. 51, no. 316, February, 1967.

——— AND DORSEY BAYNHAM, *Focus on Change: Guide to Better Schools,* Commission on the Experimental Study of the Utilization of the Staff in the Secondary School, Rand McNally & Company, Chicago, 1961, 147 pp.

SEC-TION 2

2

leadership
for
secondary
schools

INTRODUCTION   In the chapters that follow attention is given to the nature and function of leadership, selected theories of leadership, hindrances to effective leadership, competencies needed for effective leadership, and leadership in a democratic framework. In discussing these central themes consideration is given to some of the causes of complexities in administering a secondary school as well as to the principles of leadership applied in other disciplines. Ways of identifying leaders and the persistence of group leadership are reviewed.

Examples of types of leaders found in practice are presented along with a discussion of certain identifiable hindrances to leadership. The competency concept is reviewed in relation to administration.

Presented in this section are many ideas based upon research and sound practice which an effective and professional leader may use successfully in the American secondary school. Decision making is equated with administration. The future of the principalship at the secondary level is presented along with its many challenges and opportunities. Emphasis is placed upon making the secondary principalship a more professional position and one that requires a training program of breadth and depth.

CHAPTER 6

WHAT IS LEADERSHIP?

It is the purpose of this chapter to treat various meanings of leadership and their relationship to the dynamics and goals of the particular group. Also discussed will be the background of educational leadership and its complexity in the secondary school. Further, consideration will be given to some selected principles of leadership.

THE NATURE AND PURPOSE OF LEADERSHIP

The word "leadership" has a wide assortment of definitions or interpretations. It is used by some people to refer to almost every type of administrative, executive, or supervisory performance. Others use it in a more restricted sense. Leadership is defined by some in terms of attributes of the individual. Still many others consider leadership to be an aspect of organization or an interactional process by means of which the organization defines for each member his scope for action in making decisions, carrying out duties, and enlisting the cooperation of others. First, let us review the nature and purpose of leadership as given by several authorities and various groups.

Personal Traits Theory

Our society has always put a reward on leadership or thought that leaders should be valued in excess of their par or above their nominal value. The values attributed to leadership have caused us to impute to such behavior the attitude that leaders are people who are superior. The idea that the "king can do no wrong" is an illustration of this concept. A rigid class-structure system implies the same connotation. "Being born on the right side of the tracks" supports the same contention. All these concepts imply that some people are born leaders. The man in the street may view leadership largely as a matter of personal qualities. He believes there are certain persons who possess the qualities of leadership and who will be the ones to emerge as leaders in any given situation.

For many years it was thought that leaders were people who had a set of traits different from those who were destined to be followers. If this were true, the choosing of leaders would be greatly simplified. Studies by Hackman and Moon and by Myers showed that competent leaders in different situations possessed outstandingly different traits.[1,2]

Many people today hold that the traits approach to explain the meaning of leadership is grossly inadequate. This thesis is supported by Weber and Weber in their exhaustive review of research on leadership.[3]

Characteristics of Leaders

This definition of leadership is devised from studying leaders to determine what characteristics they have in common. Such an approach assumes that leadership is a function of the personality characteristics of the individual and can be assessed apart from the leadership situation or group. A wide range of leadership positions has been studied such as officers in the Armed Forces, industrial leaders, politicians, business executives, and school administrators. Most of these personality traits or characteristics are considered to be learned or acquired. Possessing these characteristics still does not mean that a person becomes a leader.

General Traits of Leaders   The outstanding study in this area was done by Stogdill, who reviewed 124 studies of the characteristics of leaders.[4] He grouped them under five headings: (1) *capacity,* including intelligence, alertness, verbal facility, and judgment; (2) *achievement,* including scholarship, knowledge, and athletic accomplishments; (3) *responsibility,*

[1] Roy C. Hackman and Rexford G. Moon, Jr., "Are Leaders and Followers Identified by Similar Criteria?" *American Psychologist,* vol. 5, pp. 312–313, July, 1950.
[2] Robert Myers, "The Development and Implications of a Conception of Leadership for Leadership Education," unpublished doctoral dissertation, University of Florida, Gainesville, Fla., 1954.
[3] C. A. Weber and Mary E. Weber, *Fundamentals of Educational Leadership,* McGraw-Hill Book Company, New York, 1955, p. 279.
[4] Ralph M. Stogdill, "Personal Factors Associated with Leadership," *Journal of Psychology,* vol. 25, p. 64, January, 1948.

including dependability, initiative, persistence, aggressiveness, self-confidence, and desire to excel; (4) *participation,* including activities, sociability, cooperation, adaptability, and humor; and (5) *status,* including socioeconomic position and popularity. If one possesses these traits, it is no guarantee that he will become a leader. However, these traits appear to be held or exhibited by people who have been judged to be leaders more often than not. Others who have related traits have demonstrated little leadership function.

With the exception of *capacity,* most of the above traits could be learned or acquired. Most of these traits are not a part of one's original equipment when he is born. The attributes of individuals approach fails to describe adequately energies of leadership as a process. When one person affects another person or group of persons in a manner that causes common direction to be given to their efforts through this one person, leadership is present.

Traits of Executives This approach to leadership is based upon studying top executives to determine what personal qualities they possessed that helped them achieve this role and be successful in it and to determine those who achieved this role but later failed in it.

Traits of the top executive are quite similar to those found in educational leaders. They both point to the leadership act as one that gets results in terms of what others do. The act of leadership motivates the work of others. It is almost impossible for a leader to demonstrate effective power over others if he does not have substantial power over himself.

A leading authority on the Thematic Apperception Test (TAT) analyzed records of executives and found that six traits distinguished the successful from the unsuccessful.[5] These were: (1) a strong desire for achievement, (2) a strong desire for social advancement, (3) a liking for their superiors, (4) decisiveness, (5) assertiveness, and (6) practicality. The TAT consists of a series of pictures of one or more persons. The person being tested is asked to compose a story about them and to tell what is going on in the pictures and what led up to this event and to predict the outcome. It was through this process that Henry was able to arrive at the executive traits. He concluded that personality factors are by far the most important ones in determining the success of the executive.

After numerous investigations, Argyris developed the following list of qualifications as being necessary for successful executive work: (1) the ability to work effectively under frustrating conditions, (2) the ability and the desire to obtain the participation of others in solving problems, (3) the ability to question one's own judgment and actions in an objective manner, (4) the ability to take knocks without undue hostility or com-

---

5 W. E. Henry, "The Business Executive: A Study in Psychodynamics of a Social Role," *American Journal of Sociology,* vol. 54, pp. 286–291, January, 1949.

plaint about persecution, (5) the ability to express hostility tactfully, (6) the ability to accept victory or defeat gracefully, (7) the ability to face adverse decisions from superiors gracefully, (8) the ability to identify oneself with the work or professional group, and (9) the ability to set realistic goals.[6] Of all these qualifications, the most significant is probably the ability to set realistic goals. Since planning and coordination take such a large proportion of an executive's time, it is imperative that he use this time in establishing goals that may be achieved.

In a study of the meaning of executive qualities, Stryker found fourteen traits that he considered essential for successful executives: (1) judgment, (2) initiative, (3) integrity, (4) foresight, (5) energy, (6) human relations, (7) decisiveness, (8) dependability, (9) emotional stability, (10) fairness, (11) ambition, (12) dedication, (13) objectivity, and (14) cooperation.[7] This list is somewhat compatible with others previously suggested.

Up to this point, most of our attention has been devoted to traits of successful executives; however, some observation and study have been done on the traits that good executives should not have, or those found in unsuccessful executives. Five types of undesirable executives described by Emmons are: (1) the egocentric who advances at the expense of others, (2) the efficiency expert who feels that personalities can be ignored, (3) the yes-man who advances by long and undistinguished service, (4) the frightened man who likes individuals but is afraid of groups, and (5) the hard boy who acts like a feudal lord.[8] Within one's own scope of operations he may have witnessed one or more of these types of unsuccessful executives.

Major executives themselves have been found to consider personality factors to be the most important cause of failure in persons holding executive positions. One such study was done by Gaudet and Carli in which they asked 300 major executives which was the more important cause of failure, personality traits or lack of knowledge pertaining to the job.[9] About 92 percent of the executives questioned stated that personality traits were the more important cause.

Despite all that has been said about traits of the successful executive, human behavior is so complicated and depends to such a large extent upon a variety of conditions that knowledge of psychological characteristics, even if accurately determined, does not enable one to make satisfactory predictions in terms of the executive. Piotrowski and Rock express

[6] Chris Argyris, "Some Characteristics of Successful Executives," *Personnel Journal*, vol. 32, pp. 50–55, June, 1953.
[7] Perrin Stryker, "On the Meaning of Executive Qualities," *Fortune*, vol. 57, pp. 116–119, 186–189, June, 1958.
[8] R. J. Emmons, "Getting Along with Your Top Executives," *Personnel Journal*, vol. 29, pp. 55–58, June, 1950.
[9] F. J. Gaudet and A. R. Carli, "Why Executives Fail," *Personnel Psychology*, vol. 10, pp. 7–21, Spring, 1957.

this same opinion as follows: "To know the psychological characteristics necessary for success and to predict success to a satisfactory degree are two different things." [10]

Traits of Military Leaders Military leadership has been defined as "the art of influencing and directing men in such a way as to obtain their willing obedience, confidence, respect, and loyal cooperation in order to accomplish the mission." [11]

Although not all-inclusive, the following traits are representative of those found to be most desirable in a military leader: bearing, physical and moral courage, decisiveness, dependability, endurance, enthusiasm, initiative, integrity, judgment, justice, knowledge, loyalty, tact, and unselfishness.

A study of the lives and careers of successful commanders reveals that they possessed many personal qualities or traits that were similar, although they did not necessarily possess these qualities to the same degree. It was the extent to which they demonstrated these traits and other individual characteristics that determined success.

In any final sense, military leadership is not considered inherent, as it depends upon traits that can be developed. It is a skill that can be acquired, developed, and practiced in varying degrees by anyone properly motivated and possessing the mental and physical ability and the moral integrity expected of a commissioned or noncommissioned officer. The development of this art is a continuing process.

A Dynamic Group Function

A rather widely accepted usage of the term "leadership," particularly within the field of educational administration, is that it is a process or act of influencing the movements of an organized group in its efforts toward goal setting and goal achievement. It is this definition of leadership that the writers purport to explain and defend as being the most helpful for secondary school principals.

Under this definition, the leader is expected to advance the group objectives, show administrative competence, motivate group activities, and contribute to the security of its members. In this sense leadership refers to a relationship between persons or to interplay among persons. The act of leadership is never alone but always occurs in relation to others.

Selected Meanings The three definitions of leadership that follow are thought to be typical of how educators view leadership. The American Association of School Administrators defines leadership as the process of

---

[10] Zygmunt A. Piotrowski and Milton R. Rock, *The Perceptanalytic Executive Scale*, Grune & Stratton, Inc., New York, 1963, p. 7.
[11] Department of the Army, *Military Leadership*, FM 22-100, June, 1961, p. 3.

getting people to think through a project and to arrive at a group decision —not to accept ideas of the leader without question.[12]

The Association for Supervision and Curriculum Development describes leadership as that action or behavior among individuals and groups which causes both the individual and the groups to move toward educational goals that are increasingly mutually acceptable to them.[13]

Another type of definition considers leadership to be a group function. Shane and Yauch define creative educational leadership as the guidance of the cooperative process of using individual and group power of school and community in order to develop socially desirable learning experiences for children and youth.[14] Here one may see leadership thought of as a group function whose purpose is to improve educational opportunity. Emphasis is placed upon the process values of enriched learning experiences. It is thought that this type of leadership might be productive of creativity in learning.

Emergent and Appointed Leaders   Although the nature of leadership is interactional, a number of studies have been made to determine the characteristics of those who hold positions of leadership. Leaders secure their positions in one of two ways. They are chosen by the group (emergent) or are designated (appointed) by some higher authority. In the former situation, at least at the outset, the leader begins with a backlog of goodwill which gives him an advantage over the imposed leader. Of course, many factors, including how he uses his leadership, will help decide whether he uses the advantage effectively.

The appointed leader has to combat the fact that his group played no part in his selection, and thus it may feel free to cooperate or reject him. This situation can exist even where individuals are not supposed to have a freedom of choice as to whether they will obey. This could be exemplified by the Armed Forces in the appointment of officers. Some leaders can secure cooperation and obedience of their subordinates under these conditions, and others cannot.

A Social Process   Leadership is a phase of the social process in which the most adaptable and useful members emerge as representing the values most desired by the group at the time. A leader is the center of the social potential of the group. In achieving this position, he must share the values held by the group and use his knowledge, intelligence, vitality, and adaptability to become the most active and acceptable member. In the final analysis, the effectiveness of a leader is to be measured only in terms

[12] *The American School Superintendency*, American Association of School Administrators, Washington, D.C., 1952, p. 79.
[13] *Leadership for Improving Instruction*, Association for Supervision and Curriculum Development, Washington, D.C., 1960, p. 7.
[14] Harold G. Shane and Wilbur A. Yauch, *Creative School Administration*, Holt, Rinehart and Winston, Inc., New York, 1954, p. 12.

of the performance of groups that work under his supervision. The qualities, characteristics, and skills required in a leader are determined to a large extent by the demands of the situation in which he is to function as a leader. Characteristics related to leadership must be as varied as the situations which are likely to develop for a group. As group goals change, so will the characteristics of a person likely to be selected or likely to succeed as a leader.

THE BACKGROUND OF EDUCATIONAL LEADERSHIP

In order to understand educational leadership at the secondary school level, it is necessary to comprehend several factors associated with its early development.

Origin and Development of School Officials

The origin of the secondary school principalship in this country may be traced back to the Latin grammar school of colonial New England. In the original Thirteen Colonies of this country schools were maintained by religious bodies. Later the churches relinquished control of the schools, and the responsibility was assumed by the town governments. During this time the local communities were in complete control of education since the colonial charters and state constitutions made no provisions for education. Because many communities neglected to assume their responsibility for public education, the colonies and later the states, came to recognize the need for some central control. In Massachusetts the law of 1647 required the selectmen, later to become board members, to maintain both an elementary and a grammar school in every town of fifty or more householders. These selectmen became the first lay representatives of the community charged with the management of the schools. These men found themselves surrounded with increasing school and nonschool problems. Special committees were then created which were responsible to the town selectmen. Gradually the school committee evolved into a separate status, and with that practice the school board proper came into existence.[15]

Functions of School Officials

The functions of school officials are generally classified as legislative, executive, and appraisal or evaluative. At first the school board performed all three functions. In time, expanding school enrollments, the ever-growing complexity of school management, and the creation under state constitutions of state school systems helped end the very simple organization of early public schools under school committees and town

[15] James D. Lacey, "An Analysis of the Respective Duties and Functions of Selected Florida Superintendents and School Boards," unpublished doctoral dissertation, University of Miami, Coral Gables, Fla., 1962, p. 13.

jurisdiction. These constitutions permitted the legislatures to establish local school systems as governmental units apart from other local government. Education then became the responsibility of the various states.

Need for Professional Leadership

There were two basic reasons why local boards of education needed to secure professional leadership and assistance. First, the members of the boards of education were involved in making their own livelihoods and could not spare the necessary time. Second, the complexity and intensity of administrative problems were beyond the solution and capabilities of lay boards. Slowly the board of education relinquished its responsibilities to a teacher or a public-spirited person. Eventually, this person became known as the superintendent of schools. By 1837 the first superintendents (city) were appointed in Buffalo and in Louisville. These appointments were made after schools had been operated for nearly 200 years almost as independent units with principals and head teachers in charge under the general supervision of school boards or committees.

Over the years school boards have delegated the superintendent the authority to execute its policies and the responsibility of translating them into sound educational programs. This trend is evident, although state laws give practically all powers and duties pertaining to the administration of the schools to the board and give few of them to the superintendent. The board of education should give the superintendent the job of executing all decisions of the board and should support him in all reasonable performance of the task.

Increased Authority and Responsibility for Principals

The high school principalship in American education is its oldest administrative position. In terms of origin it exceeds both the elementary school principalship and the superintendency. In the days when the selectmen operated public schools, the general rule was that if a school had more than one teacher, a principal teacher or head teacher was appointed.

The duties of the early head teachers, sometimes called masters, were widely diversified. They were given little time for actual administrative tasks. Frequently principal teachers would conduct school committee members and other guests on a tour or inspection of the schools. Often principals were expected to teach almost a full teaching load in addition to being principal.

If one analyzes the duties performed by the early high school principals, he immediately realizes that this position was not thought of in the beginning as a professional position. As the secondary schools grew in enrollment and size of faculty, principals assumed additional responsibilities. Among these were the preparation of a schedule for students and one for teachers. A host of reports concerning attendance, courses of study, disciplinary problems, and the like became the responsibility of the principal.

During the latter part of the nineteenth century there was an increasing tendency to recognize a profession of educational administration. Yet, it is only fair to say that this recognition by the general public did not take place quickly. This new development carried with it the responsibility for the principal's increased professionalization and more released time from teaching to perform the many tasks assigned to him by the school district.

The secondary principalship evolved out of the status of a teacher who was in addition little more than a clerk and part-time principal to a more complicated position of professional leadership over a period of time dating back to about 1890. From about the year of 1890 until the present time, each year and each decade have produced increased pupil enrollments and greater variations in pupil backgrounds. Also the life of the pupils outside of school has become more complicated. Today it is difficult if not almost impossible for youth of high school age who have not graduated from high school to secure satisfactory employment. In the United States as a whole, two-thirds of the unemployed have less than a high school education. For additional information see Chapter 4.

Accompanying this tremendous change in makeup of the high school population has been a need for teachers to develop new skills and methods for challenging all American youth who attend high school. In their quest for help, they have sought much assistance from secondary principals. In addition, school curriculums were broadened and redefined, and new courses of study introduced. All these demands upon the secondary schools made additional mandates upon principals. They had to become more than office boys or secretaries. Principals, too, needed additional training and new experiences in order to give help to teachers. An educational leader today demands more than just knowing how to operate a school: He must provide genuine help and guidance for teachers who are attempting to improve.

In recognition of the many demands made upon secondary principals, great improvement has been made in their qualifications, methods of selection, and types of assignment. Generally, increased authority and responsibility have been delegated more widely to the professionally trained secondary principal.

COMPLEXITY OF LEADERSHIP IN
SECONDARY ADMINISTRATION

Perhaps there is no field in which the difficulties of leadership are more pronounced than in educational administration. This is particularly true of the secondary school principalship.

Demands of the Federal and State Governments

Nowhere among our social institutions is there a more acute awareness of the responsibilities of one institution to build for its constituents an understanding and appreciation of our essential functions as citizens than in the American secondary school. The high school is no longer the passive institution it was once apparently thought to be. There is hardly an influence that affects adult society which is not reflected in the high school in some manner. The plan of organization for the secondary school must indicate an appreciation of national needs and goals. The unemployment of youth, the increasing number of dropouts, pressures from home and college to succeed in academic work, providing for the slow learners, challenging the gifted pupils, and the increase in roughhouse behavior of pupils particularly in large cities all add to administrative problems.

With the increased mobility of the population, the very framework of our social order may be attacked as poorly educated youth move from one region of the United States to another.

Many state governments have become concerned about similar problems, including the varying capacities of individuals and the great emphasis upon physical sciences almost to the exclusion or at the expense of the humanities, social sciences, and the arts. The growing difficulty high school graduates encounter in seeking college admission, together with other problems, offers a tremendous challenge that secondary administrators have to face.

Larger Attendance Units

The twentieth-century development of large attendance units has added to the problem. As the size of schools to be administered has grown from small enrollments of 250 to 500 pupils to large and complex high schools with 2,000 to 3,000 and sometimes 5,000 pupils, the organization has become difficult and detailed. More people, both lay and professional, have to be dealt with in planning and administering such an organization. Likewise, the slogan or belief of educating all American youths to their capacities has brought about the need for more and better planning and leadership.

The increase in size of attendance units has brought about the need for increased delegation of authority and responsibility to subordinates and the creation of new administrative positions at the secondary school level.

Increased Services

Another contributing factor to the complexity of leadership in the secondary school has been the increased school services that accompany the larger attendance units, huge faculties, and the increasing number of administrative personnel essential to sound administration. Those services assumed by today's modern secondary schools include guidance and counseling, pupil transportation, lunchroom programs, dental and physical health needs, and other areas of specialized operations for the welfare of students.

Population Growth and Inflation

If present growth rates persist, it is fair to estimate that the population of the United States will have increased by 1970 to 215 million, and perhaps by 1980 it may reach 265 million. This unprecedented growth accompanied by a desire for increased education by many youth plus the added number of years that youth remain in school contributes to the population explosion taking place in the public schools. Recently it was proclaimed that one out of three persons in America is in public schools or colleges. This means that schools wil be operating on budgets which are developed in competition with other local and state agencies.

For the past decade and a half the public secondary school has experienced tremendous population gains with the accompanying factor of inflation. Many buildings were planned at one unit cost and built at a much higher unit cost. Public pressures have mounted. With increased expenditures for education and buildings, the public has become more interested in being involved in planning the school program and buildings of the schools at the secondary level. A major task of educational leadership is to restore to the public a sense of security and confidence in its schools. The prerogative of deciding for itself what kind of men and women it wants its youth to become and what type of culture it wishes to promote still belongs to the public.

Interdependence of Individuals in Modern Society

The factors mentioned above tend to contribute to the complexity of leadership in the secondary school; however, it should be remembered that since the time of Plato, philosophers and scientists of Western culture have given thought to the problem of leadership, but none have developed blueprints. During recent years, psychologists and sociologists have been increasingly active in their endeavors to introduce the methods and knowledge of the social sciences into the study of leadership. This ever-expanding interest apparently springs from the assumption that the effectiveness of group performance is determined largely by leadership structure. Consequently, the high degree of interdependence of individuals within modern society has augmented the importance of teamwork and the demands for increased skill in leadership.

PRINCIPLES OF LEADERSHIP

To synthesize all the basic principles of leadership found in the literature would be to engage in an almost endless task; however, it is the purpose of this section to bring into sharp focus some of the convictions held by persons who exercise leadership principles in various groups. It is believed that most of the principles of leadership presented herein are applicable to educational leaders.

Educational Administration Leadership Principles

This type of administrative structure is based upon both inward and outward convictions. Perhaps no group in the field of educational administration has studied so thoroughly and reported so accurately in the area of leadership as the National Conference of Professors of Educational Administration. They envisioned inward and outward convictions as being held by school administrators.

Inward Convictions At its fourth national conference, the professors of educational administration studied administrative leadership and found that school administrators who display democratic leadership appear to hold convictions like these: [16]

1. The welfare of the group is assured by the welfare of each individual.
2. Decisions reached through the cooperative use of intelligence are, in total, more valid than decisions made by individuals.
3. Every idea is entitled to a fair hearing.
4. Every person can make a unique and important contribution.
5. Growth comes from within the group rather than from without.
6. Democracy is a way of living.
7. Democratic methods are efficient methods.
8. Individuals are dependable.

Outward Convictions When inward convictions are expressed in action, one has the outward signs of democratic leadership. These were expressed

[16] National Conference of Professors of Educational Administration, *Providing and Improving Administrative Leadership for America's Schools*, Fourth Report, Bureau of Publications, Teachers College, Columbia University, New York, 1951, p. 19.

by the National Conference of Professors of Educational Administration as follows: [17]

1. Its processes increase the powers of individuals to adjust, to solve problems, to gain satisfactory expression, to maintain emotional poise, and to grow in attitudes and mature in behavior.
2. Its effectiveness is measured by what happens to people.
3. It grows out of the action of a group working on a problem and does not belong to any one individual as a privilege.
4. It comes from within the group and not from some outside source.
5. It develops and uses for the common good the potentialities of each member of the group.
6. It shares the formulation of policies and decisions with every person concerned with or to be effected by the decisions, insofar as possible.
7. It assists the group in arriving at a consensus.

Military Leadership Principles

Certain fundamentals are customarily followed by successful military leaders in making decisions and taking action. The fundamentals used for the proper exercise of command are known as leadership principles. The Department of the Army has listed what it terms leadership principles as follows: [18]

1. Be technically and tactically proficient
2. Know yourself and seek self-improvement
3. Know your men and look out for their welfare
4. Keep your men informed
5. Set the example
6. Insure that the task is understood, supervised, and accomplished
7. Train your men as a team
8. Make sound and timely decisions
9. Develop a sense of responsibility among subordinates
10. Employ your command in accordance with its capabilities
11. See responsibility and take responsibility for your action

Perhaps no one would suggest that a secondary school be operated or administered in the same manner as the Army of the United States; however, many of the principles of leadership enumerated here as being essential for effective military leadership have some application to secondary school administration. For example, the making of sound and timely decisions and the developing of a sense of responsibility among subordinates are both done in a related manner in educational administration.

[17] *Ibid.*, p. 20.
[18] Department of the Army, *Military Leadership*, FM 22-100, June, 1961, pp. 28–37.

Naval Leadership Principles

Early in May, 1958, the Secretary of the Navy directed naval efforts to a course consistent with the changing nature of the leadership requirement. This was done by signing of general order No. 21 which formalized and made explicit a program for the teaching and application of sound naval leadership. The spirit of this general order was undertaken by the Aviation Supply Office through a program designed to support and carry out the best of the traditional methods of teaching leadership—by precept and example—and also includes the modern techniques of formal education as follows: [19]

1. The formal classroom phase brings together officers and civilian supervisors to achieve thorough integration of civilian and military leadership which is the key to successful operations in a shore activity largely staffed by civilians.
2. These seminars enable supervisors at all echelons to learn while they practice and while they teach.
3. The program adopts the teaching methods of the old timers and softens possible resistance to a direct approach to leadership training.
4. The case study method is widely used for instruction.
5. Sets an example of professional knowledge, industry, tough and ethical thinking, devotion to the Navy's purpose, and willingness to assume responsibility.
6. Makes a close and useful observation of subordinates in action and "under fire."
7. Lets the "Indian" who did the spade work show himself and his good effort before the tops in the organization.

Many other important elements of leadership are exercised by the Navy in its leadership training courses. For the most part, the highlights seem to center upon those discussed here.

General Principles of Leadership

Other general principles of leadership have been discovered by a number of authorities in psychology, social psychology, and sociology. Among the more significant principles considered to be in the public domain are the following:

1. The performance of the leadership function is essential to a group's satisfactory progress toward goal achievement.
2. Emergent leaders will appear more often in groups where the status leader does not perform his leadership function.

[19] T. W. Jones (ed.), "A.S.O.S. Leadership Program," *Monthly Newsletter*, September, 1961, pp. 24–27.

3. Emergent leaders often demonstrate a degree of expertness with the problem confronting the group.
4. Group leadership tends to reduce the amount of group and individual tension as friendly interpersonal relationships among group members are encouraged.
5. Great men are considered to possess leadership qualifications by their peers.
6. A leader's behavior is determined in part by the task on which the group is working.
7. Emergent leaders tend to be more authoritarian than designated leaders.
8. A leader gives the group information on how to carry out its activities.
9. A leader will initiate activities directed toward achieving the group's goal.
10. Groups are inclined to select an individual who can be depended on for the leadership position.
11. Those least likely to be awarded leadership status are not necessarily those who manifest the least amount of initiative.

An analysis of the principles listed above indicates that these principles of leadership cannot be generalized to all types of groups irrespective of their purposes or goals. Rather, these principles may be used when applicable.

SUMMARY

Although a number of definitions of leadership are reviewed, the authors define leadership as a process or act of influencing the movements of an organized group in its effort toward goal setting and goal achievement.

The secondary school principalship evolved out of the status of a teacher who was in addition little more than a clerk and part-time principal to a more complicated position of professional leadership over a period of time dating back to about 1890. Over the years increased authority and responsibility have been delegated more widely to the professionally trained secondary principal.

Due to increased demands of federal and state governments, larger attendance units, increased services, population growth, inflation, and the interdependence of individuals in a modern society, the leadership role of the secondary principal is very complex. Modern principals may find the principles of leadership used in other disciplines of great help in attempting the solution of present-day problems.

SUGGESTED EXERCISES

1. Give your definition of leadership, and compare it with those included in this chapter.

2. Do you believe that leaders are born? Made? Support your belief with evidence.

3. Compare the traits of successful and unsuccessful executives.

4. How has educational leadership in the public schools evolved? What part did need for professional assistance play?

5. Justify the practice of giving increased authority and responsibility to principals.

6. What factors contribute to the complexity of leadership at the secondary school level? Compare those discussed by the authors with the difficulties in your school.

7. Define *principles of leadership*. Contrast the inward and outward convictions expressed in principles in this chapter.

8. How do the principles of leadership exercised by the Army and Navy compare? How can a secondary principal profit from a study of their practices?

9. Suggest principles of leadership you feel essential to administering a secondary school.

SELECTED REFERENCES

Leadership for Improving Instruction, Yearbook, The Association for Supervision and Curriculum Development, Washington, D.C., 1960.

BROWNE, C. G., AND THOMAS S. COHN, *The Study of Leadership,* The Interstate Printers and Publishers, Inc., Danville, Ill., 1958.

BURSK, E. C., "Case of the Product Priority: Excerpts from Cases in Marketing Management," *Harvard Business Review,* vol. 44, pp. 6–8, March, 1966.

CAMPBELL, ROALD F., AND RUSSELL T. GREGG (eds.), *Administrative Behavior in Education,* Harper & Row, Publishers, Incorporated, New York, 1957, chap. 8.

HELLER, W. R., "Spotting the Seed of Success," *Nation's Business,* vol. 54, pp. 78–80, April, 1966.

HUMPHREY, HUBERT H., "Responsibilities of World Leadership" (address), *Department of State Bulletin,* vol. 54, pp. 769–772, May 16, 1966.

KEPPEL, F. R., "Aspects of Leadership" (address, Jan. 18, 1966), *Vital Speeches,* vol. 32, pp. 254–256, February 1, 1966.

MILLER, VAN (ed.), *Providing and Improving Administrative Leadership for America's Schools,* Fourth Report of the National Conference of Professors of Educational Administration, Bureau of Publications, Teachers College, Columbia University, New York, 1951.

MORPHET, EDGAR L., AND CHARLES O. RYAN (eds.), *Designing Education for the Future: No. 1. Prospective Changes in Society by 1980,* Citation Press, New York, 1967.

PIOTROWSKI, ZYGMUNT A., AND WILTON II. ROCK, *The Perceptanalytic Executive Scale,* Grune & Stratton, Inc., New York, 1963, chap. 1.

PUNKE, H. H., "Education for Leadership," *Adult Leadership,* vol. 14, pp. 297–298, March, 1966.

RICE, A. H., "Should the Principal Lead or Manage or Both? Interview with D. Beggs," *The Nation's Schools,* vol. 77, pp. 6ff., Fall, 1966.

SHARTLE, CARROLL L., *Executive Performance and Leadership,* Prentice-Hall, Inc., Englewood Cliffs, N.J., 1961, chaps. 1 and 2.

SMITH, D. W., AND W. F. WETZLER, "Rate of the School in Developing Leadership," *Education,* vol. 86, pp. 356–362, February, 1966.

TOMPKINS, ELLSWORTH, "Principal's Rate in School Improvement," *NASSP Bulletin,* vol. 49, pp. 1–4, October, 1965.

WEBER, C. A., AND MARY E. WEBER, *Fundamentals of Educational Leadership,* McGraw-Hill Book Company, New York, 1955.

CHAPTER 7

LEADERS
AND
THEORIES
OF
LEADERSHIP | The objective of this chapter is to develop the
means for identifying leaders, to discuss the persistence of group leadership, and to review the prevailing concepts of leadership with illustrations
of how they operate in educational administration.

IDENTIFICATION OF LEADERS

In line with the belief that a leader can be studied best in relation to a
total group situation, research indicates that a true group leader can be
identified only by some kind of observation of the effectiveness of his
performance in the type of group to which the leadership is related.
Several methods for identifying leaders are presented. The identification
and selection of leaders for practical situations usually involve some
combination of two or more of these approaches.

Observation

The observation of performance for leadership qualities by outside
experts qualified to judge is considered to be one of the most valid
methods. These methods have been checked through research and care-

fully controlled practical experiments. The task is usually a realistic life situation, sometimes in miniature, and the ratings are given by persons of superior rank such as military experts or administrators and supervisors who rate teachers.

The observation of performance method was used very successfully in war. One example refers to German officer candidates who were given tests in which they were required to instruct a group of soldiers or to carry out difficult commands under stress while their performance was judged by experts.[1] British officer candidates were given common tasks in groups like bridge building or some tactical test, or a "blind war" test in which two leader candidates directed opposing squads of blindfolded men on an open field. The United States Office of Strategic Services placed candidates on a large estate where they were forced to play the role of someone else. Evaluations of their performance were made by their superiors on a five-point scale. Though no scientific data are available on the validity of army methods of choosing leaders, the fact that at least three major armies found these methods practical cannot be overlooked.

Ratings by Associates

Many studies have been made of the identification of leaders by some method of rating by associates. Among the more significant for this purpose is one by Soderquist and another by Swab and Peters.[2,3] Both point out that ratings by associates are valid methods of selecting leaders. One of the conclusions reached by Soderquist was that the best judges of responses are the members of the group who are the objects of the responses rather than outsiders. One of the best pieces of evidence in favor of this concept is the report on the combat success of 185 second lieutenants in the Marine Corps as reported by Eaton.[4]

Although no significant relationship was discovered between composite numerical marks secured at Officer Candidate School and combat success, rating by associates was found to have a closer correlation to the opinion held by senior combat officers than any other measure. The evidence reported strongly points to the conclusion that the men themselves are more capable of picking their own leaders than are instructors and training officers. This point of view coincides with current concepts of leadership and implies that very serious consideration should be given to the possibility of using more democratic methods of selecting leaders.

[1] J. W. Eaton, "Experiments in Testing for Leadership," *American Journal of Sociology*, vol. 52, pp. 523–535, May, 1947.
[2] H. O. Soderquist, "Validity of the Management of Social Traits of High School Pupils by the Method of Rating by Associates," *Journal of Educational Research*, vol. 31, pp. 29–44, September, 1937.
[3] J. C. Swab and C. C. Peters, "The Reliability and Validity of Estimates (Ratings) as Measuring Tools," *Journal of Educational Sociology*, vol. 7, pp. 224–232, December, 1933.
[4] Eaton, *op. cit.*, pp. 30–35.

Sociometric Techniques

This method of selecting leaders relegates the choice of the leader to the individuals of the group and is consistent with the democratic approach. It was used by Jennings[5] in ascertaining the direction of interpersonal responses made by girls in choosing roommates in college. She arranged for group conferences before choices were made to encourage the subjects to collaborate in the plan of research and to volunteer to give the information. Her instructions were: "You will observe that your paper is divided into 8 squares or boxes. In the first 'Yes' box, marked 'live with,' write in the names of whatever girls there are anywhere on the campus or in your own house whom you would prefer to live with." The choices were charted, and those who attracted the most positive choices were considered those whom others naturally followed in the defined situations.

The sociometric technique was used by Zeleny, who asked cadet pilot-observers in training to indicate how they felt about flying with other cadets in their flight.[6] After obtaining the responses and other information from a group, the degree of acceptance of each cadet could be shown in a table. This technique is applicable to other dynamic group situations.

Psychological Testing

No single instrument is available which can serve as a best predictor of effectiveness for choosing a leader. Individual and group tests of mental ability, aptitude, and personality have been used by psychologists and educators to assess leadership-predicting potential. However, the process of measuring and predicting leadership ability remains relatively inexact.

Nevertheless, considerable effort has been expended in the use of psychological tests to discover the extent to which a prospective high school principal possesses administrative potential. Obviously a secondary school principal today should possess better than average intelligence and be able to use his intelligence effectively in his work.

A prospective administrator may be examined on one of the following group tests which provide acceptable norms for adults:

1. Army General Classification Test: First Civilian Edition. Science Research Associates, Inc., Chicago.
2. California Short Form Test of Mental Maturity, Adv. Form. California Test Bureau, Los Angeles.
3. Ohio State University Psychological Examination, Form 21. The Ohio State University Press, Columbus, Ohio.

[5] Helen H. Jennings, "Leadership Training through the Sociodrama," *National Association of Deans of Women Journal*, vol. 10, pp. 112–119, March, 1947.
[6] L. D. Zeleny, "Selection of Compatible Flying Partners," *American Journal of Sociology*, vol. 52, pp. 424–431, March, 1947.

In a study of a large sample of school administrators, Hopper and Bills found the median intelligence quotient to be 127, and the range of scores in the group was from 109 to 133.[7] The prospective administrator who scores below this range has little or no opportunity for success as a secondary school principal.

A few tests are in existence that give promise of predictive value in measuring administrative potential in various factors of intelligence. Among these are:

1. Cooperative English Test, Form C², Educational Testing Service, Princeton, N.J. (Reading Comprehension)
2. Miller Analogies Test, The Psychological Corporation, New York (Scholastic Aptitude)
3. Watson-Glaser Critical Thinking Appraisal, Harcourt, Brace & World, Inc., New York (To draw accurate inferences from related data)

Studies at the University of Texas reported by McIntyre indicate that prospective graduate students in the field of educational administration should score above 55 on the combined percentile scores for these three tests if they are to be seriously considered as candidates.[8]

Measurement of personality traits is less exacting than those in the area of native capacity or intelligence. Even though a small number of studies have tried to relate administrative effectiveness to personality inventory scores, the results are not valid enough to support the making of broad generalizations.

In an experiment in selecting leaders, McIntyre found some relationship between the traits of administrators and scores made on the Guilford-Martin Inventories which purport to measure a number of personality traits.[9] McIntyre discovered that effective administrators scored consistently high in such traits as sociability, freedom from depression, masculinity, freedom from inferiority feelings, freedom from nervousness, objectivity, and cooperativeness. Since this study did not include females, no conclusions should be made with regard to women.

Gibb reported several studies in which the Bernreuter Personality Inventory was used to relate personality traits to leadership behavior.[10] A general conclusion was that leaders tend to score higher than nonleaders in the areas of self-confidence, sociability, and dominance and lower in the area of introversion.

Despite the fact that the testing of personality traits is less exacting

[7] Robert L. Hopper and R. E. Bills, "What's a Good Administrator Made of?" *School Executive*, vol. 74, p. 93, March, 1955.
[8] Kenneth E. McIntyre, *An Experiment in Recruiting and Selecting Leaders for Education*, Southwest School Administration Center, Austin, Tex., 1956, pp. 29–35.
[9] *Ibid.*, pp. 31–34.
[10] Cecil A. Gibb, "Leadership," *Handbook of Social Psychology*, Addison-Wesley Publishing Company, Inc., Reading, Mass., 1954, vol. II, pp. 886–888.

than measurement in some other areas, it is evident that an effective secondary school principal must understand himself if he is to be a successful leader. A prospective or active secondary administrator may find value in the use of these inventories.

Principles of Testing

In order to find principles of testing for leadership that one might use, a survey of the field indicates that Eaton has established the most usable and worthwhile ones as follows: [11]

1. The testing situation should be set up with reference to a precise criterion of leadership.
2. The sociodramatic activities should contain an identifiable number of components involving the demonstration of a number of specific skills.
3. The situation should be simple rather than complex.
4. Each response of the one rated should be evaluated in some numerical weight.
5. Ratings should be made by associates as well as by observers.
6. Final results should not be expressed in too exact gradations—perhaps in deciles or quartiles of the total test population.

These principles for testing indicate that no one really considers this process a refined one. At most, it is a screening which eliminates many persons who obviously could not become successful leaders.

Interview

An interview may be defined as a conversation with a purpose. The method of conducting an interview is influenced to a considerable extent by the purpose of the interview. Some interviews are directed primarily toward obtaining information, some primarily toward giving help, but most involve a combination of the two.

In identifying leaders, the interview is used in most instances to coordinate data with observed behavior. In many instances it is the culminating experience involved in identification and selection.

The interview is used in screening applicants for advanced graduate work in educational administration. For example, at Temple University the educational administration applicants for the Certificate of Advanced Graduate Study and the Doctor of Education degree are required to take screening examinations before they are permitted to file formal applications to the college of education and to the department of educational administration.[12] Further, they must be interviewed orally by members of the department of educational administration, as a part of the admission

[11] Eaton, *op. cit.*, p. 533.
[12] The Department of Educational Administration, *Programs and Services*, Temple University, Philadelphia, 1964, p. 7.

process, in order to supplement application data and to estimate their personal and professional qualifications for doing advanced study.

PERSISTENCE OF GROUP LEADERSHIP

The human group is much more than a static structure. Its dynamic character is revealed in many ways. One who exercises leadership within a group deals with a product that is the process in a particular situation, and the ability of the leader to persist is therefore of considerable interest. Evidence from research indicates that the persistence of group leadership is dependent upon two basic factors: (1) the stability of the group structure and (2) the flexibility of the leader.

Stability of Group Structure

Where the group structure is relatively stable, a leader who earns his way to the center of the social field may be expected to maintain his status for some time. In a study of measurement and prediction of leadership, Page found a correlation of .667 between first-year and fourth-year leadership rankings of West Point cadets.[13] Generally, in a stable society or group, leadership, once attained, tends to persist.

Adaptability of a Leader

When leaders change groups or when the group structures change, the nonadaptable leaders tend to be replaced by those making a better adjustment to the social field. In a study of the persistence of leadership, Courtenay compared the post-high school activities of 100 paired leaders and nonleaders and discovered a considerable loss in leadership status of leaders and an increase in status for high school nonleaders.[14] Thus, different group structures tended to bring forth new leadership.

A leader today may not be a leader tomorrow unless he is flexible enough to adjust to groups with many different structures. A review of research shows that outstanding leaders have demonstrated considerable ability to make adjustments. One example is a research by Remmlein, who pointed out that all but 14 percent of school leaders held office in more than one group.[15] Outstanding leaders tend to dominate many different groups in the same community of groups. They are adaptable or flexible enough to adjust themselves to the structures of many groups.

---

[13] D. P. Page, "Measurement and Prediction of Leadership," *American Journal of Sociology*, vol. 41, pp. 31–43, July, 1935.
[14] Mary E. Courtenay, "Persistence of Leadership," *School Review*, vol. 46, pp. 97–107, February, 1938.
[15] Madaline K. Remmlein, "Analysis of Leaders among High School Seniors," *Journal of Experimental Education*, vol. 6, pp. 413–422, June, 1938.

SOME TECHNIQUES OF LEADERSHIP

The leader seeks positive reactions toward him from the followers. The nature of the behavior that obtains these responses has been a major subject of research in many areas. Given an opportunity to indicate the kind of behavior they liked in an officer, servicemen reported that he must show an interest in soldier welfare, make prompt decisions, teach well, show good judgment, avoid bossing men around when there was no good reason for it, be appreciative of good work done, and give orders clearly.[16] Although this was a questionnaire study, it is important because it reveals successful types of behavior in a meaningful situation.

A leader is one who fits into a particular dynamic group situation in such a way as to contribute to the more complete satisfaction of the needs of the members of the group than any other member. Studies by Lippitt in the United States show that human needs are more completely satisfied in a democratic social group than in an autocratically organized one.[17] The results of a similar study performed in a totalitarian culture would be of considerable interest for comparative purposes.

CONCEPTS OF LEADERSHIP AND THEIR RELATION TO EDUCATIONAL ADMINISTRATION

Concepts of leadership found in the literature vary all the way from incidental and accidental ones to concepts based upon extreme authoritarianism. Some writers have described the extreme boundaries as chaos and autocracy. To say that confusion exists in the minds of the public would perhaps be an understatement. Certainly wide differences of opinion or different beliefs about leadership are easy to find.

Leadership versus Being Pleasant

Leadership involves more than just being pleasant and easy to get along with. Merely getting together people who are concerned over a common problem and serving them coffee and doughnuts and avoiding all conflicting points of view does little to get to the heart of an administrative problem. Improvement in almost any aspect of administration or teaching involves getting a number of people to change the way they are doing things. This type of change demands a leadership that encourages the personnel involved to think through what is being suggested by the group or others and to understand why changes are being made. This type of planning calls for the establishment of acceptable goals and

16 Editorial, "How Soldiers Rate Officers," *Science Digest*, vol. 13, pp. 23–24, April, 1943.
17 Ronald Lippitt, "An Experimental Study of the Effect of Democratic and Authoritarian Group Atmospheres," *Studies in Topological and Vector Psychology 1*, University of Iowa, Studies in Child Welfare, vol. 16, pp. 43–195, 1940.

obtainable means of pursuing those goals. If a principal desires to see changes in the way he works with teachers and in the way these people work together, he must be willing to undergo a reeducation himself.

Although most authorities in educational administration would probably agree that being pleasant and at the same time firm is a desirable consideration, few would feel that this attitude is an adequate basis for leadership in the secondary school. The high school principal articulates the school with the society it serves. In order to relate the school to society's demands, it is essential to remember that a leader's behavior is influenced, to some extent, by the institutional setting within which he functions.

One should be wary of accepting a leader's statement of how he plans to behave as an indication of his actual behavior. Likewise, a leader's belief in how he should behave is not necessarily associated with how his subordinates perceive his behavior.[18] However, it is not uncommon for leaders to exhibit more ability than their followers judge them to exhibit.

Leaders usually are superior to nonleaders in their ability to evaluate group opinion of familiar and relevant issues. One substantiating study was made by Chowdhry and Newcomb.[19] They compared leaders and nonleaders on their ability to estimate opinions of their own group. The groups consisted of a religious organization, a political organization, a medical sorority, and a medical fraternity. In this study the leaders greatly excelled in their ability to determine how their followers felt about important topics without having to ask members how they felt. Also leaders were more cognizant of the goals of the group than nonleaders. Part of this may be explained by the fact that the leader often has channels of communication open and that his attitude and personality may also make it possible for him to be in fuller communication with other members than nonleaders.

Formal Leaders versus Functional Leaders

The formal leader may be thought of as being synonymous with the status leader. In the formal leader situation one thinks of a person granted or endowed with authority, position, and title. This theory implies that one who holds a spot or place in an organizational chart is automatically a leader. This place usually carries with it a title which signifies the position on the table of organization. It is felt by those who accept this type of leadership that its holder will of necessity have to be a leader. Likewise formal leadership may be thought to end with the term

[18] Andrew W. Halpin, "The Leader Behavior and Leadership Ideology of Educational Administrators and Aircraft Commanders," *Harvard Educational Review*, vol. 25, pp. 18–32, Winter, 1955.
[19] Kmala Chowdhry and Theodore M. Newcomb, "The Relative Abilities of Leaders and Non-Leaders to Estimate Opinions of Their Own Groups," *Journal of Abnormal and Social Psychology*, vol. 47, pp. 51–57, January, 1952.

of office or position. Many people are unable to distinguish between the man and the job in this type of leadership.

To some extent a secondary principal in the American public school system may be said to occupy such a position. In governmental functions it may well be the mayor or the city manager who occupies a position in the organizational chart which to many is synonymous with formal leadership. Often individuals in the formal or status leadership positions are unable to or do not live up to the expectations of the office. This is not necessarily due to the organization but may be due to the inability of the individual concerned.

In fact one often hears the comment, "educate the best 15 percent of high school graduates and ignore the rest." Of course the implication is clear that only leadership by the elite will be effective since the great majority of people are not wise enough to govern themselves or others. Some people would call this great mass of humanity followers. Many public school administrators subscribe to this theory. They often refer to "my school," "my faculty," "my custodian," and "my school plant." Many of them hand down policies to be followed and more or less demand cooperation from their subordinates. In the same tone of argument some administrators would feel that leaders are born not made. Most of the leadership of this type comes from the legal powers vested in them rather than from what they have to contribute to the group.

Another theory of leadership that may be found in practice is called functional or operational leadership. In some instances it may be referred to as situational leadership. This type of leadership is based upon situations where the individual and the group are in interaction. Here the emphasis is focused upon the situation and the characteristics of the group rather than on the traits of the leader or the individual members of the group.

This type of leadership is grounded upon the process or act of influencing the activities of an organized group in its efforts toward establishing goals and in achieving them. Under this theory a leader contributes to the ongoing process in terms of his own special abilities and realizes that his ideas have no priority simply because he has some official title. The functional leader helps by attempting to discover with the group its most effective ways of working together and how special abilities may best be used. His suggestions to the group are evaluated by the same criteria as those of other members.

The functional leader owes his position to the efforts he expends in behalf of the group. He is the coordinator of the actions of the group. It is fully recognized, however, that he accomplishes goals through working with others and by learning their desires and helping the group attack its problems. This type of leadership seeks to learn from the activities of the group what direction is sought and attempts to get contributions from the group.

The functional leader may assume the responsibility for establishing and maintaining group morale, for helping members feel secure, for giving praise for work that is done well, and for improving the general welfare of the group. Educational changes made under this type of leadership generally exist after the leader has left. This type of leader does not confuse the word "official" with leadership.

Indecisive Leaders versus Automatic Decision Makers

At one time or another many of us have seen leaders who were indecisive. By "indecisive" is meant that the leader hesitates to make a decision; he is bewildered, embarrassed, and suspends action on issues that often need immediate attention. Frequently under this theory of leadership the principal may wait with wishful eyes and ears hoping that no irritated parent will appear on the scene before the end of the day or that no telephone call will force him into having to make a decision about administering the secondary school without long and uncertain delay. It may well be that leaders under this theory of operation use committees and the term "the principal's office" to assign responsibility for unpleasant tasks that are done under the name of the school.

In seeking to avoid a flagrant display of authority, these principals go to the extreme end of the continuum and fail to assume their properly assigned responsibilities. Secondary schools that are administered under this leadership style usually are poorly organized, and faculty and staff members seldom know where they stand with regard to their responsibilities and with regard to their administrative relationships. This type of education can hardly be considered effective or acceptable in our modern age.

In contrast to the indecisive decision maker, one finds the automatic decision maker. Under this type of leadership one may find a secondary administrator whose predetermination is that all problems and issues have answers and who feels that it is his duty and responsibility to make decisions quickly and definitely. This style of leadership permits the secondary principal to make many decisions alone that might better be handled by the entire faculty. For example, a disciplinary problem that occurs in the cafeteria due to poor acoustical treatment which encourages noise may be handled by the principal through a memorandum to the faculty stating new rules, or he may call a faculty meeting in which he tells the faculty how to solve the problem according to his way of thinking. In many instances where principals seize the authority of their office to mandate changes concerning local school administration, there is an underlying element of insecurity. This may be accompanied by the attitude "take my word for it." It may be said that a member of such a faculty can ask the principal for an answer and always be assured that he will receive an answer. It goes without saying that the response may be based on blind impulse. Administrators are expected to make decisions but only after they have gathered and analyzed all the facts possible.

Authoritarian Leaders versus Democratic Leaders

So much has been said, discussed, and written about these two theories that it is rather difficult to separate the wheat from the chaff. Nevertheless, it is imperative at this time to give an extensive and fair evaluation of both theories. Leadership theories are not always clear-cut and are not generally white or black without some gray in between. Therefore it is necessary to dispel some popular notions as well as to discuss active ingredients.

Under the theory of authoritarian leadership one finds that the basic belief of the administrator is that he must tell others what to do. After all, he is the appointed head of the school and thinks that he knows what is best. This is the oldest concept concerning management of schools in existence. The principal, under this theory, is limited in power only by state laws, board of education rules, and local administrative controls. Traditionally this is the concept in America under which secondary schools grew and developed. This tradition has been difficult to cast aside.

Secondary principals working under this theory have felt that it was a personal weakness to admit that there are questions to which they do not have answers. They often combat this situation by developing and attempting to enforce detailed rules of operational procedure. Often rules are developed to answer almost any type of trivial question, many of which may never arise. These principals like to avoid controversial problems and issues by substituting rules and regulations. Many such administrators fear loss of control or loss of status. The authoritarian leader wants all persons, including the faculty members, students, parents, and others considered to be subordinates, to be fully aware of the fact that he is in control.

Some authoritarians attempt to explain their actions by referring to any other plan of administration as a waste of time and by saying that faculty members are not qualified to participate. More often than not, this attempt is based upon poor planning and is characterized to a high degree by lack of confidence in the faculty. These principals do not see this action as detrimental in any way but feel that they are operating efficiently controlled schools.

Selected features of control within these schools are often exaggerated. Control may be confused with desired educational outcomes. One of the writers visited such a secondary school recently. The principal was a retired colonel of the U.S. Army who had taken two graduate courses which entitled him to a provisional certificate in that particular state. In the outer lobby was a machine where teachers had punch-in and punch-out cards with a time clock so that the principal would know exactly when teachers arrived and departed. Practically all the students were in formations or lines when either entering or leaving the buildings at intermission periods. There was evidence of tenseness in classrooms as the principal boasted, "We have absolute peace and quiet here at all times." The regimentation in the school cafeteria, the corridors, the classrooms, and the faculty meetings gave evidence that the principal had honest intentions and thought he was administering an efficient school.

Rather than an efficient school, pupils were most likely being taught to ignore orders when not under direct supervision. Unnatural and artificial responses usually follow such a theory of administration. Direct obedience without toleration on the part of the faculty stifles initiative and restricts creativity. In the example cited, the pupils felt that the principal was sincere but too severe and too much guided by rules.

Another fear that authoritarian leaders can have is that of permitting any faculty member to receive widespread recognition and praise for some particular achievement. Although an excellent teacher may secure this kind of recognition, it will be reduced by the principal to the extent that it conflicts with what he thinks is his status or position.

Another side of administering secondary schools under the authoritarian theory may well be presented. The tremendous insecurity manifested by administrators who operate under this concept may be due in part to the lack of know-how or to the insufficient knowledge of the administrative process. If one analyzes the background and training of principals who are on the job and have been for a decade or two, it becomes apparent that many of them grew up in homes where the father ruled with an iron hand. They attended places of worship where they were told what to think. These same principals observed the government operating at local and state levels with little regard for any administrative process save know and tell. Institutions of higher education gave some courses in administration which were characterized by the words "administer your schools as I tell you." Very few opportunities have been afforded some principals to acquire the necessary skills to manage a secondary school with anything other than an authoritarian approach.

Respect for individuals and confidence in coworkers are basic premises of democratic leadership. In order for a faculty to have confidence in its principal, it is axiomatic that the principal must begin by exemplifying his confidence in the faculty. Confidence seems to beget confidence. In the individual school, the principal is a delegated representative of the superintendent and the leader of the professional faculty and staff as well. Success for the principal is dependent to a large extent upon his capacity to motivate colleagues to work cooperatively to attain cooperatively developed goals.

An administrator who operates under the theory of democratic leadership finds himself in conflict with much of the theory and practice used to describe authoritarian leadership. First, the basic belief is not to tell others what to do but rather to lead others to make intelligent decisions. He works toward earning the respect of coworkers through demonstrated action and judgment. Position or authority would be rated very low on his list of how he proposes to accomplish leadership goals. However, the principal would still be expected to operate under existing laws and the state board of education rules.

Under this theory of leadership, rules are used when necessary but not as a substitute for avoiding controversial issues or problems that need attention. The process of seeking the solution is given almost as much attention as the answer to a problem. Persons to be affected by the solution are involved in the process. These principals have no excessive fear of loss of status, for control and respect are earned, not automatically attached to a position or office. The word "coworker" is substituted for "subordinate."

Democratic leaders generally hold that planning, both short-range and long-range, is the essence of efficient administration. Representatives of personnel involved in the problems concerned are essential to the making of policies or evaluation of results under this theory of operation. Likewise the efficient use of personnel through good selection processes and through the assignment of personnel to areas of their specialties and aptitudes would improve the school program.

When the democratic process is employed, control of the school is not solely dependent upon extensive use of rigid rules and regulations, but great dependence is given to ideas shared by representatives from parents, teachers, and students as well. Administrative problems may become faculty problems. Teaching materials may be determined cooperatively rather than in the office of the principal. Faculties can be encouraged to have a voice in operations that affect their welfare directly.

One of the most interesting and efficient plans yet discovered by secondary principals for the participation of faculty is through the use of what is frequently called the advisory council. This body also goes by other names such as advisory committee to the principal or educational advisory committee. This committee or council would have as its major objective to recommend policy to the principal. This body may be elected from the faculty at large without regard to departmentalization since department heads are usually an arm of the principal and a part of his executive cabinet. The advisory committee may find that a part of its work is to help the principal screen problems that are to be submitted to respective areas or departments for consideration. Their duties and responsibilities as well as the limits of their authority should be explained early so that members have a clear understanding as to their functions and limitations. Perhaps the size of this group should be from five to nine members, depending upon the size of the faculty. Just as a senior class sponsor would prepare a group of senior students to elect class officers, so should the principal stress the type of activity this committee should be concerned with and its significance. Faculties should make every effort possible to elect persons who are interested, informed, and willing to participate. The selection of uninterested persons may cause defeat of one of the prime ways of administering a secondary school with some element of democracy.

Channels of communication must be kept open. It should be possible for teachers to suggest topics for consideration by the principal and his advisory group. If the occasion is deemed necessary, teachers should be permitted to submit typed reports or requests for action without their names attached. In most instances this would not become necessary. The principal has a vote and is chairman of the committee. He is still obligated to give his best advice and suggest courses of action which are within the law. He may veto an advisory committee's recommendation; however, it would not be wise to do this so often as to destroy the confidence of the body. Usually the principal will be working so closely with the advisory committee that he gives his ideas and suggestions in such a manner that voting upon many issues will not be necessary. Many of them can be settled through discussion and general agreement or common consent. This type of relationship does not prohibit a vote or a veto if the advisory committee members have strong feelings about a particular problem.

The degree of democratic process involved in making decisions about schools can be developed only within the limitations of the ability and the experience of the various people involved. The more able the individuals involved are, the more likely they can assume the accompanying responsibilities incumbent upon people who make decisions. Perhaps a good plan would be to begin with the most advanced and satisfying theory of leadership that may be used with a given school faculty and to seek to advance to higher levels as rapidly as is deemed wise.

Of the several theories of leadership, the writers consider democratic leadership as the one offering the most challenge and as the one most difficult to place in operation. Although all the prevailing theories discussed may be found in practice, it is reasonable to assume that the democratic theory is gaining in practice and is endorsed by a majority of efficient school principals and also by professors of educational administration.

There are great demands for strong and effective leadership within our secondary schools, and it is necessary for a principal to have an acceptable framework for viewing leadership behavior. Americans are living in an age that is characterized by change. One needs only to read the newspapers to become cognizant of this fact. Our population is becoming more mobile; our rate of juvenile delinquency is increasing; our education for world understanding is inadequate; and change seems to be one of our few constants. Therefore, many of the theories of leadership described here have little chance for success in today's world.

SUMMARY

A leader can be identified by some kind of observation of the effectiveness of his performance in the type of group to which the leadership is related. Leaders are often identified by observation, sociometric techniques, psychological testing, and interviews or through some combination of these procedures.

When the group structure is relatively stable, a leader may be expected to maintain his status for some time. When group structures change, the nonadjustable leaders tend to be replaced by those making a better adjustment to the social field. Research indicates that outstanding leaders have demonstrated considerable ability to make adjustments. Human needs tend to be satisfied more completely in the United States in a democratic social setting than in an autocratically organized one.

Improvement in almost any aspect of administration or teaching involves getting a number of people to change the way they perform certain activities. This kind of planning calls for the definition of acceptable goals and obtainable means of pursuing these goals.

Leaders usually are superior to nonleaders in their ability to evaluate group opinion of familiar and relevant issues. A functional leader is the coordinator of the action of the group. He accomplishes goals through working with others and by learning their desires and by helping the group attack problems. Indecisive leaders often suspend action on important issues that need immediate attention. They fail to assume their properly assigned responsibilities. By contrast the automatic decision maker often has a predetermination that all problems and issues have answers and feels that his rightful duty and responsibility is to make decisions quickly and definitely.

The authoritarian leader may believe that his job is to tell others what to do. This type of leader may feel that it is a personal weakness to admit that there are questions to which he does not have answers. Further, he expects that all subordinates must be aware that he is in control. A democratic leader finds himself in conflict with much of the theory and practice associated with authoritarian leadership. The democratic leader works toward earning the respect of coworkers through demonstrated action and judgment. He uses rules when necessary but not as a substitute for avoiding controversial problems that need attention. This type of leader feels that planning is the essence of efficient administration.

SUGGESTED EXERCISES

1. Discuss the various methods of identifying educational leaders presented in this chapter.

2. Suggest other ways of identifying leaders in educational administration.

3. Compare yourself against the criteria for identification of leaders in administration.

4. How reliable are tests in predicting administrative performance? Can you suggest other standardized tests that may be used to predict administrative potential?

5. What does the phrase "stability of group structure" mean to you?

6. Prepare a list of techniques of leadership with which you feel a secondary school principal should be acquainted.

7. Give illustrations of the various theories of leadership discussed in this chapter. Can you add others?

8. How do democratic leaders differ from other leaders in regard to their approach to secondary administration?

SELECTED REFERENCES

BAUGMAN, G. D., AND A. MAYRHOFER, "Leadership Training Project: A Final Report," *Journal of Secondary Education,* vol. 40, pp. 369–372, December, 1965.

BRUNER, JEROME S., "Education as a Social Invention," *Saturday Review,* vol. 49, pp. 70–72, February 19, 1966.

DOWNEY, LAWRENCE W., "The Secondary School Principal," in *Preparation Programs for School Administrators: Common and Specialized Learnings,* Seventh UCEA Career Development Seminar, Michigan State University, East Lansing, Mich., 1963, chap. 8.

ENGLEMAN, F. E., AND OTHERS, *Vignettes on the Theory and Practice of School Administration,* The Macmillan Company, New York, 1963.

GIBB, CECIL A., "Leadership," *Handbook of Social Psychology,* Addison-Wesley Publishing Company, Inc., Reading, Mass., 1954, vol. II.

HALPIN, ANDREW W., *Administrative Theory in Education,* The Macmillan Company, New York, 1967.

HOPPER, ROBERT L., AND R. D. BILLS, "What's a Good Administrator Made of?" *School Executive,* vol. 74, p. 93, March, 1955.

KIMBALL, J. T. "Age of the Intuitive Manager," *Dun's Review and Modern Industry*, vol. 87, pp. 42–43, January, 1966.

MCINTYRE, KENNETH E., *An Experiment in Recruiting and Selecting Leaders for Education*, Southwest School Administration Center, Austin, Tex., 1956.

MOORE, HOLLIS A., JR., *Studies in School Administration: A Report on the CPEA*, American Association of School Administrators, Washington, D.C., 1957.

OKERSON, D., AND E. HOISETH, "Our Metropolitan Locals: A Suggestion for Progress," *Minnesota Journal of Education*, vol. 46, p. 22, March, 1966.

OVSIEW, LEON, "Administrative Leadership and the Theory of Incremental Gain in Education Budget-making," *Canadian Education and Research Digest*, vol. 5, pp. 335–345, December, 1965.

SAUNDERS, R. L., AND OTHERS, *A Theory of Educational Leadership*, Charles E. Merrill Books, Inc., Columbus, Ohio, 1966.

STOLZ, R. W. "Executive Development: New Perspective," *Harvard Business Review*, vol. 44, pp. 133–136, May, 1966.

SYPHER, A. H., "Why Bureaucrats Rate Programs above People," *Nation's Business*, vol. 54, pp. 29–30, March, 1966.

WEINER, J. B., "Management of Litton Industries," *Dun's Review and Modern Industry*, vol. 87, pp. 32–33, May, 1966.

WHITE, K., "Personality Characteristics of Educational Leaders: A Comparison of Administrators and Researchers," *The School Review*, vol. 73, pp. 292–300, Autumn, 1965.

CHAPTER 8

HINDRANCES TO EFFECTIVE LEADERSHIP

There are many seemingly recurring obstacles that militate against effective leadership. To attempt to name all would make an extensive array. For the purpose of this discussion we will restrict ourselves to those that are in the foremost light and are thought to be surmountable. Among the obstacles to effective leadership in the secondary schools are the traditional atmosphere, the fear of theory, poorly defined goals and responsibilities, difficulties involved in initiating action, the various perceptions of the principal's role, doing what is popular, differences in beliefs about education, and ineffective selection of principals.

TRADITIONAL ATMOSPHERE

Resistors to Change

In order to develop a modern concept of leadership, the administrator at the secondary school level frequently must begin by overcoming the traditional atmosphere that is prevalent in the minds of the community people and the faculty. Generally, this tradition resists change in any form and looks upon change as being almost a catastrophe. Changes in the instructional program are never automatic. They must be preceded by careful preparation on the part of administrators and teachers responsible for their innovation. This calls for leadership that will enable schools beginning new projects to begin at a level of progress that has been attained by some other enlightened school district. Changes in school programs are not made just to satisfy a whim or to be in step with the times but must be constructed upon solid foundations and have continuous evaluation. Thus, preparation for change by the leader and the participants must be a continuous process and one in which conditioning takes place.

Fear of Shared Responsibilities

Faculty personnel who have become accustomed to taking orders from administrators do not hasten to welcome with open arms the greater freedom and responsibilities given or permitted by a more democratic administrator. This reluctance may not be due to indifference or unwillingness on the part of the participants but can be a result of fear of shared responsibilities and cooperative development which calls for more reading and thinking on their part than merely following orders or carrying out plans made by someone else. Also fear may involve the idea that the principal is abandoning his responsibilities and that anarchy and discord will result from a more modern concept of secondary administration. These teachers feel that if they have no part in making a decision, then they have no responsibility for the outcome of the decision. Therefore, taking orders is much easier in that they do not have to feel responsible for an unfavorable or unsatisfactory outcome.

Public Confusion over Efficiency

In a democracy, administrators and teachers cannot isolate themselves from the community in which they work or from the profession to which they belong. This is evidenced by the fact that there is almost a continual expansion of the school plant and facilities and the constant demand for a better prepared and higher-paid teaching faculty in America. Although many schools enjoy this abiding faith exhibited by their community citizens, some become very confused about what is an efficient school. Leading citizens may support the idea that an efficiently operated high school can be achieved only if autocratic practices are used. Parents often do not understand that children can be taught effectively in a school where a democratic climate prevails. Some parents are impatient with results gained in this manner. Too, some boards of education have often expressed their delight with a new secondary principal who tells the faculty what policies will operate rather than have a principal who will work out the policies cooperatively with the faculty.

FEAR OF THEORY

A Lack of Understanding

The word "theory" appears to create anxiety among many persons who are earnestly interested in improving public education. To consider theory in relation to improving leadership that involves changing practices relative to learning is unacceptable to a large number of administrators as well as to some teachers. In common usage *theory* may be defined as abstract principles which explain a set of related facts that are applicable to a defined field of inquiry. In most educational endeavors theory precedes improved practices. Thus, theory is something to be understood rather than feared by administrators and teachers alike.

Relationship of Theory and Practice

Actually, our theory of public education and our theory of educational administration are two aspects of a theory that explains the institution as a whole. One deals with the nature of education as a public service, and the other with the process of organizing and administering that service. Any theory of administration must take into consideration the purposes it is to serve and the nature of the work that has to be done in order to attain these purposes. Almost any good administrative practice is based upon a sound theory, and likewise many theories are derived from the use of new practices. The application of theory to practice represents one of the highest levels of thinking in educational administration. It is an essential part of administration and deserves to be comprehended.

Social Theory and Political Philosophies

A theory of administration should harmonize with the social and political philosophies of a country. In America, the kind of education the young receive will be reflected in how they feel about their citizenship and about life in a democracy. In a country in which the political and social life are governed by totalitarian leadership, the type of education its youth should receive ought to be reflected in their citizenship and their attitudes toward their country and nation. Public schools have an obligation to their own states and nation as well as to individuals. Education is a state function, and many things that are essential for state and national security and advancement should be a part of the public school experience of children. Therefore, it would seem to make sense to administer our secondary schools as laboratories of democracy and to somewhat reduce the fear of theory.

POORLY DEFINED GOALS AND RESPONSIBILITIES

Few if any actions that a secondary school principal may take can cause as much harm or delay or prohibit progress to the extent that poorly defined goals and responsibilities can. This disclaimer is extensive and knows few bounds. It is a type of professional sin that cannot be long tolerated in today's modern secondary school.

Establishing New Goals

In the everyday school operation it is possible for the major goals, especially if they are poorly defined, to become lost among the maze of immediate activities. One of the largest and most significant responsibilities with which the secondary school principal may be charged is that of keeping the administrative team and faculty keenly aware of school purposes or goals. It may become essential at times to assist individual members of the administrative staff to keep these purposes in sight. The attainment and fulfillment of certain goals may make necessary the establishment of new goals from time to time.

A basic statement of ultimate goals is not sufficient, although it might well serve as a starting point for a faculty in defining the goals or purposes of a school. The goals must be rather specific in order that they may help determine what experiences are to be provided for pupils and in order that the faculty may make a decision as to whether or not they have been achieved. As a result of evaluation, faculty members may change the learning experiences or the school purposes or even, in some cases, both. If new goals need to be established, the principal must lead the faculty in this process as goal definition is a significant part of the educational process.

For example, maintaining good physical and mental health was for many years accepted as a purpose of the secondary school. Experiences were provided for pupils in the secondary schools to enhance this purpose. More recently, this purpose has been enlarged to include maintaining good health and physical fitness. This broader goal required the secondary schools to change their learning experiences in many areas such as in physical education, athletics, and medical services.

Job Definitions

When responsibilities are not defined adequately, it is inevitable that conflicts and misunderstandings will result. Within the secondary school, the principal is the leader as well as the legal commander-in-chief. He must make certain that there are job definitions so that conflicts arising from misunderstandings about responsibilities are kept to a minimum. In addition, he must provide some type of machinery for resolving the conflicts that do appear although responsibilities have already been defined. With the increasing size of the administrative and supervisory staff working in the administrative office, conflicts in duties are certain to develop. One way of dealing with these conflicts is to have each member of the team whose duties conflict list his own responsibilities and then have the two persons meet with the principal and resolve areas of conflict. In many instances one will find that administrative personnel have been assigned or have accepted responsibility for areas of work that involve reporting to their superiors. Other types of responsibility may involve actions that an administrator may need to take but that require the permission of some other administrative person or group. Whether the conflict is between two persons or more, it can be cleared up if the parties involved are willing to seek a solution through persons outside the conflict area.

Delegated Responsibilities

Irrespective of whether decisions are made by the faculty, by a committee, or by an individual, the principal is held responsible for seeing that decisions are made and action taken. In order to avoid the routine of office management, principals should learn to delegate authority to others. This permits the principal to use his time in a more organized fashion. It relieves him from doing all the detail work, much of which can be taken care of by clerks. Some principals are unable to delegate responsibility. They try to see every caller, spend much time visiting, avoid a regular schedule of work, and often neglect to confide in staff members or to draw upon their abilities in developing policies for the school. This type of principal generally has poorly defined policies for his coworkers in the administrative family. If he is unable to define and delegate his own work, it is rather unlikely that he will be able to see clearly the work of the administrative team. Thus conflicts will arise and personalities may become involved because of poor job definition.

DIFFICULTIES INVOLVED IN INITIATING ACTION

Involve Interested and Capable People

No serious-minded principal can be content merely with keeping the status quo in his school. Yet, change just for the sake of change is not worthy of its name. Helpful changes demand that the principal work carefully with the faculty so that changes can come about without unnecessary controversy. To provide leadership that brings about such change requires that meetings be planned so that only those having a common concern and interest are invited to participate. For example, if a controversial question arises in faculty meetings that concerns only the senior class, then it may not be necessary to have all the high school faculty discuss some detail that can be handled by the class officers and senior class sponsor and/or principal. Or if the homeroom teachers of the tenth grade are concerned about a particular problem that can be postponed to a later date for a more detailed examination by those concerned, the entire time of the whole faculty should not be used for such problems.

Avoid Hurried Faculty Decisions

Another type of difficulty arises when faculty members are hurried or pushed into making a decision about a particular problem before they are ready. At the same time, the principal cannot wait unduly for action on a problem that calls for immediate attention. "As the principal goes, so goes the faculty" is a saying worth remembering. It is indeed his job to initiate change and action. This requires him to be a person who is sensitive to human relations and informed so that he is able to discover when the faculty is ready to act and when it needs additional time for study.

It may well be that the principal has been thinking and discussing with others his school problems and fails to realize that the faculty is ill-prepared to think through a problem that is brought to their attention for the first time. It is his responsibility to share with the faculty information which he possesses about a problem or situation before he rightly expects the group to analyze that problem in its true prospective and to suggest alternatives.

Unwillingness of Faculty to Try Out New Ideas

Most of the comments so far have been predicated upon the principal's having the ability to initiate change and action. Some difficulties in initiating change and action programs stem from members of the faculty. Fear of change or action that may make new demands upon their time and require them to learn new methods or techniques or additional content in subject fields causes many teachers to "grandstand" or to profess beliefs they do not necessarily want to support in order to thwart proposed changes. Calling attention to possible weaknesses of the proposal, telling how other schools have tried the suggested plan with little or no success, and appearing to doubt the validity of the suggested plan of action can delay and sometimes defeat the principal in his attempts to bring about changes that are necessary if the school is to keep pace with the technological developments of our society. In many instances the real issue is the inability or unwillingness of the faculty to accept its responsibility to try out new ideas.

Give Recognition for Successes

In other cases, faculties are willing to discuss new plans for action and are willing to vote for their acceptance but are very slow to put them into operation. Again, this may be based more upon a desire to please the principal and to be known as a cooperative teacher than upon a desire to accept a planned program for action that requires them to assume new responsibilities and to be relieved of some former responsibilities. Willingness to support a plan which a faculty has had a part in planning is not enough. The faculty needs to have additional help and assurance as it goes about initiating action. Recognition should be given for successes rather than failures. Assistance should be given where and when it is needed.

It is significant to create an atmosphere of teamwork in which participants feel that they will be given due credit for ideas and work. Recognizing success need not be done publicly but should be verbally given to those who have contributed the most and worked the hardest. A failure to commend faculty members for work well done tends to leave the participant with a question about the value of his own performance and to make him feel that he is a part of a big machine which does little for the dignity and worth of the human individual. Of course, insincere flattery is as bad as no recognition at all. It creates an illusion on the part of the participant that he is doing better than he is. This leads to the destruction of confidence between the two and to a lack of trust. Honesty is the best policy even when it hurts.

PERCEPTIONS OF THE PRINCIPAL'S ROLE

How the Principal Views His Job

There are great demands for strong leadership within our secondary schools, and it is essential for a principal to have an acceptable framework for looking at leadership behavior. Most administrators are afraid to use a framework for self-evaluation other than democratic because they may immediately be labeled autocratic. Some administrators lack the courage to say that they received their training under autocratic methods and do not know how to operate a school except by the autocratic process. One of the major obstacles to successful secondary administration is the way the principal views his job and the often very different way it is visualized by his faculty and members of the community. A complicating factor is the desire and willingness of the principal to adjust to what is expected of him by his superiors and by his subordinates. He may lack the necessary skills to perform the job in the manner that is expected.

How the Faculty Views His Job

One of the writers is acquainted with a principal who received his doctor's degree from a teachers college and was somewhat confused about the democratic process versus the autocratic process. He was so eager to please his superiors by adopting what he thought to be democratic processes that he became very autocratic about having practices he considered democratic actually carried out. One of these concerned the idea that all conferences with parents must be held in the classroom with the teacher sitting on one side of a specially provided table and the parent on the other side. In the words of the principal, "We must not permit parents to think that we are undemocratic." The principal had it expressly understood that this was the *one way* in which parent conferences could be held.

This example illustrates how the principal felt and what he thought his functions were, but it does not show the faculty reactions, which were many and negative. The faculty members felt that the principal was interfering with an instructional function which could be handled in several ways. They did not envision parental conferences as having to be held in one way. They felt that each teacher should work out his own efficient manner for the interview. The faculty did not think of the principal's role as one in which he was to dictate a method of operation under the guise of democracy. Faculty members felt that what they expected on the part of the principal in this case was very different from the principal's own perceptions. In the final analysis, the principal must work with and through his faculty. He cannot spare the time, even if he knows the answers, to give detailed instructions to well-trained faculty members.

How the Community Views His Job

The exact amount of time a principal should spend in community activities is not a matter of common agreement, but the amount he does spend is conditioned by many factors. Among these are what the community expects from him. How the community views the job of the principal inevitably influences his plan of action. Few, if any, principals in today's large high schools spend a disproportionate amount of time in community service; if they do, they are prohibited from furnishing leadership for expanding faculties and the instructional programs. The amount of time to be spent in community service is conditioned greatly by the administrator's philosophy of administration as well as by the community's expectations.

A few principals still see their role in terms of getting things done. This perception of the job leaves undefined many operational procedures which may in themselves be detrimental to the objectives of secondary education. Trivia may become the most important aspect of administration under this perception. If getting action becomes the most sought after goal, it is likely that the administrative process itself will suffer. Ways of promoting action and securing desirable results must be considered as a part of the process.

In order to develop perceptiveness about the administrative process at the secondary school level, principals should begin by defining their own jobs. Despite the present-day knowledge of the social sciences, this complete knowledge cannot be developed into guides for dealing with administrative processes. Culbertson points out that sciences can provide important understandings through such concepts as community power structure; [1] however, they cannot give a complete answer to administrators on how and to what extent the power structure can be manipulated. Again, the administrator must come face to face with community attitudes toward public education and relate them in some acceptable manner to his own perception of his position.

DOING WHAT IS POPULAR

Assuming That All Teachers Are Enthusiastic about Change

It is very easy for a secondary school principal to become strongly motivated and to permit his enthusiasm for a new insight into a problem, say, that of the curriculum, to lead him to assume that his teachers will be equally enthusiastic.[2] This tendency is the source of many faddist movements that plague the secondary schools today. Often teachers have not had ample motivation or are not as interested as the principal in attacking a problem in the manner suggested by the principal. After all, many different backgrounds, experiences, and training are represented by most secondary school faculties. It is a mistake to assume that they are always interested in following or sharing the spirit of fervidness exhibited by the principal.

Others Do It, Therefore It Must Be Good

To base one's ideas about change upon what others are doing, without stopping to consider whether it is needed or desirable for one's own individual school, is to be misled by popular notion. To embark suddenly upon some new program or method without first surveying the capacities

[1] Jack A. Culbertson, "Implications for Program Change," in *Preparing Administrators: New Perspectives,* University Council for Educational Administration, Columbus, Ohio, 1962, p. 161.
[2] Philip G. Smith and H. Gordon Hullfish, *Reflective Thinking,* Dodd, Mead & Company, Inc., New York, 1961, p. 240.

of the faculty for such changes is to invite trouble. Take some popular approach to education today such as team teaching. It requires more than two people's or the administrator's deciding that they will exchange teaching periods in two selected subject fields. It may involve the development of new and different skills on the part of the faculty members who will participate. It may involve schedule changes, personality differences, and a host of details that have to be adjusted before it can work satisfactorily in a particular school. It is much more complex than just imitating some school or reproducing and using materials found to work in other situations. This approach to change represents a faulty premise.

Solving One Problem and Creating Others

It is common for schools that are not satisfied to remain in a status quo position to submit to the lure of ideas that are currently popular. If it is a practice in some of the better-known schools to handle discipline in a certain manner and if a particular school has a related disciplinary problem, the latter will likely try to copy the other schools in its approach. Such a blind approach may solve the particular problem but create greater problems. In an instance with which the authors are familiar, it was customary to send troublemakers or pupils who disrupted classes to the library for the remainder of the period in question. The feeling of the principal was shared by the faculty members who had this problem. However, this temporary relief granted the teacher in question failed to resolve the problem since an increasing number of pupils found being sent to the library as punishment not really punishment but a relief from any class they considered boring, and it also provided the student with time for library work that ordinarily would have to be done after school.

DIVERGENCES IN BELIEFS ABOUT EDUCATION

Beliefs Affect Behavior

What one believes about education, both curriculum and methodology, influences his behavior in terms of adjusting to or participating in change within the framework of the school. According to Neagley and Evans, many teachers hold strong beliefs about educational procedures and cannot honestly support practices which are contrary to what they believe.[3] As a result of training and experience, teachers become conditioned to believe as they do and may resist change because the change suggested is in conflict, in part if not fully, with what they believe about education. A belief generally runs deeper than the words which are used to express it. Perhaps there is no such thing as a merely verbal belief.

[3] Ross L. Neagley and N. Dean Evans, *Handbook for Effective Supervision*, Prentice-Hall, Inc., Englewood Cliffs, N.J., 1964, p. 120.

Confusion about Beliefs

When a person professes to believe but is unwilling to act, he may, of course, be honestly confused. This can, and often is, the case with a teacher who has been asked to give up a certain type of activity and to take on another. For example, there is often honest disagreement about how learning takes place with high school students. One teacher may believe that learning is enhanced by lectures, extreme pressures for rote memory work, emphasis upon drill and workbooks; that anyone can learn anything if he tries hard enough; and that education must be an unpleasant experience. Another teacher may believe in almost the opposite approach and view learning as a process where the learner participates, where several methods of instruction may be used, where schoolwork is thought of as a normal and pleasant experience, and where the interest, capacity, and social and physical development of the pupil are considered in planning and carrying out school experiences.

INEFFECTIVE SELECTION OF PRINCIPALS

It is not the purpose of this section to elaborate on proper methods for the selection of principals, rather it is contended that ineffective selection creates problems that inhibit progress and change.

Inadequate Supply of Competent Candidates during World War II and the Korean War Years

At a time when so many young and able-bodied men were called to the defense of their country, local school systems had relatively little choice in deciding who would be the high school principal when theirs was drafted into service. This statement is not intended to impugn in any manner the many fine choices that were made during this period. Longevity of service plus being of the male sex, married, and available were factors that were substituted for competence in educational administration. One of the writers is acquainted with a high school principal who was selected during the war years and given tenure after three years. He is now working as a principal in the smallest school in a large district. He has been transferred to three different schools within the system, but his incompetence always shows up in his working relations with others. This incompetence is hardly the type that one would wish to contest in court for dismissal after tolerating it for so many years. Yet, it is often said of this man, "He has inhibited teachers and progress in each school where he has served as principal." Had the local superintendent of schools not recommended his employment, the board of education and superintendent would perhaps have had to replace him with another of his equal.

Local Person Given Preference over Competent Person from Outside

It is the responsibility of the superintendent of schools to nominate to the board of education for employment the most competent person available for the salary that can be offered a principal. In recent years some large school districts have tended to omit from consideration persons outside the school system or have required a specific number (often three to five) years of teaching experience within a particular system before an individual may become eligible for a school principalship. This procedure of selection automatically leaves out many administrators who have already proved their competence elsewhere. While this practice may improve morale within the local system, it fails to help the school system secure the best qualified person for the position in all instances. No school district should isolate itself to the extent that all administrators and supervisors are chosen from within the system. Limiting the choice of personnel for the principalship to local persons tends to encourage inbreeding and to promote the selection of a yes-man rather than someone who has proved competence and has ideas to contribute.

Selection Based on One Special Talent

In the process of selecting a high school principal, it is easy to overrate a special talent of one person. For example, a baseball, basketball, or football coach may be able to develop skills in boys that produce winning teams. Band leaders may be able to arouse enthusiasm and to win contests with their well-trained bands. The teacher of science may be able in this age of technology to have a number of merit scholarship winners. All these and other similar types of specific skills can be seen and appreciated by the public and by members of the board of education. Likewise, a spirited group of lay supporters can often influence the local board in its final choice of who will be the principal. The criterion for selection then may be based upon one special talent rather than a competency pattern that is expected of an administrator. Possessing one special talent, along with others, is of great advantage, but a high school principalship may require an entirely different set of competencies than those of the person who is especially skilled in one area.

SUMMARY

Many factors hinder effective leadership at the secondary school level. Among these are tradition, fear of shared responsibilities, and public confusion over the meaning of efficiency.

The fear of theory is another hindrance because it is often misunderstood or does not relate to the social and political philosophies of the country. Likewise, poorly defined goals and responsibilities delay the action which a secondary principal may take. This hindrance is particularly pertinent when one recognizes that the principal is held responsible for seeing that decisions are made and action taken.

The array of problems associated with initiating action in a secondary school can be a hindrance. The faculty may hesitate or be reluctant to try out new ideas for fear of their own failure.

The manner in which the role of the principal is perceived by the faculty, the community, and by the principal himself affects the leadership within the school either negatively or positively. The principal should take care that by solving one problem, he does not create others. The differences in beliefs about education make progress difficult at times.

Perhaps the greatest deterrent to effective leadership is the ineffective selection of principals. This process has been abetted by an inadequate supply of competent candidates, giving preference to local candidates with minimum qualifications over competent persons from outside the district, and making selections based on one special talent held by the candidate.

SUGGESTED EXERCISES

1.   Make a list of obstacles to effective leadership which you feel exist in your school. Compare them with those given in this chapter.

2.   Interview several secondary school principals, and obtain their ideas about obstacles to leadership.

3.   What can be done to overcome some of the most difficult hindrances?

4.   Contrast change as it takes place in secondary administration with the way it operates in government, law, and medicine.

5.   Interview five to ten experienced teachers in your school system, and discover what they believe can be done to improve leadership and remove obstacles to change.

6.   What factors associated with change do you find most disturbing? Why?

SELECTED REFERENCES

ANDREE, R. G., "Schools under Pressure," *Middle States Association of College and Secondary Schools Proceedings,* 1964, pp. 77–86.

BRICKMAN, W. W., "Leadership and Scholarship: Concerning Report of the Carnegie Corporation of New York," *School and Society,* vol. 94, p. 116, March 5, 1966.

CARR, W. G., "Principals and Professional Negotiation," *National Education Association Journal,* vol. 55, pp. 45–46, May, 1966.

CULBERTSON, JACK, AND STEPHEN HENCLEY, *Preparing New Administrators: New Perspectives,* University Council for Educational Administration, Columbus, Ohio, 1962, chap. 10.

GARBER, L. O., "How to Free Superintendents from Negotiation Hazards," *The Nation's Schools,* vol. 77, p. 139, March, 1966.

IRWIN, P. H., AND F. W. LANGHAM, JR., "Change Seekers: Management of Change," *Harvard Business Review,* vol. 44, pp. 81–92, January, 1966.

Leadership for Improving Instruction, The Association for Supervision and Curriculum Development, Washington, D.C., 1960.

NEAGLEY, ROSS L., AND DEAN N. EVANS, *Handbook for Effective Supervision of Instruction,* Prentice-Hall, Inc., Englewood Cliffs, N.J., 1964, chap. 8.

NELSON, W. E., "Take Time to Teach Student Leaders," *Journal of Health, Physical Education, Recreation,* vol. 37, p. 22, April, 1966.

PIERCE, TRUMAN M., AND A. D. ALBRIGHT, *A Profession in Transition: A Nine-year Story of Improving Educational Administration in the South,* Southern States Cooperative Program in Educational Administration, 1960, chap. 7.

SCHLEH, E. C., "Dangerous Supervisory Gap," *Dun's Review and Modern Industry,* vol. 87, pp. 57–58, February, 1956.

SMITH, PHILIP G., AND H. GORDON HULLFISH, *Reflective Thinking,* Dodd, Mead & Company, Inc., New York, 1961, chap. 14.

CHAPTER 9

COMPETENCIES NEEDED FOR LEADERSHIP

The purpose of this chapter is to discuss the competency concept and the efforts expended to develop competency patterns in educational administration with special emphasis upon the secondary principalship. Also discussed are personal and professional competencies, recruitment and selection, and improved certification requirements.

THE COMPETENCY CONCEPT

One may see evidence of competency and incompetency daily. A competent typist can produce letters with a minimum of errors. A competent waiter has a pleasing personality, takes orders quickly and accurately, and delivers the food and beverage promptly to the proper individuals. A competent physician can diagnose accurately concerning diseases. He prescribes the appropriate medicines, and checks constantly to see how his patient is improving as a result of the prescriptions. He finds out whether the patient is regaining his health. The typist, the waiter, or the physician who performs his job efficiently and successfully is generally regarded as being competent. Thus one may see that persons have distinguishable characteristics which may be regarded as competencies.

EFFORTS TO DEVELOP COMPETENCY PATTERNS

Competency in any occupation or profession is highly desirable, and attempting to educate persons to be competent is a justifiable goal. The idea of competency is not restricted to professional educators, and attempts have been made in several occupations and professions to describe it. As may be expected, competency may make different demands upon individuals in one occupation or profession from those in another profession. Therefore competency in any profession must be described in relationship to the job to be performed. There remains a wide disagreement in the description of competency among the professions.

Description of Traits

A very common way of designating competency is by describing the traits or dominant characteristics which an individual should have in order to perform a particular job. For example, one might list the traits of an insurance salesman. Yet, if one were to list the traits expected of a successful electrician, he would find different requirements. Due to the generality of such traits this method of designating competency has little to offer in school administration.

The attempt to identify competencies rather than traits as a basis for leadership does not deny that traits exist but proposes an additional dimension: that the holder of such traits is able to demonstrate that he can apply knowledge to situations.

Formula Approach

One of the best-known examples of the formula approach is Richard's Formula for Job Success.[1] This formula was developed to obtain competent industrial workers at the Brighton Mills, Passaic, New Jersey. It attempted to determine what personal qualities were essential for job competency. The manipulations of a worker's hands and tools were analyzed. Although the formula finally died from overexpansion, it did much to focus the attention of people on job performance.

Job Analysis

The objective of job analysis is to break down any particular business activity into distinct and essential actions. Each action is then evaluated in terms of what it contributes to the ultimate objective. Although the

[1] John A. McCarthy, *Vocational Education: America's Greatest Resource*, American Technical Society, Chicago, 1951, pp. 199–207.

actual abilities of the workers have not been improved, what they now do counts for more because much lost motion has been eliminated.

COMPETENCY STUDIES IN EDUCATIONAL ADMINISTRATION

The principal of a modern secondary school needs certain competencies in order to do his job effectively. The word "competencies" is being used instead of "traits" since it is a more comprehensive term and denotes a relationship to effective administrative behavior. One may be a possessor of many admirable traits but still be unable to use his traits as a leader in a wide number of situations. The total behavior pattern of the principal should be stated in terms of competencies. A *competency* may be defined as an agent that contributes to or is a part of the total effective administrative behavior.

A number of studies have been made of competencies and competency patterns. Although these studies are not in complete agreement on details, there is substantial agreement in many areas.

Moore's Study

After making an extensive summary of the studies in school administration under the auspices of the Cooperative Project in Educational Administration, Hollis A. Moore, Jr., found that there is no general agreement on the differentiation between the role of the principal as contrasted with the role of the superintendent.[2] Most of the competencies expected of superintendents should also be applicable to principals. Perhaps this takes on special meaning when one recalls that up until now most superintendents were principals before becoming superintendents.

Southern States Cooperative Project

Thinking of educational administration in terms of a competency pattern is not new. This pattern was developed by a group of universities that took part in the Southern States Cooperative Project in Educational Administration. The work of this group culminated in a publication which deals with the competency pattern in educational administration and its uses in the Southern region.[3] This report was based upon 5 years of study and shows the competency pattern as consisting of a theory of educational administration, the job of educational administration, and the know-how of educational administration. The materials included in

---

[2] Hollis A. Moore, Jr., *Studies in School Administration: A Report on the CPEA*, American Association of School Administrators, Washington, D.C., 1957, p. 30.

[3] Southern States Cooperative Program in Educational Administration, *Better Teaching in School Administration: A Competency Approach to Improving Institutional Preparation Programs in Educational Administration*, McQuiddy Printing Co., Nashville, Tenn., 1950–1955, 279 pp.

this publication are suggestive in nature and are not set forth as final products in any sense of the word.

University of Tennessee Studies

One of the major concerns of the Kellogg research project carried on by the department of educational administration and supervision at the University of Tennessee from 1955 through 1958 was the determination of behavioral characteristics of effective and ineffective school administrators.[4] Statements of such behavioral characteristics were combined into a single instrument which came to be known as the Tennessee Rating Guide. The January, 1959, revision of the Tennessee Rating Guide consists of six major divisions: (1) interpersonal relations, (2) intelligent operation, (3) emotional stability, (4) ethical and moral strength, (5) adequacy of communication, and (6) operation as a citizen. Contained within each major division are a series of questions relating to behavior. Under each question there are five specific statements of behavioral characteristics representing varying degrees of effectiveness. The following example taken from the "operation as a citizen" division further explains the organization.

C.   *What is his attitude toward minority groups in the school community?*
  1.   Insists that minority points of view be appropriately represented in community-school decisions
  2.   Upholds right of most minority viewpoints to be represented but neglects consideration of those that are extreme
  3.   Follows a hands-off policy in regard to minority groups in the community
  4.   Tends to ignore the existence of minority groups in the community
  5.   Indicates that minority groups have no right to representation in community-school affairs

There have been six major studies relating to the validation of the guide. Among these is a study by Coker that was conducted to determine the validity of the rating guide in differentiating between effective and ineffective school principals.[5] In the study a four-member committee, which had intimate knowledge of the operational behavior of the subjects under consideration, selected two groups, each composed of sixteen principals. One group was composed of "effective" principals, and the other group, of "ineffective" principals. A team of two raters, who were thoroughly familiar with the rating guide, rated each of the thirty-two

[4] Orin B. Graff, for the Department of Educational Administration and Supervision, *Characteristics of School Administrators*, A Kellogg Project, University of Tennessee, Knoxville, Tenn., 1959, 106 pp.
[5] Phyllis Coker, "A Study of the Use of the Tennessee Rating Guide as a Means of Differentiating between Effective and Ineffective School Administrators," unpublished master's thesis, The University of Tennessee, Knoxville, Tenn., 1956.

principals using the rating guide. The thirty-two principals were combined into one group when the raters performed.

It was found that the rating guide as a whole clearly differentiated between the effective group and the ineffective group. The mean scores for the effective group on all sections of the rating guide was 4.3 with the range being from 4.1 to 4.6. The mean score for the ineffective group on all sections of the rating guide was 2.8 with the range being from 2.2 to 3.3. The scores were based on a one-to-five scale with the higher scores indicating the more desirable characteristics.

Another study to validate the behavioral characteristics of school administrators was made by Gentry.[6] The purpose of his study was to identify patterns of behavioral characteristics of selected administrators. Twenty-five professors of educational administration from various sectors of the United States were asked to select three competent practicing public administrators to serve as raters. Each rater was asked to rate one of the most effective school administrators and one of the most ineffective school administrators whom he knew intimately. His sample included fifty-five effective and fifty-five ineffective school administrators. From a comparative analysis of the ratings of the two groups Gentry concluded:

1. The effective administrators rated had common characteristics which tend to differentiate them from the ineffective administrators rated.
2. A rating of four or better characterized the effective administrator.
3. The ineffective administrators rated had common characteristics which tend to differentiate them from the effective administrators rated.
4. A rating of three or less characterized the ineffective administrator.

Based on the research evidence, it appears that the revised Tennessee Rating Guide (1959) is a valid instrument when used by a competent rater for the purpose of distinguishing between effective and ineffective school administrators or potential administrators.

Woodard's Study

An exhaustive study of competencies needed by superintendents, principals, and supervisors, was made by Woodard.[7] His review of the literature revealed 203 competencies as essential for either of the three positions. He found that 70 percent of these competencies were common to three types of positions and that 84 percent of the competencies listed as necessary for the principal were also noted as being necessary for the superintendent. Further, Woodard compared the findings of the litera-

[6] Harold W. Gentry, "Patterns of Behavioral Characteristics Exhibited by School Administrators," unpublished doctoral dissertation, The University of Tennessee, Knoxville, Tenn., 1957, pp. 94–95.
[7] Prince B. Woodard, "A Study of Competencies Needed by School Administrators and Supervisors in Virginia with Implications for Pre-service Education," unpublished doctor's dissertation, The University of Virginia, Charlottesville, Va., 1953.

ture with those of selected juries of superintendents, principals, and supervisors and found them to be virtually identical.

PERSONAL AND PROFESSIONAL COMPETENCIES

Despite the various studies about competency, there are many unanswered questions. In fact, one aspect that is still difficult is the ascertaining of the competency of the middle group of school administrators who do not fit into either the effective or ineffective group. Also, in several instances it is almost impossible to determine whether a competency is of a personal or a professional nature. However, for the sake of discussion, the authors have attempted such a division.

Personal Competencies

The personal competencies thought desirable for the secondary principalship have been grouped under the headings that follow.

The secondary principal should possess adequate personal qualities. He should have good physical and mental health. So much of his work is with others and involves face-to-face relationships that he ought to be relatively free of any unusual or pronounced physical abnormalities. A person operating in this sphere of leadership should have a high degree of intelligence. There is a close relationship between intelligence and leadership ability. This is not to say that all persons who are very intelligent will make effective principals. A principal ought to have an acceptable personality in terms of his total behavior pattern. As a part of his social disposition it is desirable that he exhibit a sense of humor and not be easily brought to periods of high temper flare-ups.

The secondary principal should be of good moral character and have basic integrity. Historically our society has demanded that persons who hold administrative and teaching positions be of good moral character and possess basic integrity. Associated with these demands have been the need for understanding problems which involve ethics and character since the teaching of moral and spiritual values is done in our public schools. Most of the qualities expected of teachers can be desired of the principal such as fairness, patience, and persistence.

Professional Competencies

The professional competencies discussed in this section are not thought of as being compiled into an exhaustive list, but the ones presented are believed to be somewhat representative of what research indicates the needs are.

A leader of the secondary school should have a wide background of undergraduate or graduate work which gives an understanding about the

nature of learning and specific learnings related to his own teaching field.
He needs an understanding of adolescent growth and development, teaching methods, curriculum development, counseling and guidance, tests and measurements, government, role of the school in society, the purposes of education, sociology, economics, and many related disciplines.

The principal of a secondary school should have a deep understanding of the technical aspects of educational administration. This phase of education will be geared to his graduate program and should include all the aspects of administration for which he will need knowledge and skills. Some of the areas discovered by Woodard include the following: [8]

Function and scope of public education
Related disciplines
Communications
Educational foundations
Human relations
Personnel administration
Community relations
School organization and management
Financial and budgetary services
School plant: construction, operation, and maintenance
Curriculum
Instructional and guidance activities
Supervisory services
Evaluation and research
Related educational agencies

In addition to possessing competencies in these areas, the principal should be able to relate his knowledge and skills in a meaningful way.
The principal should be able, as a result of his total graduate program, to be qualified for the highest certificate required by his state. As a part of his graduate program a principal should have opportunities to gain new insights through field experiences.[9] These may include practicums where he is permitted to handle some type of administrative problems and practices while he is still teaching and preparing for the principalship. Another type of field experience would be the internship. Here the prospective principal is permitted to serve one semester or more in a public school system where he is an assistant to a principal. He becomes involved in almost every administrative activity and learns to apply theory to practice through the guidance of an experienced principal.

A leader of a secondary school should possess an adequate background of experience. It is difficult if not impossible to separate experience from

[8] *Ibid.*, p. 9.
[9] These field experiences are a part of the training program of The Department of Educational Administration, Temple University, Philadelphia.

education, but it is done here for emphasis. The secondary school principal will probably have taught in the secondary school and will have some knowledge of what adolescent boys and girls are like. Too, he will have gained as a part of his experience some understanding of the school and its relationship to the community and have some general acquaintance with administrative problems that arose in the schools where he taught. To say that a specific number of years of teaching experience is required would be somewhat questionable; however, a minimum of three years would seem helpful.

Experiences other than teaching such as military service, governmental work, camp work, church work, and kinds of experience where the principal was in charge of others or assumed leadership roles are highly desirable. It is thought by many professors of educational administration that married men have better professional opportunities than single men. Perhaps this thought is based upon the idea that a stable home organization contributes to the effectiveness of a principal.

The secondary principal should have a good understanding of related disciplines. Being knowledgeable in the disciplines of economics, sociology, public administration, public finance, and political science can contribute greatly to the principal's integration of knowledge. Many of the problems faced by secondary principals are related to these disciplines and to others such as history, communications, and the newer developments having to do with automation.

The principal of a secondary school should be able to work effectively with both individuals and groups. In the performance of functions related to his office the principal will be in contact daily with large numbers of individuals. It is imperative that he be approachable and schedule his time in such a manner as to permit and possibly encourage faculty members to confer with him about real problems that impede teaching effectiveness. In dealing with individuals, be they students, parents, or teachers, the principal must be constantly aware that behavior is a relative thing and that an unusual response or behavioral pattern exhibited by anyone at a given time may be due to stress or emotional strain, and therefore he must reserve judgment and always be considerate of others. It is his task to help the individual concerned rather than to rebuke or condemn him.

Working with groups has received great emphasis in recent years. The principal's role entails helping the group identify its goals and helping it in its achievement of these goals. The principal should initiate action in time to meet the schedules assigned to him by the central office or by the state department of instruction. One measure of a successful principal is his ability to work with others and to lead them to accomplish their mutually developed objectives. It is essential that the secondary principal have a basic interest in people since he spends so much time working with them in contrast to time spent with machines.

The principal of a secondary school should be able to adjust his knowledge and thinking to situational patterns. Each principal works within some kind of community setting, with some type of power structure, and with his own professional and personal attributes to administer a school. Some schools are large and located in urban areas. Other schools are small and located in rural or semirural areas. The mores, customs, traditions, habits, and attitudes of the people who reside in the attendance unit and whose children attend the public high school are to be considered in the administrative process. The qualifications and experiences of the faculty and administrative assistants are part of the overall picture that must be taken into account when policies and practices are developed. This is not to say that the principal adjusts his thinking to the level of the community's, but suggests that he must begin at the level of operation where the faculty and community are operating and move forward as rapidly as is feasible under the present conditions.

RECRUITMENT AND SELECTION

Recruitment

It is difficult to separate recruitment from selection as some phases of both processes overlap. Recruitment is thought of as involving the process of finding candidates to fill a job description and vacancy within a school system.

Job Description One of the first steps to be taken in recruiting principals is to develop job descriptions for each vacancy in secondary administration. These likely will be drawn up by the superintendent of schools or someone delegated by him and approved by the board of education. A typical job description may include the following: the nature of the position, the community setting, the school, the general offerings or program, the staff, the requirements for the position, the salary, the starting date, and the person to whom the application should be submitted. The following example illustrates the thoroughness with which some school systems approach the job description.

Agencies to Be Canvassed Among the agencies to be contacted are college and university placement offices, commercial placement offices, departments of educational administration, the National Association of Secondary School Principals, and state departments of education. Most of these groups, particularly college and university placement offices and commercial offices, strive to keep in close touch with all schools within their sphere of influence that have vacancies in administrative positions. Candidates for positions in educational administration should maintain

Dresden School District [10]
Hanover, N.H.

HIGH SCHOOL
PRINCIPALSHIP
OPENING

Hanover High School
Hanover, N.H.

THE POSITION   The position is that of Principal of the Hanover Junior-Senior High School, the nation's first interstate high school. Hanover, N.H., and Norwich, Vt., have recently combined to form an interstate school district, grades 7–12, called the Dresden School District. The principal will have the authority and the responsibility for the total administration of the high school. Functions include: budget building and budget administration, supply ordering, internal accounting, staff and pupil personnel leadership, curriculum supervision and, most important, curriculum development. The principal will have a well-equipped office and two secretaries.

THE COMMUNITY   Hanover and Norwich are contiguous New England towns located in the picturesque Connecticut River Valley. Three institutions in Hanover by their nature influence the school population and the community as a whole: Dartmouth College; the Hitchcock Clinic and the Mary Hitchcock Memorial Hospital (with affiliated Medical and Nursing Schools); the Cold Regions Research and Engineering Laboratory of the U.S. Defense Department. The high level cultural environment of the area owes much to the high percentage of professional people employed by these institutions. Drama, symphony, art displays, plays and concerts, the Baker (Dartmouth) Library, the Hopkins Center (an $11 million facility which includes concert halls, theaters, art galleries, etc.) all combine to make this community a cultural center for the entire area. Spectator sports for the Dartmouth Athletic program and many outdoor activities —golf, skiing, skating, camping, hiking, boating, hunting, fishing—make the community an excellent recreational area.

THE SCHOOL   Hanover High School is generally considered to be one of the finest high schools in New England. The community is an academic-professional community and support for the schools is excellent. Per pupil costs for the high school approximate $775.00. The school is a comprehensive high school with an anticipated enrollment of between 725 and 800 students. Teachers' salaries are the highest in N.H. and among the highest in Northern New England. Financial support is excellent (e.g., Textbooks: $13,000.00; Teaching Supplies: $12,350.00,

[10] Used by permission of the Dresden School District.

etc.). In general, the community insists on and supports a high quality educational program.

REQUIREMENTS Candidates must meet N.H. certification requirements. Prefer candidates well beyond the master's degree (CAGS or near doctorate). Candidate should have an academic major, several years of teaching and/or administrative experience, graduate study in administration and must be a real student of the secondary school curriculum.

SALARY The salary will depend upon the person, his training, and his experience, but will probably not exceed $12,000.00.

STARTING DATE Approximately August 1, 1964.

APPLY TO Dr. William G. Zimmerman, Jr., Superintendent of Schools, Hanover, N.H.

an active, up-to-date file of confidential credentials in the placement office of their own choosing. The most natural place would be the college or university at which they received their last graduate degree or did their most recent study. In most private universities there is a small registration fee assessed to help defray expenses. Placement officers are in a significant position to provide prospective employers of administrative personnel with the credentials of interested and qualified persons. This service can be provided for persons who apply for positions both within and outside their own school systems.

Selection

The selection process includes careful screening of candidates after many data have been collected and assembled. The purpose is to choose the person who most nearly meets the requirements established in the job description.

Trends A study of practices in ninety-eight school districts with populations larger than 100,000 revealed several trends in the selection and appointment of principals.[11] These were: (1) encouraging teachers in the system to prepare themselves for administrative certification and to apply for available jobs; (2) making the initial appointment as assistant principal, frequently to obtain evidence of leadership and personal qualities and to ensure a proper orientation to educational administration within the particular system; and (3) giving an examination, either written or oral, to determine the fitness of the candidate for the position. This survey of practices was conducted in 1957 and pertained to the larger school districts.

In a study done by McNamara in the Commonwealth of Pennsylvania, it was found that the chief school administrator was the

[11] Robert W. Strickler, "The Evaluation of the Public School Principal," *NASSP Bulletin*, vol. 41, pp. 55–58, February, 1957.

person primarily responsible for evaluating candidates for the secondary school principalship.[12] The superintendent of schools nominates candidates for the high school principalship in 86 percent of the districts in the state. The teaching staff was rarely consulted or involved in any way in choosing a principal.

Suggested Procedures As indicated earlier, the very large high school districts tend to select secondary principals from within the district with the idea that this increases morale. The reverse of this can also happen. One of the writers is acquainted with a large metropolitan school district in which candidates for the principalship are requested to fill out specific forms and to give pertinent data about themselves, to take several examinations, and to submit to interviews with several administrators present. The interview usually reduces the number of candidates considerably, and about one-third of the applicants are successful in obtaining principalships in the district. The two-thirds who tried but were unsuccessful have a tendency to become jealous, unhappy, and often work against their own school administrators or in some instances seek employment in another district. Restricting one's range of selection to the personnel within a particular district implies that all the capable and qualified persons from which to choose are already in the district and that the only job of the administrator is to find them.

The selection procedures recommended by the authors are as follows: (1) write job descriptions for the secondary principalships; (2) seek qualified and competent applicants both from within the system and from outside the system; (3) search for the person who most nearly meets the job description; (4) gather extensive data on each applicant through tests, confidential papers, letters of recommendations, telephone conversations with former coworkers, and group interviews; (5) where feasible, involve representatives from the faculty to supplement the superintendent, the board, and other administrative personnel in the process; and (6) notify all applicants of the final selection when it has been made prior to a general public announcement.

These procedures are not infallible but do offer some guidelines in the selection process. It would appear that involving several people in the screening process would tend to bring out opportunities for applicants to respond to a variety of questions and situations that otherwise might go uncovered. Likewise, having a broader participation in the screening tends to help the applicants see what is expected of them if they are selected to take the position. Further, it provides them with opportunities to question more people about the nature of the position itself.

[12] Robert A. McNamara, "A Study of the Practices and Procedures in the Selection, Examination, and Appointment of Secondary School Principals in Pennsylvania," unpublished doctoral dissertation, University of Pittsburgh, Pittsburgh, Pa., 1956.

BETTER CERTIFICATION REQUIREMENTS

Recent Improvements

Despite the fact that the qualifications of the average secondary school principal are higher than state certification requirements, the increasing significance and responsibilities of this position in the American public school system have set the stage for the belief that the office requires special preparation. Prior to 1930 only seven states required preparation beyond that required for teaching, but these requirements for certification improved so rapidly that by 1957 forty-six states required either a secondary school principal's certificate or a general certificate for all types of administrative positions.[13] Most states require at least the master's degree, with some states requiring graduate work beyond the master's degree. For example, in Pennsylvania the secondary school principal must complete a planned program of 45 semester hours of graduate work.

Future Plans

The National Association of Secondary School Principals' Committee on Screening and Experience Standards for the certification of high school principals recommended rather definite standards for the certification of high school principals.[14] Included in the proposal were plans calling for a general education background, specialized professional preparation equivalent to the master's degree, required renewal of the beginning certificate after 3 years, and an advanced professional certificate which could be renewed every 5 to 10 years.

The American Association of School Administrators, through its Committee for the Advancement of School Administration, has been working diligently to discover new ways of promoting and improving educational administration. This group exists primarily for superintendents of schools. Since January, 1964, active membership in the AASA has been restricted to those persons who have completed 2 years of graduate study in a university program designed especially to prepare school administrators and accredited by the National Council for Accreditation of Teacher Education. While these requirements do not apply directly to high school principals, the implications for all educational administrators is abundantly clear. It is expected that the National Association of Secondary School Principals will follow suit within the near future.

Certification requirements for the secondary principalship are not as

[13] Robert B. Howsam and Edgar L. Morphet, "Certification of Educational Administrators," *Journal of Teacher Education*, vol. 9, pp. 75–96, March, 1958.
[14] Dan H. Eikenberry, "Training and Experience Standards for Principals of Secondary Schools," *NASSP Bulletin*, vol. 35, pp. 5–62, November, 1951.

high as they should be for the functions of leadership now assigned to the modern secondary school principal. Many of the larger and wealthier school systems have imposed their own requirements for secondary principals which are well above and beyond those set by the respective states. In several instances the requirements call for a minimum of 60 semester hours of graduate work in a planned program. In a few instances the doctor's degree is required, particularly in laboratory and university schools where a great deal of experimentation is being conducted.

The responsibility and leadership roles of secondary principals who head high schools with 5,000 or more pupils exceed those of many superintendents of small school systems with 1,500 to 2,500 pupils in the entire system. While the gains in certification improvement are not overwhelming, they do represent the substantial progress that has been made over the past 35 years, and the principalship is fast becoming a profession.

SUMMARY

Competency in almost any profession may be described in relation to the job to be done. Several efforts have been made to identify competency patterns in areas other than educational administration.

There is considerable evidence that the role of the secondary principal is similar to that of the superintendent. Both professional and personal competencies for the secondary principal may be spelled out rather clearly.

Recruitment and selection of secondary principals have been performed by superintendents of schools. Faculties have participated in a limited fashion in this process. Suggested procedures for recruitment and selection of principals are presented in detail.

Although vastly improved in the last decade, certification requirements for the secondary principalship are not as high as they should be. This is particularly true when one considers the responsibilities and leadership roles of secondary principals in high schools with more than five thousand students.

SUGGESTED EXERCISES

1. Give your definition of competency, and compare it with the one presented by the authors.

2. Why is it difficult to identify competency patterns as exhibited by others?

3. Can you suggest other studies of competency that might be helpful in educational administration?

4. Enumerate the personal qualities you feel a secondary school principal should have. Compare your own competencies in these areas with those you suggested.

5. What professional competencies should the secondary principal possess? Again, compare your own competencies with those expected of the person who becomes a principal.

6. Outline a program of graduate work that you think would be practical and helpful for a secondary principal.

7. How would the principals you know measure up if they were checked by the criteria suggested in this chapter for personal and professional competencies?

8. Distinguish between recruitment and selection.

9. Draw up your own plan for the recruitment and selection of five high school principals for secondary schools each with more than 3,500 pupils. What would you include in the job descriptions?

10. What role should certification play in improving secondary school administration?

SELECTED REFERENCES

ANDREWS, J. H. M., "School Organization Climate: Some Validity Studies," *Canadian Education and Research Digest,* vol. 5, pp. 317–334, December, 1965.

BAUGHMAN, M. D., "School Administration: Beatitude for Beleaguered Bigwigs," *Phi Delta Kappan,* vol. 47, pp. 317–319, February, 1966.

BRICKMAN, W. W., "Leadership and Scholarship," *School and Society,* vol. 94, p. 116, March 5, 1966.

CULBERTSON, JACK A., AND STEPHEN HENCLEY (eds.), *Preparing Administrators: New Perspectives,* University Council for Educational Administration, Columbus, Ohio, 1962.

DAVISON, H. M., AND R. R. RENNER, "Discovering Leadership Guidelines: An Empirical Approach to the Principles of School Administration," *NASSP Bulletin,* vol. 49, October, 1965, pp. 18–25.

FERGUSON, L. L., "Better Management of Managers' Careers," *Harvard Business Review,* vol. 44, pp. 139–152, March, 1966.

GARDNER, J. W., "Need for Leaders, Excerpts from Anti-leadership Vaccine," *Science,* vol. 151, p. 283, January 21, 1966.

HENCLEY, STEPHEN P. (ed.), *The Internship in Administrative Preparation,* The University Council for Educational Administration and the Committee for the Advancement of School Administration, Columbus, Ohio, and Washington, D.C., 1963.

JENNINGS, E. E., "You Can't Succeed in Business by Merely Trying," *Nation's Business,* vol. 54, pp. 110–112, May, 1966.

LEU, DONALD J., AND HERBERT C. RUDMAN (eds.), *Preparation Programs for School Administrators,* Seventh UCEA Career Development Seminar, Michigan State University, 1963.

MACY, J. W., JR., "New Computerized Age: Use of Computers in Washington," *Saturday Review,* vol. 49, pp. 23–25, July 23, 1966.

McINTYRE, KENNETH E., *Learning in a Block-of-time Program,* Southwest School Administration Center, Austin, Tex., 1957.

176 LEADERSHIP FOR SECONDARY SCHOOLS

PIERCE, TRUMAN M., AND A. D. ALBRIGHT, *A Profession in Transition: A Nine-year Story of Improving Educational Administration in the South,* The Southern States Cooperative Program in Educational Administration, Nashville, Tenn., 1960.

WALTERS, R. W., JR., "How to Keep the Go-getters," *Nation's Business,* vol. 54, p. 47, June, 1966.

CHAPTER 10

LEADERSHIP IN A DEMOCRATIC FRAMEWORK

Perhaps it is true that every member of a democratic structure may be a leader on some issue or problem or at some particular time or other. Likewise he may be a follower at some time or other. It is well known that no one can be a leader in everything all the time. Legal authority and responsibility are often thought of as being synonymous with leadership based upon authority of knowledge. Although the secondary principal should have a broad background and be well trained, he cannot know all there is to know about every phase of the secondary school. He must rely upon his associates who have special knowledge about specific areas for their advice and suggestions. A well-qualified art teacher ought to be more of an authority in his field than a secondary principal. A similar conclusion may be drawn in regard to many other areas of specialization.

In order to treat adequately this phase of leadership, it is necessary to consider the following aspects: the school as a workshop of democracy, the role of the secondary principal, professionalism and leadership, the necessity of decision making, and the future of the principalship. Examples will be given as they are needed to explain points of view.

WORKSHOP OF DEMOCRACY

Reflected in the School Program

If the secondary school campus is to be a laboratory in which students learn greater proficiency in the skills of democratic living through actually living democratically, the school program should reflect this self-government in its activities and also in the objectives of the school. The school itself should be democratically organized, with students, teachers, and parents taking part in the planning of group life and school activities. The procedure would begin in the kindergarten and be gradually increased as the students pass from grade to grade. Of course the professional staff would carry the heavy burden of the planning and would involve laymen on whatever levels they are able to operate.

Boards of Education Must See the Need for Leadership

Certain prerequisites are essential in order that a secondary school can operate as a workshop of democracy. First, boards of education and school superintendents must recognize the importance of having a school principal do a real job of leadership rather than perform clerical tasks. This concept includes the appointment of principals because they are highly qualified and not merely because they are being rewarded for long service as a teacher in one particular school. Also involved in this belief is the choosing of a principal who will give democratic administration an opportunity to work.

In this context, superintendents must delegate the necessary authority and responsibility for principals to use their leadership effectively. Over the years the scope and duties connected with administering secondary schools have increased at a tremendous pace where they have been delegated properly to the principals.

Choose Principals Who Can and Will Practice Democracy

Principals should attempt to translate into practice the best ideas the staff can develop. This point has been argued for many years and was well stated by John Dewey in 1903:

> Until the public school system is organized in such a way that every teacher has some regular and representative way in which he or she can register judgment upon matters of educational importance, with the assurance that this judgment will somehow affect the school system, the assertion that the present system is not, from the internal standpoint, democratic, seems to be justified. Either we come here upon some fixed and inherent limitation of the demo-

cratic principle, or else we find in this fact an obvious discrepancy between conduct of the school and the conduct of social life—a discrepancy so great as to demand immediate and persistent effort at reform.[1]

The person who heads the secondary school makes it largely what it is. If the principal does not know how to use the faculty and to stimulate their thinking, the school will never achieve its potential. A well-qualified principal, on the other hand, may make it possible for an individual school and its faculty to overcome many obstacles and to produce an efficient school that gets the job done.

Principal Should Free Teachers for Creative Tasks

A fourth prerequisite for making the secondary school a laboratory of democracy is the freeing of teachers by the principal for instruction that is creative and imaginative. Under this type of administration, teachers may help pupils learn to evaluate conflicting claims, weigh evidence, search for the truth, detect propaganda, and arrive at independent judgments. If the teacher himself is an instrument of autocracy, it will be impossible for him to demonstrate to the class the spirit and intent of democracy.

THE ROLE OF THE PRINCIPAL

Instructional Leader

The principal should be thought of as an instructional leader, a staff officer, and as head of his faculty. He is the administrative official to whom all teachers are directly responsible. The principal is held responsible for improving the instructional program in his school. He is responsible for promoting teacher growth and efficiency and for securing maximum use of supervisory services. He must coordinate the work of the staff officers with the instructional program within his individual school. He is charged with the responsibility in many schools of securing and helping to keep well-qualified teachers. It is the job of the principal to develop and maintain high morale among his faculty members. He is responsible for planning the school year along with his administrative staff and faculty. The principal has as one of his functions the administering of student activities and their evaluation. It is his job to help administer the guidance and counseling program, although much of the responsibility may be delegated to assistants. Evaluating, grading, and reporting are important phases of instruction that demand leadership

[1] John Dewey, "Democracy in Education," *The Elementary School Teacher*, vol. 3, pp. 194–195, December, 1903.

from the principal. He must understand the nature and purpose of supervision and be able to organize and administer these services.

Public Relations and Special Services

The principal is the key person in the program for promoting public relations. He must be able to analyze the social and community setting including power structures and pressure groups. He will lead his staff to participate in the general programs for the entire district and will also carry out a program adapted to his individual school. In most schools the principal is responsible for planning and administering such special services as the cafeteria, health, school library, and transportation. His role in each of these phases will depend upon the structure of his school district. The operation of the school office is a function of the principal. He is supposed to carry out certain prescribed operations and many that are optional, but he is charged with the duty of seeing that the school office contributes to the efficient operation of the school.

School Facilities and Research and Development

Administering school facilities occupies a part of the duties which principals assume or are assigned. This may involve the management of present facilities, the utilization of space, operation and maintenance, and the planning of new facilities. A part of the time a secondary principal spends in his work should be devoted to research and development which may be helpful in providing the insights so necessary for initiating changes that are felt desirable in school practices. He should be well acquainted with the best educational research and literature available and be particularly well informed concerning valid principles of administration which may be helpful in the performance of his leadership role.

Reexamine His Own Perception of the Job

The complexity of the field of secondary administration has become so marked and the knowledge so involved that the principal must have a knowledge of leadership that extends far beyond the mere mechanics of operating a school. It is imperative that the routine and mechanical processes be delegated to assistants in order that time may be found for the significant job of leadership which is so badly needed. All administrative behavior must in the long run contribute to the improvement of the instructional program. What one sees in a situation and how he feels about himself in relationship to the situation determines, to a great extent, what he does. Therefore constant reexamination of perceptions held by the principal should be made. The principal must function as an educational leader in the school and community if these ends are to be achieved.

AN EFFECTIVE LEADER IS A PROFESSIONAL

Responsible for Self-growth

The secondary principal of today must be a professional in every sense of the word. He has to be a student of education and educational administrative problems. He finds the time for an analytical study of his functions and responsibilities. He assumes the responsibility for self-growth and development.

Opportunities for continued professional growth are not limited to taking formal courses in universities and colleges. The involvement of the principal in staff selection and orientation, in using the staff to develop programs, and in interpreting the needs of the community to staff and administrative officers are all activities that call for continued professional growth. Becoming an ongoing part of a professional organization is one of the better ways to develop new understandings and skills.

Allies with Professional Organizations

The professional leader takes advantage of such local, state, regional, and national organizations as can help him grow and develop and keep professionally alive. The national organization for principals is called the National Association of Secondary School Principals and is a vital and dynamic source of growth for an educational leader. Likewise the Association for Supervision and Curriculum Development is an organization which provides many opportunities for principals to keep up-to-date in curriculum practices and supervisory functions. In addition, local and state groups assist principals in sharing information and dealing with different types of common problems.

Producer and Consumer of Research

The professional must read widely, both in his own field and in related disciplines. It is also helpful if he is a producer of research as well as a consumer. The secondary principal should write for professional journals and become involved in research projects that help him seek new truths and express himself in writing for publication.

Goals of School Come First

An effective leader places the goals of the school before his own personal goals. In helping the staff achieve the school goals, he may at the same time be fulfilling partially his own goals. It is the job of the professional to bring out the best in his faculty and staff. He must know how to use human resources in an effective manner. On occasion this may mean that he will be expected to recommend members of his staff for promotion to better positions which may even be outside his own school district. Even though this recommendation means a temporary loss for his school, he is professional and feels no bitterness but is glad to help people advance to higher levels of achievement since this is part of his work.

Knows How to Use Human Resources

A professional leader recognizes that people are different and knows that this applies to his own staff. He feels the need for understanding the strong and weak points of each faculty member. He works with these people as individuals and avoids holding petty personal faults against them and against other colleagues. No "black book" of errors is kept, nor is any effort made to remind people of their mistakes. Instead, the effective leader capitalizes on the strengths of the people with whom he works and helps them with achievement.

Displays Ethical Relations

An effective leader displays ethical relations in all aspects of his work and dealings with people. There is no room for encouraging gossip or rumor spreading. There is no double-talk or dual standards for different faculty members. The professional deals honestly and fairly with all people. He is genuinely interested in people and their problems. He is a good listener and does not try to offer suggestions without first having heard the person's story and having gathered sufficient data upon which to make some recommendations. Although many teacher problems may at first glance seem trivial, he takes time to hear all sides to the story. No effort is expended on the part of the effective leader to manipulate people to get them to think like him. Adequate data, conditions, situations, and personnel involved help provide sources upon which decisions are made rather than to manipulate people from one side of the road to the other.

Has Confidence in Staff

Since status leaders usually have to prove themselves despite having titles and official assignments, it is desirable to operate on a level where the administrator puts complete trust in his staff and expects the same from them. This is quite different from the method of operation used by principals who feel that they are above question by their faculties, that their official title represents authority in the strongest sense, that loyalty is a one-way street—running from the top to the bottom of the organization—and that any disagreement is a violation of confidence.

Knows How to Use Consultants

A professional recognizes that there are times when he and his staff need help from the outside. This awareness is based upon trained observation and insights into problem solving. Under a condition of need, the effective leader does not hesitate to seek help by contacting his administrative superiors, the state department of education, university and college specialists, consultants in the area of the specific problems concerned, and of course his own faculty. A professional does not think of calling for special help as a manifestation of a weakness of his office or his faculty but thinks of it instead as a necessary step for intelligent action.

Cares about the Welfare of His Staff

An effective leader is concerned about the welfare of his faculty. He wants to know that they are adequately paid. His desire is for them to have pleasant facilities and working conditions which encourage efficiency. A professional is concerned that his faculty has adequate and sufficient welfare provisions such as leaves of absence, tenure, promotional machinery, and health insurance. It is the desire of an effective leader that his staff has assignments and teaching loads that are reasonable, and he strives toward this end. He can provide a stimulating environment and clearly defined personnel policies that help in the achievement of this goal.

Is a Career Person

Lastly, an effective leader is a professional and a career person. He is not someone filling in the job until something better comes along in business, industry, or in other fields. He is a person who chooses educational administration as a lifelong career and is cognizant of the many shortcomings and the many benefits that accompany the position. He knows what the position demands in time, energy, and sacrifice. Likewise, the professional knows the many rewards that come from continuous application of one's ability toward defined goals. He is well aware that the range of his effect on education will be decided largely by his own perception of opportunities intrinsic in the secondary principalship.

DECISION MAKING IS NECESSARY

A Part of the Administrative Process

In the past few years the literature of educational administration has been replete with regard to consideration of decision making as a part of the administrative process. The dictionary states that a decision is a settling or deciding, as of a controversy, by giving a judgment on the matter, also the judgment given. Also a decision can be defined as a calculated choice from among a large number of well-known and possibly competing alternatives or choices. Decision making is a step in the administrative process whereby choices are made which stimulate action. Another way of defining decision making for the administrator is deciding upon a course of procedure or action. Of course the need for someone or some group to choose a plan of action must exist before decision makers can be stimulated to activity. Decision making may also be used synonymously with problem solving in regard to choosing paths of action by educational leaders.

Identifying Problems and Recognizing Alternatives

In order to attack a problem, it must be defined; data must be gathered concerning it; alternatives must be considered; a proposed course of action must be selected; and the proposed decision must be implemented. In defining the problem, it must be recognized that the administrator's personality and experiences tend to condition him so that he does not see the same problems as others do. It is here that he should be able to see the problem more clearly as a result of the viewpoints of the many people who are attempting to help him. Each person who is involved in the problem solving tends to analyze the problem as he views it through his own background of training and experience and value system. This influences the kind and type of data chosen concerning the solution of a problem. As solutions are hypothesized, the consequences of each must be examined closely. One may find that the decision reached is only a partial solution or that the alternative chosen cannot be administered effectively. Another member of the same group may be satisfied with the proposed choice. Therefore, before a decision is reached or the preferred solution is finally accepted, it is wise to ensure that the possible outcomes of each alternative have been weighed carefully in order that the choice made will seem to fit the solution better than other alternatives.

Making Decisions in the Light of Knowledge

Once an alternative or choice of action has been made, it should be immediately implemented. This may call for other administrative decisions to be made and for policies to be developed to carry forward the plan chosen. Not all decision making is shared with the staff; however, neither is it something that should be done by the principal alone. Some decisions will be simple and may not demand the help of others, but many of the problems with which the secondary principal comes into contact will cause him to think of and to use many people in the process.

One might ask the question, what kinds of administrative decisions are secondary principals asked to make? The following list will introduce the type of difficulties encountered by some principals:

1. Which of the three teachers suggested by the members of the English department shall I nominate to the superintendent?
2. Should Mr. Jones have his increment withheld?
3. How many pupil stations will be needed in the new science laboratory?
4. Should the principal have a policy committee in addition to his department heads?
5. How can the supervision in the lunchroom be improved?
6. Should the high school explore the possibility of student activities after school?
7. What should be done with regard to the personal conflict between the head custodian and his staff?
8. Should Miss Schwartz be recommended for continuing contract?
9. Should all ninth-grade girls take home economics?
10. How can the PTA be assisted to see that its role is one of cooperation and advisement?

As one views this list, he is likely to note that the secondary administrator has a variety of problems about which decisions must be made. In making decisions, whether by himself or with the aid of the faculty, he must work within the legal framework of education as established by law, policies, and procedures. Many times action will be dependent upon setting a time limit. Some decisions have to be made by a certain time. It is the duty of the principal to see that deadlines are met.

Almost any decision or action made concerning secondary schools involves the relationship of this action to other related areas. In other words, one has to guard constantly that he is not solving one problem by a certain decision and thereby creating two new problems. A teacher may request the principal to permit him to leave school on Friday before the end of the school day to keep an appointment that he has had for several months with the dentist. The principal may see no immediate good reason for denying him this privilege. After granting such a privilege, he may discover that other requests are made for using the last period for personal reasons of teachers.

Helping Develop Criteria for Decisions

Decision making should not be thought of in management terms as opposed to administrative problem solving. First, management seeks to define what rules and regulations are necessary to perform certain functions and then to see that the manager carries out these rules. At this time it is not possible to reduce recurring problems and situations to mathematical models. It is probably impossible to duplicate social tradition and values, institutional environment, and individual judgment as the framework within which human problem solving must operate. Administering a secondary school involves more than problem solving based upon a set of management rules. Decision making is based in part upon helping to make the rules and regulations which may become criteria by which decisions are reached. Policy making by the local board of education with the help of the superintendent and others gives guides for helping principals in decision making. They, too, can help change the rules if the rules are found wanting.

Drawing upon Knowledge of Other Disciplines

It is true that decisions about school matters have to be made. They should be made in the light of all the knowledge one is able to muster. The professional secondary school principal holds a precarious position. He is open to view by the public while the parents and the public seem to become further and further removed from an understanding of the psychological factors involved in learning, the social goals of learning, the methods of learning, and the subject-matter content of learning. In order to meet these complex conditions effectively, the secondary administrator must draw upon disciplines or related fields such as economics, sociology, history, social psychology, and political science, as well as all that can be learned about the process of administration itself. The secondary principal must be a professional in every aspect of his work and as a leader of people.

THE FUTURE OF THE PRINCIPALSHIP

Tomorrow's Principal

The high school principalship of the future is a professional position that calls for specific preparation on the part of those who seek to fill it successfully. It will constitute a calling which will be truly professional and require not only distinctly superior professional and personal competencies, but also continued technical professional training. The secondary principal of the near future will be afforded responsibility and prestige equivalent to that of the generally recognized professions of medicine, law, and dentistry. Public citizens' groups and persons in educational positions of responsibility have long thought of secondary principals as having been chosen for their professional competencies rather than for their ability to control unruly children and to keep the school in operation.

Educational administration may not be considered a profession by many of those who are outside of it. But by definition and purpose it meets most of the requirements of educational administration as a profession as outlined by Moore. In his study of school administration, he listed the following criteria:

1. Admission is based on guarantee of a standard of competence of people who apply.
2. An extra large dose of graduate, professional training is needed. (Several states, along with AASA's Committee for the Advancement of School Administration, go along with two graduate years as the minimum.)
3. The ultimate purpose of the professional job must be significant service to society at large.
4. A profession is never a stepping stone to a position in some other occupation.
5. There must be a high salary return to the individual and stature in the eyes of the public. . . .
6. Long hours of work can be expected. . . .
7. A profession must be a learned calling, based on intellectual study.
8. The duties must be distinctive from those of any other profession and must be known generally just to the persons who practice the professional calling.[2]

Although secondary administration at this time may not fulfill all the above requirements of a profession, there is mounting evidence that the status of the future secondary principal will be improved greatly as school boards tend to select the most capable individuals available to head our high schools in the future.

Opportunities and Rewards

Where the principal's professional and personal competencies are demonstrated successfully, and he assumes the role of a professional leader, he will be respected as one of the most important leaders in the life of the school and community. The general American public has great confidence in the secondary school and what it can do for youth despite the many weaknesses it may possess. There is a great opportunity in the principalship for young men and women who understand the significance of the secondary school's services to youth and to the state and to the nation.

To develop the competence to perform effectively the varied and difficult functions of a modern secondary school principal is a challenge worthy of the highest devotion to duty for any aspirant. He may secure the position after serving in other minor administrative capacities or serving as the principal of a small junior high school or small secondary school and then after this experience may be appointed to a high school principalship. In many instances, the high school principalship is an excellent training ground for superintendents since most of the same

[2] Hollis A. Moore, Jr., "Professional Status: Opinion Poll," *The Nation's Schools*, vol. 62, p. 37, July, 1958.

competencies required for the principalship are also required for the superintendency.

Better salaries, improved working conditions, intangible rewards, and the feeling of accomplishment are all factors that add to the satisfaction of serving as a high school principal. The opportunities for leading and directing the growth of others are very stimulating. For anyone who desires outlets of expression for his personality and imagination and enjoys the challenge of an important profession, the secondary principalship provides a stimulating opportunity.

SUMMARY

The modern secondary school provides opportunities for democratic living through its objectives and its activities. This is as it should be in America. The school ought to be a workshop of democracy.

Boards of education must see the need for employing principals who are highly qualified and who provide leadership that encourages students to practice and live democratically at school. Principals should be able to free teachers from petty restrictions and enhance instruction that is creative and imaginative.

The principal is the instructional leader. He must be able to comprehend and to organize the supervisory process. His leadership in all aspects of the secondary school should be oriented toward instructional improvement. In order to provide this leadership, he will be concerned with school facilities, research and development, public relations, special services, teacher growth and efficiency, student activities, guidance and counseling, and a host of other related areas.

An effective principal is responsible for self-growth, joins appropriate professional organizations, and is both a producer and consumer of research. He places the goals of the school ahead of his personal goals, knows how to use people effectively, and displays ethical relations. An efficient principal has confidence in the faculty, knows how to use consultants wisely, is concerned about the welfare of the staff, and is a career person.

Decision making is necessary for the principal and is a part of the administrative process. The high school principal of tomorrow will need special preparation for the position and continuous in-service training at a sophisticated level. Despite the high level of expectation, the principalship offers many challenging opportunities and satisfying rewards. The secondary principalship can be a rewarding career position.

SUGGESTED EXERCISES

1. Explain ways in which a principal can help his school to become a workshop of democracy.

2. How can one help a board of education see that the role of the principal is one of leadership and not a clerical function?

3. Describe what you consider to be the role of the principal in regard to his being an effective instructional leader.

4. Outline ways in which the principal may reexamine his own perception of his position.

5. When is a principal a professional? How can ethics of prospective principals be discovered?

6. Define decision making and give examples.

7. Suggest activities in which principals should engage to improve their ability to make decisions and to improve professionally.

8. Compare the expectations of future principals with what has been expected of them in the past.

9. What opportunities abound for the young and capable high school principals of tomorrow?

SELECTED REFERENCES

ARGYRIS, CHRIS, "Interpersonal Barriers to Decision Making," *Harvard Business Review,* vol. 44, pp. 84–97, March, 1966.

CORNELL, S. D., "Education for the Modern Age" (address, February 25, 1966), *Vital Speeches,* vol. 32, pp. 372–376, April 1, 1966.

COSTIN, R. G., "Ideal Principal," *Journal of Secondary Education,* vol. 40, pp. 259–262, October, 1965.

ELLIS, J. R., "Call for Leadership: Time for a Civil Responsibility Movement," *The Teachers College Journal,* vol. 37, pp. 159–160, January, 1966.

GRIFFITHS, DANIEL E., *Human Relations in School Administration,* Appleton-Century-Crofts, Inc., New York, 1956.

GROSS, NEIL, AND R. E. HERRIOTT, "EPL of Elementary Principals: A Study of Executive Professional Leadership," *The Nation's Elementary Principal,* vol. 45, pp. 66–71, April, 1966.

HAGMAN, HARLAN L., AND ALFRED SCHWARTZ, *Administration in Profile for School Executives,* Harper & Row, Publishers, Incorporated, New York, 1955, chaps. 2 and 10.

HALPIN, ANDREW W., *Theory and Research in Administration,* The Macmillan Company, New York, 1966.

HODGKINSON, H. L., *Educational Decisions: A Casebook,* Prentice-Hall, Inc., Englewood Cliffs, N.J., 1963.

JACOBS, J. W., "Leadership Behavior of the Secondary School Principal," *NASSP Bulletin,* vol. 49, pp. 13–17, October, 1965.

KEEFE, JOSEPH A., "The Course to Democratic Participation," *NASSP Bulletin,* vol. 45, pp. 36–39, February, 1961.

LANGFORD, H. E., "Workshop Trains PSEA Leaders," *Pennsylvania School Journal,* vol. 114, p. 69, October, 1965.

LONSWAY, F. A., "Focus on the Individual in School Administration," *NASSP Bulletin,* vol. 49, pp. 80–86, September, 1965.

MASON, J. G., "No Not Another Committee," *Nation's Business,* vol. 53, pp. 80–81, December, 1965.

MEYERS, M. S., "Conditions for Manager Motivation: Survey of Manager Motivation at Texas Instruments," *Harvard Business Review,* vol. 44, pp. 58–71, January, 1966.

MORTENSEN, C. D., "Should the Discussion Group Have an Assigned Leader?" *The Speech Teacher,* vol. 15, pp. 34–41, January, 1966.

Professional Administrators for America's Schools, The American Association of School Administrators, Washington, D.C., 1960.

ROYAL, RAYMOND E., "Decision Making in the Middle Echelons of Public Education," *NASSP Bulletin,* vol. 45, pp. 85–87, February, 1961.

SACH, BENJAMIN M., *Educational Administration: A Behavioral Approach,* Houghton Mifflin Company, Boston, 1966.

SAUNDERS, ROBERT L., RAY C. PHILLIPS, AND HAROLD T. JOHNSON, *A Theory of Educational Leadership,* Charles E. Merrill Books, Inc., Columbus, Ohio, 1966.

SHERRILL, R. G., "Brass Pyramid," *Nation,* vol. 203, pp. 49–51, July 11, 1966.

SMALTER, D. J., AND R. L. RUGGLES, JR., "Six Lessons from the Pentagon," *Harvard Business Review,* vol. 44, pp. 64–75, March, 1966.

TALBOT, A. R., "Needed: A New Breed of School Superintendent," *Harper's,* vol. 232, pp. 81–82, February, 1966.

SEC-TION 3

instructional program

INTRODUCTION Section I provided the setting for administering schools through tracing historical antecedents of American secondary schools. It further cast an image of present-day secondary schools in terms of multiple sets of societal demands, and it described the modern concept of organization whose primary criterion is adaptability.

Section II dealt primarily with the phenomenon of leadership. It focused on the role of the one identified as the educational leader of the school, that is, the secondary principal.

Section III will treat the educational program. It seeks to bring the reader to the heart of what schools are for and what they try to do. Although it is inappropriate to say that one phase of the administrative process is any more important than another, it is an incontestable fact that those who administer schools require an adequate understanding of a specific body of knowledge about the instructional program.

Chapter 11 will treat the instructional program from the curriculum point of view. It will tie together these two complementary processes—curriculum and instruction. Chapter 12 comes to terms with a phase of the instructional program which is constant, necessary, yet constantly presenting difficulties. This is the area of measuring, evaluating, and reporting student learning. Chapter 13 looks at the instructional materials necessary to do the kind of job that must be done. It is concerned with major changes in the philosophy and technology of instructional materials. Chapter 14 deals with nonclassroom educational activities. This area is the frosting on the educational cake. However, far from being a "frill," it will be shown that this program is related directly to the instructional program. Chapter 15 will handle the logistical aspect of administration, that is, the matter of total scheduling of students, teachers, curriculum, and educational spaces. An extremely technical matter in the modern age, this phase too bears a direct relationship to the instructional program and must be managed competently by secondary school administrators.

Chapter 16 unifies this section by treating the improvement of educational programs and services. It places the major responsibility for improvement squarely upon the principal. Through the organization of well-designed supervision and in-service programs, the principal works through others with a fierce determination to upgrade constantly his school's educational program.

CHAPTER 11

THE EDUCATIONAL PROGRAMS IN SECONDARY SCHOOLS

Other chapters of this book have attempted to present the historical background of secondary education, the kind of secondary education which it is believed that society needs and wants, and the characteristics of good secondary schools found in the United States today. It is from these sources that one must infer the purposes of secondary education for the United States and for a locality at this time. These purposes or objectives must be realistic and possible to achieve. To be achieved, purposes must be understood and accepted by those who will attempt to carry them out—educators; those upon whom the purposes will bear most directly—students; and those whose moral and financial support will be required—citizens.

The purposes of any high school, new or old, should be stated by its faculty in terms of how they perceive community needs and desires. So it is that the faculty of a secondary school will need to study, with lay and student assistance, the purposes of the school in an era when changes in population, and social activity occur with astonishing rapidity. Purposes of all schools must be evaluated continually so that the resulting curricular offerings and instructional methods are in tune with the needs and desires of the times.

Having determined the purposes for secondary schools in any community, steps must be taken to achieve them. To achieve these purposes, one must certainly be concerned with teaching appropriate knowledges and skills to young people.

RELATIONSHIP OF CURRICULUM AND INSTRUCTION

One of the difficulties which beset the teaching profession is the lack of precise definitions of terms used. For example, throughout the literature the terms "curriculum" and "instruction" are frequently used as if they were synonymous. We believe that they are inextricably related, but are substantially different.

It is the point of view of this chapter that *curriculum* is the total of all the intended learning experiences that youth have under the supervision of the school. The experiences are sometimes grouped under headings called courses or subjects. These subjects constitute *what* is to be taught. On the other hand, the means or process by which teachers lead, guide, and direct students to have worthwhile learning experiences is *instruction*. Instruction might be considered the *how* of providing learning experiences. The two together make up the educational program offered by the school. Further definitions are given later in the chapter.

It can thus be seen that attempts to improve the educational opportunities available in the school must be concerned with both curricular and instructional aspects.

It would seem worthwhile to examine first the curricular aspect in the secondary school. To the average layman "curriculum" means groups of learning experiences as organized into courses or subjects. In fact, most people think of the curriculum as "all the courses offered." To fulfill society's demand that schools teach for citizenship, certain courses will be required of all students. Sometimes these required courses are referred to as *general education*.

To become good citizens, students need to acquire written and oral communications skills as well as to be good listeners. They need to know the historic traditions of our country, its ideals, and the relationship of our system of government to the free-enterprise system of economics. They need to acquire basic computational skills and a knowledge and understanding of essential mathematical concepts. They should also appreciate the role of science in their lives and learn the scientific facts essential to health and survival. Concern for the development of a sound body as well as a sound mind leads to requirements in health and physical education for all students. In summary, it may be stated that general education is that part of the total educational program which the student needs just because he is a human being and a member of society.

It would seem obvious then that general education studies should also provide all students with experiences in music, art, philosophy (developing of human values), and the household and practical arts. The methods of grouping of students, grading standards, and teaching procedures may be different in the general education class required of all students.

Specialized Education

The long-range goals of high school students will vary. Upon graduation some will want to go to 4-year colleges or universities, some will want to enter 2-year or less post-high school programs, while others will immediately enter the world of work. For this reason, the modern high school must provide specialized patterns of subjects to meet individual needs.

The student under the careful guidance of trained counselors, who work in close cooperation with parents, selects the appropriate pattern of courses consistent with his abilities and goals and the graduation requirements of the school. Although the planning of each student's program is an individual matter, subjects are arranged into sequential patterns for groups of students with similar elections. Thus programs or courses of study are set up in most schools.

Most schools have developed a statement regarding secondary school course selection and programs. In this statement, minimum graduation requirements including general education requirements and a description of the programs in specialized areas are usually given.

Planning Whether the student will be eligible for admission to a particular college or job may depend upon the selection of the proper subjects and, of course, upon the quality of the work done in these classes. Selecting the subjects he will take in high school is so important to the student that it demands his most careful consideration. Students should seek the advice of parents, teachers, counselors, and any other person who is qualified to help. The student should be expected to consider his subject selection carefully.

Evaluation of Programs

One of the more effective ways to evaluate the curriculum available at this time is to use the *Evaluative Criteria* for the study of high schools seeking accreditation by their regional accrediting association.

That the evaluation of these high schools has been beneficial is borne out by the improvements that have been made in their educational programs. Flexibility of scheduling has been increased, improvements have been made in ability grouping procedures, and additional course offerings to meet newly discovered needs of students have been provided.

The extremely high percentage of secondary school graduates that now goes on for higher education indicates that greater emphasis must be placed on academic programs. It is probable that needs of the student body for the future will require an increasing emphasis on academics.

The courses which should be included in the curricular offerings of any high school, and the justification for their inclusion in the list are given in the following by subject areas:

Subject Areas

The major subject areas which are recommended for most secondary schools today are discussed briefly below.

English Course offerings in this subject area are designed to develop the ability to communicate effectively. Communication means thinking, speaking, writing, and listening in our own language. English is a part of general education and is required in every high school grade. A balance should be sought between instruction in literature and in grammar.

Elective subjects offered in this area will probably include: journalism, speech, dramatics, creative writing, developmental reading, and world literature. The authors recommend their inclusion along with the required English courses.

Foreign Language The purpose of foreign language instruction is to assist the student to develop the ability to understand, speak, read, and write in the selected language. Connected with the language goal is the goal of seeking an appreciation of other peoples and cultures. It is generally recommended that the high school study of foreign languages should provide at least 3 years of instruction in one language. The European origins of most of our people and culture will probably cause these languages to be those most often taught. In addition to the traditional offerings of Latin, French, Spanish, and German, recent world events have caused a demand for instruction in the Chinese and Russian languages. When the demand is sufficient to justify adding other foreign languages, the authors recommend their inclusion, but only if competent teachers can be secured.

Mathematics Citizens in our society must be able to communicate in terms of numbers as well as in words. Mathematics instruction should seek to develop an understanding of the number system, skills in computation, and an ability to use symbols that stand for quantities. Instruction should stress the acquisition of meaning for solving number problems met in everyday life.

Recent studies in this area have brought about great reorganization of content. Termed "new," "modern," or "contemporary" mathematics and developed by scholars in the field, it provides much opportunity for change.

While basic skills of mathematics would come under the heading of general education, advanced courses are required for college entrance. How advanced and in what areas depends to some extent on the colleges to which admission is sought and the programs to be pursued in college.

Sciences The sciences contain organized bodies of knowledge and require the acquisition of certain skills as well if one is to attain true mastery. In the sciences, the student must acquire facts about natural laws and phenomena and also must develop skill in the use of the scientific method of thinking and solving problems. Many of the problems which students will need to solve have to do with health and survival in a technological culture.

In addition to general science, most modern secondary schools offer biology, chemistry, physics, and advanced placement in these areas. Earth science courses, physical sciences, and a discrete course in astronomy or astrophysics may be found in some high schools.

Just as in the field of mathematics, the content of the sciences has been reorganized by study groups of scholars and educators. Thus "modern biology" will be different from the older traditional biology course. Other sciences have undergone similar revision.

The authors recommend the following offerings in the sciences:

General Science
Biology I, II
Chemistry I, II
Physics I, II
Physical Science (1 year)
Advanced Placement Courses (determined by demand)

Social Studies As the name implies, the social studies are concerned with the ways in which people live with each other, adjust to their environment, and develop their cultures. The purposes of the social studies are to assist the student to acquire those skills, habits, and attitudes needed by the citizen in the American democratic society.

Subject areas grouped under this heading are history, geography, government, economics, sociology, anthropology, and psychology. (The latter is classified as a science by some persons.)

It is recommended that the modern high school offer:

World History
United States History (State History may be included where required by law)

United States Government (State Government may be included where required by law)
World Geography
Economics
Modern European History
Sociology
Psychology

Art Art experience affords the student an opportunity to develop his powers of creativity and help him grow in sound aesthetic judgment and in the appreciations which ensue. The trend in the United States is to make art experiences a part of the general education provided all students. The development of artistic skills should follow as the primary objectives are pursued and should not be allowed to crush the creative exploration of students.

It is recommended that the following courses be offered in the visual arts:

Foundations in Art (Art I)
Artistic Design (Art II)
Exploration in Art (Art III)
Three Dimensional Art (Art IV)
Crafts I, II

Music Music education is another field of endeavor which points up the aesthetic activities of man. Such activities are valuable for their enhancement of life and the expression of creativity. Music instruction should be designed to foster improvisation on the part of all students. Attention to opportunities for exploration in music will bring about more appreciation of music than any other way. The barrier between performers and nonperformers in music should be removed.

Music educators as well as parents and school administrators recognize that music will become a vocation for some students, that the discovery and development of musical talent is as important a cultural benefit to society as scientific talent, and that musical performing groups benefit school morale and foster community interest in the schools.

Opportunities for musical experience should be provided in:

1. Glee clubs—boys', girls', and mixed; choirs and madrigal groups; other combinations
2. Orchestra, band, ensembles, and other smaller groupings that should give experiences in instrumental music
3. Combinations of vocal and instrumental talent in cantatas, operettas, music festival, etc.

It is suggested that in addition to inclusion in the curriculum, music experiences be included in the activity program of the modern secondary school.

Provisions should be made for:

Music Exploration
Music Theory
Music Harmony
Chorus
Glee Club
Marching Band
Concert Band
Orchestra
Beginning Instruments
Advanced Ensembles

Home Economics Homemaking education is a more descriptive term for this area. Everyone will have to make a home for himself, if not for others, too. Because the family unit in our society also assumes the presence of the male, it is natural that boys in high school also be prepared for their role in homemaking. The goals or purposes in homemaking education are to develop skills and understandings essential to the well-being of persons and families, the improvement of homes and homelife, and the preservation of values significant to the family unit.

Because of the complexity of modern living and the consequent change in the family unit from one of production to one of consumption and because of the increasing number of working wives and mothers, the old cooking and sewing (or foods and clothing) classes are not adequate as the scope of the program.

The contemporary view is that preparation for home and family living must include the following areas:

Human Development and the Family
Home Management and Family Economics
Food and Nutrition
Housing
Textiles and Clothing

To make it possible for all students to receive some homemaking instruction as a part of general education, there should be considerable flexibility to accommodate individual and community needs.

For those students who choose to concentrate or major in this area, a sequential program should be provided. These students may be preparing for employment opportunities, for college entrance in the field, or for personal development.

The following offerings are recommended:

Home Economics I	Personal and Child Development
Home Economics II	Personal and Family Management
Home Economics III	Personal and Family Relationships

*Special Courses:*ᵗ
  Nutrition and Meal Management
  Housing and Furnishings
  Child Development
  Clothing and Textiles
  Money Management
  Family Relations

Business Education This area has as a major purpose the preparation of students for successful participation in business. The nature of the participation can be either vocational or nonvocational. Thus the business subjects may contribute either to the general or to the specialized education of students or to both. However, the nature of the sequential program in business education is such as to focus on the development of salable skills. The number of secretaries and other business personnel needed by the numerous governmental offices as well as area business and industrial concerns would seem to indicate a ready market for such salable skills.

Specialized tracks are centered in bookkeeping, office practice, secretarial, and distributive education.

The authors suggest that the following courses be offered if enrollment justifies:

General Business
Business Mathematics
Typing I, II
Shorthand I, II
Bookkeeping I, II
Office Machines
Automatic Data Processing
Distributive Education
Personal Typing (for nonmajors)

Industrial Arts Because of the fact that we live in an industrial-technical society, youth need to learn about the influences which industry has on present-day living. Thus the industrial arts have a place in the general education of all students to help them gain an understanding about industrial production, consumption, products, processes, materials, mechanics, tools, machines, and design. Development of craft skills for avocational and leisure-time pursuits is also important.

A recent persistent trend in this area has been to separate rather sharply the general education–based industrial arts from vocational trade and industrial training. The latter is moving more and more toward a cooperative training program with industrial employers and unions. The increased emphasis on technical training has caused the Industrial Cooperative Training programs to extend into post-high school years. Preparation in broad fields such as electronics is becoming the pattern rather than preparation for a specific job.

The authors recommend the study of the local demand and need for the following:

Industrial Arts:
   Home Mechanics and Repair (open to girls)
   Industrial Arts I, II
   Mechanical Drawing I, II
   Metal Shop I, II
   Woodworking I, II

Special Areas:
   Auto Mechanics
   Carpentry
   Printing
   Electricity
   Masonry
   Electronics

Health and Physical Education   Although traditionally health and physical education have been linked together as one, they are, in fact, dissimilar and should be treated as separate subject areas.

Health education usually is taught as a classroom subject and treats such areas as public health, first aid, personal hygiene, physiology, and the study of the bodily processes. Physical education attempts to develop physical fitness through activities. These activities are designed to promote coordination and control of muscles, stamina, and other motor skills.

A program of corrective physical activity to assist those with physical handicaps should be planned in cooperation with competent medical personnel. Such a program has been mandated recently in Pennsylvania.

One way in which physical activity for developmental programs is provided is through sports, games, and rhythmics. Provisions for sports will range from intramural sports to varsity athletics, free playtime, and field days.

Recent trends in physical education indicate a growing concern for the physical fitness of all students with a lessening of emphasis upon competitive team sports. Coeducational classes in physical education are increasing in number and in the variety of activities engaged in on this basis.

It is recommended that the following be offered:

Health Science (1 or 2 years)
Physical Education 9, 10, 11, 12
Corrective Physical Education
Extensive Intramural Programs for Boys and Girls
Driver Education

FOUNDATIONS OF CURRICULUM AND INSTRUCTION

Definitions

The words "curriculum" and "instruction" are controversial among educators. Many scholars use the terms to describe a very narrow aspect of the educational program, but the terms have earned a much broader meaning in most recent publications. *Curriculum* is defined in its broadest sense as what is to be taught or learned, while *instruction* has been defined as the process of implementing the curriculum.[1] The stated definition of "curriculum" refers to curriculum for the individual, society, and the subject. It is not necessary to differentiate when referring to any one aspect of the definition. These modern definitions serve to bring together all directly related student functions within the school under the heading of curriculum. As a result of the acceptance of this meaning of curriculum the instructional phase has become much wider in scope and will be dealt with separately.

Curriculum Determinants

The factors which are allowed to determine the curriculum within a school system should come from the nature of the learner and the needs and demands of society. Many factors are taken into consideration during the developmental phase of any curriculum. Some of these appear as part of the criteria upon which every curriculum is based. Some of these are national, state, and local regulations, the needs of the student, the goals set forth by the community and the livelihood of its members.[2] Other curriculum determinants are peculiar to the system for which the curriculum was developed. While many secondary schools take the conservative role and offer only mandatory subjects and well-established courses which are felt to be necessary, others have become much more liberal. The curriculum in systems taking the latter approach is identified by the courses which have been instituted to prepare the

---

[1] *New Curriculum Developments,* Association for Supervision and Curriculum Development, Washington, D.C., 1965, p. 5.
[2] Kimball Wiles, *The Changing Curriculum of the American High School,* Prentice-Hall, Inc., Englewood Cliffs, N.J., 1962, pp. 69–70.

student for life outside the local community. In addition, subjects that provide for a greater depth in learning, special programs for both the gifted and the handicapped, and a well-rounded extracurricular program will be parts of the progressive curriculum. The factors which determine the makeup of the modern curriculum are far-reaching since each system attempts to provide the finest education for all its people.

Curriculum Objectives

One of the most important tasks in preparing a curriculum is the formulation of objectives. Although objectives should outline the specific goals for which the community wishes to strive, obstacles often arise within the implementation phase. There is a definite need for more realism in writing objectives. To be realistic, each objective should describe the proposed method of reaching, through instruction, the desired goal. The writing of objectives tends to set the conditions for the completion of other administrative tasks in the development of a closely adhered to philosophy. The same factors must be considered in the establishment of objectives as were considered in determining the curriculum offering.

Objectives may be stated as functions of the school or as changes in, or developments in, students. In stating the objectives as functions, emphasis is placed on actions and purposes of the school as an agency. In some cases these objectives would imply what is to be taught, but it is also possible to have statements that do not carry such specific identifications. Objectives stated as changes in, or developments in, students might be aimed toward character traits or improving behavioral characteristics.[3] Understandings, skills, attitudes, interests, and appreciations are also commonplace. These latter categories of specific types of learning outcomes are particularly convenient when dealing with school subjects and are frequently used in curriculum guides or resource units.

Statements of educational goals should be looked at in terms of how they can be implemented. It is one thing to state objectives, but it is another thing to have in mind effective methods of accomplishing these objectives.

Objectives for local use should be written in local systems with participation by representatives of the community. These statements should always be flexible and tentative in character and should be in a continuous process of development.

Statements developed by national organizations or state departments of public instruction may serve as guidelines. Committees working at the state level in the various instructional fields may help local groups by indicating the specific purposes for curriculum guides and resource units.

[3] Robert W. Heath (ed.), *New Curricula*, Harper & Row, Publishers, Incorporated, New York, 1964, p. 5.

But in all cases, the local group should make the decision on what it accepts, modifies, or omits.

The question of what the schools should teach has been a problem in all societies. Throughout the years, most have agreed that knowledge and skills are the things to be taught. The problem arises as to just what knowledge and skills should be taught. Other questions in this area are: For what purpose do we teach this knowledge? To whom do we teach this knowledge? and When do we teach this knowledge?

The National Committee on Education, as reported in *Schools for the Sixties,* suggests six fundamental values that it believes should serve as criteria for assessing present-day practices and for planning for improvement in our secondary schools. They are:

1. Respect for the worth and dignity of every individual;
2. Encouragement of variability;
3. Equality of opportunity for all children;
4. Faith in man's ability to make rational decisions;
5. Shared responsibility for the common good;
6. Respect for moral and spiritual values and ethical standards of conduct.[4]

The same committee proceeded to make some recommendations. Two of the more important of these include the following:

1. School systems should allocate an appropriate proportion of their annual operating budgets, not less than one percent, for the support of research, experimentation, and innovation. Adequate time should be provided for each staff member to participate in curriculum planning, research, evaluation, and other activities designed to improve the instructional program.
2. Adequately staffed and supported regional curriculum and instructional centers should be encouraged. These centers, located mainly in universities, should work in partnership with local schools to initiate innovation and conduct experimentation and research to improve the instructional program of the public schools.[5]

Because of the tremendous pressures of today's society, there is a continuing demand for a reassessment of curriculum content. There are changes taking place in economic life, in the expanding role of the government, in the growth of world population, and in the upward surge of independence of colonial peoples which put pressure on our society to reevaluate and change portions of the curriculum.

Since it is the policy of the United States educational system to provide education for every child from the elementary through the secondary grades, we have the responsibility to develop the curriculum to the fullest

4 National Education Association, *Schools for the Sixties,* New York, McGraw-Hill Book Company, 1963, pp. 7 and 8.
5 *Ibid.,* p. 22.

possible extent. This idea was expressed well in the report of the NEA Project on Instruction:

> It is not in the might of the military, the productivity of industry, or the efficiency of transportation and communication that the true greatness of America lies. Rather it is in the high esteem accorded to the individual personality. Here, indeed, is our greatest contribution to men everywhere. And here is America's secret weapon. Our philosophy from the beginning, our deepest convictions, and our highest ideals have sought to clothe the individual with a sense of dignity, to recognize his potentialities, to unloose his creative powers, and to stimulate his initiative. It was on this platform that Jefferson, Lincoln, Adams, and Wilson rose to greatness.[6]

TYPES OF CURRICULUM ORGANIZATION

Definitions

There are numerous definitions of curriculum organization. To some people curriculum is synonymous with a course of study. *Curriculum* has been defined also as a sequence of potential experiences set up in the school for the purpose of disciplining children in the thinking and acting in groups.[7] Further, curriculum has been defined as a systematic arrangement of a number of courses into a unit group for a particular group of pupils, for example, the college preparatory curriculum. It is also used by many to include all the provisions for learning activities, guidance, subject activities, and courses of instruction.[8]

> "Curriculum" has been used, historically, to refer to selected portions of accumulated knowledge, classified into separate subjects, or disciplines, and transmitted to students in convenient administrative units, called "courses." The curriculum of a school, then, referred variously to the collection of all such courses offered by the school, or to groups of related courses, such as the "business curriculum," or "college-preparatory curriculum." [9]

Characteristics of Each Type of Curriculum

Subject-centered Curriculum Curriculum has been classified in various ways. The most generally used pattern of curriculum is the subject-centered curriculum. The school day is divided into from five to eight periods. One period is allotted for each subject such as English, history, mathematics, science, languages, or physical education, each taught independently.

[6] *Deciding What to Teach*, National Education Association, Washington, D.C., 1963, p. 51.
[7] B. Othanel Smith, William O. Stanley, and J. Harlan Shores, *Foundations of Curriculum Development*, Harcourt, Brace & World, Inc., New York, 1950, p. 4.
[8] Harl R. Douglass, *Modern Administration of Secondary Schools*, Ginn and Company, Boston, 1954, p. 135.
[9] James W. Thornton, Jr., and John R. Wright, *Secondary School Curriculum*, Charles E. Merrill Books, Inc., Columbus, Ohio, 1963, p. 3.

The subjects are arranged in logical sequence for each grade level. There are variations, but most secondary schools follow the Algebra I, Plane Geometry, Algebra II, the Solid Geometry and Trigonometry (or Advanced Algebra or Calculus) sequence. The time for each period is 45 to 55 minutes.

The traditional curriculum has been expanded into tracks in some of the more advanced school systems. A track may be thought of as a level of instruction in a subject which is geared to a student's achievement. Tracks are widely used in the academic field. The St. Louis, Missouri, school system uses several tracks which are more suited to the individual student's capacity to handle the specific subjects. The traditional pattern is not changed, but rather the subjects are upgraded for the more gifted children.[10]

The organizational argument for the separate subject curriculum is that it is organized by experts with the most knowledge to organize it and in a logical order. It provides a choice of methods suited to the teacher.[11]

Broad Fields Curriculum The second type of curriculum that is widely used is the broad fields curriculum. This is a combination of two or more subjects or closely related areas. For example, a school may combine English, journalism, and speech.

The broad fields curriculum aims to integrate learning experiences by cutting across traditional subject-matter boundaries. In an attempt to help pupils discover relationships more easily, a number of subjects are combined into one broad area of study.[12] Instead of teaching civics, sociology, economics, history, and geography as separate subjects, in the broad fields curriculum they are brought together and taught as a single area, social studies. Another example would be to combine English, journalism, dramatics, literature, creative writing, and speech.

Correlated Curriculum When two or more subjects are fused together, such as medieval history and medieval art or American history and American literature, and they are taught at the same time with their individual identities retained, the pattern is known as correlated subjects. Correlation can be achieved through systematic preparation of curriculum content or through an agreement among teachers in the various areas.[13] "About one-third of the classes organized along new patterns of curriculum retain the individual subject-matter divisions, and may be considered to be merely correlated with each other."[14] The basis of the

[10] "A Curriculum Guide for Mathematics: Kindergarten to Grade 12," St. Louis Public Schools, St. Louis, Mo., 1965.
[11] Ward G. Reeder, *The Fundamentals of Public School Administration*, 4th ed., The Macmillan Company, New York, 1958, p. 49.
[12] Sidney P. Rollins and Adolph Unruh, *Introduction to Secondary Education*, Rand McNally & Company, Chicago, 1963, p. 44.
[13] *Ibid.*, p. 45.
[14] Thornton and Wright, *op. cit.*, p. 105.

correlated curriculum is that two subjects which appear to have close relationships are taught so that each adds to pupil achievement in the other.

Core Curriculum   The core curriculum is built around a core of required subjects. These subjects are the common learning (or general education) subjects. These are the subjects needed by all the students regardless of their future educational or vocational plans. For example, the basic essentials of reading, writing, and the computational skills.

The core curriculum encourages experimentation and the use of modern methods. It requires guidance, flexible schedules, and democratic procedures in classroom management. Usually the pupils and the teacher plan together what is to be accomplished.

Many modern curriculum specialists think of the core curriculum as the required block of the total curriculum. Usually content is taken from the English and social studies areas and taught to a group of children by the same teacher during at least two periods per day. The same teacher usually does guidance work as well. An example of this is found in the ESSO classes of Arlington County, Virginia. ESSO stands for English, social studies, and orientation.

Recent studies found that core programs were concentrated in five states: Maryland, California, New York, Pennsylvania, and Michigan. Between one-half and two-thirds of the core classes were found in grades seven, eight, or nine.[15]

The broad fields, fused pattern, correlated pattern, or block patterns are often confused or misnamed "core." Too often, the term "teaching method" is used synonymously with the term "curriculum patterns." The core curriculum is not a teaching method. The core curriculum is a pattern of curriculum organization. The core curriculum itself has many variations. Basically it represents an attempt to provide a set of learning experiences that are necessary for all pupils.[16]

One of the chief problems of the core curriculum is the lack of adequately trained teachers. The core curriculum has ended in failure in many schools due to a lack of teachers with the special knowledge and special skills required for broad general education and for group dynamics.

The Experience Curriculum   According to Rollins and Unruh:

The child-centered curriculum and the activity curriculum are synonymous. The experience curriculum assumes that the skills and attitudes that are valuable to a pupil in solving a problem or satisfying a need are those that are learned best and most effectively by the pupil. Therefore, the curriculum can-

15 *Ibid.*, p. 105.
16 Rollins and Unruh, *op. cit.*, p. 47.

not be planned in advance since each group will be different. The curriculum is planned for and by each class as needs and interests develop.[17]

Basic to the effectiveness of the experience curriculum is the ability of the teacher to discover the needs and interests of the children.

The Purpose-centered Curriculum   This is a new type of curriculum where all learning experiences in each of the subject fields are selected from the purposes of a 6-year high school. The content of each subject is built around the purposes previously developed. The purpose-centered curriculum is an integrated subject-matter pattern.[18]

Samford in his book, *Secondary Education,* stated that integration is a misnomer when applied to curriculum. He accused some writers of using it when they really were thinking of a practice resembling fusion or correlation. "Integration, to them, goes a step farther and ignores subject-matter boundaries completely." [19] However, integration here means organizing the curriculum according to what the child requires rather than in terms of a sequence of subjects in a prescribed curriculum.

Rollins and Unruh provided an explanation of the purpose-centered curriculum. They stated that the skills, knowledge, and understanding in each of the subject fields should be identified and then coded on an IBM card. Once the cards are run through a sorter, it is possible to group pupils on the basis of the elements of, for example, English they have yet to master. Such groups, then, are organized according to the needs of these pupils. In this manner a curriculum is developed for each pupil; yet these pupils can be taught in groups of varying sizes.

The content for each of the subject fields can be divided into that part of the content which all pupils should experience and that part which should be available to those pupils who want it or need it.

> The purpose centered curriculum is based on the premise that it is possible to place in a sequence all the experiences to which pupils are exposed in each of the subject fields. The purpose centered curriculum is committed to a genuine consideration of differences among individuals, and the development of a curriculum organization that will, in fact, make it possible to provide an individual program for each child.[20]

Curriculum Guides

In order to prevent gaps in the instructional experiences provided to students in any of the subject areas, curriculum guides or courses of study have been or are being developed at state and local levels. These guides outline the recommended objectives, scope, and sequence of learning

---

[17] *Ibid.,* p. 52.
[18] *Ibid.,* p. 62.
[19] Clarence Samford *et al., Secondary Education,* Wm. C. Brown Co., Dubuque, Iowa, 1963, p. 66.
[20] Rollins and Unruh, *op. cit.,* p. 66.

experiences essential to mastery of knowledge and skills in the subject. They also usually include suggested materials and evaluation techniques.

The authors caution administrators and faculty to study carefully any state curriculum guides so that they may be adapted to the particular needs of the local community. In no case should these guides be used so narrowly as to impede the creativity and imaginativeness of students and faculty.

ROLE OF THE PRINCIPAL IN EDUCATIONAL PLANNING

Primacy of the Instructional Leadership Responsibility

The prime justification for the position of principal in the school is to give leadership to the teaching-learning process. If the principal spends the major portion of his time at that endeavor, he is placing the emphasis where it belongs. If, however, he spends most of his time counting the lunch money, seeing that the playing field is lined, and other similar housekeeping chores, he is not fulfilling the major role his profession and society expect him to play.

Many principals have been appointed to their positions on bases other than their training and competence for the educational leadership role. This does not excuse them, however, from accepting their responsibility for instructional leadership. Regardless of the circumstances surrounding the appointment of an individual to the principalship, once he has accepted that position, he is obligated to fill it in the most responsible manner. Other sections of this book consider the leadership function and describe preparation programs for the principalship in more depth than can be done here.

If the principal is to be the instructional leader in his school he must certainly have knowledge and skill and the inclination to use them to determine:

1. How learning takes place
2. The basis for selection and organization of learning experiences
3. The nature of the growth and development of human beings
4. How to work with people

The principal must lead to utilize the human, physical, and social resources of the community to maximize the educational opportunities for its youth.

The major assistance that a principal can give to his faculty is to manifest concern for curriculum improvement. If he constantly points out that his most important function in the school is improving the quality of the living and learning experiences of pupils, teachers will be eager to put their efforts toward the improvement of instruction and curriculum.

A good teacher will be even better if he has the sympathetic interest, cooperation, and encouragement of an understanding principal. A principal should also give the teacher freedom to experiment, encouragement to try out a new idea, flexibility of scheduling, and show a readiness to commend every success. Curriculum work will then become the accepted activity, and teachers will not hesitate to become active in this field.

The principal should see curriculum development as a cooperative endeavor. Every principal, when he makes a decision concerning the school program, is exercising his legal responsibility. He can make these decisions on his own or share in their making with his faculty. It has been shown that when he involves his staff in making decisions, better decisions are made. The principal has to secure the teachers' understanding and support if he is going to be able to convince them of the value of a change, for teachers often have to be convinced of the value of a change before they are willing to accept it. Schools in which decisions concerning curriculum are shared make more changes and make a greater variety of changes than schools in which the principals keep the decision-making process to themselves.

The public also must be informed of reasons for changes in the curriculum. The principal must take an active part in seeing that the curriculum is designed to meet the needs of the local community. He must see that the proper school personnel are available for informing the public of the importance of a curriculum change. A curriculum change will not be successful unless the faculty and the local community can be made to understand why it must be made and unless they can have a hand in making the change.

The principal is not only responsible for curriculum work in the school, but is also responsible for helping the members of his staff use all resources that are available to them in the system. He should not view central office supervisors as threats to his leadership. He should talk over any differing perceptions concerning respective functions so that difficulties will not arise and curriculum work is not blocked by personality clashes. He should take the initiative in talking through with supervisors what type of program is to be developed and what contributions each person can make.

Another part of the principal's role is to develop a structure for curriculum change. He must ensure close cooperation among all departments by coordinating functions. A planning committee of the faculty can be formed which will plan faculty meetings and in-service education. This group can use suggestions from the total faculty to project the kind of curriculum study that makes improvement possible. In a larger faculty, a committee known as the curriculum coordinating committee can be formed. This would be in conjunction with the planning committee. It would be responsible for looking at the total program and recommending projects for the faculty to undertake to improve the curriculum. Whatever organizational structure is used, the principal should take the initiative in helping the faculty plan, organize, and execute curriculum work. Extended treatment of this subject is given in Chapter 16.

The definition of the areas in which he has the power to make decisions that he is willing to share with the staff is a part of the principal's role in curriculum making. He knows what limits are placed upon the individual school. He knows where he can make decisions. It is his responsibility to let the faculty know the limitations of their authority. He must let the faculty know in what areas they can make curriculum decisions and where they cannot make them. If he does not do this, he will have a frustrated faculty that will not be able to work enthusiastically in a curriculum development program.

In the decision-making process, the principal's role is to guard against making decisions without thinking through all the aspects of the problem. Time must be provided and procedures established by which problems are defined, evidence is collected, and proposals made before any final decision is reached. He must recognize that data-collecting and analyzing periods are times in which the faculty will make the greatest growth. He must see that the curriculum development procedures are a major portion of the in-service program and will not be frustrated by the time spent in arriving at proposals and decisions.

Implementing the decisions reached is the final phase of the curriculum and instructional improvement program. Unless steps are taken to put the decisions into operation, the time and effort spent on improvement will be useless, and teachers will lose interest.

Steps in Evaluation and Revision

The principal's role does not cease once the new developments have been initiated. The principal must be concerned with the task of constantly evaluating the curriculum in terms of well-defined objectives to determine pupil progress and teacher effectiveness.

The basis for evaluation should be the degree to which students have attained reasonable goals which reflect the generalized desires of society and the specific demands of the local community.

The educational product should be evaluated in terms of the "school's philosophy, its individually expressed purposes and objectives, the nature of the students with whom it has to deal, the needs of the community which it serves, and the nature of the American democracy of which it is a part." [21]

21 "Evaluation of Secondary Schools," *General Report of the Cooperative Study of Secondary School Standards*, Washington, D.C., 1939, p. 57.

Precise measurement of the degree to which these goals are met is not possible, but estimates of program success can be made when they are based upon as valid a collection of information as possible and when competent professional judgment is used.

Many instruments and devices are now available for obtaining this information. Measuring achievement is no longer the only assessment of student growth. Devices for encompassing areas of social adjustment, physical and mental health, attitudes, appreciation, critical thinking, and vocational interests are also available. Instruments used to gather information range from highly refined standardized products to informal personal judgments.

In order for program evaluation to be valid, objectivity is desirable, and therefore the measurement procedures noted above are needed. It must be remembered, however, that the results of measurement are quantitative and that the scores derived have no meaning until values are placed on them. Some important objectives cannot be measured easily but must also be evaluated. Pertinent and reliable data are symptomatic and presumptive evidence of the ideals, beliefs, values, and standards of the school program.

The primary purpose of all program measurement and evaluation is to continue favorable practices, to eliminate or modify less desirable phases of the existing program, and to give direction to future planning.

Relationship of Guidance Program

The guidance program in the secondary school exists to assist students in making wise selections among alternatives, and in making the most of their capabilities. Another important function of the guidance program is to furnish feedback to the principal and his staff about the adequacy of the instructional program in the school. Test results should be reviewed for the lessons that can be learned about how well the needs of youth are being met and/or how good a job of teaching is being done.

From the follow-up studies which are conducted of college-bound and noncollege-bound graduates and of dropouts, strengths as well as weaknesses in the programs may be discovered.

Information from the above sources should be "cranked into" the curricular and instructional development programs as described in the preceding section of this chapter.

SUMMARY

The educational program is composed of *curriculum,* which is composed of all the intended experiences that youth have under the supervision of the school, and *instruction,* which is the means or process by which teachers guide, lead, and direct students to worthwhile learning experiences.

Some of the courses offered in secondary schools will be required of all and are classified as *general education*. Other subjects are relative to the goals of certain students only and are called *specialized education*.

The major subject areas were described briefly, and minimum offerings were recommended for each area.

Curriculum determinants are those factors which influence the makeup of the modern curriculum. They include needs of the student, community goals, state and local regulations, and national concerns. Other determinants may be peculiar to a local school system.

The roles of national, state, and local levels in the development of educational objectives were identified.

Types of curriculum were classified as subject-centered, broad fields, correlated, core, experience, and purpose-centered.

Curriculum guides are recommended only when they are adapted carefully to the particular needs of the local community. The better ones result when the guides are developed locally.

The principal's role in educational planning was emphasized as being of prime importance. The continuing nature of that role means that evaluation and revision of the curriculum must also be continuous.

The authors point up the value of feedback from the guidance program to help in curriculum and instructional development.

SUGGESTED EXERCISES

1. Poll your associates and ask them to define the terms "curriculum" and "instruction." Compare the definitions and discuss the differences and similarities found.

2. Secure the courses of study from a high school and look for the stated objectives which should accompany each guide. List the criteria which you think could be used to evaluate such objectives.

3. Obtain a copy of the most recent *Evaluative Criteria* for regional accreditation, and study the criteria for evaluating the curriculum and the total educational program. Which ones would you agree are appropriate? What others do you think should be added?

4. What recent innovations relating to curriculum and instruction do you find in the literature? What were the forces which prompted these innovations?

5. Visit one of the regional educational research laboratories established under public law 89-10, and become acquainted with some of the new directions in education. How many are related to new curriculums and new instructional methods? Would they work in your school system? Why or why not?

SELECTED REFERENCES

BROUDY, HARRY S., B. OTHANEL SMITH, AND JOE R. BURNETT, *Democracy and Excellence in American Secondary Education,* Rand McNally & Company, Chicago, 1963, chaps. 1, 2, and 7.

CONANT, JAMES B., *The Comprehensive High School,* McGraw-Hill Book Company, New York, 1967, 95 pp., chaps. 3 and 4.

Imperatives in Education, Yearbook of The American Association of School Administrators, Washington, D.C., 1966, 180 pp.

NEAGLEY, ROSS L., AND N. DEAN EVANS, *Handbook for Effective Curriculum Development,* Prentice-Hall, Inc., Englewood Cliffs, N.J., 1967.

NEA Project on Instruction, Several reports and studies.

RICE, DAVID, "Employment and Occupations in the Seventies," *Educational Leadership,* vol. 22, no. 4, January, 1965.

SMITH, B. OTHANEL, WILLIAM O. STANLEY, AND J. HARLAN SHORES, *Fundamentals of Curriculum Development,* rev. ed., Harcourt, Brace & World, Inc., New York, 1957, 685 pp.

SULKIN, SIDNEY, "The Challenge Summarized," *NASSP Bulletin,* vol. 50, no. 311, September, 1966.

TYLER, RALPH W., "New Dimensions in Curriculum Development," *Phi Delta Kappan,* vol. 48, no. 1, September, 1966.

CHAPTER 12

MEASURING, EVALUATING, AND REPORTING STUDENT PROGRESS

The intent of this chapter is to examine critically the process of measuring, evaluating, and reporting student progress. Although virtually everyone agrees that there must be some yardstick for charting individual student learning, there is a wide area of disagreement on methods for accomplishment of this pervasive educational task. The complex of activities centering about this universal need of schools becomes the subject of this chapter.

MEASUREMENT AND EVALUATION

The measurement, evaluation, and reporting of student progress is an area which touches all the principal participants in the school process directly. Parents, students, teachers, and administrators all have important concerns with whatever system the school uses. Parents typically see themselves projected through whatever meaning they attach to the reports which their children bring home from the school. Students typically orient their real worlds around the rewards and punishments of marks. Teachers are under continuing pressure to measure, record, grade, and evaluate their students' scholarly efforts. School administrators devote considerable amounts of time mediating disputes, interpreting meanings, and striving for improved systems, all centering about this same process.

The cycle of measurement, evaluation, and reporting demands competence on the part of those who would administer secondary schools. Wide horizons of understanding are required. A complete evaluating system within a secondary school must encompass several areas of professional educational knowledge. It must touch upon curriculum content, educational philosophy, learning theory, child and adolescent psychology, and educational measurement. Because of its dependence on these special areas of knowledge, the reporting of student progress is a complex matter.

First it is necessary to distinguish between the processes of measurement and evaluation. *Measurement* is the process of assessing quantity. *Evaluation* is the process of assessing quality to the dimension being measured. One cannot evaluate a student's progress in school unless the trait or aspect under evaluation is first held up to some standard unit of measure for comparison. In education these standard units of measurement are generally crude; and this fact, no doubt, partially accounts for the constant difficulty encountered in educational measurement.

In employing educational measurement, there is the classical assumption that if a thing exists, it can be measured in some way. However rough and crude some of our educational measures may be, this assumption nevertheless obtains. It is not too difficult to measure a student's ability to type. It can be reported, for example, that he can type 35 words per minute over a 5-minute trial, committing no more than three errors. However, when it comes to such a thing as critical thinking, there are few valid measures. Yet critical thinking is an important intellectual skill to be taught by the school experience, and it is an important concept which does, indeed, exist. Therefore, if one can only develop appropriate instruments, he is then able to measure students' progress in this dimension.

In spite of the several inherent difficulties, educational measurement attempts to identify a trait or a characteristic or a skill and find some method of measuring its relative quantity. For example, a teacher constructs a twenty-item matching test in history. The items can be reliably scored, yielding raw scores from 0 to 20. This raw score is then assumed to be a measure of the student's learning on that particular body of historical content. However, even this requires a prior assumption. The raw score achieved by the student on the twenty-item history test is only a sample of his knowledge of history. Whatever faith is placed on the extent to which the sample is a true measure of his knowledge depends upon the construction of the twenty-item test. The point to be kept in mind—and one which is frequently ignored by teachers—is that the test itself is only a sampling of his historical knowledge. But to evaluate a student's performance on this test requires the application of his score to a graded scale of some sort. The raw score itself, or even the raw score multiplied by a factor of 5 to produce a percentage of correct responses, is not an evaluation. Scoring remains with the measurement process. Evaluation enters when the teacher makes a judgment on the quality of that particular score, or "grade," as it may be called.

Most teachers might assume that the student who scored twenty correct answers on this history test would achieve an "excellent" grade. In all probability this would represent excellent achievement; but our point is that there is nothing inherent in the score itself which makes it excellent, good, fair, or poor. Sometimes, the achievement of twenty correct out of twenty might represent a minimum level of achievement. There could be situations where the test could rightly demand absolute mastery. Anything less, even nineteen out of twenty, or 95 percent could be failure. On the other hand, in other testing situations, a score of ten out of twenty could represent excellent achievement. Evaluation is the application of quality to a quantitative score.

By analogy, the concept of speeding in driving an automobile must be related to a set of accompanying conditions. Driving 20 miles per hour on icy pavement is more truly speeding than is 60 miles per hour on a turnpike. Unfortunately, some law enforcement officials fail to appreciate this fundamental truth, as have some teachers.

The other common term in the measurement and evaluation process is grading. *Grading* is the ordering of a set of common tasks, or performances, completed by students. In the illustration of the twenty-item history test, the assignment of gradations from one to twenty, or zero to 100 percent is the grading process.

The complete cycle of evaluating pupil progress proceeds from the measurement of a task or attribute and the translation of this measure into a graded scale to the final application of a qualitative judgment in the form of evaluation.

Purposes of Evaluation

A fundamental question in this process is what purposes are served by the evaluation process? The process serves all the major reference groups of the school, that is, the students, their parents, the teachers, and the administration. In addition, the evaluation process serves society in general and its various subsystems which have interests in the school.

Consider first the student since he should always remain the school's central focus. The evaluation system should provide the student with (1) information on his performance in relation to other students, (2) information which will assist the student in redirecting his learning efforts so that he can improve his performance, and (3) motivation to put forth his best efforts. By providing a means for diagnosing learning difficulties, the evaluation system makes it possible for teachers to design specific learning activities for students in order that they may overcome their diagnosed difficulties.

The evaluation system should serve as one means for self-evaluation for the teacher to determine his own effectiveness. Suppose, for example, that a teacher designs a unit test covering certain content which he feels he has presented well during the past few weeks. His class, on this test, attains a median score of 55 percent, with his best students scoring 70 percent. If, in such a situation as this, the teacher expected his class to average 70 percent or better, he must now realize that either his teaching during this period of time was less effective than usual, or his expectations for performance were unduly high. Another real possibility is, of course, that all students have "let down" during this period. In order to serve well, the evaluation system must lend itself to be used by the teacher for the purpose of assessing teaching effectiveness as well as student efforts.

The evaluation system also serves the parents. It provides them information which they hope will tell them how their children perform in school in relation to others. They also want to know what kind of traits and attitudes their children are exhibiting in the school situation. Parents expect that by means of the evaluation system, they will be able to acquire useful predictions of their children's anticipated life careers, i.e., what kinds of work they can be suited for, whether or not they can expect to be admitted to college, and how well they apply themselves to responsible tasks.

Evaluation also serves the school administration. The school administration, represented by the superintendent and his central office staff, the board of education, and the school principals, is responsible for making overall judgments about the quality of the educational program. Each of these members of the administrative team carries a different responsibility, but each is concerned with evaluative aspects of the educational program. At the broadest level, the board of education adopts broad policies which, it hopes, will serve the best interests of the entire educational system. The superintendent, working through his line administrators (assistant superintendent and principals), works to coordinate the implementation of these policies. At the building level, where the program actually occurs, principals supervise the implementation of these policies. Since each administrator wages a continuing search for improvement, he depends upon evaluative knowledge of the school's program. For this reason, the system of student evaluation should lend itself to interpretation by responsible administrators in making reports and judgments about the school system.

Beyond the immediate confines of the school itself, the evaluation system serves purposes for units of the society. Higher education uses the school's system of evaluation to make judgments of its own about who should be admitted to their institutions. As the pressure for admission to colleges continues to climb, it seems likely that this particular purpose will not diminish in importance for the modern secondary school. Potential employers, too, look to the secondary school to furnish evaluation of the school's products.

GRADING SYSTEMS

Since all schools are committed to the concept of the measurement and evaluation of student growth, they must necessarily develop systems of grading. The *grading system* would be defined as that system which enables the various indices of curricular measurement to be translated into a hierarchy of evaluative symbols. Through its expression, the student, his teacher, and his parents are able to make an assessment of his growth along some particular dimension under consideration. In a letter grading system there are usually five levels representing the evaluative concepts of excellent, good, fair, poor, and failing. A percentage system derives grades on the basis that students are expected to demonstrate successful completion of a predetermined percentage of the tasks given. Other grading systems may be based on simply two categories of student performance, satisfactory or unsatisfactory, pass or fail, acceptable or unacceptable. Grading is the language of evaluation.

Rather than advocate the use of one particular grading system, it seems more to the point to center on the meaning and implications of various systems. Whatever system is employed, it is paramount that it be well understood by all who use it and, further, that this system be congruent with the existing purposes within the school.

Role of the Administrator in Grading

The administration of the modern secondary school must assume keen interest in grading. The secondary administrator can use the evaluation system as an instrument of instructional improvement. Through it, he has an opportunity to examine several significant phases of his school program.

The secondary administrator can study the issue of reliability. Reliability, that is, the extent to which grades given from class to class are the same for equal quality achievement, is a major problem in all grading systems. One means of examining reliability is to construct a *grade distribution table*. This can be done by tabulating the number and percentage of grades given by subject or by teacher. By this device various questions can be explored. For example, if the grading system uses a letter grade of C as average, one would expect to find approximately 50 percent of the grades given to be C's. If the grade distribution chart reveals that this is not the case, explanatory hypotheses can be sought. Or, if there are ability-grouped "tracks" and the grading system is supposed to be based on relative achievement within the track, there should be approximately equal percentages of high and low grades in all ability levels. Or, if there is the converse assumption that the grading system remains independent of the tracking system, one would expect top-ability groups to earn mostly A's and B's, with no or only rare D's or F's. Figure 12-1, from Abington High School, in Abington, Pennsylvania, illustrates a typical grade distribution chart.

Objective data, presented in tabular form, and perhaps placed on acetate transparencies for overhead projection, can be used to initiate faculty discussions on grading and its implications.

The principal can also work on the problem of validity. *Validity* is the extent to which a measurement actually measures the item it claims to measure. Since the principal is vitally concerned with refining the purposes of the school, he can likewise investigate whether the current measures being taken are valid indicators of fulfillment of the school's stated purposes.

The problem is that for some very worthwhile objectives ways of assessment are not yet developed. For example, the NEA Project on Instruction recommends teaching students about controversial issues.[1] Students need to learn not only about the issues themselves but something about how to evaluate contradictory sources of information. This objective seems critical for intelligent citizenship in a world where mass communication increasingly shapes public opinion. It is not too difficult to teach a body of information about certain controversial issues, but it is much more difficult to teach students how to judge the source of their information. This becomes an aspect of critical thinking. This is a continuing problem in education. New learning objectives are constantly being added to the school without their accompanying means of measurement.

It is not only in the social studies area that this same problem of lack of valid measures for objectives exists. In a study reported by Heath, a sample of high school classes using the Physical Science Study Committee (PSSC) course was compared with samples of similar classes using conventionally taught courses.[2] Under investigation in this study were "cognitive preferences." It was hypothesized that PSSC students would demonstrate a stronger cognitive preference for "fundamental principles,"

[1] *Deciding What to Teach*, National Education Association, Washington, D.C., 1963, p. 175.
[2] Robert W. Heath, "Curriculum, Cognition, and Educational Measurement," *Educational and Psychological Measurement*, vol. 24, no. 2, pp. 239-253, Summer, 1964.

ABINGTON HIGH SCHOOL
SOUTH CAMPUS
Abington, Pennsylvania

STUDY OF GRADE DISTRIBUTION IN RELATION TO ABILITY GROUPING—FIRST SEMESTER 1964-65

Table I

Ability Group One

Grades	U.S. History No.	%	Pol. Sci/Ec. No.	%	World Cult. No.	%	Chemistry No.	%	R-Math III No.	%	M-Math III No.	%	Totals No.	%
A	34	20	46	48	4	6	20	23	18	26	15	15	137	23
B	85	50	41	43	46	73	31	35	34	50	31	30	268	46
C	45	27	8	8	12	19	21	24	14	20	46	45	146	25
D	3	2	—	—	1	2	4	5	3	4	10	10	21	4
F	2	1	1	1	—	—	11	13	—	—	—	—	14	2
Totals	169	100	96	100	63	100	87	100	69	100	102	100	586	100

Table II

Ability Group Two

Grades	U.S. History No.	%	Pol. Sci/Ec. No.	%	World Cult. No.	%	Chemistry No.	%	R-Math III No.	%	M-Math III No.	%	Totals No.	%
A	19	4	10	6	14	6	27	10	2	2	15	8	87	6
B	151	33	50	31	78	33	59	23	15	12	62	34	415	29
C	141	31	52	33	87	37	75	29	56	46	60	33	471	33
D	78	17	41	26	46	19	40	16	36	30	28	15	269	20
F	73	15	6	4	12	5	57	22	12	10	17	10	177	12
Totals	462	100	159	100	237	100	258	100	121	100	182	100	1,419	100

Fig. 12-1. Study of Grade Distribution in Relation to Ability Grouping (Reproduced by permission of Abington School District, Abington, Pennsylvania).

and "critical questioning of information," than conventionally taught control groups; and further that control group students would exhibit cognitive preferences relating to "memory for specific facts or terms" and "practical application" to a greater extent than the PSSC groups. The findings produced positive relationships on both hypotheses, indicating that PSSC students were responding to the new program in physics, which stresses fundamental processes and inquiry more than vocabulary and application. However, when both groups were tested on the Cooperative Physics Test, Form Z, a test designed for conventionally taught high school physics, the difference between the means of two groups was only slight.

This example from the research study reiterates our contention that some of the most worthwhile objectives are not measured because adequate instruments are not developed. Some take the position that since measurement of many learning objectives is difficult, it shouldn't even be attempted. Our position is to admit the grave difficulties but to push on, unrelenting in search for objective measurement.

Thus, the responsibility to examine the validity of whatever measures are available falls most directly upon the secondary principal. He, better than anyone else in the building or in the central office is in a position to look at his school's program in terms of what it attempts to do for students.

Role of the Teacher

The teacher plays a central role in grading students. School administration may lay out excellent policies and procedures on grading, but implementation depends on the teacher. In the final analysis the teacher is probably the greatest factor in the grading process. Therefore, it is of signal importance that teachers understand the system intended to be used in the school. Clear understanding is important since even under the best of conditions, measurement contains error. Refining the process consists principally in reducing the sources of potential error. The teacher is one of the prime sources of error. This is not to say that teachers are especially prone to mistakes; it is simply that even the most objective of measurement processes must account for the phenomenon of error.

If a grading system is to minimize potential teacher error and increase reliability, it should meet the following criteria:

1. It should contain as few separate operations as possible. The teacher should not be required to copy over a series of grades to enter for an additional set of records. Each copying step largely increases the chances of error. One advantage of using data proc-

essed information for grading and report cards is that teachers perform but few mechanical operations.

2. The evaluative symbols used should denote only one dimension of performance. If letter grades are used to denote academic achievement, student effort should not be reflected in this grade. If student effort is shown, a separate symbol should be used.

3. The system should be thoroughly understood by all who use it, especially by teachers who actually assign the grades. It should be a part of an administrator's responsibility to ensure that new teachers in the school acquire a complete understanding of what the grading system means.

Role of the Parents

Since this book is written for administrators rather than parents, this section intends to suggest how principals can view parents' attitudes toward their children's grades.

Parents' attitudes toward grading are determined primarily by opinions formed during their own school years. Since the grading system cannot help but be a reflection of the underlying educational philosophy of the school, a great many modern parents will have difficulty interpreting modern grading systems. The trouble is not so much that parents can't look at a report card and tell you what it means, as it is that what they tell you it means is not what the school may have intended. Therefore, one of the genuine contributions an administrator can make is to assist parents in developing an understanding of the school's grading system. Teachers, too, of course, participate in this process, but it is the administrator who can undertake this as one particular objective of his public relations program. He can purposefully set out to raise the level of understanding of his supporting parent groups. Special meetings, programs, newsletters, and conferences can assist in this process.

Parents can play an important role in the development of changes in grading systems. Should a school or district initiate a study for the purpose of changing an existing system, parents can be useful in serving with the professional committee. Some may contend that the development of a grading system is strictly a professional matter and that, as such, lay parents have no place in this process. While work on developing grading systems is certainly high-order professional work, this does not negate the wisdom of parental participation. Parents serving in this capacity will arrive at new levels of respect for the professional expertness of teachers; and teachers will find that parents can provide valuable information by their reaction to proposed grading changes.[3]

[3] H. V. Phelps, "How to Design a Report Card Parents Can Understand: Westside Community Schools," *School Management*, vol. 8, pp. 72–74, May, 1964.

Basic Issues on Grading Systems

Controversy over the relative worth of grading systems is of long standing. Inspection of the professional literature of many education journals will illustrate that this subject is superbly capable of generating sharp disputes within the profession. Unfortunately most journal articles on the subject tend to concentrate on condemnation of existing systems while promoting the merits of their own systems.

Granting that the area is fraught with the hazards of endless philosophical argumentation, it is the authors' position that such conflict is unnecessary. Rather, we suggest an examination of the questions which the grading process seeks to answer. Once these are secured, the particular method of grading is of less concern.

How well is Johnny doing? This is the fundamental question that grading seeks to answer. Grading, we said, is the communication system which attempts to answer this question for each student in each dimension of the curriculum which the school feels is significant enough to be reported. As a special-purpose language, grading must employ abstract symbols to represent reality. Once there is agreement and general understanding of the symbols to be used, grades will then communicate. To communicate the reality of how well Johnny is doing, we need to know how well he is doing in comparison to what or whom and when and on what evidence and against what yardstick we are measuring Johnny. There are at least five different standards of comparison. First, his achievement can be measured against his own prior achievement, that is, he can be measured against himself. Second, he can be measured against the others in that particular classroom or section. Third, he can be compared with others in the same level in the same school. Fourth, he can be measured against others at the same academic level but in different schools, that is, against all tenth-grade English students in the entire city. Fifth, John's performance can be measured against a kind of normative national standard for similar students. The choice of standard will profoundly influence the grade Johnny receives.

The problem for the secondary school is to adopt one of these as the standard for its grading and then make an extensive effort to ensure that all who use the system employ the same base. It is at this very point about which many heated discussions arise over the meaning of the marks and grades given. Each disputant will argue strongly that his interpretation is preferred. We submit that it is less a matter of right and more a matter of mutual agreement.

Even the question of *when* requires consideration. In secondary schools, the academic year is divided into four to eight grading periods. At the end of each period a student is awarded a grade for the period just completed. Presumably this grade represents typical achievement over that period of time. Using only the arithmetical mean, grades achieved in the early part of marking periods are equally weighted with those achieved at the end. But the question remains, *when* is the actual period of grading? Consider the student, for example, who initially achieves outstanding grades for the first half of the year, but who during the second half steadily drops in achievement. By using the average concept, his achievement for this year would probably be an "average" grade. But does this give useful information? The opposite story could be illustrated. The time-honored "average" concept in grading systems is useful, provided that those using it understand that it is an arithmetic mean. As one measure of central tendency it cannot convey anything other than statistical properties of the mean.[4]

To overcome this problem some schools are attempting to utilize achievement trends. A student's achievement plotted over a period of time, portrays a trend. As in the above illustrative cases, trends would be more meaningful than averages. The trend, maintained cumulatively gives a different answer to the question of "when" in grading. Figures 12-2 through 12-4 illustrate one possible method of utilizing graphic trends in reporting student achievement.

In Figure 12-2 Johnny began the year with a C, then climbed to a B, dipped to a C, and finished on a strong upward trend heading for a

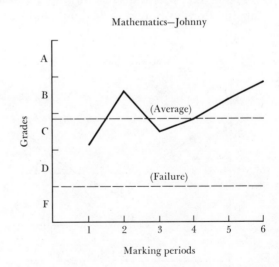

Fig. 12-2. Illustration of Graphic Reporting: Mathematics.

[4] The *median* and the *mode* are also accepted measures of central tendency. Each concept has different uses. Schools seem to rely exclusively on the *arithmetic mean* as the most appropriate measure for all situations.

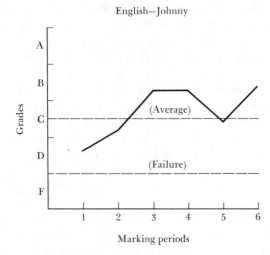

Fig. 12-3. Graphic Reporting: English.

high B. His average would be close to a B but still in the C range. With information of this type graphically portrayed, his parents and mathematics teacher would be able to provide explanatory information to help interpret this pattern.

Figure 12-3 tells the story in graphic form of Johnny's slow start in English. Previously Johnny had only mild enthusiasm for the "dry" sub-

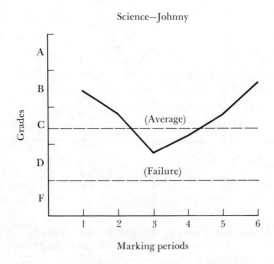

Fig. 12-4. Graphic Reporting: Science.

ject, as he expressed it. But this year, Mr. Romans was able to kindle a spark in Johnny and made him begin to appreciate the functional value of English communication as well as some of the great ideas contained in English prose. His interest and achievement climbed hand in hand, with one dipping exception during the end of the basketball season, when Johnny just didn't put in time enough on English.

From Figure 12-4, we see that Johnny had his ups and downs in science, too, this year. He started off strongly, as he had always done in science. But toward the middle of the year the topics seemed to become more difficult for him. He even slumped to the D level at midyear. His spirits were low, and his mother and father were furious. A conference with the guidance counselor was arranged. Some special after-school sessions were arranged with the help of Johnny's science teacher. This seemed to help, and Johnny finished the year at the same level he started.

These simple stories about our proverbial Johnny merely illustrate the type of information and interpretation possible through the use of the chart form of reporting. Many variations of this basic model are possible. All subject areas can be plotted simultaneously, using differing color codes or line types. Or, average class performance can be plotted along with the individual student's plotting, in order to provide a clear comparison with the rest of the group.

One reason why this type of reporting is infrequent is that it is considered too complex for the average parent. It may have been complex for the parent of the last generation, but the present generation is well-exposed to interpretation of graphs and charts through the daily press. Even if they fail to understand it, they would probably understand it no less than they would any symbol of reporting.

In addition to the *who, what,* and *when* problems in grading, there is also the basic issue centering about which dimensions of performance will be considered. In a sense, this issue is simply an extension of the *what* issue previously discussed. To use English, for example, what is the base upon which the grade is given? Specifically what dimensions of a student's performance in English will go into the composite rating expressed by whatever symbol is used? Is it knowledge of grammar usage as demonstrated on quizzes and tests? Is it the usage patterns displayed in ordinary discourse? Is it his ability to organize and present a formal speech or debate? Is it his ability to express himself in meaningful and essentially correct prose? Is it his recognition of certain pieces of written English, as great works of literature? We could go on listing various sub-skills and abilities all contained under the heading of English. Of course the English teacher will reply, "Well, it's really all of these and other dimensions which make up a student's performance in English. We generally try to blend them together."

And as if this were not complex enough, the problem is further compounded by the long-standing confusion over the influence to be granted for the student's attitude. Teachers find it nearly impossible not to be influenced by the student's attitude when they make grading decisions. Should this be an influencing factor?

Recognition of this problem has led many districts to create dual or multiple marking systems, where they use one symbol for what they consider strictly academic achievement and another for an evaluation of a student's attitude, effort, or conduct in that subject.[5]

Another fundamental and continually vexing problem existing in schools is the relative variability in ease of measurement of different school objectives. Some curriculum areas lend themselves to measurement much easier than others. It is relatively easy to determine that a student can do six chin-ups in a physical education class. It is less objective but still reasonably objective to determine when he can carry on a simple conversation in beginning French and even when he can do simple algebraic problems. But, it is much more difficult and much less reliable to state with confidence what this student can do in his history class.

Another dimension to this same problem is present in the difficulty in measuring intellectual skill as distinct from factual knowledge. Recognizing the importance of this distinction, the test makers are working hard to develop instruments which will measure these skills.[6]

Because many of the school's important objectives are at the present time immeasurable, there is a constant danger that those items most measurable will receive most attention. Sociologists have observed that when organizations take frequent measures of their efficiency, there tends to be stimulation of those elements of production which lend themselves to measurement, but not necessarily at the same standard of quality.[7] Schools could easily fall victim to this phenomenon by being so eager to demonstrate to all how efficient they are that they overmeasure the things which can be easily measured but, worst of all, tend to neglect some equally important but less measurable objectives.

To the extent that these basic issues remain unresolved within a secondary school, there will remain a myriad of resulting problems. As Mauritz Johnson, Jr., suggests, a policy needs to be formulated, in order to solve the "mess in marks." [8]

[5] Raymond H. Muessig, "The Mystery of Grading and Reporting," *Education*, vol. 83, pp. 90–93, October, 1962; also Morton Alpren, "A Fair Grading System," *Clearing House*, vol. 35, pp. 113–114, October, 1960.

[6] Henry Moughamian, "General Overview of Trends in Testing," *Review of Educational Research*, vol. 35, no. 1, pp. 5–16, February, 1965.

[7] Amitai Etzioni, *Modern Organizations*, Prentice-Hall, Inc., Englewood Cliffs, N.J., 1964, p. 9.

[8] Mauritz Johnson, Jr., "Solving the Mess in Marks," *Education Digest*, vol. 27, pp. 12–14, February, 1962.

Research on Grading

Educational research on grading has principally taken the form of descriptive survey research.[9] The goal of this type of research is mainly to describe, as accurately as possible, current practices. In fact, much of educational research has been of this type. While useful in identifying prevailing practice, survey research does not tell which practices are superior. With respect to grading, the researches have tended to catalog the ebb and flow of various grading systems.

Among the long-term trends of prevailing practice of grading are these:

1. increased recognition that marking and grading practices ought to reflect educational objectives
2. increase in the use of grading systems which attempt to recognize a broader range of student performance
3. increased recognition that a single "mark" cannot accurately express the desired information
4. a continuing trend away from the use of percentage points as the basis for grades, with an accompanying standardization trend toward the 5-point grade system.
5. a clear trend to involve both parents and teachers in the development of new marking and grading systems
6. recognition that the major unresolved issue is the determination of the basis of marking and grading [10]

A comprehensive survey on marking, as reported by Terwilliger, reviewed the marking practices and policies of a national sample of 129 public secondary schools.[11] Using a questionnaire, Terwilliger secured data from teachers and administrators on their grading systems.

Data were secured on practices and policies on the "primary basis" for grading, the type of grading system used, the possible effect of student behavior on grades, the method of computing class rank, types of weighting formulas for determining average grades, and the effect of homework on grades, among other items. Although warning his reader that his sample of 129 was too small to be considered normative for the entire United States, Terwilliger concludes that "what is truly needed is a revolution in marking." [12] His battle cry for revolution is based on the findings which showed that there is widespread variation among schools

[9] For an excellent description of survey research, see, Carter V. Good, *Essentials of Educational Research*, Appleton-Century-Crofts, Inc., New York, 1966, chap. 5.
[10] Chester W. Harris (ed.), *Encyclopedia of Educational Research*, 3d ed., The Macmillan Company, New York, 1960, pp. 783–789.
[11] James S. Terwilliger, "Self-reported Marking Practices and Policies in Public Secondary Schools," *NASSP Bulletin*, no. 308, pp. 5–37, March, 1966.
[12] *Ibid.*, p. 36.

concerning the primary basis for marking. Not only that, 22 percent of the schools reported that they had no policy governing the basis. There appeared to be an equal lack of uniformity over the part student effort plays in grades received, as well as the effect of homework. Perhaps even more serious for the college bound, at least, is the confusion surrounding the use of "class rank." In those schools reporting homogeneous grouping, or tracks, only 25 percent had apparently accounted for tracking in their grading systems. Also, for actual computation of class rank, 38 percent of the reporting sample included marks for all subjects, 34 percent included only academic subjects, 10 percent included subjects requiring "outside preparation," while 12 percent employed still other criteria.[13]

The research on grading has, for several decades, shown a wide range of grading practices in public secondary schools. While few would seriously propose a national standardized grading system for all secondary schools, the continued existence of widely divergent practices and policies does harm students since many of society's rewards and punishments are based on school grading records. Chief among the unresolved and critically important issues concerning grading is the determination of the primary basis for grading. Is it strictly intellectual achievement? Is it intellectual achievement tempered by a student's attitude, deportment, and willingness to conform to the school's ways? Is it the student's own profile of growth, measured only against his own capacity? These and other questions raise fundamental, difficult, but not unresolvable problems.

A Suggested Grading Program

The optimistic allegation that grading questions are not unresolvable is based on a suggested procedure which could be followed by a secondary principal. This procedure would be implemented in several steps, as outlined below.

Setting the Stage   A principal can set the stage for approaching the grading problem by first, quietly, on his own, making a survey of his present situation. This means a thorough examination of the presently used system to determine the extent to which teachers understand it, adhere to it, and feel comfortable with it. This may also involve statistical tabulations of percentage of grades given by track (if this system is used) and by subject and by teacher. When the principal has his facts firmly in presentable form, he can share them with his faculty at a meeting devoted to this topic. His task here is neither to prescribe nor accuse: It is only to raise fundamental issues and provide an objective basis for subsequent discussion.

The Grading Committee   The formulation of a grading committee is the next step in working toward the goal of resolving, at the local level, the

13 *Ibid.*, p. 35.

grading problem. The committee should consist of interested teachers, a representative guidance counselor, and either the principal himself or his assistant. Its membership should total no more than seven or eight, in order to facilitate group action. It should be given the general charge to evaluate the current grading system and make subsequent recommendations for change, if any are called for.

This committee assignment will be given a high priority, and those participating will not be expected to serve on other major committees during the course of the grading committee's life. Assuming that the committee might meet less frequently than weekly but more frequently than monthly, the major part of an academic year will be required for this task.

The administrator will consider himself a member of the group, but, hopefully, he will serve to initiate it and then turn the leadership reins over to one of the members. He will remain an important resource to the committee, but he must not dominate it or attempt to manipulate members toward a favorite system of his own.

Committee Feedback System The chief operating feature of this committee is its continual feedback to the faculty. At faculty meetings, progress reports can be given. As each major area is covered, committee members can communicate the results of the committee's thinking to all faculty members, and they can also systematically seek out faculty members' feelings and attitudes on key issues. By diligent attention to this feedback feature, the committee can minimize the likelihood that the faculty will not accept their final product.

To illustrate how this can work, assume that the committee is working on the issue of how to consider a student's behavior in class in relation to the grade given. Individual committee members can each canvass, systematically but informally, their assigned faculty members, to secure their thinking on this particular issue. After each has completed his interviewing assignment, the results are compiled and compared at a committee meeting. If there are serious schisms, they will appear; and the committee then will either have to seek resolution of the divisions or else seek to change some faculty members' outlook on the issue.

While the use of a committee to study and make recommendations is a time-tested technique in all organizations, the feedback mechanism has enjoyed a more limited use.

Implementation Once the grading committee's recommendations have been presented to the faculty, its duty is complete. Upon acceptance by the faculty and by any other group of persons involved in major policy decisions of this type, implementation becomes an administrative function. The recommendations may provide for trial periods or partial adoptions on an experimental basis, or they may call for complete adoption. The administrators will need to set up ways of evaluating the new system so that minor modifications or "bugs" can be worked out administratively, or should they prove to be major, they might require revision by the grading committee.

What the secondary principal has done in instituting this procedure on grading is simply to create the climate of awareness of the existence of a problem, set up an organization of concerned teachers to work on it, and then allow this group to freely, creatively, and with the authority granted from participation in the feedback system, recommend a new system for the school.

At this point, cognizance should be given to the assumption that this procedure occurs in one secondary school under its immediate administrative leadership. Complete independence of action of this type may not be possible and probably isn't desirable in districts where there is more than one secondary school. Nonetheless the process can be the same. It may originate under impetus from the central office and involve the entire district. Even so, the basic model of the operating committee with its feedback channels can work nevertheless, although its decision making will be slower since the lines of communication will be broader.

One cannot expect the use of a grading committee to become a curative for the several ills of a grading system; yet this device can provide workable machinery for making intelligent revisions which will be more likely to receive support from those teachers who will use the grading system. This will be a giant step forward.

REPORTING TECHNIQUES

Reporting is considered a form of communication between two or more persons or groups. Communication can take a variety of forms, and the content of messages communicated can employ various communicative symbols. The goal of this process is to achieve a close congruence between the sender and receiver of the communication. On the surface, it would seem that the communication of student progress would be a relatively uncomplicated matter. The school simply reports what the student does or does not do, using its appropriate symbols, and the parents receive them and understand them in the same form as they were intended. From both the practical side of experience in parent interpretation of school reports and from the theoretical side of communications research, there is agreement that communication's apparent simplicity is beguilingly false.

The matter of reporting student progress in school depends upon symbols. As we have already demonstrated, it is a very complex matter to design symbols which guarantee reliability of meaning from one person to another. Even the A given in tenth-grade English by Miss Jones is not necessarily the same as the A given in tenth-grade English by Miss Smith. And it is at this level, among teachers in the same subject field, that there is probably the greatest agreement. No wonder, then, that by the time students, other teachers, administrators, counselors, and parents are involved in trying to understand an evaluative symbol, each is likely to derive a different interpretation. Therefore, the school's efforts to create an understanding of the agreed-upon meaning of the communication symbols will promote wider understanding. The broader the understanding of the messages being communicated by the reporting process, the greater the likelihood that the purposes of reporting can be realized.

Clear communication is one objective of a good reporting system. The first portion of this chapter dealt with various aspects of measurement, grading, and evaluating student progress in the secondary school. Our attention now focuses on the reporting (and use) of this information. As was pointed out initially, the evaluating process serves each major reference group within the school; that is, students, teachers, and other school personnel, as well as parents. While the student himself is the focus of the entire process, the information needed by each reference group differs.

Students need reports of their progress in school so that they can adjust their own performances. Indeed, this aspect, sometimes considered as "motivation through marks," appears uppermost to many students and teachers. Students need to know to what extent their efforts—or perhaps lack of efforts—have been successful. Teachers need to issue evaluation reports not only to furnish the student with his needed information, but also to gauge their own teaching effectiveness and to judge the adequacy of the school curriculum. Counselors require reports of student progress in order to furnish realistic occupational guidance. Administrators require reports of student progress in order to assemble comparative data upon which they can appraise the entire school's progress. And of course parents require reports of student progress. They entrust their children to the school for 6 hours a day for the purpose of learning and expect a report of the extent to which both the school and their children are fulfilling their respective responsibilities. To accomplish each group's reporting needs and requirements, many different forms and techniques are necessary. Perhaps a convenient way of classifying these reports is by the two main groups concerned—the home and the school.

School Reports

The average American secondary school is likely to have dozens of different reports and report forms. Probably, the longer the school has existed, the more reports it maintains.

Reports are necessary and functional to the internal communication of the school. Every report has, or at sometime had, its legitimate purpose. Once created, forms and reports can acquire a value unto themselves, as distinct from their purpose. When this not infrequent condition occurs, the rational purpose of some report or record becomes subverted by the emphasis placed upon the making of the report itself. Schools can fall victim to this typically bureaucratic illness as easily as any large and complex organization.[14]

The implication for the secondary administrator is clear. Scrutinize carefully each reporting form. What was its original purpose? Is that purpose still current? Does this report adequately serve this purpose? Is time and effort required to make the report justified? By putting reports to this hard test, the administrator may find that he can harmlessly eliminate some and revise others.

Schools are required to keep accurate reports of attendance. By law, attendance at public school is compulsory. Even as secondary school students reach the end of mandated attendance age, attendance remains compulsory. It is only enrollment which becomes optional. If he enrolls, a student must attend. In addition to student accounting purposes, records need to be kept for the purposes of determining state financial aid. Reasons such as these provide sufficient grounds to justify schools' efforts to account and record students' attendance (and give particular attention to nonattendance) day by day and, in fact, hour by hour.

Schools are also expected to maintain records on each student's academic progress through the school system. At the very least, this record will indicate the student's evaluative marks received each year he was in school. Secondary schools are expected to be able to furnish prospective employers and higher educational institutions with these kinds of reports.

In addition, secondary schools generally maintain a comprehensive set of supplemental records on each student. These can include health history and record of examinations, illnesses and special health problems, dental records carrying complete evaluation of all thirty-two teeth, special talent records such as music or art, performances on a multitude of tests, anecdotal accounts of incidents considered as significant bits of behavior, and photographs. Combined into a year-by-year account, these cumulative records can assist counselors, teachers, and administrators in providing improved guidance for each student. However, the essential point is that reports and records must serve purposes other than their own creation and completion. A record of tests taken, scored, and filed away efficiently in a locked file accomplishes nothing. Record use is the key to wise administration of record keeping.

Home Reports

Home reports are those communications sent from school to home whose intent is to inform the receivers on some aspect of the student's school progress. They may be intended primarily for the student,

---

[14] For a humorous extension of this phenomenon see Bel Kaufman, *Up the Down Staircase*, Prentice-Hall, Inc., Englewood Cliffs, N.J., 1964.

primarily for his parents, or for both. The communication may deal with the student's overall school evaluation, or it may deal with selected phases of academic achievement, social development, or emotional development.

The report card is the time-honored workhorse of home-school communication. Throughout the history of American education it has been this 4- by 6-, or 3- by 5-, or 5- by 8-inch piece of card stock, full of evaluative symbols, which has carried the hopes and dreams of millions of students and their anxious parents. Typically sent home four to six times a year, this situation has become institutionalized in American life. Cartoons in popular magazines, television comedians, and after-dinner speakers continually find the moment of confrontation, when the student presents his report card to a parent, a rich source of humor. Yet present-day secondary school students often fail to appreciate the potential so widely exploited in the world of humor. For it is at this point that his parents receive the school's official word as to how well he has done in school during the last period.

The issuing of the report card is a moment of triumph or despair for many parents as well as for their children. Parents are prone to see themselves projected through the reputations their children make in school. If the report indicates success, parents undeniably feel proud. If it indicates less than success, they immediately seek causes. Is it the child's own lack of effort? Is it an inherent lack of ability? And if this is the case, from which side of the family does this unfortunate lack arise? Is it the school's fault? (Don't they give my child the help he needs?) A multitude of anxious questions like these immediately arise to those parents for whom school achievement is very important.

Although the report card has been attacked by both educators and some parents as being the cause of many school problems, it continues in almost universal use. The variety of size, form and type of information contained is nearly infinite. However, most contain certain basic elements. First there is the subject-by-subject evaluative symbol of academic progress. The symbol may be numerical percentages or letter designations or other symbols to which are attached particular evaluations. At the present, the use of the five-letter system, ABCDE or ABCDF, is the modal pattern. The card will also generally contain a legend to explain the meaning of the symbols used. Most report cards will contain some symbolic expression of the student's social behavior. This may be tied to performance within a subject field, or it may be general deportment. There may be a page of descriptions of types of typical behavior with spaces for teachers to enter checks for those characteristically representative of the student. The card will also report attendance and tardiness, both excused and unexcused. Most cards provide for a parent's signature and expect the card to be returned signed, as evidence that the report did, indeed, get home and was seen but not necessarily approved.

Along with identification information for the student, class, year, school, and school district, many cards contain some message from the school administration. These then, are the basic elements of most report cards.

With the increasing use of electronic data processing in schools, the nonreturning report card is gaining favor. Under this method, the machine prints out each student's report card each reporting period and provides a take-home copy as well as a record copy. This eliminates a great deal of clerical work for homeroom teachers and appears to be well received.

The major implication for the secondary administrator is that he should be able to place the emphasis on what the report means to the student and his parents. Regardless of the intention of the report as sent by the school, the receiver may not acquire the identical message. The administration's task becomes the challenge to improve this communication channel. There are two ways this is possible. First, the reporting system itself can be modified so that it meets the objectives intended for it. And second, the receivers of reports can be taught to understand the intentions of reports.

Official Warning Notices

Most secondary schools find it desirable to employ some kind of a written form to notify students and their parents in the event of impending failure. Used between marking periods, it principally serves to alert the student that he is presently on a failing course and that he must significantly alter his performance in order to avoid the failure at the approaching marking period.

Other official notices may also be used by schools. Some use forms to notify parents of serious disciplinary infractions. Whenever a student is suspended from school for a period, a written notice accompanies this severe action. In short, schools design official report forms to fit any type of recurring situation which they want to make an official record of and to ensure that both the student and the home are duly informed of these acts or conditions.

Formal Conferences

Although the secondary school typically depends less upon the formal conference to accomplish its reporting objectives than the elementary school, it remains a useful method of communication. Formal conferences are arranged between parents and members of the school staff on either a problem-centered or a regular basis.

The problem-centered conference is initiated either by the parent or school and attempts to resolve an issue or seek possible solutions to a diagnosed problem. For example, Johnny receives a warning notice in mathematics. Much alarmed, his parents call the guidance office and arrange for a conference with Johnny's mathematics teacher. There, his parents learn that Johnny has recently been spending most of his out-of-school time practicing baseball in the community league. Together, parents and teacher map out a plan to remedy the current problem.

The regular conference occurs, not because of some problem diagnosed in school or at home but as a fulfillment of a regular planned conference program. It may be once a semester or once a year that the reporting policy calls for a parent-teacher conference. It may be with a guidance counselor, with one or more of the subject teachers, or a conference with several teachers in sequence during the same day or evening. Although the scheduling of parent conferences in the secondary school is complex due to the potential number of teacher conferees, these programs have proved valuable. When conferences supplement the report cards or other formal means of reporting, parents and teachers gain a great deal of useful information which they can both use to serve the student.

Informal Conferences

A frequently used source of parent-teacher reporting is informal conferences. Generally these grow out of what might be termed casual meetings. For example, Mrs. Smith happens to encounter her daughter's English teacher in the school foyer. They exchange pleasantries and soon Mrs. Smith asks, "How is Sally doing this term?" Teachers encounter this type of questioning in many places. Some teachers are annoyed by this type of invasion of their personal time. They can, of course, curtly reply, "I would be glad to discuss this with you if you make an appointment through the office." However, such replies are not likely to further that parent's desire to confer with the teacher. Understanding is needed on both sides.

Informal Notes

Teachers also find occasions to write brief notes to parents when reporting on some particular incident which concerns students. This is most appropriate when a prior relationship has been established, so that the informally written note represents an extension of something previously discussed or reported upon. One of the best uses of informal notes is when teachers tell parents how well their children did on some piece of work or performance. One caution of which administrators should be aware is that hastily written communications can be a frightful source of misunderstanding, even though well-intentioned.

Formal Letters and Narrative Reports

Few systems regularly use narrative reports at the secondary level. There are probably two major reasons accounting for this. First, objective, informative, and well-written reports are difficult to write, and second, they require a great deal of time. Nevertheless, in the hands of a good teacher who can also communicate well in writing, a narrative report or letter is an excellent means of supplying information to parents. As a reporting technique, such reports are most practically used by administrators or guidance counselors.

Telephone Calls

Because of its omnipresence, telephone communication is a constant of modern life. Although the telephone as a formal reporting technique in schools is not often used, this is, nevertheless, one more method whereby information is often exchanged between home and school. Most of the communication exchange relates to simple routine information, such as "Is tomorrow a school holiday?" or "When do report cards come out?" Still, the telephone is an indispensable instrument for furthering many phases of home-school reporting. Parents are often inclined to call the school, ask for a teacher, counselor, or principal when some incident has disturbed them. Parent explosions on the telephone are a part of every school administrator's life. Ideally, the receiver of such calls attempts to arrange a face-to-face conference if the matter is serious enough to warrant one. In most cases, the sting is taken out of parental wrath by patient listening.

The school also employs the telephone as an instrument of reporting. Particularly in the case of attendance reporting, school offices make telephone calls to homes when students are not accounted for in school. Some schools follow a regular practice of daily telephoning to all homes when the absence is unaccounted. Such a practice requires cooperative parents, who establish the habit of informing the school in the morning when students are absent; then the school's secretary or attendance clerk simply checks out those unaccounted. Such a practice also requires homes with phones, an assumption many times mistakenly taken for granted. Where rigorously followed, this system acts as an important spur to good attendance. Rather than resenting such close checking, understanding parents come to appreciate such personal concern for their children.

Homework

Homework is usually not considered as a means of school-home reporting. Yet, it is, in reality, one method by which many parents acquire reports on their children's progress in school. For those parents who give the time and attention, checking homework is an excellent source of information about the type of curriculum followed and about the child's ability to perform in this area. This is just one reason why the type of homework assignments given can be a powerful instrument for either good or poor public understanding. Indiscriminately assigned, the laborious busywork type of homework not only does the student no good, it can result in severe loss of confidence in the school on the part of a discerning parent who examines it.

PROMOTION AND PROMOTION POLICIES

A student's vertical movement through the school is what is commonly called *promotion*. The use of this term implies a set of values surrounding its use for this purpose. Promotion denotes advancement and reward. As a student successfully completes certain tasks, he thereby wins the right to promotion to the next level, whatever that may be. Upon reaching the zenith of the public secondary school, the successful student is then formally *graduated* from the school. In this fashion, the vertical climb from entrance to graduation is marked by successive promotion hurdles. Graduation becomes the ceremony marking the successful running of the course, attested to by public ceremony and a symbolic certificate called a diploma. In general, this represents the traditional notion of entrance, promotion, and graduation.

Connected with promotion is the matter of entrance. Traditionally the successful completion of the eighth-grade grammar school was required for entrance into the 4-year high school. With the advent of the junior high school in the 1930s, it became the vehicle for high school entrance; and in similar fashion the 6-year elementary school became the requirement for entry into the junior high school.

Throughout the earlier period of American secondary education one probable reason for maintaining the successful completion of the grammar school as a requirement for admission into the high school was an effort to keep high academic standards. The high school had as its primary goal the preparation of a select group of youngsters for the academic college. As was pointed out in Chapter 2, during the late 1890s and 1900s, such a narrow goal for secondary education no longer fitted the needs of a rapidly developing nation. Nevertheless, some of the traditional ideas surrounding promotion remain as vestigial leftovers of a bygone era.

Modern secondary public schools are not selective institutions. They may nevertheless insist upon rigorous academic standards, but they try to accommodate all American youth. This includes the dull and the bright, the badly behaved and the well-behaved. With a firm commitment to this system it is no longer justified to establish entrance requirements to screen out "unfit" students. No student is unfit. Any student retains his eligibility as long as he demonstrates a reasonable amount of effort and normal social behavior.

As an operating policy, it is recommended that the junior high school, or middle school, as the case may be, simply admit all students recommended for admission by the sending school. Within a single school district this simple policy works well. It may cause a few problems when students enter from other districts where the program has been meager. Here, the receiving school must attempt to determine the incoming student's optimum level of placement and work out the best individual school placement for him.

A promotion policy which is in harmony with modern concepts of secondary education is one which has, as its determining criterion, the best interests of the student. It works on the principle that the most important consideration is the long run interest of each individual student. With this primary criterion, promotion or failure is less reward and punishment and more guidance oriented. A year of school is seen as both a right and a privilege. It is a right for every student, established for him by the state constitution, entitling him to a secondary education till the age of twenty-one if he chooses. As long as he conforms to reasonable standards of acceptable social behavior and as long as he puts forth enough effort in his schoolwork to justify his instructor's time, he is entitled to public schooling. Secondary public education is also a privilege in that it gives to all who will take it an opportunity for a broad and enriching secondary education. A year spent in school costs the public about $600 for a secondary student. It is a special favor granted by the society to this adolescent. It gives him a special place to spend his time, not requiring him to be on his own in the labor market or the armed services. The secondary school is a specially designed institution for American youth. From this point of view then, providing an adolescent with an extra year of public secondary school, more than the normal, is seen as a special privilege, rather than a punishing sentence.

The above view is not, unfortunately, accepted by a great many. Much of society, including teachers, administrators, parents, and students, cling to an image of the public secondary school as a place from which students are expected to try their utmost to get away. When they conform to the academic and social standards set down for them, students are rewarded by passage to the next grade, and finally they win the right to leave altogether—they graduate.

Operating from a philosophic base such as this, the promotion policy becomes a question of professional guidance from which each student can profit most. The grade designations are less important. What is paramount is a determination of what group or what grade or what "phase" [15]

[15] The nongraded high school at Melbourne, Fla., uses phases as a system of classifying students.

will enable the student to get the most out of school. This may mean some shifting ahead and some moving back.

At this point it may be useful to distinguish between elective and required courses. Standards for passing or failure need to differ between these two types of courses. For required courses, which all students take, there need to be standards which can fit all students along the complete ability spectrum. It is an utter disregard of rationality as well as human decency to attempt to hold students to any standard of academic achievement which they cannot possibly maintain. Failure in this sense is unjust. The approach is rather to adjust the content, pace, and teaching methodology to fit the level of students being instructed in required courses. As long as a student is accurately placed and putting forth reasonable effort, he should pass the course. In elective courses, it is reasonable and justified to maintain the necessary level of achievement to master those subjects. This same recommendation is listed by Conant in his *The American High School Today*.[16]

Graduation

Since the American secondary school has virtually achieved the goal of universal education, the meaning of graduation has become somewhat blurred. The award of the high school diploma formerly meant that its possessor had successfully passed a series of courses comprising a curriculum. If it was the college preparatory curriculum, graduation meant that the student was prepared and qualified to enter a 4-year college. If it was the commercial or business curriculum, the student was prepared and qualified to enter the world of business as an office employee.

Major changes in both the secondary school and the world of work as well as in the colleges have caused readjustments in the meaning of graduation. As we have pointed out, the secondary school is less selective. Even though the dropout problem is still acute, high schools are issuing diplomas to many students whose ability and achievement level is in the lower half of the range. The world of work has thrown up high school graduation as the minimum entrance requirement for even the most menial jobs. With the great crush for entrance into college, there is less reliance upon presentation of a diploma as evidence of qualification for college and more on percentile scores on nationally standardized tests. The mere possession of a high school diploma does not and cannot mean what it was intended to mean a generation ago. The successful completion of the high school program has to represent different things for different students.

Graduation from an American high school should mean, first, that the

[16] James B. Conant, *The American High School Today*, McGraw-Hill Book Company, New York, 1959, p. 48.

student has met a reasonable standard of attendance and social behavior during his attending years. He has learned to apply himself to his tasks with appropriate maturity. It means that he has completed a number of constants in the curriculum. These center about written and spoken communication and his cultural heritage, that is, the subjects of English and the communication arts and the social studies. His completion of these areas is no guarantee of mastery to any predetermined level. It only means that he has had that many units of instruction. The school's goal in the language arts, for example, is not that everyone shall graduate reading at the twelfth-grade level but that everyone will graduate with the highest achievement level of which he is capable. This will mean that some will be able to read at the level of advanced graduate students, while others will be able to barely read at the sixth-grade level.

Graduation from high school should also mean that the student is specifically prepared to take the next step in his life. For the college bound it means that they are prepared and capable of serious study at the undergraduate level. For the graduates of vocational programs, it means that they are prepared to succeed at the entry-level job. For all students, it means that they are prepared to take on the responsibilities of adult life, free from immediate social control.

The general society—colleges, employers, etc.—needs to understand what possession of the high school diploma does mean in today's comprehensive high schools.

The secondary principal can play an important role in creating understanding of the meaning of graduation in his particular school and community. He will need to start within his school, with his faculty. He can promote an understanding of the meaning of graduation by including this as a topic of study for a faculty meeting. To the extent that he achieves some degree of across-the-board understanding and agreement, he can then attempt to influence his supporting community.

SUMMARY

This chapter has explored the topic of measuring, evaluating, and reporting student progress in today's secondary schools. Throughout this chapter there has been the recurring theme of purpose—that evaluation must be related to purposes. This is a difficult area to administer well. It is difficult because, on the one hand, issues on evaluation lead directly into deep questions, and on the other hand, the evaluation area is replete with strong traditions, deeply rooted in an image of education which is no longer relevant to the present age.

The principal's most appropriate role is to exercise his leadership skills rather than to attempt to impose his ideas. Through patient work with his faculty and accompanying work outside the school in the community, the principal can lead his staff and his community into building an evaluation system which is consistent with the purposes of the school, agreed upon by his staff, and understood by his community.

SUGGESTED EXERCISES

1. Search the literature of educational psychology and learning theory to test the degree of support for the oft-repeated contention that students are motivated to learn by the device of marks.

2. As a class, collect a sample of secondary school report cards. Test the extent to which they reflect the trends reported in this chapter. Also attempt to determine the basis upon which the grades are given.

3. As a class project, design an ideal reporting system.

4. Survey nearby schools and list all the various report forms used that have to do with student evaluation. Evaluate each form in terms of the purpose it is supposed to serve.

5. Design a class research project, using a small sample of citizens. Ask them, through personal interview, "What should high school graduation mean?"

SELECTED REFERENCES

Coombs, Robert H., and Vernon Davis, "Social Class, Scholastic Aspiration and Academic Achievement," *The Pacific Sociologist Review,* vol. 8, no. 2, pp. 96–100, Fall, 1965.

Faunce, Roland C., and Carroll L. Munshaw, *Teaching and Learning in Secondary Schools,* Wadsworth Publishing Co., Belmont, Calif., 1964, 438 pp.

Findley, Warren G. (ed.), *The Impact and Improvement of School Testing Programs,* Sixty-second Yearbook, Part II, National Society for the Study of Education, The University of Chicago Press, Chicago, 1963, 304 pp.

Humphreys, Phila, "The Schools Concern in Non-promotion," *Theory into Practice,* vol. 4, no. 3., pp. 88–89, Ohio State University, June, 1965.

Moughamian, Henry, "General Overview of Trends in Testing," *Review of Educational Research,* vol. 35, no. 1, pp. 5–16, February, 1965.

Remmers, H. H., N. L. Gage, and J. F. Rummel, *A Practical Introduction to Measurement and Evaluation,* Harper & Row, Publishers, Incorporated, New York 1960, 370 pp.

Strom, Robert D., "Academic Achievement and Mental Health," *Journal of Secondary Education,* vol. 39, pp. 348–355. December, 1964.

Terwilliger, James S., "Self-reported Marking Practices and Policies in Public Secondary Schools," *NASSP Bulletin,* no. 308, pp. 5–37, March, 1966.

U.S. Department of Health, Education and Welfare, *Pupil Marks and School Marking Systems: A Selected Bibliography,* 1963, 22 pp.

CHAPTER **13**

INSTRUCTIONAL
MATERIALS
AND
SERVICES | This chapter will outline the major types
of instructional materials and services available to secondary schools. As a
specialized study area, it contains powerful educational ideas and a wide
range of teaching materials.

First, attention is directed to the underlying philosophy of instructional materials.

AN UNDERLYING PHILOSOPHY OF INSTRUCTIONAL MATERIALS

Three major ideas converge to form the basis for a modern philosophy
of instructional materials. These three are (1) the knowledge explosion,
(2) the transference of learning responsibility, and (3) modern technology.
Each major idea contains implications for all phases of the instructional
program, but it is within the area of instructional materials and services
that they have a most direct and necessary connection.

The Knowledge Explosion

The modern world is in the midst of a knowledge explosion. The branches of the physical sciences are leading the way. It has been estimated that 90 percent of all the scientists who have ever lived are present on the contemporary scene.[1] The social sciences, too—psychology, sociology, anthropology, economics, and politics—have added greatly to what Stuart Chase, 20 years ago, called "knowledge in the storehouse."[2] It is not only those fields called scientific which are expanding by the production of new knowledge. History, as the chronicle of man's past, is constantly sifting and revising its perspective. The relatively straightforward story of Columbus's discovery of America in 1492, which every school child has been brought up on, has been cast in a new light by careful scholars' published reports establishing strong claims to a much earlier discovery of the continent of North America.[3] Writers create new literature constantly, and literary scholars review and reinterpret the old. The gifted design new art forms. Theologists who specialize in examination of man's relationship to a Supreme Being are constantly in the midst of reexamination and suggest new dimensions. A great deal of this new knowledge finds its way into published books. By 1964, the United States alone was publishing more than twenty-eight thousand titles.[4] There is no field of knowledge exempt from an accelerated rate of expansion.

An unintended by-product of the knowledge explosion is the paradox of specialization. Prior to the nineteenth century, the world's accumulated knowledge grew slowly. The formal educational institutions (chiefly the universities) could turn out "educated men" who could be expert in several different branches of knowledge and well-informed in all. As we move into the latter half of the twentieth century, this "Renaissance man" image appears no longer possible of attainment by even the most gifted. Branches of knowledge spawn subfields, or specializations. The sociologist is not simply a sociologist; he may specialize in urban sociology, criminal sociology, marriage and the family, bureaucracy, economic systems, educational sociology, social change and diffusion, the sociology of religion, the sociology of the aged, social demography, social stratification, and numerous others. In order to stay up-to-date in one of these subbranches requires full-time attention. But, in spite of the rapid accumulation of highly specialized knowledge, the need to synthesize and relate

[1] Arthur D. Nelson, "Medical Education and the Knowledge Explosion," *Temple University Alumni Review*, Philadelphia, Fall, 1965, p. 30.
[2] Stuart Chase, *The Proper Study of Mankind*, Harper & Row, Publishers, Incorporated, New York, 1948, chap. 5.
[3] R. A. Skelton *et al.*, *The Vinland Map and the Tartar Relation*, Yale University Press, New Haven, Conn., 1965; also Associated Press, *The Philadelphia Inquirer*, "Welsh Claim Discovery of America," Oct. 6, 1966.
[4] Sara K. Srygley, "A New Look at the Older Media," *NASSP Bulletin*, no. 306, p. 27, January, 1966.

all knowledge appears to be more necessary than ever. Thus we have this unintended paradox of the knowledge explosion.

For those whose specialty is the transmission of knowledge through formal education, that is, teachers and school administrators, this problem will become increasingly critical. What is needed, apparently, is a means of learning how to learn and relearn throughout life.

The Transference of Learning Responsibility

A second major idea bearing on instructional materials is the transference of learning responsibility from the teacher to the student. An older notion of education conceived of knowledge primarily as a certain set of definite facts. This set was the possession of the teacher. It was his responsibility, as the holder of the knowledge, to pass it on, in a rather direct manner, to his students. His students, while they were expected to be disciplined, that is, well-behaved and cause only a minimum of trouble, were really not required to do much more than absorb as much as they could. Under this concept of education the emphasis was upon the teaching process by which the body of knowledge was transferred from teacher to student. It was axiomatic to state that the student could know only what the teacher taught. The surest indication of how well the student had learned was for him to demonstrate the extent to which he could reproduce, either verbally or in writing, the same knowledge that his instructor had dutifully presented. Many secondary schools and most of our universities still appear to cling to this basic model of instruction.

With the present and future explosion of knowledge, this former model of the teaching-learning process is inadequate. It is inadequate because much of that knowledge which high school students will need in their adult life does not yet exist. Thus present-day teachers cannot hope to rely solely on their personal fund of knowledge. As many have said, we must prepare students to learn that which we ourselves do not yet know.

The direction for a solution of this apparent teaching dilemma lies in the model of instruction employed. It is through transference of responsibility from teacher to student. Major emphasis will focus upon the learner, rather than the teacher. This instructional model wins liberation from the restrictions of teachers who must deal only with present knowledge. The emphasis is upon the learner's acquiring the skills by which learning itself is acquired rather than upon his attempting to master the teacher's present-day knowledge holdings.

Lest some contend that we have relegated teaching to an unimportant role, let us hasten to state that, under this model of teaching-learning, the role of teaching becomes vastly more complex. The teacher becomes the director of learning experiences for each student. In this role, he constantly leads students into greater depths of self-learning, self-motivation, and self-discipline. It means that the teacher strives for the goal of increased student competence in the acquisition of more knowledge, rather than the worn-out goal of repetitious demonstration of the teacher's own knowledge. It means greatly increased attention to the skills of knowledge building.

The implication for instructional materials which can be rather directly drawn from this transference of learning responsibility is that instructional materials themselves assume greater importance than ever before. If a learner is to increasingly seek out his own knowledge, he must correspondingly learn to employ the raw materials of knowledge building. These raw materials, as we have called them, are, of course, not only the familiar text and reference book but also many other kinds of stored information. Periodicals, statistical reports, newspapers, films, and tapes provide a fertile source for gathering knowledge. These materials must be accessible and retrievable, and the student must learn to assimilate and generalize from them.

Modern Technology and Instructional Materials

The third major force in the development of instructional materials is the rapid advancement of technical capabilities for collection, storage, and information retrieval. Anyone who has strolled through Convention Hall Associated Exhibitors' commercial displays at the annual American Association of School Administrators convention at Atlantic City, New Jersey, cannot fail to be impressed with the advance of modern technology and education. Here, it is claimed, is the most comprehensive educational materials exhibit assembled in one place anywhere in the world. The annual conference of the National Association of Secondary School Principals also presents a large instructional materials exhibit.

The National Defense Education Act stimulated the purchase of new instructional materials, and several trends can be observed in the new technology. First the traditional audio-visual devices are continually getting smaller and simpler to use. Gone are the days when the projector was a giant, complicated, unreliable monster. Today's devices are compact, easily portable, simple to operate, and almost completely reliable. In addition to the miniaturization of devices, there is increasing freedom from the necessity of the electric cord. More and more devices are run from cord-free transistors.

By means of electronics, another significant feature is already operational in many systems. This is an electronic system which provides a linkup from student to instructor with complete feedback capabilities. Systems such as these are available for use in subject areas other than the now-familiar language laboratory. By using a system like this, an instructor can proceed with a prepared lesson (this too may be programmed into a set of synchronized audio-visual devices) and be instantly aware of each student's response to certain learning cues.[5]

There are an increased number of instructional aids, devices, or models which demonstrate or illustrate principles and generalizations. More and more, these aids are being designed for student use instead of only for teacher demonstration.

Another electronic reality is a system enabling a student to dial a lesson. He may sit in a carrel in a library or instructional materials center and by using a dial similar to a telephone dial can actually select a tape or even a video lesson tape. Then, by means of earphones and a small video screen, he has a private and completely individual lesson.

Therefore, to handle the knowledge explosion, we are shifting our focus on the learning process, transferring the responsibility for learning from teacher to learner, and at the same time developing new technologies which have and can produce tools by which students can learn.

Flexibility of Organization and Instructional Materials

In order that the capabilities of new ways of learning through modern technology can be effectively utilized, a high degree of organization flexibility becomes mandatory. Neither students nor teachers can utilize the newer materials in a school which is rigidly organized into tight little compartments where there is slavish devotion to everyone's being in his proper place at the proper time.

The actual transference of the learning responsibility from teacher to student requires an organizational plan which allows students enough freedom and flexibility to take the learning initiative. It means that they must be able to move about the building at times other than on signal from the electronic clock. If self-learning devices are available, it means that students must be allowed to use them independently, without immediate and directed supervision. Students will need large blocks of time when they can pursue learning opportunities. Teachers must be able to resist the temptation to fill every class period to the brim with class content.

Organization for this model of instruction tends to move away from tight period scheduling. It may not be necessary to move to a complete modular scheduling (see Chapter 15) in order to move toward utilization of learning resources, but it is necessary to provide flexibility of student movement throughout the building and also to provide blocks of time when students can avail themselves of opportunities for independent study.

[5] For a simple and machineless application of this idea, see Ralph L. Spencer, "In the Game or Out of the Game? A Visual Answer," *New York State Mathematics Teachers Journal*, vol. 18, no. 2, April, 1968, pp. 68–69.

In addition, there must be flexibility of curriculum. This means that the curriculum requirements in terms of material to be covered must not be so full and specific that students are denied the opportunity for assuming the learning responsibility. When each segment of the curriculum is rigidly prescribed so that all the facts to be learned are neatly stored up in an outline, students will have no opportunity to acquire the experiences they need most if they are to practice the methodologies of learning. Teachers must have sufficient freedom to allow certain deviations from course guides so that this can take place.

Those who administer secondary schools can play a determining role in arranging the school environment so that full and effective utilization of learning materials can occur. The administrator's attitude toward learning is a key variable in the tone of the school. The tone of the school will become an important determinant of how successfully learning resources are used.

Also under the heading of organization are such questions as should there be an instructional materials center as well as a library? Or, is an instructional materials center part of a library? These questions shall be taken up later in this chapter.

THE SCHOOL LIBRARY

When, in 1964, former United States Commissioner of Education Francis Keppel called schools without libraries a "national disgrace," he was speaking principally about elementary schools.[6] The situation in secondary schools was markedly better in that over 90 percent of the nation's secondary schools had libraries.[7] Yet, in spite of this, collections were often meager, numbering only a few books per student; budgeted financial support for libraries was begrudgingly given; qualified librarians were in short supply; and perhaps most serious of all, the library was often only an administrative convenience as a place to put students when they didn't have anywhere else to go.

Current thinking awards a much higher place to school libraries than did patterns of prior times. The library should be the heart of the modern school. Occupying its new central role as the heart means that the library carries a major responsibility as an indispensable organ of learning. When the transference of the learning responsibility from teacher to student becomes implemented, dependence on an adequate library is mandatory. No longer can any school in any community claim to have an adequate program unless it can also demonstrate that it has an adequate library. No longer can any community display a mildly supportive attitude

[6] Francis Keppel, "Schools without Libraries: Our National Disgrace," McCalls, November, 1964.
[7] American Association of School Libraries, "The Good School Library," American Association of School Libraries, Chicago, n.d. (Mimeographed.)

toward the establishment of a school library, for not to provide an adequate level of financial support for school library service is not to provide an adequate level of support for its *basic* rather than supplementary program.

As the heart of a school, the library is a place of heavy utilization, for each hour of the school day and for many hours beyond. Its services will be in demand by all students, not just those who have time to look up extra projects. The school library to a large extent, claims a superintendent of schools, "can be considered as the pulse of the instructional program of the school." [8] Or, as another superintendent states, in speaking of library service, "A student deprived of good library service is a student deprived of good education." [9] In short, there is widespread agreement among educators that library service is no longer an auxiliary service about which a school district debates whether or not it can be afforded. If the school administrator holds a modern conception of the school library, he will do his utmost to convince those in the position of making financial decisions about the educational program that a full-sized library program is not only desirable but necessary. A full-sized library program means an adequate collection (both book and nonbook), an adequate physical setting, and an adequate staff.

The Collection

The collection consists of all those items held by the library which are part of the learning resources. As such, each item will be recorded in the card catalog. The library collection consists of two types of materials—book and nonbook.

The American Library Association recommends a basic collection of ten books per enrolled student, with a minimum number of 6,000 regardless of the size of school.[10] To keep the collection current, the standards recommend an annual budgeted allotment of from $4 to $6 per student, or one book per student enrolled. For the typical 1,000-student secondary school, this would mean, then, a collection of 10,000 volumes and planned budgetary purchases of 1,000 new books per year. The yearly addition of 1,000 new books does not automatically mean that the library must accommodate 15,000 volumes within 5 years. An allowance for loss, wear, and obsolescence will approach 8 to 9 percent, so that there is a much slower increase in the requirements for shelf space.

An important part of the basic book collection will be the various

[8] Homer O. Elseroad, "The Superintendent's Key Role in Improving School Libraries," *NASSP Bulletin*, no. 306, p. 1. January, 1966.
[9] Wesley F. Gibbs, "The School Library: An Administrator Speaks," School Activities and the Library, reprinted by American Library Association, Chicago, 1966.
[10] *Standards for School Library Programs*, American Library Association, American Association of School Librarians, Chicago, 1960.

types of reference material. The good secondary school library will have not only several different encyclopedias but will include numerous atlases, dictionaries, yearbooks, and reference sources of many types. The collection will include a wide range of magazine periodicals, preferably at least 70 titles for junior high schools and up to 120 for senior high schools. In order to serve student research purposes, back periodicals need to be retrievable. Whereas many school libraries secure binding services and then store their bound back issues in a storeroom, more efficient use of space is accomplished through microfilming. If this procedure is followed, then the library must be equipped with a microfilm reader.

The collection may also include paperback books. Although paperbacks have a limited circulation life, they bear strong reader appeal. The number of paperbacks published each year is rapidly increasing. Particularly encouraging is the growing number of high-quality paperbacks published for young people. The school library can guide youngsters in developing their paperback tastes and encourage their purchase. Since a good many youngsters have access to considerable amounts of spending money, it seems appropriate that the library could do its share in guiding students in making a wise choice of books for individual purchase.

The collection will include *nonbook* materials. These include virtually anything which is used as materials for learning other than the books themselves. Charts, maps, globes, films, filmstrips, transparencies, audiotapes, museum exhibits, and displays are all part of the nonbook collection.

As a part of its nonbook collection, the secondary library should include an extensive vertical file of current materials. These would be significant clippings and pictures taken from newspapers and magazine articles on current subjects. For these, subject categories are developed as they are needed. The vertical file is particularly useful for supplying current information on the rapidly changing world situation. Its purpose is to gather information on a timely topic which is more up-to-date than that found in published books.

One important shift in the concept of the modern library is the inclusion of audio-visual materials as a part of library holdings. It is often a point of dispute in schools as to whether the audio-visual materials should become a part of the library or retain their accustomed independence. The outcome of this argument should depend more on the physical limitations of the existing school than strictly on an idealized conception. Many existing libraries simply could not contain the audio-visual materials even if it should be determined that they should henceforth come under the supervision and control of the library. On the other hand, we would strongly recommend that audio-visual materials be considered as part of the nonbook items by which students can learn. When they are considered in this light, it means that students must have information and access to them. They must be able to find, for example, in the card catalog, references to a particular filmstrip on their topic and be able to independently retrieve it for private showing by means of a hand viewer or other convenient device.

Microfilm and a device called a microfilm reader are finding increasing use in secondary libraries. Programmed learning devices with appropriate programs will also become part of the nonbook resources. The key to the effective use of all these materials is to convince both teachers and students that these resources are suitable learning materials and to provide facilities so that students can use them on their own without immediate teacher direction or supervision. The Knapp School Libraries Project has demonstrated that this is indeed possible, not only for secondary students, but even for elementary students in the third or fourth grade.

The Knapp Foundation

Under a grant from the Knapp Foundation, the American Association of School Librarians launched the 5-year Knapp School Libraries Project.[11] The project consists of a few selected demonstration schools at widely separated geographical locations across the country. Initially, five elementary schools were chosen as demonstration schools in New York, Washington, Indiana, Maryland, and Texas. In 1965 the project selected three secondary schools as demonstration centers. The three were the Roosevelt High School of Portland, Oregon; the Farrer Junior High School of Provo, Utah; and the River Forest High School of Oak Park, Illinois. The demonstration schools were equipped with ideal collections and matching facilities and were completely staffed. A unique feature of the Knapp project was that interested school administrators, board of education members, and librarians could apply for travel grants for visitations to a demonstration school. If the applying district met the criteria for selection, it could thus receive reimbursement for the expenses of its visiting team. By the end of the 1966–1967 school year, thousands of visitors had witnessed firsthand what a difference in the life of a school a first-class library can make.[12]

The Library Quarters

A modern library program requires certain types of physical facilities. Although many secondary principals will not have the opportunity to play a major role in determining a completely new library, nevertheless,

---

[11] Peggy Sullivan, "The Knapp School Libraries Project," *NASSP Bulletin*, no. 306, pp. 82–88, January, 1966.
[12] One of the authors was privileged to participate in one of these demonstration visits.

it is important that they be aware of the physical facilities necessary to support the newer type of program.

The most important requirement is space. Formerly, libraries were built to accommodate seating for 10 percent of the student body. Thus the 1,000-student school would typically construct a library as one large rectangular space, large enough to put rectangular tables so that 100 students could sit and supposedly study at the same time. This concept of space requirement is no longer appropriate. The large-group study idea, which was really a study hall, has been replaced by an emphasis on individual and small-group study requirements. This means that there should be spaces for truly individual study, or carrels, where students can seek deep absorption in undistracted study. Writing in *The School Library: Facilities for Independent Study in the Secondary School,* Ellsworth and Wagener recommend that the library be built to accommodate 30 percent of the student body; and that 60 percent of this space be given to individual study carrels.[13] A secondary school library then for a school of 2,000 students would require 15,000 square feet of (based on 25 square feet per reader) floor space. With 60 percent of this space for individual study carrels, this would require 9,000 square feet.

The library facilities should also provide for small groups to meet and talk together. In order not to disturb the individual study spaces, these meeting rooms need to be soundproofed. Here, groups of five to seven students would be able to work around tables, freely conversing and moving about, performing whatever tasks their project requires.

In keeping with the emphasis on independent study and with the corresponding emphasis on the use of nonbook learning resources, the facilities should include provisions for the independent use of audiovisual materials. Some libraries may be planned so that separate rooms are used for listening and viewing, or some may contain library carrels which have built-in capabilities for viewing and listening. When these capabilities are combined with taped and programmed learning devices which can be retrieved by the student from within his carrel by means of a control dial, the student can be master of his own learning resources with fingertip control.

Especially important to the success of the library is its overall atmosphere. Its atmosphere should be one which beckons all who pass by to come in and seek learning. The use of carpeting for libraries has proved a great asset to producing the desired atmosphere. Comfortable lounge-type chairs and appealing display cases for materials contribute to this as well.

13 Ralph E. Ellsworth and Hobart D. Wagener, *The School Library: Facilities for Independent Study in the Secondary School,* Educational Facilities Laboratories, Inc., New York, 1965, p. 51.

The Library Staff

As with all dimensions of education, the quality of the staff is paramount to the success of the teaching-learning process. The American Library Association *Standards* recommends one librarian for every 300 students for the first 900.[14] Few present-day secondary schools match the recommendation. Ricking estimates that there is a need for at least 25,000 additional secondary school librarians.[15]

There is a critical shortage of trained librarians across the country for every type of library service—public school, public library, and university. As school administrators who work on staff recruitment know, school librarians are most difficult to find. So widespread and long-standing is this shortage that the American Library Association has opened an office for recruitment.

Part of the recruitment problem for school librarians is that the new dimensions of librarianship call for a special combination of qualifications. To adequately serve a modern secondary school library, a person should possess a broad liberal arts background as a base of knowledge. In addition, he must have acquired the necessary professional education courses to enable him to understand the teaching-learning process as well as curriculum. Added to these qualifications is professional library training, that is, training in specific technical knowledge such as reference materials and organization of libraries. And finally, and perhaps the most difficult requirement of all, there is the demand that school librarians have that special ability to work with people in cooperative relationships. The modern school library is a service to the entire school. The extent to which the librarians are able to convince their users of the worthwhileness of their service largely determines the value of the service—and this, in no small degree depends directly upon the librarian's skill at working with people. Gone is the day when those who pursued a library career were shy, retiring introverts who sought the quiet life as "keeper of the books." Today's school librarian must be able to savor the role as one of the key members of the staff, working with and through people in dynamic human relationships. Today's librarian would be able to sit with the school's Curriculum Coordinating Committee (if there is one, or any similar group) and make a contribution as one who can be on the frontier of learning materials. Such persons are relatively scarce.

Technical Assistance

One significant development in the personnel problem is the addition of library technicians and clerks to the staff. In the past, the prevailing

[14] American Library Association, *op. cit.*
[15] Myril Ricking, "Recruiting New Librarians for the Secondary School Level," *NASSP Bulletin*, no. 306, January, 1966, p. 59.

idea was that the librarian "herself" actually performed all the necessary work of the library. ("Herself" is deliberate since the stereotype of librarian is even more female than the teacher "herself" stereotype.) This included ordering, indexing, pasting, stenciling, filing, and typing—all important tasks necessary to the complex process of getting book from jobber to shelf.

Librarians would customarily organize a Library Club of students to help in this process, but by and large the overwhelming bulk of this work fell directly on the librarian. Some were fortunate enough to work with understanding principals who lent the school secretary's service upon occasion, but most had to doggedly perform their own clerical chores. This meant, of course, that librarians had to spend up to 50 percent of their time doing clerical work. They were actually overtrained for the job. Their real professional skills of book selection, reading guidance, and study skills were underused. A modern secondary library needs at least one full-time skilled clerk who can perform the many clerical tasks for operating a library. A more advanced clerk, with training in reference work and some college background, can serve more as a technician under the direction of the professional librarian.

Centralized Processing

Another significant development in the use of library personnel is what is termed centralized processing. When applied to an entire school district composed of a number of individual libraries, centralized processing means that all the activities of ordering, cataloging, and the physical preparation of books for library use are performed by the central center rather than by each individual library. A centralized processing system completely removes from each librarian all the technical and clerical aspects of book preparation. The individual school librarian may still retain the function of book selection for his particular school, but after that is done, he simply waits until the books arrive, ready to place on the shelves. The greatest advantage of this system is that it makes much more of the librarian's time available for direct service to students and teachers. It also represents a significant financial economy since the individual cost of processing is greatly reduced by the centralization process. Teachers, administrators, and especially the public fail to appreciate the time required to place a book in the library. The American Library Association estimates that it requires an average time of 10 minutes per item to catalog and classify a book, and this is only if the printed catalog cards are used which eliminates a card-typing job.[16] Multiply this 10 minutes by the number of new books to be added in a year (possibly 1,000 or more), and it is easy to see that a large amount of time will be required. Milbrey

[16] *Standards for School Library Programs*, p. 52.

L. Jones estimates that if a school has neither central processing nor clerical help, just the time required to process 500 books would take a librarian at least 30 days; [17] the significant point is that during this time, the school is deprived of professional library service.

For districts which do not have a centralized processing system, some find satisfactory service in the commercial processing services. In any event, for any school to consider that it has modern library service, it must have some method of acquiring its new-book collection which does not require that the professional librarian spend a major proportion of his time in the detailed performance of this task. Through centralized processing and through the employment of clerks and technicians, better use of human resources can be made so that the school can enjoy the indispensable benefits of efficient and effective library service.

THE INSTRUCTIONAL MATERIALS CENTER

Some modern secondary schools have instructional materials centers *as well as* libraries; and some have instructional materials centers *instead of* libraries; and of course, there are some that have *only* libraries. It is possible that each of these three types could have entirely adequate programs of instructional materials. What is the difference, one may rightly ask?

Nicholsen defines an instructional materials center "as a collection of print and nonprint materials and equipment so selected, arranged, located and staffed as to serve the needs of teachers and students to further the purposes of the school." [18] As one will immediately realize, this is not at all different from the concept of the library, which we have already presented, as a collection of book and nonbook materials. As early as 1956 the American Library Association adopted the following as its official statement of policy on this matter:

> The American Association of School Librarians believes that the School Library, in addition to doing its vital work of individual reading guidance and development of the school curriculum, should serve the school as a center for instructional materials. Instructional materials include books—the literature of children, young people and adults—other printed materials, films, recordings, and newer media developed to aid learning.[19]

If one were to accept these pronouncements as guiding statements, the conclusion that there really is no difference between a library and an

[17] Milbrey L. Jones, "Technical Services for School Libraries," *NASSP Bulletin*, no. 306, pp. 52–58, January, 1966.

[18] Margaret E. Nicholsen, "The I.M.C.," Reprint by American Library Association from *School Libraries*, March, 1964.

[19] Official Statement distributed by American Association of School Librarians, American Library Association, Chicago, established at Miami Beach, June 21, 1956.

instructional materials center becomes inescapable. Of course, the key to resolving differences is in the varying concepts held of the library, or book part of instructional materials, and the nonbook sector of instructional materials. The debate wages sharpest around the housing, control, and maintenance of audio-visual materials.

In school libraries whose main emphasis is upon the book collection, there may be strong feelings against the inclusion of audio-visual materials as a portion of the library. School librarians may, with genuine justification, complain that they couldn't possibly supervise the distribution of the films, filmstrips, records, tapes, and all the necessary accompanying electronic equipment. They hardly have time and space for their books, as it is. If there is an audio-visual room staffed by a technician for maintenance and supervised by a staff member, it is quite likely that these personnel may feel reluctant to lose their autonomous operation to come under the wing of the library. What, then, is a way of resolving this problem of two functions, whose basic purposes are both to facilitate the instructional program?

Resolving the Dilemma

The solution to the dilemma outlined above is more a matter of adapting to present realities and less a matter of argument over libraries versus instructional materials centers.

If new construction is to be planned, this is, of course, the ideal opportunity to work out the problem in advance. Those involved in the planning (and hopefully this will include teachers, students, librarians, and principals, as well as architects and the school board) should envisage facilities to match program. If they adopt the modern philosophy of instructional materials, they can recommend facilities which will incorporate book and nonbook materials. What matters is not so much whether it is called a library, an instructional materials center, a resources center, or an independent study center as what learning concepts are being advanced.

If a secondary school already has a well-equipped library in the traditional sense and also has an effectively operating audio-visual center, it may serve the school's best interests to simply bolster each and allow them to retain their independence. Hopefully, as time goes on, these two functions will realize their need to cooperate and coordinate their services. One simple first step in this situation could be the cataloging of audio-visual holdings in the library card catalog, so that students will at least become aware that here is another source of learning materials on certain topics.

Other secondary schools may be able to make major renovations or alterations within existing building structures to incorporate an enlarged concept of a school library. One of the authors is familiar with a junior high school where this occurred with excellent results. In this 600-student school, there had been only a very small traditional library, which could seat about 25 students around rectangular tables. Located on the second floor and housing about 5,000 volumes jammed into crowded shelves, this library was seriously hampering the advancement of the school. Through the leadership efforts of the school principal, a librarian, and the supporting central administration, this school was able to convince the board of education of the necessity of a modern library program.

Through a significant alteration project, the school now has twice as much seating space as before, 8,000 volumes easily and attractively shelved, individual study carrels, listening posts for audio-visual materials, and an enticing atmosphere produced by carpeting. Most significant of all, the library is used much more than before by the students and staff. It is on its way to becoming the heart of this school. In many similar situations, it would surely be possible for administrators and librarians, working with an enlightened board of education, to significantly alter the concept of its library facilities and service—and it doesn't really matter whether they choose to call their enlarged center a library or an instructional materials center.

WHAT THE PRINCIPAL CAN DO

A recurring theme throughout this book is that the secondary principalship is a key leadership position. As such, the principal is able to make his presence felt throughout the school in many ways—ways which will make a significant difference in the instructional program. And so it is with instructional materials. What the principal says and does about these resources for learning makes a big difference in the school.

Setting the Tone

The most important thing the principal can do about proper use of learning materials is to establish a tone which will lead to their use. As we said at the beginning of this chapter, the underlying philosophy concerning instructional materials has changed greatly. The principal who exhibits an understanding of the nature of the knowledge explosion, of the shift in the responsibility from teacher to learner, and of modern instructional technology will be able to transmit some of this viewpoint to his staff. We have used the word "some" in recognition of the reality that most school faculties contain some staff members who do not, and probably can never, share many of these ideas on modern knowledge assimilation. Yet unless the principal does actively support a modern program, there is little chance that the staff will be able to make effective use of some of the newer learning resources.

Textbooks and Their Selection

The textbook remains the most widely used instructional device. Although what is called "textbook teaching" has been discredited by some, when wisely used, the textbook retains its rightful place in the secondary school. Like any workman's tool, the teacher's chief tool, the textbook, can be badly used. It can be misused as an excuse for poor lesson planning. It can be misused as a confining straitjacket prohibiting creative teaching. And it can be misused when it is held up as the final and complete book of knowledge on any subject. But in spite of these common and valid objections, there is no reason to throw away the book.

As the instructional leader of the school, the principal can be instrumental in assisting staff members to see the textbook as one aid to learning. In any given area, the textbook is written as a convenient and systematic coverage of one phase of knowledge. It has the further advantage of being written by experts who, although not infallible, have set their words down with great and systematic care, and a publisher has invested large sums of money for its publication.

In the selection of textbooks the secondary administrator can also exercise his leadership. Of course, a great deal will depend upon the state and local board options in this matter. Legally speaking, the right of textbook selection rests with the people of the state. This is generally exercised through local boards of education, although in some cases it may even be expressed through state statutes which mandate a state-approved textbook list.

Where the option remains with the local board, it will depend upon the professional staff for their textbook recommendations. In this fashion, textbook selection will normally flow downward through the district to the school, and the principal can work with his staff on this problem.

An effective way of working on textbook selection is for the secondary administrator to establish a selection committee. Either within a single school or across an entire district, this committee can be charged with the responsibility for presenting a recommendation for school or district adoption of a textbook. The administrator's role can be advisory to this committee. He can be most instrumental in helping the group develop criteria for adequate textbook selection, rather than in exercising direct influence over the particular selection itself. Once the textbook committee arrives at its recommendation, implementation becomes an administrative responsibility which is referred to the appropriate administrative channel; that is, either approval by the board of education or approval by the superintendent, or both.

An important portion of administrative responsibility for textbooks as instructional materials is the development of efficient inventory control procedures. Since this is really a matter of office management, this aspect will not be discussed here. Still, it should be recognized that a workable system for the management of textbooks, as well as all instructional materials, is an important administrative responsibility.

Support Instructional Materials Personnel

The principal can contribute significantly to the effective use of instructional materials in his school through his support of all personnel whose major responsibilities are in that area. These may be professional librarians, library assistants, library technicians, audio-visual specialists or technicians, and any others whose jobs include managing or directing instructional materials. "Support" in this context means clearly understanding these persons' jobs within the school and helping other staff members gain wider understanding of those jobs. This kind of support lets the instructional materials personnel know that their principal understands their job and wants others to understand it also. One specific help in accomplishing this is to provide time at a faculty meeting where instructional materials specialists can explain their goals in the instructional program.

Seek Adequate Financial Support

In a very real sense, the principal can be instrumental in securing adequate financial support for instructional materials of all types. In most schools, the principal bears the responsibility for submission of a tentative budget to the superintendent's office. Although it is true that many school districts operate a budget procedure which removes most of the power from the individual school administrator, many more operate on systems which allow the principal the freedom to submit his school's requests based on the particular needs of an actual program as he sees it.

If the principal is convinced of the value of a modern instructional materials program, he can expect to be much more effective in defending his requests for adequate financial support.

In support of adequate funds for library books, the principal can resist the well-intentioned but misguided attempts of parent-teacher organizations to "help out" the library. Many schools' library collections have unquestionably been helped by voluntary fund-raising efforts. As laudable as these efforts are, it is our opinion, at least, that they are self-defeating in the long run and detrimental to the interests of building an adequate level of financial support. By depending on or even encouraging fund drives for library books, a school administration admits that library books are desirable but not really essential for the program. As such, they inevitably become identified in the public mind as optional parts of the program, not worthy of tax support, but as luxuries to be purchased through private funds. The private support of libraries completely denies the use of the library as an essential teaching tool and flies in the face of a modern concept of learning.

Be Aware of Federal Legislation

The secondary administrator can exercise his leadership through keeping informed on various sections of federal legislation which enable him to add to the collection of instructional materials. The National Defense Education Act and the subsequent revisions have enabled schools to purchase on a matching-grant basis many instructional materials for use in mathematics, science, guidance, and foreign languages. The Vocational Education Act of 1963 and the Economic Opportunity Act of 1964 have been used to some extent to strengthen school libraries and instructional materials.

It was not until the Elementary and Secondary Education Act of 1965 that school libraries and school library service became eligible for federal aid. Title II of this act (89-10) deals most directly with school libraries. As Milbrey L. Jones, School Library Specialist with the U.S. Office of Education, points out, "The opportunity is also available to all school libraries to become instructional materials centers in the very richest sense, making materials of all types available in the library, as well as throughout the school." [20]

Many of these federal acts provide exceptional opportunities for creative programs adjusted to local needs. The secondary administrator aware of these acts may be able to participate in the design and administration of a local program to materially assist a major upgrading of the instructional materials program.

Protection from Controversy Charges

In spite of the intense devotion to many kinds of "freedom," many of our educational institutions have been subject to repeated attempts by various pressure groups to suppress some types of historically cherished freedoms. This type of pressure frequently strikes directly at the public school library by attempts to censor reading materials. At the secondary level, there are often vituperative charges leveled against teachers and administrators for allowing students to choose to read certain selections of literature. As Georgia Cole points out, such literary works as *Huckleberry Finn, Catcher in the Rye, Lord of the Flies, To Kill a Mockingbird,*

[20] Milbrey L. Jones, "Libraries and the 1965 Education Act," *The American School Board Journal,* vol. 151, no. 5, p. 23, November, 1965.

and innumerable other recognized works, from time to time have been subjected to attempts at restriction.[21]

The strong secondary administrator can render a real service to his teachers and librarians by rising to their defense in times of attack. As in military or athletic strategy, the best defense is often a good offense; so in handling controversy, the strongest method is to have a policy worked out in advance of the controversy's eruption. The policy would include method of book selection as well as procedures for handling complaints. Both the National Council of Teachers of English and the American Library Association have helpful materials on this matter. A principal is on much sounder ground attempting to defend the right of the professional to choose appropriate materials, backed up by a supporting policy from the board of education, than he is attempting to debate whether or not some piece of literature is suitable for secondary students.[22]

Provide a Professional Collection

A principal can work toward providing an adequate professional collection as a part of the library or instructional materials holdings. Whether these books, journals, reference materials, and sample texts are housed in the library itself or in a separate curriculum center or even as a part of a faculty lounge is a matter probably best left to be determined by the space available and the desires of the professional staff.

As the instructional leader of his school, the secondary principal can play a major role in seeing that a good collection of professional journals is on hand for teacher reference. He can ensure that adequate funds are budgeted for annual purchases of significant new books in the field. Of course, it is unrealistic to expect that each individual school will have a full professional library with collections numbering in the thousands. Still the *Standards for School Library Programs* of the American Library Association recommends a minimum basic book collection of 200 titles with a minimum of 25 professional journals. Even where there is a district curriculum library or full professional library, each school needs its own minimum professional collection.

The principal and the librarian can provide the leadership in the selection of timely materials, but they can be assisted by teachers or teacher committees. A good way of encouraging faculty use of professional materials is to involve the faculty in the selection of materials which they feel are useful to them in their work.

[21] Georgia Cole, "Controversial Areas in Library Materials," *NASSP Bulletin*, no. 306, pp. 31–36, January, 1966.
[22] Sources of information and materials useful are the following: American Library Association, Chicago; National Council of Teachers of English, Champaign, Ill.; National Education Association, Commission on Professional Rights and Responsibilities, Washington, D.C.

SUMMARY

The underlying philosophy of instructional materials is built in recognition of three facts of modern education. First, the knowledge explosion has made knowledge assimilation for any one person a major problem. Choices must be made as to what knowledge can and should be learned since one clearly can't master all or even one small segment of it. At the same time, each of us has to, in some way, come to terms with the facts of the knowledge explosion.

Second, modern education is shifting emphasis from teacher to learner. Teachers no longer attempt to give, pour out, provide, furnish, or supply the student with his knowledge. It is rather that the teacher has a special role to play in helping the learner learn the methods and tools of inquiry itself.

Third, modern technology is making it possible to capitalize on these first two facts and develop new instructional materials. These materials will greatly assist the learner to acquire the skills of knowledge building.

A school library or instructional materials center is an integral part of the learning environment which the alert secondary administrator attempts to create. In this context the library should be fully supported from public funds, just like textbooks or teachers salaries.

One of the key determinants of the type of instructional materials program any single school will have is the quality of leadership shown by the secondary principal. Since the newer image of libraries and instructional materials is not yet widely held, he can play a major role in creating planned change in the facilities, materials, staff, and usage of his school's instructional materials.

SUGGESTED EXERCISES

1. Design an actual survey of a school library service within a secondary school. Secure data on the size and type of collection and its circulation. Include information on the extent of student and faculty use. Make recommendations for improvement of library service.

2. Make a listing of nonprofessional tasks possible in instructional materials service. Include a description of the type of nonprofessional person who could do these tasks.

3. Interview several librarians from different schools. Elicit their attitudes toward the use of the library as an instructional materials center, including the storage and control of audio-visual materials.

4. Hold a class discussion on the educational implications of "the knowledge explosion."

5. Find case histories of schools which have become embroiled in heated controversy on the issue of public censorship of books. See whether they had a policy on this matter prior to the episode.

SELECTED REFERENCES

American Association of School Librarians, *Standards for School Library Programs,* American Library Association, Chicago, 1960.
American Association of School Librarians, "The Role of School Administrators in School Library Development," American Library Association, Chicago, 1962. (Mimeographed.)
ELLSWORTH, RALPH E., AND HOBART D. WAGENER, *The School Library: Facilities for Independent Study in the Secondary School,* Educational Facilities Laboratories, Inc., New York, 1965.
"Libraries in Secondary Schools: A New Look," *NASSP Bulletin,* no. 306, January, 1966.
"Special Report: School Libraries," *American School Board Journal,* vol. 151, no. 5, November, 1965.
U.S. Office of Education, "Library Research in Progress: 1959–64," U.S. Department of Health, Education and Welfare, no. 14, OE-15005014.

14

NONCLASSROOM
EDUCATIONAL
ACTIVITIES | One widely recognized characteristic of
the American public secondary schools is their attention to activities
which are deemed educational and which take place within the jurisdiction of the school, yet which occur primarily outside the classroom. These
activities are a constant reminder that there is more to school than the
regular round of classes.

This chapter intends to give its attention to this universal practice in
the secondary schools of the United States. For those who would administer secondary schools, it is important that they understand the function
of nonclassroom educational activities within the school and that they
learn how to utilize some general guidelines in administering a full
program.

WHY NONCLASSROOM ACTIVITIES?

A prerequisite to administering any phase of a secondary education
program is an understanding of its purpose and function. The choice of
the term "nonclassroom" to describe what are often called extracurricular,

cocurricular, extraclass, or out-of-class activities is deliberate. The old debate as to whether such activities are actually a part of the curriculum and therefore cocurricular or whether they are seen as optional additions to the curriculum and therefore extracurricular seems no longer relevant.

That secondary schools shall sponsor and maintain a wide range of activities is no longer seriously controversial. However, we would hasten to add, although there is no real controversy over whether or not the school shall have student activities, there often arise serious problems connected with the school's sponsorship of some of these activities.

For the purpose of this book, *nonclassroom educational activities* are those identifiable programs sponsored by the school for the educational benefit of its students, which occur adjacent to but separate from regular curriculum offerings. The use of the terms "adjacent" and "separate" is an effort to furnish nonclassroom activities with legitimacy and at the same time recognize that they function apart from the classroom program.

This concept recognizes that the entire school experience influences the student. Nonclassroom educational activities are a special group of programs which function to provide the student with channels whereby he can express his talents and interests within a sanctioned social environment in company with his peers. Activity programs support and reinforce the purposes of the school.

Nonclassroom activities furnish students with healthy outlets for constructive activity. Adolescent youngsters need opportunities to do something specific, substantive, and intrinsically interesting to them. Ideally, the entire curriculum program would fit these requirements. However, it seems a long way from reality to expect that the regular program can adequately fulfill these needs, even in the best schools. An adequate but succinct answer to the question why nonclassroom educational activities? is that, first, they complement the regular (or classroom) program, and second, they fill genuine student needs. Therefore, the school which offers a broad spectrum of nonclassroom educational activities can do a better job than one that has fewer of them.

PRINCIPLES OF NONCLASSROOM ACTIVITIES

Miller, Moyer, and Patrick present a fourfold classification of the general functions of cocurricular activities.[1] They see activities capable of classification in terms of for whom they function. They list "contributions to students," "contributions to more effective school administration," "contributions to curriculum improvement," and "contributions to the community." While all activities could be viewed (and probably should be) from the point of view of what they can and will do for the student, it is useful to think that these contributions can be made through various

[1] Franklin A. Miller, James H. Moyer, and Robert B. Patrick, *Planning Student Activities*, Prentice-Hall, Inc., Englewood Cliffs, N.J., 1956, pp. 13–26.

ways. The paramount point of departure is the individual student. All other functions subsume this one.

Activities Should Be Related to School Purposes

As a guiding principle, this means that each activity that is sponsored by the school must be able to be justified on the grounds that it is meaningfully related to one or more identifiable school purposes. The school concert band can be justified because it is directly related to the school's purpose of providing opportunity for students to participate in an enriching, aesthetic experience. It may also provide some students with an element of vocational guidance; that is, those musically talented students may find a possible career interest in music. It also provides an opportunity for students to receive peer and adult recognition for different abilities; that is, for some students the concert band may be the only area of school life in which they can excel.

The task of the secondary administrator is to be able to understand and help others understand the place of each activity in the total program and thereby make the link between the school's purpose and the activity.

Activities Should Be Built upon Genuine Student Interests

Even though the needs of youth are of primary importance, schools are adult-designed places. Society's adults decide what it is that youth must be taught, how youth must be taught, how youth must behave, when youth must attend, and what precise educational experiences youth must undergo. Hopefully, adults are wise and cognizant of genuine youth interests. However, it is easily recognized that adult ideas of youth's needs and youth's ideas of their own needs are frequently incongruent.[2]

It is through the nonclassroom educational activities program that genuine youth interests can be served. This does not mean that the school must sponsor every passing student fad as an activity. It does mean though that the criterion of interest must be applied as an operating principle. A ham radio club activity is good only as long as there are interested students. Activities will rise and fall over the years. This principle does not negate the value of some interested faculty member's promoting some new club. But if he is not successful in generating student interest, the activity will and should be allowed to gracefully die out.

Activities Must Be Controlled by the School

If an activity is to be sponsored by the school, it must be controlled by the school. Control, in this sense, means not only that there is official sanction for the activity but that it operates under professional super-

---

[2] Wayne C. Gordon, *The Social System of a High School*, The Free Press of Glencoe, New York, 1957; also James S. Coleman, *The Adolescent Society*, The Free Press of Glencoe, New York, 1961.

vision. The football team, therefore, remains under the control of the school, not under control of a local athletic booster club. Decisions about teams to be played, policies concerning who shall play, and who shall coach are educational decisions to be made by school authorities.

This consideration is especially important from the legal point of view. For any activity which the school sponsors, it assumes legal liability. In order to guard itself against the possibility of incurring liability in the event of accident, the school must demonstrate that it has taken all reasonable and prudent precautions. One fundamental precaution for any school activity is that the personnel in charge are officially and legally trained and qualified to supervise students. This concept applies even in states where the school district is legally exempt from liability suit since teachers themselves can become victims of personal negligence suits. The best protection is official sponsorship and professional supervision of all activities.

Application of this principle to activities does not prevent responsible community organizations from serving other youth interests. A community organization can provide a basketball league using the school evenings, or any number of organizations can also serve youth needs by using the school facilities. The critical difference is sponsorship. In allowing nonschool organizations use of the school for youth-serving purposes, the school's responsibility is to see that this use is in conformity with existing state law and local board policy and that the local organization is legitimate and responsible.

Activities Should Be Open to All

In order that nonclassroom educational activities serve the needs of youth and relate directly to supplement the purposes of the school, it logically follows that they should be open to all.

In applying this principle within a secondary school, the criterion becomes extent of participation by the entire student body rather than extent of participation by one segment of the student body. Applying this principle means that students are prohibited from participation only by requirements indigenous to that activity. That is, one cannot participate in the orchestra unless he can play an instrument. One cannot join the girls' chorus unless she is a girl and can sing. One cannot (and should not) be elected to membership in the National Honor Society with a poor academic record. Application of this "openness" principle means that all are eligible to win the privilege of participation, even in those activities requiring special talents.

Applying the principle of openness means that activities should be scheduled at a time which makes it possible for all students to attend. Where students are bussed to school, many activities must be scheduled during the regular school day, or if some are scheduled after school hours, bus transportation should be provided for those requiring this service. In other words, where a student lives must not determine whether or not he can participate in nonclassroom activities.

Activities Should Be Financially Supported

Acceptance of the previously mentioned principles mandates acceptance of the principle that nonclassroom educational activities should be financially supported by regular school district funds. If the activities are related to the school's purposes and are officially sponsored and organized by the school, it follows that the finances necessary for their accomplishment come from school district funds.

Adherence to this principle also helps maintain the principle of openness; that is, this aids in preventing a student's economic circumstances from determining his eligibility to participate. If costs are to be imposed directly on students for some necessary materials, they should be nominal and, then, only for the value of teaching the student proper care or respect for the item he has purchased. Otherwise, the result is a quasi-private school arrangement, in which students (their parents, actually) pay for privileges. This denies a fundamental concept of the American public school.

As fundamental as this is, this principle is often violated. Students are frequently offered a nonclassroom educational activity—at a price. Bowling at the local lane as a school-sponsored club activity would be an example, where students frequently pay for their weekly bowling. Even though the cost is reduced for students, this factor eliminates some students from participation. This, therefore, denies the principle of being open to all.

Application of this principle has implications beyond the immediate concern of the internal operation of the school. Applying the principle of regular financial support means that the staff members will receive compensation for their work. Often many parts of the activity program are actually supported by the efforts of teachers themselves. They willingly give their professional time for the sake of furthering the school's program. On the other hand, with the marked trend toward teacher organizations which bargain over conditions of work, teachers may become less willing to accept what they consider as extra duties without appropriate compensation.

Although it is counter to current trends, the best long-run policy on teacher compensation for nonclassroom activities would seem to be their inclusion as a part of the regular teaching load. This, of course, denies the concept of extra pay for extra work. But, the extra pay for extra work idea runs counter to the inclusion of nonclassroom activities as a basic part of the teacher's job description. Justification for such a position is secured on the grounds that if the activity is worthwhile enough for the school to officially sponsor and if it requires the guidance of a professional person, then it is therefore worthy of acceptance as a part of the teacher's job—without extra compensation. Although this could be considered a backward step by some teachers who have fought hard for compensation for worthwhile services they had previously furnished free, we submit that it would ultimately benefit teachers—and the educational program. With the possible exception of major sports in the senior high schools (principally football and basketball), most teacher compensation for extraclassroom educational duties is minimal and hardly equivalent to what might be considered professional compensation. Actually, a compensation of $50 to $100 for some activity requiring 50 hours of extra work is simply baby-sitting money.

TYPES OF ACTIVITIES

Six types of nonclassroom educational activities will be discussed: athletic activities, student council activities, club programs, social and assembly-type activities, community-related activities, and performing activities. Each type could be afforded an extended treatment. However, our purpose is to sketch briefly the highlights of administering these activities within the secondary school.

Athletics

Athletics is a legitimate part of a sound physical education program.[3] Within the context of nonclassroom educational activities we consider athletics as sports and game activities which take place beyond the regularly scheduled curriculum program in physical education. This includes intramural athletics, that is, those sports and games taking place within the school itself which are an outgrowth of the regular program; intermural (or sometimes called "extramural" athletics), that is, those intramural types of activities which occur between two or more schools; and the third type is the familiar interscholastic athletics, which are the highly organized team sports with established leagues. Each type of athletics has its legitimate place in the secondary school athletic program.

For the administration of nonclassroom educational activities the area of athletics often presents the secondary administrator with his greatest personal challenge. He has the challenge of threading the course between seeking a winning team in the interscholastic league and constraining athletics to its proper place within the total school. He has the challenge of promoting the goal of wide participation versus the goal of narrow development of star teams.

A constant problem area for secondary administration is to capitalize on the tremendous appeal athletics has for secondary youngsters while at

[3] Jesse F. Williams, *The Principles of Physical Education*, W. B. Saunders Company, Philadelphia, 1964, pp. 318–366.

the same time preventing this appeal from having a deleterious effect on the entire program. Coleman reports that high school athletics plays a dominant role in the status and reward system in American high schools.[4] Athletics can easily crowd out the school's intellectual interests. As a part of a study of the secondary school principalship, approximately 16,000 senior high principals were asked to indicate factors which they considered "roadblocks" hindering them from doing the job they would like to do. Fifty-one percent of the respondents to this item checked "Athletic-minded persons (especially alumni)," as one alternative roadblock.[5]

Interscholastic athletics can easily usurp the resources of a good physical education program. Overemphasis on league play in the major sports can produce championships, but it can also produce a poor physical education program in which coaches spend their time and energies with a small minority of the athletically gifted boys of the school. In England, by contrast, there is widespread support and encouragement for athletics among secondary schools, yet the goal is widespread participation rather than highly organized league play.[6]

While seeking a reasonable balance in athletic activities within his school, the secondary administrator should recognize the functions that interscholastic athletics play within the school and the community. As perceptive observers of secondary education realize, and as Coleman has clearly shown, the high school athletic program provides students with a collective goal and a sense of belonging about which they can center their immediate life interests.[7] The athletic program and its concomitant activities probably also function to keep many youth in school who would otherwise find their attendance completely without purpose.

To many communities, the local high school athletic teams provide a rallying point for community pride and loyalty. While the abuses of this spirit are too well known to require elaboration, the secondary administrator needs to recognize these frequently powerful forces operating in so many communities.

Student Council Activities

Student council activities furnish one excellent opportunity for secondary schools to create a workshop in democracy. Most secondary schools have organized some form of activity wherein the students themselves share in some aspect of decision making. The range of shared decision making is great, from practically none to a significant amount. The variability in role of student council organizations can probably be accounted

[4] James S. Coleman, *Adolescents and the Schools*, Basic Books, Inc., Publishers, New York, 1965, chap. 3, pp. 35–51.

[5] John K. Hemphill, James M. Richards, and Richard E. Peterson, *Report of the Senior High-School Principalship*, The National Association of Secondary School Principals, Washington, D.C., 1965, p. 87.

[6] George Baron, *Society Schools and Progress in England*, Pergamon Press, New York, 1965, p. 40.

[7] Coleman, *op. cit.*, p. 48.

for by the difference in philosophy. If the school is dominated by the philosophy which recognizes the wisdom of soliciting student opinions but which feels no accompanying responsibility to account for them in any viable method, then the student council organization's function will be limited to that of sounding board for student opinions. On the other hand, should the dominant philosophy see students as capable of worthy participation in self-government through actual participation in matters important to them, then the council organization is more likely to encompass broader functions.

Miller, Moyer, and Patrick differentiate between the "student council" and the "school council." [8] They see the former as developing first for the primary purpose of providing a means for students to practice leadership skills. The school council approach, which they see with greater favor, conceives of the council as having a broader function which includes that of sharing in important aspects of decision making.

For the secondary administrator, the more important point is that he work toward establishing a student organization whose purpose and function is clearly understood by the whole school.

Club Programs

A club program within a secondary school is critically dependent upon student interest. In fact, of the principles presented earlier in this chapter, club development depends most of all upon genuine student interest. There is no compelling reason why a school has to have any clubs at all, unless students want them.

Clubs, therefore, are optional fringes to the nonclassroom educational activities program. After so labeling them in cavalier fashion, we would hasten to add that they nonetheless can make an important contribution to the atmosphere of a school. For example, the authors know of a secondary school which sponsored a radio club. Under the direction of an able and interested faculty member, and with the excellent cooperation of a local radio station, this radio club provided a worthwhile activity for twenty to thirty high school youth. Not only did this provide a worthwhile activity worthy in its own right, but in this particular case it served a career guidance function for several young men who entered the radio broadcasting field directly upon completing high school. This program, unfortunately, is no longer operating because the teacher who directed it left the area and a suitable replacement has not been found.

This points up the other crucial requirement of a club program—that faculty sponsors be found. Hopefully, the administrator can bring together matching groups of interested students with a willing and interested teacher.

---

[8] Miller, Moyer, and Patrick, *op. cit.*, p. 216.

Social and Assembly-type Activities

As all of us know, who have been through an American high school, parties, dances, assemblies, and special occasions are often remembered with fond recollections. In these days of increased pressure on students to perform well academically, it is easy to lose sight of the great meaning students attach to these events. Adolescents need legitimate activities where they can socialize with one another. It seems better that the school sponsor and control these activities rather than discourage them and thereby drive them underground.

Again, it is a question of balance. The administrator of a secondary school will exercise his leadership to determine a reasonable balance between various kinds of social activities.

Although fewer and fewer secondary schools are being built with an auditorium with seating capacity for the entire student body, the school assembly still retains its worthwhile place. It furnishes an appropriate forum for many and varied activities, not only to build school spirit, but to augment and supplement the curriculum program.

Community-related Activities

Another common type of nonclassroom educational activity is what we have termed community-related activities. We have elected this term in order to stress the aspect of community relationship. This includes many kinds of contests, drives, and special projects in which, although the school may be a willing participant, some element of the community (or the larger community, in some cases) has a special interest. In this category would fall such things as an essay contest sponsored by a patriotic or veterans group, a poster contest promoting the value of drinking milk sponsored, of course, by the dairy interests, school savings programs conducted through a local bank, or a program to help the local March of Dimes campaign. Every American school receives numerous requests from representatives of a myriad of outside interests that the school participate directly. Smaller schools in smaller communities are especially prone to influences of this type, for the school may be the largest social institution in the community.

Contests, fund drives, and the like can contribute to the life of the school and the life of the community in meaningful ways. However, a large caution flag should be waved at this point. Such activities can also sap off valuable student and faculty time for projects contributing little to the school's purpose. Not only is there need to be wary of student and teacher time for these projects, there is the larger issue of commercialism in the schools.[9] When banks urge the schools to initiate a school thrift

[9] For a publication devoted entirely to this theme see *Theory into Practice*, "Commercial Pressures in Schools," vol. 4, no. 5, December, 1965, The Ohio State University, Columbus, Ohio.

program, they are likely to play up the educational lessons of thrift and play down the fact that they are asking for permission to use the public school as an accessory to private enterprise advertising. This type of activity is usually thrust upon the school by some special group which has some particular cause to champion. The school may, indeed, wish to join in championing the same cause, but the decision should be left to the school.

The school administrator's best protection against an onslaught of requests for teacher and student involvement in assorted community projects is a policy statement by the board of education. Like all policies, it needs to be a guide for action rather than a set of arbitrary rules. Such a statement can bulwark the school's position in avoiding the diffusion of its energies on peripheral projects.

There are worthwhile community-related activities which can contribute to enhancing the life of the school and matching with the schools' educational purposes, and these should be encouraged. The point is, though, that this determination is made by the proper school authorities rather than through persuasions of local pressure groups.

Performing Activities

The listing of performing activities as an additional type of nonclass-room educational activity is, from one point of view, redundant. Many of the types of activities already discussed can be considered performing activities. The football team, the school band, the debating club, the school science fair, all may contain the common element that they are performed in front of the local public. The primary reason for including this as a separate category is to make the point that it becomes all too easy for communities to come to expect that public performance is the goal of some school activities.

There is no question that the American public, and parents in particular, enjoy and want to see their children publicly perform a skill the school has taught them. Parent-teacher organizations recognize that the one unfailing technique of getting parents into a school building is to lure them with a student performance. As commendable as this tendency is, school administrators need to play the watchdog role in order that the demands of public performance do not outweigh the educational value of the activity.

As has already been made clear from the discussion of high school athletics, this problem is especially acute. Marching bands, too, often become victims to the expectations of public performance. The community may expect the band director and students, at the simple behest of a phone call, to give up a school holiday in order to march in the local parade. The school principal should be able to mediate demands for community performances with educational values.

THE PRINCIPAL'S ROLE IN NONCLASSROOM ACTIVITIES

At this point consideration will be given to the part the principal can play in administering this phase of the total educational enterprise. In turn, we shall examine how the principal (or his assistants) can function through the areas of (1) support, (2) staffing, (3) supervision and control, (4) fiscal accounting, and (5) evaluation.

Support

As he does in nearly every phase of the operation of the school, the modern secondary principal lends support to the area of nonclassroom educational activities. "Support" in this sense connotes that he seeks to maintain each part of this program so that the program has a chance to accomplish its legitimate objectives. Teachers who sponsor musical activities, athletic activities, school publications, cheerleaders, etc., are all very much aware of the presence or absence of principal support. The problem a principal may have is not to oversupport some types and undersupport others, in reflection of his own background and prior experience with some types of activities.

Support by the secondary principal takes the form of exhibiting personal attention to and interest in each of the student activities. Some principals, particularly in smaller communities, are likely to feel that they must personally attend every athletic event, every concert, every play, and every dance. Although this is one evidence of support, it is also unnecessary. It is appropriate that the principal or his assistant attend some of these functions, but he need not develop the feeling that his attendance is essential for the sake of either the community at large or the student body itself. The principal who feels he must attend every function in order to ensure that "things will go well," either has an inflated notion of his own importance to the school or else is promoting excessive paternalistic dependence. The inevitable result is that such an administrator will neglect other phases of his job because he won't have time and energy for them.

Principals can support the nonclassroom educational program by lending the weight of administrative authority to the program at certain key times. For example, the authors recall a situation wherein the high school held an annual spring musical concert. While the principal gave nominal support for this program, he failed to understand support in another way. In addition to the expected extra work in preparing for the concert program, each year the music teachers had to personally arrange the stage, set up the chairs, and make all the physical arrangements. It would have been a simple matter for the principal to make extra custodial help available during the necessary hours for these tasks; yet this help never came. The music teachers were made to feel that anything connected with this program was their own personal responsibility.

Principal support, therefore, can be keenly felt by those charged with supervising activities. Principals can indicate support in many ways, from attendance to seeking financial support through budgeted funds.

Staffing

In all phases of administrative activity, staffing is a vital function. The principal can play a determining role in matching the needs of the activity programs to individual faculty interests. One useful device for helping bring this about is maintaining a resources file as a part of the principal's personnel records. In large secondary schools with professional staffs of more than one hundred, it becomes difficult for a principal to know each staff member's possible areas of interest. The teacher's ability and interest in extra-educational activities is generally solicited on teacher application forms, but principals often never get to see these forms when the major hiring function is performed by the central office.

One additional caution in the area of staffing is in order. Concerning athletics, there is little justification for the employment of a coach who is incidentally a teacher. Principals are obliged to staff their classrooms with teachers first, then fill coaching positions.

Supervision and Control

In order that the school's nonclassroom educational activities meet the principles outlined in the first portion of this chapter, it is necessary that the principal exercise supervision and control. It is particularly necessary to meet the principle of control by the school and the principle that activities are open to all. Supervision and control in this context do not imply that the principal personally oversees each activity and issues frequent orders demanding compliance. Rather, it does require that the principal establish adequate systems of supervision and control.

It is fundamental to all school programs that they operate with the benefit of teacher supervision, that is, that each activity occur under the direct control of a teacher. The principal's task in this regard is to ensure that each activity has a teacher supervisor and that those who supervise thoroughly understand their supervisory responsibilities.

This element of teacher supervision is sometimes interpreted as meaning that any time students are doing anything in the school, a teacher must be physically present to be sure the students are behaving properly. Such a strict interpretation of student supervision may well satisfy an excessively negligence-conscious administrator, but it is unlikely to give students an opportunity to demonstrate maturing responsibility. Good judgment becomes paramount. It would be poor teacher judgment to allow a gymnastics club to practice on flying rings, parallel bars, and the vaulting horse without close personal supervision. It should be safe and appropriate, however, to allow the school newspaper staff to work together at certain times without the sponsor's being present. Students are not likely to learn responsibility unless the school provides real opportunities for practice.

The principal needs to be cognizant of another dimension of control, that is, a system which controls which students participate in activities and when. Some schools find that a point system operates as an effective control mechanism. The principal's task is to ensure that whatever system is in operation is effective in terms of the objectives of the activity program.

Fiscal Accounting

Another of the activity task areas to which the principal must direct his attention is the handling of funds. The amount of money actually handled in the various activity or extraclass funds within some high schools reaches thousands of dollars. Knezevich and Folkes report activity funds reaching as high as $100,000 per year in some schools.[10] Needless to say, funds like these need to be handled with propriety and system.

One question surrounding the collection and use of monies from various activity funds is, to whom do they belong? Is it considered strictly student money, and as such is it subject only to whatever safeguards the organization imposes on its fund handlers? Or, since the activity takes place as a legitimate part of the school program, is the money subject to the same safeguards and constraints as is regular board of education tax money? Somewhat over half the states list statutes regulating these funds.[11] Legal opinion clearly inclines toward the inclusion of activity or extraclass funds as public money.[12] The fact that these funds originate from nontax sources does not invalidate the position that they are to be considered public monies. Even where the law does not specify, the local board of education is considered responsible since it must ultimately control all the legal matters.

The U.S. Office of Education has issued a guide for accounting for funds derived from nonclassroom activities.[13] This has been approved by the American Association of School Administrators, the Association of School Business Officials, the Council of Chief State School Officers, the

---

[10] Stephen J. Knezevich and John Guy Folkes, *Business Management of Local School Systems*, Harper & Row, Publishers, Incorporated, New York, 1960, p. 189.

[11] *Ibid.*

[12] William H. Roe, *School Business Management*, McGraw-Hill Book Company, New York, 1961, p. 118.

[13] Everett V. Samuelson, George W. Tankard, Jr., and Hoyt W. Pope, *Fiscal Accounting for School Activities*, Bulletin 1959, no. 21, U.S. Government Printing Office, Washington, D.C., 109 pp.

National Association of Secondary School Principals, and the Department of Elementary School Principals of the National Education Association.

Whether or not the state statutes require it, a secondary principal is well advised to administer his school's funds carefully. At the very least, this means utilizing a system of receipts, securing storage of temporary funds, swift bank deposits (preferably within 24 hours), control procedures on check writing and authorization of expenditures, and standard accounting records.

Evaluation of the Program

Just as he turns his attention toward evaluation of the entire classroom education program, the competent secondary administrator attempts to judge systematically the effects of the nonclassroom educational activity program. His point of major reference for evaluation must be the objectives for the nonclassroom program. Evaluation must be related to objectives.

Actually, it is easier to evaluate a school's nonclassroom activity program than it is the classroom program. Some of the criteria are relatively straightforward and measurable. The administrator can determine, for example, what percentage of the student body the programs are reaching. From these statistics, other kinds of information can be derived. Do boys participate more (or less) than girls? Is there more participation at different class levels? Is the program promoting the social mingling of students, or do their choices reflect social elite groups? Over a period of 2 or 3 years, do students elect various types of activities, or do they tend to channel their interests? Many kinds of important questions can be answered from these data, which furnish a solid basis for making evaluative judgments.

Evaluation is not a one-man job. The principal may wish to initiate a faculty committee to launch an evaluative study. Such a group would include representation from among faculty sponsors of different types of activities. After making its study, the group could report to the faculty and make recommendations for changes in the existing program.

SUMMARY

Nonclassroom educational activities are a special set of programs whose purpose is to provide the student with channels through which he can express his talents and interests within a sanctioned social environment in company with his peers. Properly planned and executed, these activities enhance and reinforce the purposes of the school. Capitalizing upon the strong adolescent tendency to band together for activities which are intrinsically interesting to them, the nonclassroom educational program creates an atmosphere of zest and relevancy within the American secondary school.

So that the activity program can bolster, rather than impede, the school's basic program objectives, five guiding principles require adherence. First, activities should be meaningfully related to school purposes; second, activities should be built upon genuine student interests; third, activities must be controlled by the school; fourth, activities should be open to all; and fifth, activities should be financially supported.

Types of activities are classified as athletics activities, student council activities, club programs, social and assembly-type activities, community-related activities, and performing activities.

Central focus was given to the principal's role in the administration of these diverse types of nonclassroom activities. Administration by the principal takes the form of support, staffing, supervision and control systems, fiscal accounting, and evaluation.

SUGGESTED EXERCISES

1. Develop a checklist instrument which might be used to survey and evaluate a school's activity program.

2. Collect a series of incidents of problems arising out of the nonclassroom program. Analyze each incident in view of the five guiding principles presented in this chapter.

3. Through comparative education sources, report on the handling of activities in England, or some other nation for which current information is available.

4. As a class, discuss each member's recollections of his own high school experiences with the activity program. Test the general proposition that these programs provide a distinct social organization within the school.

5. Survey a group of nearby secondary schools in order to develop a listing of number of kinds of activities currently available.

SELECTED REFERENCES

ANDERSON, LESTER W., AND LAUREN A. VAN DYKE, Secondary School Administration, Houghton Mifflin Company, Boston, 1963.

COLEMAN, JAMES S., Adolescents and the Schools, Basic Books, Inc., Publishers, New York, 1965.

GORDON, WAYNE C., The Social System of a High School, The Free Press of Glencoe, New York, 1957.

MILLER, FRANKLIN A., JAMES H. MOYER, AND ROBERT B. PATRICK, Planning Student Activities, Prentice-Hall, Inc., Englewood Cliffs, N.J., 1956.

SAMUELSON, EVERETT V., GEORGE W. TANKARD, JR., AND HOYT W. POPE, Fiscal Accounting for School Activities, Bulletin 1959, no. 21, U.S. Government Printing Office, Washington, D.C., 1959.

CHAPTER 15

SCHEDULING OF PROGRAMS, SERVICES, AND ACTIVITIES

PURPOSE OF SCHEDULING

Scheduling is a result of planning, organizing, and evaluating. It requires that certain choices be made among various alternatives. It may incorporate flexibility so that certain choices are allowed to be delayed to a later time. Everyone schedules to a certain extent, although perhaps not everyone does so in a formal manner. The most commonly thought of schedule is one involving arrival and departure times of trains, buses, and planes. If a person knows that a plane leaves the airport at 9:05 A.M., he must consider all that he must do ahead of time so that he will arrive at the departure gate in time to board the plane. He may jot down a series of tasks to be done and the times required to accomplish those tasks, or he may make mental notes of these tasks and times. Regardless of the formality or informality of the scheduling done, it is done to accomplish a purpose or purposes. Accomplishment of purposes usually requires careful planning so that people and/or materials are brought together at the proper places at the proper times and in the desired number and condition.

The principal in the modern secondary school has planning to do which is generally so complex that it demands that the plans or schedules which result are placed on paper. Other reasons for putting schedules or plans on paper are for ease in communicating them to others and for making a record of them for future use.

What Is Scheduled?

Although the principal may be scheduling things from time to time, he more often is scheduling people, and the things he schedules may be events in which many people are involved and from which other schedules must be developed. For instance, when the decision is made to schedule the performance dates for next year's junior class play for December 6 through December 8, certain other people must plan and schedule their activities accordingly. Because so many other people are affected by such decisions, almost all scheduling done in the school should be cooperative in nature.

If the junior class play is to be held for three successive nights in the auditorium, it is obvious that other major events must not be scheduled which could conflict on those same nights. Planners must also consider the time needed for rehearsals, building of stage settings, etc., which may prevent other use of the auditorium at certain times.

If events are to take place and since events must happen in certain locations or spaces, then the use of certain spaces in the school must be planned on a scheduled basis.

It can be seen that the job of scheduling many events; many people, including students, teachers, specialists, and custodians; many facilities; and many jobs to be done is an Herculean task. In most textbooks dealing with secondary school administration the term "scheduling" is used in the specific sense referring to the master teaching schedule and student programs derived from it.

It is the thesis of the authors of this book that the teaching schedule is only one end product of the planning, organizing, and evaluating which goes on in the modern secondary school. The school calendar must be adopted and many subsidiary schedules must be established before the teaching schedule can be developed. Any schedule so developed is a collection of decisions which have been made and fitted into a pattern.

Who Does Scheduling?

While almost everyone would agree that the responsibility for scheduling in the modern secondary school is the principal's, a fewer number would probably recognize that this does not mean he does the job all by himself. If he does try to make all the decisions by himself and to present the finished product to his staff as a fait accompli, he will probably reap a harvest of lowered staff morale and a host of schedule conflicts. In keeping with the philosophy of leadership expressed in Chapters 6 through 10, those who are to be affected by decisions should have a part in making them. This means that the decisions made in order to build the master schedule should be made on a cooperative basis by teachers, specialists, administrators, and even parents and students at levels where they have the competence to do so.

Change the Schedule Every Year?

If the theme of Chapter 5 is to be carried out—organizing the secondary school for adaptability—there is little doubt but that conditions will have changed from last year. Last year's schedule was built on the basis of decisions made last year—or even earlier, so the results of evaluations made during this year should be considered. In this day of computerized capability, the time-consuming and laborious manipulation of colored bits of paper is no longer necessary to build the master schedule. Even the modest-sized high school some distance from a large city and possessing no computer of its own can have computer assistance at a reasonable cost. It should be recognized that a computer is only a machine and does only those manipulations which it is programmed to do. The information about length of periods, lunch periods, teacher and room assignments, class sizes, etc., must be based on decisions made by the principal and his staff. This information must be fed into the computer as part of the programming or provided to those who will do the scheduling by more traditional hand methods.

PRELIMINARY STEPS IN SCHEDULE BUILDING

The description of the preliminary steps in scheduling which follows is not intended to be exhaustive, but indicative only of the breadth and depth of the planning which goes into getting ready for a new year to come.

Review of Current and Past Year's Plans

Before the time that school opens in September each year, the principal and his staff should begin their evaluation of the new year's plans, provisions, and procedures. The evaluation begins to roll when school opens and the students are there to be a part of the evaluation. It really shifts into high gear as October and November bring first teacher evaluations, the first student grading period, and some experience with the calendar and the teaching schedule. As required reports are being prepared for district and state offices during this period, the principal and his staff should begin asking such questions as: What can we do better next year? What have we learned from past years and so far this year? How can we do it better? What is a feasible priority to set on what needs improvement? These questions need to be considered throughout the year.

The authors hope that by the time the reader has come this far in his profession and in this book, he will believe in the long-run efficiency of involving people in the decision-making process. Thus the principal will utilize faculty competencies in the evaluation process.

In the nontechnical aspects students and parents should likewise be involved in evaluating the programs, services, and activities of the school. Educators cannot help youth adapt to an ever-changing world without consulting others who are concerned.

Guidance and counseling personnel of the school by their very training and their considerable responsibilities for youth must be an integral part of the evaluation team. One of their greatest contributions can be in the feedback of information they can provide to the faculty and the administrators about students from their unique contacts with them. Testing, conferences, interviews, and follow-up studies of graduates, dropouts, and even transfers can yield much that is relevant to evaluation.

The evaluative process is probably best thought of as the active participation of all members of faculty and staff to improve the school. Faculty participation may be accomplished through faculty meetings, committees, questionnaires, or a combination of all three, plus others which can be devised by imaginative educators.

The Framework for Scheduling

No faculty or administrator can make decisions about programs, services, or activities and consider only local needs. There is a larger framework within which any secondary school administrator and faculty must work. This framework includes such factors as:

1. District, state, regional, and even national objectives
2. State curriculum mandates
3. Special program time requirements
4. Space and facilities limitations
5. Regional accrediting association requirements

There are many more pieces to this framework, but the above should convince even the greatest advocate of freedom that educators are not free to follow their vision to create.

Preliminary Scheduling Decisions

Before work can begin on developing the new master schedule for the next year, certain decisions must be made. Answers to such questions as the following must be sought:

1. What shall be our school calendar next year?
2. What changes should be made in the programs, services, and activities to be offered?

3. What plan for grouping of students shall be adopted?
4. What shall be the length of the school day?
5. How many class periods shall be provided, and what will be their length?
6. What shall be the sizes of classes in different subjects?
7. Will we use team teaching?
8. How many lunch periods will we need?
9. Shall there be study halls for all? for some? for none?
10. How many teaching periods will each teacher be assigned?
11. How many periods for supervision shall each department chairman be given?
12. What time or other compensation will be given to staff members for sponsoring major activities?

Student Program and Course Selection

The principal, vice-principals, deans, counselors, and teachers all have responsibility in leading young people to make wise decisions about their futures. It is on the basis of what professional educators know about each student's abilities, aspirations, and achievements that program advisement is done. What program an eighth grader probably ought to take in the ninth and through the balance of his stay in school, and what courses —required and elective—each student should take to accomplish his goals are concerns of all school personnel and, of course, of the student and his parents.

One of the distinguishing features of the American system of secondary education is that the student is not restricted to the program, stream, or track which he elects at any particular time in his educational experience. If he elects in the eighth grade to begin a vocational program in the ninth grade, he can change to a general, business education, or a college preparatory course at almost any new semester. He must, of course, meet the graduation requirements for the new program of study to which he elects to change.

An example of a 4-year planning sheet for students is shown in Figure 15-1. While the planning sheet shown in Figure 15-1 will be used mainly with eighth graders planning for their 4 years "for record" in the senior high school, it can be used for program planning in any of the secondary grades. Such a 4-year plan sheet is not only a protection to the student to be sure he gets what he needs and wants to graduate, it is also an aid to long-range planning for the principal and his faculty.

In Figure 15-2 a combination program and course selection sheet is shown. The sheet may be kept intact for the checking of program against requirements, and/or the lower portion cut off to use for filing the pro-

(Grades 9 through 12)

(Print) Last Name	First Name	Course

Homeroom	Homeroom Teacher	Grade Next Year

Plans for Future _____

Grade 9		Grade 10		Grade 11		Grade 12	
SUBJECTS	CR.	SUBJECTS	CR.	SUBJECTS	CR.	SUBJECTS	CR.
English I		English II		English III		English IV	
Soc. St. 9		Biology I		U. S. History		Soc. St. 12	
Phys. Ed.		Phys. Ed.		Phys. Ed.		Phys. Ed.	
CREDITS		CREDITS		CREDITS		CREDITS	

TOTAL CREDITS

_____   _____
Adviser's Signature   Parent's Signature

Fig. 15-1. Any Senior High School Four-year Student Planning Sheet.

gram, and/or to be punched on tape or computer cards. Courses taken successfully (or unsuccessfully) during summer school can alter registration for certain courses substantially.

Summary of Registrations

The course selections for the next year made by students with the advice of teachers, counselors, and parents must then be tallied so that the administration will know the expected registration for each subject and thus the number of sections which must be offered. The number of sections needed may have implications for staffing needs for the coming year. Recruiting plans may need to be made in conjunction with the central office personnel officer to secure teachers and specialists with the proper training to augment the faculty.

Total registrations for each subject can be summarized on one sheet along with the sections needed and teachers to be assigned to those sections. An example of such a sheet is shown in Figure 15-3.

Date_____   Circle your grade   9   10   11   12

Name_____   Phone_____
      (Last)   (First)   (Middle)

	Program to date	Gr	Gr	Cr
9th Grade	English I Social Studies Phys. Ed. Summer School:			
10th Grade	English Phys. Ed. Summer School:			
11th Grade	English Phys. Ed. Summer School:			

Birthdate_____
            (Month)   (Day)   (Year)

Birthplace_____
               (City)   (State)

Father's Full Name:

_____

Mother's Full Name:

_____

or Guardian_____

Address_____
            (No. or Box)   (St. or Rt.)

City_____

Zip Code_____

**COURSES YOU WILL TAKE IN SUMMER
SCHOOL THIS YEAR**

_____

_____

SELECTION FOR NEXT SEPTEMBER

Name_____   Changes will be difficult to obtain   Grade_____

	First Semester				Second Semester		
*Per	Subject	*Rm	*Teacher	*Per.	Subject	*Rm	*Teacher

Advising Teacher_____   Parent's Signature_____

*To be filled out by adviser only

Fig. 15-2. Any High School Program and Course Selection.

SUBJECT	TOTAL REGISTRATION	SECTIONS NEEDED	TEACHER ASSIGNMENTS
Advanced English	20	1	Adams (1)
Business English	44	2	Charles (2)
English 12	90	4	Adams (2) Baker (1) Forest (1)
English 11	146	6	Adams (1) Baker (3) Dunn (2)
English 10	162	7	Dunn (2) Evans (2) Hart (3)
English 9	218	8	Good (3) Jones (3) Lord (2)
U.S. & State Gov't	130	5	Forest (3) Irving (2)
U.S. & State History	140	6	Good (2) Jones (2) Lord (2)
World History	78	3	Dunn (1) Novak (1) Hart (1)
World Geography	215	8	Paul (2) Novak (4) Zeus (2)
Physics	52	3	Ross (1) Smith (2)
Chemistry	74	5	Ross (1) Smith (2) Vann (2)
Biology	156	6	Smith (1) Vann (3) Keith (2)
Earth Science	98	4	Keith (3) Xavier (1)
General Science	245	9	Xavier (3) Irving (3) Moody (2) Glenn (1)
Advanced Math	9	1	Ross (1)
Trig.-Solid	59	3	Young (2) Moody (1)
Plane Geometry	87	4	Young (2) Moody (2)
Algebra II	105	5	Ross (1) Young (1) Glenn (2) Unitas (1)
Algebra I	122	5	Glenn (2) Zeus (3)
General Math	131	5	Unitas (3) Toole (2)
Latin IV	10	1	Vergili (1)
Latin III	12	1	Ciceroni (1)
Latin II	83	4	Vergili (2) Ciceroni (2)
Latin I	87	4	Vergili (2) Ciceroni (2)
French IV	14	1	DuPont (1)
French III	18	1	Rousseau (1)
French II	102	4	DuPont (2) Rousseau (2)
French I	106	4	DuPont (2) Rousseau (2)
Office Training	21	1	Charles (1)
Typing II	50	2	Royal (2)
Typing I	88	3	Royal (3)
Bookkeeping II	21	1	Ledger (1)
Bookkeeping I	28	1	Ledger (1)
Shorthand II	42	2	Ledger (1) Charles (1)
Shorthand I	46	2	Ledger (2)
Business Economics	26	1	Charles (1)
Business Math	50	2	Quintin (2)
General Business	68	3	Wilson (2) Unitas (1)

(Partial Listing of Subjects Only)

Fig. 15-3. Sample Total Registration and Teacher-assignment Sheet.

BUILDING THE MASTER SCHEDULE

Methods of Schedule Making

The two basic methods of schedule making are to deal with students either as groups taking like subjects or as individuals.

A group schedule is built by making a careful determination of the number of groups of pupils taking the same sets of subjects and by dividing them into the required number of sections. In the lower grades of junior high school or any school where the number of electives is at a minimum this is the simplest method of scheduling. Sometimes the group method is referred to as the "block" method because groups of students stay together through blocks of time in the daily schedule. All eighth-grade pupils could be assigned to a group after a pattern such as 8_1, 8_2, 8_3, and 8_4 and may stay together all day, going to different rooms for different subjects. Some advocates of this method feel that it perpetuates the feeling of belonging to a home group and continues somewhat the elementary self-contained classroom group of students. Only the room and the teacher change for different subjects; the makeup of the students remains the same.

There are, of course, any possible numbers of ways to modify the above plan and still call it a group method.

As soon as any electives are allowed to students, this immediately breaks up the group for the number of periods during the day in which electives are allowed. In traditionally organized junior high schools, the seventh and eighth grades are allowed very few or no electives. Electives are usually limited to one, and all electives are taken the same period. In fact the so-called electives may be no elective at all, but just a rotation plan. For example, during the period of the day for electives the 8_1 group boys may go with the 8_3 boys to woodshop, while 8_2 boys and 8_4 boys would go to metal shop. The 8_1 girls and 8_2 girls might go to sewing classes, while the 8_3 and 8_4 girls are in foods classes. The groups may then switch subjects for the second half of the semester. If the experiences to be provided during the elective period are more than two a semester, then the time spent in each would be less. The authors would advise, however, that the number of weeks spent in each elective be the same length as one or more normal grading periods of the school.

In the group or block method the physical education classes for boys and girls would be held the same period, but could use different facilities and different teachers. Coeducational instruction for certain activities seems to be increasing, however.

The higher up one goes in the secondary school grades, the more likely one is to find that specialization of programs, and the number of electives available make block or group scheduling increasingly difficult, if not impossible. The larger the school, the more likely it is that specialization will be broader and that more electives will be available also.

For such schools as described above, the individual or mosaic method of scheduling combined with a conflict sheet is probably used most extensively. Under this method the class sections needed in each subject are placed in the periods where the schedule makers determine that the smallest number of conflicts is likely to result for the individual student.[1]

It is necessary to realize that in using the mosaic method, a class section in any subject is put together on the basis of individual course selections made by students and by any grouping procedures followed in the school. Under such a plan there is a possibility of a number of conflicts between student subject selections and scheduling arrangements of the subject sections. The number of conflicts can be dramatically reduced if a conflict sheet is used *before* the final placement of subjects on the master schedule. Ordinarily, the multiple-section subjects give very little trouble as far as conflicts are concerned. It is the one-section and double-period classes that cause the most conflicts.

The Conflict Sheet   The conflict sheet plots those one-section classes which if placed in the same period would result in conflicts. Figure 15-4 is a sample of a conflict sheet for single-section classes only.

The individual student preliminary registration cards are checked for each student and one-section classes are plotted on a tentative schedule. On the sample conflict sheet where tally marks appear, there will be that many conflicts if those classes are placed on the schedule for the same period.

Having discovered where conflicts would appear, the schedule makers would then change the placement of those one-section classes so as to eliminate the conflicts.

The hand-made conflict sheet described above can be prepared for a high school of twelve hundred by a competent clerk in 4 to 6 hours.[2] If a computer is used to develop a conflict sheet, one can determine not only how many conflicts there are in the tentative schedule, but also who the students are with those conflicts. This information can be helpful in locating those students to have them select different courses if all conflicts cannot be resolved. It should be noted that most single-section classes are electives, and therefore the student must select from alternatives.

[1] Paul B. Jacobson, William C. Reavis, and James D. Logsdon, *The Effective School Principal*, 2d ed., Prentice-Hall, Inc., Englewood Cliffs, N.J., 1963, p. 69.
[2] *Ibid.*, p. 70.

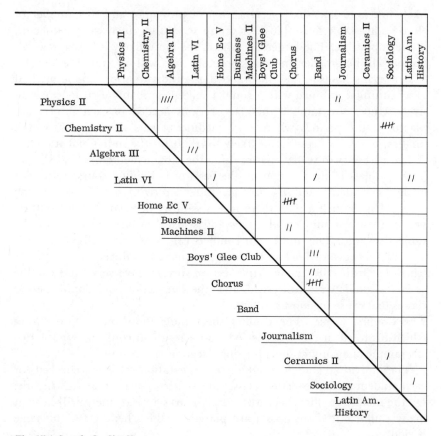

Fig. 15-4. Sample Conflict Sheet.

Placement of Subjects on the Schedule

From student registrations the schedule makers know how many sections of each subject are needed and from the conflict sheet they know what single-section courses should not be placed during the same period. If schedule makers are using a hand method rather than a computer for scheduling, they could proceed somewhat as described below.

Because of the larger size of most high schools today, it is advisable to place the periods and times across the top of the page and the teachers' names down the left side of the page. Several pages must be used in the large high school because of the number of teachers involved. Figure 15-5 is a portion of a master teaching schedule which shows teaching as well as other assignments.

In placing subjects on the schedule sheet, it is also advisable to begin

Teachers	Home Room	\multicolumn{6}{c}{PERIODS}

Teachers	Home Room	1	2	3	LUNCH	4	5	6
Algohm, Jane	9th	English I	English I	English II		Planning	English II	English I
Baker, Sally	9th	Planning	U. S. History	Senior Problems		U. S. History	World History	U. S. History
Basdrotti, Nick	9th	Biology II	Planning	Biology I		Biology I	Earth Science	Earth Science
Bergdorf, Paul	10th	Algebra I	Algebra II	Algebra II		Algebra I	Planning	General Math
Ciani, Pat	–	Attendance	Ind. Arts I	Ind. Arts IV		Ind. Arts III	Ind. Arts II	Planning
Crenshaw, Phyllis	10th	Latin I	Latin I	Planning		Latin II	Latin I	Latin II
Eckard, Arthur	12th	Chemistry I	Chemistry I	Supervision		Supervision	Physics I	Bio-chemistry
Fehr, Hal	11th	Boys' P. E.	Boys' P. E.	Boys' P. E.		Driver Ed.	Boys' P. E.	Boys' P. E.
Goshorn, Mary	10th	Girls' P. E.	Girls' P. E.	Girls' P. E.		Health	Girls' P. E.	Girls' P. E.

Fig. 15-5. Portion of a Master Teaching Schedule 1968–1969.

with the highest grade in the school because there are usually more crucial problems with that group. After plotting the subjects taken by seniors, the schedule makers move down to juniors, sophomores, and freshmen, in turn.

Some schedule makers prefer to group teachers by department in order to check off the courses and sections required in each department more easily. Others like to list teachers alphabetically with no department distinctions. Jacobson, Reavis, and Logsdon suggest using a separate page for each grade and then combining them to make the master schedule.[3]

Room and special facility assignments must also be made a part of the master schedule.

Student Daily Schedules

Having plotted all the courses on the master schedule and having made room and special facility assignments to teachers, it is now necessary to make out the daily program for each student. The individual student schedule can be made out either by hand or by computer. An example is shown in Figure 15-6. Several copies should be made of each student's schedule.

Student No.	Name	Class	School Yr.	Sem.	Home Room
1784	BARNES, FRANK L.	9th	67	1	304

Period	Subject	Room	Teacher
1	English I	127	Algohm
2	Algebra I	304	Bergdorf
3	Biology I	411	Basdrotti
4	Study Hall	128	Staff
5	Art	235	Clark
6	Cafeteria	20	–
7	Phys. Ed.	100	Fehr
8	Shop-Wood	214	Johnson

Fig. 15-6. Student Schedule.

After students have been assigned to courses from the master schedule, class lists or rosters must be provided each teacher for each period class.

Testing the Next Year's Schedule

Some secondary school administrators like to test the newly constructed master schedule by taking a half day in late spring and having students follow their schedules for the next year. This can be done on a day when

[3] *Ibid.*, p. 76.

Seniors are on "Senior Day" or practicing for final exercises. It may also be possible to have students from the feeder schools come for that day and go through a final realistic orientation for their move to a new school the following year.

During the summer months transfers into the school should be invited to come to the school for advisement and program and course selection. Their individual schedules can then be mailed to them, so they will be ready to attend classes the first day of school in the fall. Schedules of in-migrant students and adjustments to student schedules because of summer school will necessitate a working crew in the modern secondary school during most of the summer months.

Other Schedules Needed

Now that the master schedule has been built, it is necessary to provide a bell schedule, activity period schedule, lunchroom and bus duty schedules, assembly program schedule, and many more so that the communication of plans to teachers and students can be accomplished. Such schedules may be furnished on single sheets or incorporated into student and teacher handbooks.

SUMMARY

Almost everyone does scheduling of some kind. It is necessary to plan to accomplish the objectives of an institution so that people and/or materials are brought together at the proper places at the proper times and in the desired quantities and qualities. This requires careful scheduling.

The modern secondary school program is complex, and therefore many decisions affecting many people must be made. The way in which these decisions are made is as important as the actual decisions themselves. Because so many people are affected by the decisions made in scheduling, the schedule-making process in a school should be cooperative in nature.

There are many preliminary steps which must be taken before the actual building of the master schedule can take place. Evaluation must be made of current and past years' plans and schedules by involving the people who were affected, teachers, students, administrators, specialists, and parents. Guidance and counseling personnel have particular responsibilities in gathering the data needed upon which to make decisions. One of the more important of these is the advisement of students concerning their program and course selection. The planning of the student's program is an important process and should involve parents as well.

The preliminary registrations sheet contains the tally of the subject selections made by individual students. Dividing the total registrations for each subject offering by the teacher/pupil ratio for that subject will indicate how many sections must be provided in order to meet the demand.

The two major methods of scheduling are the group method and the individual method. The large modern high school with a diversity of offerings usually requires the use of the individual method combined with a conflict sheet. The conflict sheet is a means of predicting where conflicts would occur among single-section courses if they were scheduled during the same period.

The steps in scheduling were then described in some detail. Samples of a student 4-year plan sheet, a conflict sheet, a portion of a master teaching schedule, and a student schedule were shown. Some administrators arrange to test the following year's schedule by taking a half day in late spring and by having students follow that schedule. Only a few minutes are taken for each class period, and advocates of this plan believe it well worth the time spent.

In-migrants to the school attendance area are offered program and course selection advisement during the summer, and their individual school schedules are mailed to them before school opens.

Bell schedules, activity period schedules, bus and noon duty schedules, and many more must also be developed. The master teaching schedule is only one of many schedules which must be devised for the complex modern secondary school. Its prime importance, however, is not denied.

SUGGESTED EXERCISES

1. Secure copies or a listing of all the kinds of schedules to be found in one high school. Working backward from these schedules, see whether you can infer the purposes which each is to assist in attaining.

2. Take the numbers of students registered for each course from the preliminary registration summary shown in Figure 15-3, and determine what pupil/teacher ratio was used in each case. Subtract five students from the pupil/teacher ratios thus discovered, and see how many more teachers will be required. Multiply the number of additional teachers needed by the current median teacher's salary in your district to find out how much it can cost to reduce teacher/pupil ratio.

3. What justifications, if any, do you accept for advocating physical education classes of seventy students but limiting advanced language classes or shop classes to fourteen to sixteen?

4. Make a list of the activities which might be found in a junior high school of 850 students and in a senior high school of 1,600 students. Select a week in a particular month, and attempt to plan times and places for these activities.

5. Draw up a plan for evaluating last year's plans and schedules using a faculty committee or committees. On what basis would you recommend assignment of teachers and other staff to these committees? What would be the steps and time schedules you would propose for this evaluation?

SELECTED REFERENCES

Austin, David B., and Noble Gividen, *The High School Principal and Staff Develop the Master Schedule,* Bureau of Publications, Teachers College, Columbia University, New York, 1960, 107 pp.

Bush, Robert N., and Dwight W. Allen, *A New Design for High School Education,* McGraw-Hill Book Company, New York, 1964, 197 pp.

D'Antuono, Anthony, and William S. McCallum, Jr., "Constructing the Master Schedule by Computer," *NASSP Bulletin,* vol. 49, no. 303, October, 1965.

Elicker, Paul E., *The Administration of Junior and Senior High Schools,* Prentice-Hall, Inc., Englewood Cliffs, N.J., 1964, 270 pp., chap. 8.

Gladstone, Igor M., "Modified Scheduling and Foreign Languages," *NASSP Bulletin,* vol. 50, no. 313, November, 1966.

Jacobson, Paul B., W. C. Reavis, and James D. Logsdon, *The Effective School Principal,* 2d ed., Prentice-Hall, Inc., Englewood Cliffs, N.J., 1963, 532 pp., chap. 4.

Ovard, Glen F., *Administration of the Changing Secondary School,* The Macmillan Company, New York, 1966, 531 pp., chap. 7.

Patterson, Wade N., "Variable Period Scheduling," *NASSP Bulletin,* vol. 49, no. 303, October, 1965.

CHAPTER **16**

IMPROVING
EDUCATIONAL
PROGRAMS
AND
SERVICES | The central thesis of this chapter is that the prime function of administration is to conduct an unrelenting search for improvement of the instructional program. A program of formal secondary education for all American youth is the purpose for which the school exists. Just as the modern industrial corporation vigorously pursues its profit yield for the sake of its stockholders, so does the modern secondary school strive aggressively for increased yield of learning for its clients, the boys and girls. Just as the corporation establishes facilitating objectives which serve to create the conditions under which the central goal can be better achieved, so the secondary school establishes facilitating objectives which lead toward the primary goal. Thus, the *raison d'être* for administration is its contribution to the educational program.

RESPONSIBILITY FOR IMPROVEMENT

The Principal

Final justification for the principal's services is provided by the quality of his contribution to the facilitation of the instructional program. Unless this ultimate accounting is faced, there is little need to employ someone called "principal." It would be better use of human resources to secure the services of a high caliber clerk or an office manager who could arrange schedules, order supplies, check attendance, balance the petty cash fund, and monitor the cafeteria. As necessary as such duties are to the efficient operation of a school, they are nevertheless clerical in nature and could well be performed by someone with considerably less training than a principal and at less than half his annual salary. Such a contention places a heavy obligation upon the principal to demonstrate to all—the student, the faculty, and the community—that he does play a major role with a decided impact on the educational program. His impact should be felt in matters more important than the immediate day-to-day operation.

Among all those who share, with varying degrees of involvement, the responsibility for improvement of any given school's program, none has a greater personal responsibility than the principal.

The Central Office Staff

The role of the central office in improvement of educational programs and services will depend to a large extent on the organizational structure of the district. Yet, just as the principal bears the primary responsibility for his school, the central administration, or the superintendent, bears this same responsibility for the entire district.

If the organizational structure of the district is highly centralized and if most important decisions are made centrally, it is likely that the role of the individual principal will be diminished in importance, and the position may not include the major role suggested above. Should the structure be largely decentralized, the principal will be, in effect, the superintendent for the school. Pure cases of either model are rare. Most districts range in between, centering more or less about the centrally coordinated model, where individual building principals are given considerable autonomy and where the central office provides coordination and services rather than inspection and command.[1]

The State Department of Education

It has already been clearly established in Chapter 5 that within each state the constitutional responsibility for public education rests with the state itself. Expressing the people's will through the state legislature is an administrative body generally called the state department of education.

As repositories of the legal authority for education within the states, each state must accept the overall responsibility for program improve-

---

[1] Daniel E. Griffiths, David L. Clark, D. Richard Wynn, and Lawrence Iannoccone, *Organizing Schools for Effective Education*, The Interstate Press, Danville, Ill., 1962.

ment. By working through strong and competently staffed state departments of education, this responsibility can be more closely met.

Department Heads

The organizational structure of a secondary school typically but not necessarily includes the position of heads of departments. Senior high schools are most likely organized on this basis, whereas junior high schools may not be. In either junior or senior high schools, when the staff becomes large enough so that a department consists of seven to ten members, the appointment of a department head is recommended. With larger staffs the principal must depend on department heads to assist in supervision.

Under the department head organization, the principal delegates certain duties and corresponding authority to his department heads. He may not, however, delegate the final authority since under any unit control organization, whether it be a school, a hospital, or a factory, the final responsibility remains with the unit head, or, in this case, the principal.

The role of the department head varies considerably in secondary schools. Some department heads' functions are limited to compilation of budget requests from department members. Others may be granted a much broader role, which includes supervision. Regardless of the type of role the structure of the school suggests for department heads, their purpose is the same—improvement of the instructional program.

Teachers

From one point of view it seems unnecessary to mention that teachers, too, share in this responsibility for program improvement. Since this is their primary task, it seems redundant to overstate the case. Yet, from another point of view, it is important to establish clearly that teachers share this overall responsibility. In too many situations, teachers are either not invited to share or else are not willing to participate in efforts at overall improvement. What is meant goes beyond the idea of each teacher's simply doing his own best job, by himself, in his own classroom. The focus of program improvement is the individual student. What the program does for him is the key. Teachers must adopt this point of view and accept the responsibility for overall program improvement.

The implication for the secondary administrator is clear. If he desires to increase a feeling for improvement responsibility among his staff, department heads, and teachers, he must work not only to create the structure but also to foster the climate. This means encouraging department heads to assume greater responsibility. It means trying to instill departments with a feeling of unity of purpose and to give each member opportunities to work cooperatively with others.

The Federal Government

Historically speaking, the federal government has not played a major role in shaping American education. Until recently, most Americans have felt that public education is, and should be, primarily a state and local responsibility. However, as early as 1785, the Northwest Ordinance established precedent for federal concern for public schools. While the intervening years have produced many sections of federal legislation which deal with specific segments of public education, prior to 1965 none of the acts were as sweeping in size and scope as the Elementary and Secondary Education Acts of 1965. With these acts and the follow-up legislation of 1966, 1967, and 1968, a new era had clearly arrived. Scholars, statesmen, and the general public are assaying the new relationship as it becomes increasingly clear that there is now, not only federal interest in, but also federal responsibility for certain phases of public (and nonpublic) school programs. A new partnership is being forged between the three major partners—the local district, the state, and the federal government.[2]

The implication for secondary administration is that those charged with leadership of the local schools must, first of all, be well informed not only as to the specific provisions of various federal titles but also as to the nature of the evolving set of relationships. It also means that local administrators must seize the initiative in analyzing local needs and creating programs which might qualify for federal financing.

Others Responsible for Improvement of Programs

In addition to those charged with the administration and operation of the schools, from the local level to the federal level, there are other agencies and organizations interested in the improvement of educational programs. In fact, it might well be said that in modern America, due to a recognition that education is a concern of all the people, a great many organizations and special groups have the responsibility for the improvement of public educational programs.

The colleges and universities of higher education represent a major societal institution which assumes part of the burden of responsibility for program improvement. Higher education contributes to program improvement both through leading the advance as a producer of new knowledge and as a training ground for those who will teach in and administer

[2] Roald F. Campbell and Gerald R. Sroufe, "Toward a Rationale for Federal-State-Local Relations in Education," *Phi Delta Kappan*, vol. 47, no. 1, September, 1965; also W. W. Wayson, "The Political Revolution in Education, 1965," *Phi Delta Kappan*, vol. 47, no. 7, pp. 333–339, March, 1966; also Nicholas A. Masters and Lawrence K. Pettit, "Some Changing Patterns in Educational Policy Making," *Educational Administration Quarterly*, vol. ii, no. 2, pp. 81–100, Spring, 1966.

the public schools. In some communities, this recognition of mutual responsibility has taken on new dimensions of local cooperation.[3]

Another set of groups sharing in improvement of education is the entire group of professional associations dealing with education. One report of these associations lists their number as approximately four hundred, that is, those associations organized on a regional and national basis.[4] Organized variously by level of education, subject discipline, or any combination of educational interests, these associations play important roles in the improvement of educational programs.

An example of the type of interest followed by a professional organization is the National Education Association's Project on Instruction. Established in 1959, the project set the long-range goal of issuing a series of carefully constructed recommendations which could serve to guide not only the profession but the general public as well. These recommendations, if implemented, would directly raise the quality of instruction in the public schools. A national committee was appointed, consisting of teachers, school administrators, and university professors. This group then formulated the broad outlines of the project. The project attempted to develop definitive answers to twelve central questions in American education. These questions were as follows:

DECISION MAKING   Who should make what decisions about education?
RESEARCH, EXPERIMENTATION, AND INNOVATION   How can an extensive program of educational research, experimentation, and innovation be developed?
EDUCATING ALL CHILDREN AND YOUTH   How can the instructional program of the school be designed to develop the individual potentialities of all members of the school population within the framework of a society that values both unity and diversity?
ESTABLISHING PRIORITIES FOR THE SCHOOL   What are the distinctive responsibilities of the school in contrast to those that are distinctive to the family, the church, industry, and various youth-serving agencies?
What responsibilities should the school share with other institutions and with other youth-serving agencies?
What, then, should be included in the school program?
What should be excluded from it?
THE SCHOOL'S ROLE IN DEALING WITH NATIONAL PROBLEMS RELATED TO YOUTH   What is the school's role in dealing with serious national problems such as youth unemployment and juvenile delinquency?
TEACHING ABOUT CONTROVERSIAL ISSUES AND ABOUT COM-

[3] Temple University's College of Education has established several programs well illustrating this concept of a large urban university's dedication to and involvement in the educational problems of the urban area. See Temple University "Report of the President, 1964–65," Philadelphia.
[4] John M. Groebli, "An Abstract of National Organizations in the Education Profession at Mid-twentieth Century: Present Status and Future Development," Phi Delta Kappa, 1964. (Mimeographed.)

MUNISM   What is the school's role in teaching about controversial issues and about communism and other ideologies?

A BALANCED PROGRAM   How can the school provide a balanced program for the individual and maintain it amidst various pressures for specialization?

SELECTING CONTENT   How can schools make wise selections of content from the ever-growing body of available knowledge?

ORGANIZING CONTENT   How should the content of the curriculum be organized?

ORGANIZING THE CURRICULUM   How should the curriculum of the school be organized to give appropriate direction to the instructional process?

ORGANIZING THE SCHOOL AND THE CLASSROOM   How should the school and the classroom be organized to make the most effective use of the time and talents of students and teachers?

INSTRUCTIONAL MATERIALS, TECHNOLOGY, SPACE   How can the quality of instructional materials be improved?

How can the products of modern technology be used effectively?

How can space be designed and used to support the instructional program? [5]

Implementation of the resulting recommendations is chiefly left to each district. Many of these publications make excellent reading for the secondary principal and could be effectively utilized as subjects for local improvement programs.

By means of their professional journals, their research reports, their conferences, and their requirements for membership, these professional associations exert a force for improvement of educational programs.

To recognize those who have responsibility for program improvement in American secondary schools, one must present an extensive listing of organizations and groups having diverse interests. In contrast to most nations, the United States' system is characterized by diversity and diffusion of responsibility. Some see this as a severe failing. To others it remains the bulwark of strength and quality. This issue itself lies beyond the scope of this book. For our purpose, it seems most relevant to place the primary responsibility for program improvement on those who administer the secondary program at the local level. At once one becomes enmeshed in the circle of responsibility since it depends upon the local board to be wise enough to hire capable administrators. And it behooves the local citizens to be sufficiently prudent therefore to elect capable board of education members. Thus the cycle continues.

[5] National Education Association, *Deciding What to Teach*, Project on Instruction, 1963, p. 2. Other Project publications include *Education in a Changing Society*, 166 pp.; *Planning and Organizing for Teaching*, 190 pp. Also auxiliary publications: *The Scholars Look at the Schools*: A Report of the Disciplines Seminar, 64 pp.; *The Principals Look at the Schools*: A Status Study of Selected Instructional Practices, 76 pp.; *Current Curriculum Studies in Academic Subjects*, 102 pp.; *From Bookshelves to Action*: A Guide to Using the Recommendations of the NEA Project on Instruction, 32 pp. All published by The National Education Association, Washington, D.C.

THE NATURE AND PURPOSE OF SUPERVISION

What Is Supervision?

Supervision is one of the necessary functions of administration. The term "supervision" is perhaps typical of the semantic difficulty that is unfortunately present in the field of education. Supervision means different things to different observers, even within the professional education field. While it is customary to consider supervision and administration separately and as discrete processes, it seems more useful to think of supervision as encompassed within administration.

The total process of organizing, managing, directing, coordinating, and evaluating a formal organization is what it meant by *administration*. Supervision is one of a subset of functions required by the administrative process. From this point of view, *supervision* is that subdivision of the total process of educational administration which is devoted principally to increasing the effectiveness of those who are engaged in the direct performance of the central task of the educational enterprise. It deals with improvement of on-the-job performance of teachers, administrators, and all classifications of professional workers. Of course, supervision is equally a part of the necessary administrative functions of noninstructional personnel as well as instructors, but the focus here is on the latter.

By defining supervision in this somewhat narrower sense than is generally the case in the professional literature, it acquires a more precise meaning. Broader definitions which create a broad umbrella under which everything affecting the instructional program is considered as belonging to supervision, lose something because they are too general. The authors prefer a definition by which one can readily shrug off some educational activities, important as they may be, to other tasks of administration. Perhaps this point can be made clearer by looking at items which do not belong to supervision.

Improved salaries, better pension plans, and related fringe benefits may contribute toward improvement of the program through attracting better personnel, but these are considered a part of the personnel function of administration rather than a part of supervision. A new organizational plan, such as a team teaching arrangement, could contribute to the improvement of the program but is a matter of within-school organization rather than supervision, although there is a close relationship. Supervision therefore centers about what teachers do in the performance of their assigned roles and has, as its central function, a continual search for improvement in their performance. Our concept of supervision is broad as well as narrow. Its breadth derives from the inclusion of many diverse types of behaviors on the part of those who would supervise.

Its narrowness grows out of its restriction in focus; that is, it is focused about the performance of those who deal directly with the teaching process.

The principal or department head or assistant superintendent for instruction or supervisor is performing the supervision role when he confers with teachers about their work in the classroom in either formal or informal situations. He is performing supervision when he points out research findings to a teacher, and he is acting in a supervisory capacity when he arranges for a teacher to attend an educational conference. Rather than prescribe a comprehensive list of supervisory activities, the point here is to establish a clear concept that supervision consists of many types of specific behaviors. As long as they center about the teacher's job in the classroom and are directed toward continual enhancement of this vital process, the administrator is carrying out his responsibility for supervision.

Value of Supervision

Although often contentions are made severely challenging the value of supervision itself, it would be contended that it is not only valuable but a critical function within every school. Those most opposed to supervision feel that it is unnecessary in an organization, such as a modern secondary school, staffed by qualified and competent teachers and, further, that it is an undemocratic infringement upon academic freedom. Such contentions, it is maintained, stand in error on two major accounts. First, schools, like business and industrial organizations, employ large numbers of people who, by the very nature of their work assignments, work in interdependent and cooperative ways. The teacher in a modern school is not an independent professional who simply supplies the complete program for students. Teachers must work together in prescribed organizational structures. As long as this elementary condition exists (which we suspect will be as long as we have organized human effort), someone must be granted authority and responsibility for the supervisory process. The charge that supervision is undemocratic and contrary to principles of academic freedom is supported only when supervision is performed badly. As long as it is dedicated to its essential task and respects the rights of all concerned, there appears to be no conflict.

A well-administered supervisory program in a modern secondary school can be the cornerstone of program improvement. In spite of modern curriculum guides, the latest audiovisual devices, or the most enlightened organizational plans, without adequate teacher role-performance, the quality of the educational program will suffer irreparably. Modern supervision is aimed directly at the maintenance and improvement of the instructional process.

Supervision as Instructional Leadership

Since Chapters 6 through 10 dealt with leadership, there is no need to treat concepts of leadership here. It is appropriate, though, to make it unmistakably clear that it is from the administrative function of supervision that educational leadership takes its highest challenge. It is through engaging in specific leadership behavior that the secondary principal can be most effective in executing the supervisory function.

Although the administrator has, by the authority of his position, certain administrative prerogatives granting him the right to engage in certain supervisory behavior, such as observing the instructional process or calling a meeting of a department, he must earn the right to be a respected leader. Only as the principal's faculty perceives him as an effective leader can he actually become effective in the supervisory process. Their perception of his leadership is the crucial factor in determining how effectively he can perform his supervisory role. In his official position, the principal is the appointed leader; yet he may or may not be granted the status of emergent leader.[6]

ORGANIZING A SUPERVISORY PROGRAM

Since supervision is an integral part of the administrative process, it follows that it can benefit from systematic planning and organization, as will any function of administration. The failure to recognize that supervision lends itself to planning may, in no small part, account for the failure of many supervisory programs.

The Human Relations Emphasis

To realize that administrators have not always recognized the importance of good human relations seems inconceivable. Yet, what is known as the "human relations movement" in the history of administration began only in the 1930s.[7] It was this famous series of research, directed by Harvard University at the Hawthorne Works of the Western Electric Company in Chicago, which first empirically found that the attention workers received was of more significance than the physical conditions of the workplace.[8] This series led to further work into the importance of what is now called human relations.

Now thoroughly espoused by management in American industry and administration in American education, the necessity of maintaining a

---

[6] For a review of these concepts of "appointed and emergent leaders," see Chap. 6.

[7] Edwin E. Witte, "The Evolution of Managerial Ideas in Industrial Relations," *Bulletin* 27, New York State School of Industrial and Labor Relations, Cornell University, Ithaca, N.Y., 1958, p. 13.

[8] The interested reader who desires a concise discussion of the Hawthorne Studies can consult Henry A. Landsberger, *Hawthorne Revisited*, Cornell University, Ithaca, N.Y., 1958, 116 pp.

favorable climate of human relations is well-recognized. For the supervisory process, the establishment of good human relations is a necessity. As was pointed out earlier, supervision is dependent upon leadership, and leadership is dependent upon good human relations. However, good human relations alone is not a sufficient condition for achievement of all tasks. A sound plan is also paramount. This plan, in keeping with the purpose of supervision itself, will directly confront the area of making desirable changes in what teachers do. It recognizes the essential element of a favorable climate of human relations between the supervisor and supervised.

Forms of Supervisory Organization

The form of supervisory organization existing within a given secondary school will be partially dependent upon the organizational structure of the school district. The principal's role can vary significantly from district to district. If there is a high degree of building autonomy in the decentralized district, the building principal may have not only the primary but also the sole responsibility for the supervision process in his building. At the other extreme, in a highly centralized organization, the role of the principal may be limited to scheduling supervisory visits between central office supervisors and his own teachers. As was suggested before, the centrally coordinated model is preferred by most authorities.

Under the centrally coordinated model, the building principal has primary responsibility for supervision within his building. He will probably be able to call on one or more members of the superintendent's central staff for assistance in his supervisory program, but the responsibility remains his. Central staff members serve as resource personnel, offering specialized supervised services, as in the case of a music supervisor, or general supervision, as in case of the director of secondary education.

One of the salient factors of the supervisory organization is the role assigned to department heads. Some secondary schools relegate department heads to minor duties and restrict their activities to routines such as gathering supply requisitions from departmental members or maintaining an inventory of departmental books and instructional supplies. Under such a pattern, the department head is an honorary chairman, appointed principally on the basis of seniority. In this position the department head does not participate in the supervision program in any effective manner. His contribution is severely limited. By saying that when department heads have limited responsibilities, their supervisory effectiveness is equally limited, it is not intended to imply that this form of departmental organization is universally unsuited. The point is clear, though, that such departmental organization contributes little to the supervisory program and that department heads would not be considered members of the supervisory team.

Other schools grant department heads broad powers. The most crucial power that any supervisor can possess is the power to write official recommendations for reemployment or dismissal. When department heads are given this responsibility, they become strong power figures. Depending upon their qualifications and competencies, this organization may be effective. It possesses inherent disadvantages, for it creates an additional authority level.

A middle position for department heads is the one in which they serve in a staff rather than a line relationship to the building principal. This means that department heads assume coordinating functions within their departments as a service both to the principal and the teachers within the department. A department head is generally released from teaching one or more periods a day for his departmental duties. With this lighter load he can provide assistance to new teachers and work on developing new curriculum materials for departmental use.

In considering which is the preferred model of supervisory organization within a secondary school, the purpose of the authors is not to prescribe a particular form. Much will depend upon the size of the staff. A principal responsible for 25 teachers can utilize a different organization from one with 125 teachers. It seems better to point out that secondary administrators should be aware of a variety of possible supervisory organizations and that if they are in a position to make changes, they should work toward the form of organization which will work out best within each school and school district.

The Assistant Principal

Another important position in the supervisory organization is the assistant principal. This position includes associate principals as well as those bearing the title of assistant to the principal. Although there is a great deal of variation here, too, the position of assistant principal generally implies that this person is one who is directly subordinate to the principal and carries certain specific duties such as discipline, attendance supervision, budget requisitions, etc. The title of associate principal implies a more nearly coequal status with the principal. While still subordinate to the principal, the associate is more likely to generally share all duties with the principal. The title of assistant to the principal is generally given to one who has limited administrative responsibility. He may be an intern or one who is in training for greater administrative responsibility. Whether or not a principal has any of these assistants makes considerable difference in the kind of supervisory organization possible. If his school organization includes an experienced and competent associate principal, the principal can share the supervisory duties.

SUPERVISORY TECHNIQUES

Classroom Observation

Classroom observation is one technique in the repertoire of supervision. Having previously defined supervision in terms of increasing the effectiveness of the teaching staff, it follows that supervisory activities must include direct observation of the teaching process. There are also indirect and perhaps equally effective techniques of supervision, but it seems difficult to conceive of a realistic supervisory program which is not built on the firm foundation of classroom observation.

A classroom observation is defined as at least one full period of instruction. By this definition, the "in-and-out" technique does not qualify. There may be other defensible reasons for administrative popping in and out of teachers' classrooms, but improving the supervision process is not one of them. With a full period of instruction, the observer has the advantage of witnessing a complete period of instruction. This is a considerable advantage since the supervision process is concerned with the quality of instruction, and the instruction process operates within the framework of the instructional period. Therefore, the observer has the responsibility to witness the entire process since its meaning for students is derived from the total period rather than from one segment of it. Perhaps another way of expressing this idea is to say that a teacher's lesson is one indivisible unit. To observe only a portion of it is to increase the probability of inaccurate observation and to breed misunderstanding.

Can a secondary principal observe a class in a subject field in which he has perhaps less knowledge than the students being taught? Although many teachers and some administrators will answer negatively, the authors' affirmation is positive. The secondary principal can and should observe the teaching process in subject areas where he has only general knowledge. However, in so doing, he must be cautious about what evaluations he makes on his observations. One who observes classrooms as a part of the supervisory process must make judgments only on those items about which he is competent. Any principal should be, and in fact must be, qualified to observe and subsequently make professional evaluations of the *teaching process*. He may need expert help in evaluating the worth of the content of subject matter, but if he is to fulfill his supervisory responsibility, the secondary administrator must be trained to make careful observations of what actually happens in a classroom.

What does happen in classrooms? Officially, teachers teach and, hopefully, students learn. But it is considerably more complex than that. There are at least five discrete elements capable of observation within a classroom: physical conditions, student behavior, teacher behavior, academic content, and something commonly termed "climate for learning." Admittedly, these elements are not equally capable of reliable observation. Physical conditions lend themselves better to objective observation than does climate for learning.

The physical conditions of the rooms that are of interest here are those items the teacher can control. While it is often said that teachers should maintain a desirable temperature in the classroom and moderate amounts of fresh air, most modern schools have entrusted control of these elements in automated sensing devices such as thermostats and humidistats. The observer of the physical environment should take stock of the room as a potential learning environment. What has this teacher done to make the physical environment more conducive to learning? Bulletin boards, seating arrangements, decorations, arrangements, and availability of resource materials are generally within the teacher's control and can be arranged to enhance the learning environment.

Principals and supervisors have traditionally used student behavior as a primary barometer of teacher effectiveness. Here, the term "student behavior" is intended to mean behavior in its inclusive sense, not simply the notion of discipline. How are the students reacting to the learning environment? Their degree of attention in the lesson is relatively easy to determine. What attitudes do they exhibit by their behavior, both verbal and nonverbal? What kinds of questions do they raise? How do they react to one another? How many students within the class actually participate? What are the nonparticipants doing? Some observers find a checklist useful. With this, they catalog the incidence of certain behavioral acts within a given period of time. Harris, writing in *Supervisory Behavior in Education,* suggests several techniques of observing what happens in a classroom.[9] One technique is the Pupil Response Analyzer. This provides a coding system for recording the types of responses made by pupils during an observed period. He employs a classification system for responses according to the following code: *a.* solitary response, *b.* controlled response, *c.* uncontrolled response, *d.* spontaneous response, *e.* mass response. Once an observer gains an understanding of the category into which each response fits, it becomes relatively simple to keep an observational tally during an entire lesson. The value of an observational record of this type is that it can provide objective data on what actually happened during an instructional period. The question of what appropriate types of pupil response are can become a subject for discussion between

9 Ben M. Harris, *Supervisory Behavior in Education,* Prentice-Hall, Inc., Englewood Cliffs, N.J., 1963, chap. 5.

teacher and supervisor, with the obvious advantage of having measurable data to discuss.

Teacher behavior is the third element that can be observed in the classroom. Even though teacher behavior has been the central focus of much of the literature of supervision for a long time, there is renewed and fresh interest in this. Whereas in earlier years the emphasis in teacher observation was on acquiring a global, overall impression of the quality of teaching, present-day trends emphasize objective observation techniques. Accompanying this is a major effort to search out definitions for the act of teaching itself. Teaching has always been recognized as a complex act consisting of many and varied activities on the part of the one called "teacher." Yet, to date there is no major agreement as to just what constitutes teaching. As Green states: "At the outset, one must recognize then, that the concept of teaching is molecular. That is, as an activity, teaching can best be understood not as a single activity, but as a whole family of activities within which some members appear to be of more central significance than others." [10] It is because teaching is not a unidimensional activity that makes it particularly difficult for two observers to see the same things. But, it is for this same reason that increased efforts are being made to define the elements of teaching in terms of observable bits of behavior.[11]

One example of the increased thrust toward developing methods for objective measurement of teacher behavior would be what is termed "interaction analysis." The most widely employed system of interaction analysis is the Flanders system. It is a system for classifying verbal behavior in the classroom.

Categories of teacher talk are (1) accepts feeling, (2) praises or encourages, (3) accepts or uses ideas of student, (4) asks questions, (5) lectures, (6) gives directions, and (7) criticizes or justifies authority. Categories of student talk are (8) student-talk response and (9) student-talk initiation. There is also a tenth category for recording periods of silence or confusion.[12]

Interaction observers are trained to record verbal behavior every 3 seconds for a specified period of time. These data are then summarized by entering them in a ten-row by ten-column matrix. This matrix provides objective patterns of the proportion of behavior entered into each cell and also the pattern of sequences.

Interaction analysis is a descriptive rather than an evaluative system

[10] Thomas F. Green, "A Typology of the Teaching Concept," *Studies in Philosophy and Education,* vol. 3, no. 4, p. 286, Winter, 1964–1965.
[11] Arno Bellack, *The Language of the Classroom,* Bureau of Publications, Teachers College, Columbia University, New York, 1964.
[12] Edmund J. Amidon and Evan Powell, "Interaction Analysis as a Feedback System in Teacher Preparation," The Supervisor as Agent for Change in Teaching, papers from ASCD Eleventh Curriculum Research Institute, Washington, D.C., 1966, pp. 44–56.

for measuring teacher and student behavior. It has been used with reported success in teacher training. Its greatest potential seems to be its use as a tool for teacher self-evaluation.

Some teachers and administrators protest against this trend on the grounds that teaching is inexact, creative, and immeasurable. It will probably be a long time before teaching can accurately be defined and measured; but the responsibility of supervision demands that the effort be made. And of course, the very notion of improvement includes the assumption of some standard of desirability.

The fourth discrete element capable of observation in a classroom is the academic content. It is here the principal may have the least competence. With the rapid expansion of knowledge it is difficult if not impossible for anyone to remain knowledgeable in each of the fields taught in the modern secondary school. All who have received the fundamentals of a good secondary education as well as a liberal arts college education possess the elements of common knowledge. This level of general education is satisfactory for functioning everyday life, but it is inadequate for judging the accuracy of knowledge being taught as a part of the secondary curriculum. This level of knowledge is a specialty of the teacher in that subject or the special subject supervisor. It is important that the secondary administrator recognize that, in all probability, his knowledge in many of the content fields is certainly less adequate than the teacher's and may also be less than the students'. The administrator can test his own knowledge within the special field against that which he observes being taught, but he must learn to depend on others for an evaluation of this content. These others would include department heads, special subject supervisors, consultants, and authorities in that field.

The fifth element present within each classroom, less objective, less definable, but nonetheless real and discernible, has been termed climate for learning. Perhaps this is the subjective feeling resulting from a synthesis of the other more objective elements. At any rate, any qualified and experienced observer of classrooms will be able to take his own reading on the climate for learning. Possibly this represents the art of teaching, that portion of it which refuses to be systematized and classified.

By being aware of these five elements present in a classroom, the secondary administrator can successfully utilize classroom observation as one valuable supervisory technique.

Formal Conferences

Formal conferences form an integral part of the supervision process. Perhaps the use of the term "formal" is not the most appropriate here, but it is used to establish clearly that such conferences are held at an appointed time, a specified place, and for a definite purpose. The actual tone of the interaction between supervisor and supervised may be as friendly, chatty, or informal as seems appropriate at the moment; nevertheless, it is formal in that it is a planned portion in the supervision process.

It is axiomatic to state that formal conferences should follow classroom observations. Ideally, the sooner the better, for reasons which are self-evident. In practice, principals find this difficult to accomplish. Other conflicting and important commitments for both teacher and principal frequently intervene to delay the conference following a classroom observation. Because this is such a common problem for practicing administrators, this is an even stronger reason for making the conferences formal and allocating them first priority among competing claims for time.

It is in the human dynamics of the teacher-principal (or teacher-assistant principal or teacher-supervisor) conference that some of the highest professional skills are called forth. Many teachers—and alas, too many administrators—approach this conference with the traditional notion that the supervisor now tells the supervised what was good and what was bad. This same line sagely suggests that the supervisor ought to mix the bad in with the good, always starting and ending with the good, in such a clever fashion that the supervised is pleased by the good and not too upset by the bad. The authors submit that these shallow subterfuges built on manipulative tricks are not only readily apparent to the supervised but also are ineffective techniques of supervision. Rather, we would recommend a simpler and more straightforward approach, based not on gimmicks but on the sincere mutual understanding of the roles of supervisor and the supervised.

A successful teacher-principal conference following classroom observation depends upon a number of preconditions. Principally, it depends upon a reasonable degree of role congruency, that is, that both supervisor and supervised accept the other's expected role. It further depends upon the "organizational climate," [13] which contributes to the teacher's expectations concerning the conference and its meaning within that school and that school system. As such conditions are fulfilled, profitable conferences become more likely.

Whereas the older notion of the observation and follow-up conference cast the principal in the role of judge, present thinking suggests that more fruitful conferences result when the principal assumes a role containing several dimensions. He can be an objective reporter of what went on in the classroom, an analyzer of the instructional process, and a clarifier of instructional goals, as well as a supporter of the teacher's professional dignity.

[13] Andrew W. Halpin and Don B. Croft, *The Organizational Climate of Schools,* Midwest Administration Center, University of Chicago, 1963.

It is important that the one in control of the conference, that is, the principal acting in his capacity as supervisor, keep in mind the general purpose of the conference.[14] Since supervision was defined in terms of increasing the effectiveness of those who teach, the conference must therefore be judged by the extent to which learning occurs on the part of the one doing the teaching. Good conferences should result in increased capacity for growth among teachers. It means not so much that they have now been told the real truth of how to do a better job of teaching, but more that they now have a clearer self-concept and an increased capacity for self-learning.

The principal and teacher discuss the observation together, each contributing his perceptions. In this way the outcome is likely to be a new understanding on the part of both observer and observed rather than a one-way expectation on the part of the observer that it is the observed who must do all the changing. If the principal has observed specific teaching behavior which to him appears to be ineffective, he can share this observation, too, but he must always invite the teacher's explanation of the same behavior. If this is done in a professional manner, backed by specific references to the actual classroom situation, the likelihood of its acceptance by the teacher as an accurate observation is greatly increased. It is within a framework built upon professional integrity and a clear understanding of one another's roles that the goal of instructional improvement can be advanced through formal conferences.

Formal conferences should not be restricted to a time following classroom observations. They are valuable at any time. The most important point for a secondary administrator to recognize in organizing his supervisory program is the need for such conferences and to plan for them. His planning of this work is as essential as the teacher's lesson planning. For either to proceed without planning is analogous to sailing blind upon the sea.

Informal Conferences

The listing of informal conferences as one technique in the principal's repertoire of supervision is to recognize that his influence pervades the school. For fear of misunderstanding, we would hasten to add that there is no intention that the principal play an omnipresent "snoopervisory" role. Rather, it is that the perceptive principal is constantly on duty while in school. He is a keen observer. As he goes about the building, he cannot help observing students, teachers, custodians, cafeteria workers, building conditions, bulletin board displays, student artwork—in short, everything

[14] James J. Jones, "The Individual Conference in Supervision," *The Teachers College Journal,* vol. 28, no. 1, pp. 10–11, October, 1956.

which may be a sample of the total learning environment which is his primary responsibility.

As the principal moves through the building, he presents students, teachers, and nonteachers with a convenient opportunity to speak with him. It may be only a brief question concerning some routine information, but it may also be an invitation to come and see something that the student, or teacher, or custodian has done of which he is rather proud. Golden opportunities for informal tension-free conferences grow out of his building travels. Should an informal doorway conference appear to be moving to a point where the more private conference is preferred, it is a simple matter to say, "Yes, I can see that may be a problem, come into the office, and we'll talk about it."

Successful practicing administrators place a high value on these informal conferences. They spend much time circulating through their buildings in order to create the contributing conditions.

Student Opinions

Were one to recommend that school administrators solicit student opinions on the quality of teaching, he would, in all probability, receive little support for such an outrageous idea. Yet, the placement of this topic under the heading of supervisory techniques implies that student opinions are useful under certain conditions.

The first condition, for the use of student opinions is that the teacher himself do the seeking. If he goes about this in a direct and sincere manner, with appropriate safeguards to preserve absolute student anonymity, students can furnish useful feedback. It is a simple matter to design forms for classroom use in collecting student opinions. The teacher may wish to know the students' opinions on such items as whether the marking system is fair, how heavy the homework load is, whether his own teaching presentation is clear, and whether there is an overall feeling of student satisfaction or dissatisfaction. In addition, he can elicit specific suggestions for improvement.

Some teachers may object to the idea of using student opinion as a technique for improving teaching. They will argue that students (no matter what their age) are immature and incapable of making good judgments about the quality of the instruction they receive. Further, it is often contended that the use of this technique by a teacher is sure to be seen by students as a sign of teacher weakness. Such protestations are based on an unrealistic understanding of students as well as on a misunderstanding of the purpose of assessing student opinion. Students are capable of making good judgments. In fact, they do make judgments, all the time, good or bad. They make them to their peers and their parents and anyone who will listen. What is often misunderstood is that teachers are not bound to accept student opinions as accurate judgments. Teachers would do well, though, to accept such judgments as valid expressions of opinion. The opinions may be accurate or inaccurate, wise or foolish. Right or wrong, what students think is important. One caution is in order. Any teacher who uses student opinion must realize that there may be some very negative feelings expressed by students. He should not be unduly sensitive to these expressions.

A principal can encourage his staff to experiment with student feedback systems and thus take a considerable step forward in establishing what is so often called the open climate. Hopefully, as teachers use this device, they might report their experiences to the principal, and some may even wish to share the student opinions with him.

Conference Attendance

Another supervisory technique is the encouragement of staff members to enlarge their horizons through school visits and attendance at educational conferences.

Most forward-looking school districts have policies which allow excused time for teachers to perform this kind of visiting. The alert principal can use this policy as an effective supervisory device. Suppose, for example, that he has been working with his staff on the development of a new organizational plan such as team teaching. If he knows of a school nearby which is noted for its team teaching, he can arrange for some of his interested teachers to visit there for a day. Teachers find this interschool visitation extremely helpful in developing new teaching concepts. Rarely do they return from visits convinced that the observed innovation should be put into effect in their own school. They do frequently observe portions of programs which seem feasible for their own use. Above all, visitations provide teachers with a much needed chance to observe others doing the same kind of work. It helps them acquire some much needed objectivity.

The principal can utilize the educational conference in much the same manner. For example, he may send one or more of his English teachers to a conference where the linguistics approach is to be explained. Highlights from visits and conferences make excellent agenda material for faculty meetings.

Faculty Meetings

Faculty meetings can be extremely effective supervision devices. Faculty meetings can also be dull, uninspiring, and thought of as a complete waste of time by many teachers. They need not be this way. Principals may need to hold faculty meetings for strictly communication and informational purposes upon occasion, but the faculty meeting device is not the most effective way to communicate strictly routine information. Hopefully, every meeting contains elements of what could be termed professional matters. These might relate to new developments in some subject field, new organizational plans, research reports, or reports on current educational legislation.

Many principals have found success in developing meaningful faculty meetings by working through a faculty committee. The title of this committee isn't important. It might be called a faculty meeting committee or a principal's advisory committee. What is important is that this committee work with the principal and the faculty in developing plans for worthwhile meetings. The use of such a committee generally means that other faculty members will become participants in the meetings. The principal retains his same prerogatives but has involved others in the planning and participation in the meetings. When carefully planned and organized, this approach to faculty meetings can become an effective supervisory technique.

Evaluation of the Supervisory Program Earlier in the chapter, supervision was defined as that subdivision of the total process of educational administration which is devoted principally to increasing the effectiveness of those who are engaged in the direct performance of the central task of the educational enterprise. Therefore, to evaluate this dimension of administrative performance, it is necessary to assess the relative gains made in this central task. Since this cannot be measured directly, indirect measures and inferences must be adopted. The administrators of a secondary school must attempt to assess the extent to which the supervisory program is succeeding in improving the quality of instruction.

One usable criterion is the amount of critical information the principal has at his command. As he assesses each member of his teaching staff, how much objective knowledge can he marshal concerning this member's teaching program? Based upon evidence collected during direct observation, what are the characteristic teaching behaviors of this teacher? How many formal conferences have been held? What was the content of these conferences? What information was exchanged? Were there mutual agreements reached on specific aspects of this teacher's program? What appears to be the pattern of growth experienced by this teacher, at this time of the year, compared with a year ago, or two years ago? When a principal is able to answer, for himself, or perhaps for a formal report, these questions in a confident manner, it is one clear sign that his supervisory program is effective.

Another usable criterion of the effectiveness of the supervisory program is the combined opinions of those being supervised. In the same spirit that it was suggested that teachers make use of students' opinions about the classroom teaching program, a similar procedure is useful to the principal. Through the development of a systematic feedback device, he can secure his staff's perception of the effectiveness of the supervisory program and, in particular, their collective perception of his role in this process.

A third source of knowledge for evaluation of the supervisory program may be found by tapping the resources of the central office. Assuming that the central office of the school district considers that it has a service function (not merely inspection and command—and this is probably principally dependent upon the chief school administrator), the secondary principal can request from his immediate superior, a frank evaluation of several aspects of his school program, including the supervisory program.

IN–SERVICE PROGRAMS FOR INSTRUCTIONAL STAFF

An in-service program for the instructional staff is a special activity sponsored by the school district which has as its central purpose the improvement of instruction. This is a rather broad definition of in-service activities, but it is narrow enough to eliminate some kinds of activities. Faculty meetings, for example, would not be considered in-service since there is the assumption that such meetings are a regular part of the faculty program, although, as we shall point out later, faculty meetings can be the convenient springboard for cooperative planning of in-service programs, and the content of some faculty meetings can be a part of an ongoing in-service program. The notion of in-service is that special training is given to teachers who are already on the job. It may be distinguished from preservice training since that is concerned with the preparation for teaching prior to entry into the profession. By contrast, then, in-service training is devoted to the continual upgrading of the existing instructional staff.

University courses and graduate programs taken by teachers while in service are also excluded from consideration as in-service. Such a division is purely arbitrary, of course, but the authors' preference is to consider such courses under the label of professional advancement.

In-service programs work chiefly through two avenues. First, some in-service programs hope for instructional improvement by upgrading the skill of the teachers. Second, other programs aim for instructional improvement by increasing the quality of the content of what is taught. Thus, in-service education effects improvement through two fundamental elements of professional education: instruction and curriculum.

The Scope of In-service Programs

The scope of in-service programs is wide, ranging from brief one-shot meetings to year-long seminars. Their content may be equally varied, from down-to-earth workshops which provide practical teaching hints to philosophic lectures by renowned figures. Their attendance may be mandatory or by invitation. Participating numbers may be as few as ten or less, or mass meetings of thousands. Their appeal to teachers may be encouragingly high, or it may be dismally low. Most significant of all, their payoff to the instructional program, may be definitely discernible, or it may be nothing at all. With such a broad scope, it isn't feasible to issue pronouncements on which programs are preferable to others. A more useful approach is to consider some of the factors in selecting desirable forms.

Within any given school district in-service programs can take several organizational forms. At the widest level, a program could be planned to serve the entire instructional staff on a one-meeting basis. It could bring the complete faculty together at some central point. Naturally, this depends completely upon the size of the total organization and upon the facilities available. Still, at the district level, in-service programs can be organized both horizontally, that is cutting across levels, for example all primary teachers, or vertically, as in the case of librarians who serve all levels. Another organizational model includes committee representation, centering about some particular aspect of instruction. This might include a group of fifteen teachers, for example, representing mathematics teachers from different schools, who are organized on an ad hoc basis for one purpose: to review new textbooks. One of the clearest advantages of an organizational plan which brings staff together from different schools is that it helps create a sense of districtwide unity of purpose. It is also an excellent opportunity for cross-fertilization of ideas throughout the district. Its obvious drawback is the physical problem of getting together at a common meeting point.

Within the individual school, there may be an in-service program occurring as a self-contained unit. It may have grown out of recognized needs or areas of interest within that school. This model overcomes the common meeting place problem but is subject to the limitations of the resources of one school and one staff. However, it has strong advantages since it may be a significant contributor to faculty unity and is easiest to relate directly to that school's particular program.

The question of whether attendance at in-service sessions should be required by administrative order or should be voluntary on a professional choice basis is best answered from the point of the purpose and nature of the meeting. As long as meetings are held within the established time limits of the staff's working day, boards of education have generally taken the position that the administration can require attendance at in-service meetings. However, when one keeps in mind the purposes of in-service education, there is much to suggest that more genuine changes in teaching behavior and improvements in curriculum content can be accomplished by teachers who consider themselves as professionals working on a task which they have shared in the determination of and one to which they have willingly come. The old adage about the horse being led to water may be disturbingly appropriate.

THE TYPES OF IN–SERVICE PROGRAMS

For convenience in-service programs were classified on the basis of their content. Whereas the *scope* generally dealt with the scheme of organization, the *type* is concerned with what the programs center about. A fourfold typology can be employed: Moving from the broadest to narrowest, we include (1) philosophical-theoretical, (2) curriculum, (3) instructional materials, and (4) special problem-centered in-service programs. Each shall be considered in turn.

Philosophical-theoretical

Philosophical-theoretical is the designation given to in-service programs whose content is broad, dealing with philosophies of education and/or broad theoretical concepts. Should an individual school be planning an evaluation team visit, a prerequisite is the development of a statement of philosophy and fundamental purposes. Such programs would necessarily include the entire instructional staff or else representatives from different subject areas. Although this type of in-service program is usually conducted at the individual school level, it is also possible to hold programs at a districtwide level. The authors know of a school district which sponsored a series of three half-day seminars devoted to the theme of individualizing instruction and secured nationally known lecturers to give general presentations to be followed up by group discussions.

Curriculum In-service

In-service programs centered about the *curriculum* are probably the most widely used. Generally on a representative basis curriculum projects are handled most often by a committee whose purpose is to update a local curriculum guide. A committee may be comprehensive in that it considers one subdivision of the curriculum from kindergarten through senior high school, or it may only consider one division, i.e., junior high mathematics.

Instructional Materials In-service

In-service programs built about *instructional materials* most typically consider new texts, new audio-visual devices, or special methods of working with new materials. The division between curriculum groups and instructional materials groups is often combined into one committee's function; for example, a senior high social studies committee may rewrite a curriculum guide and then select new texts and materials which best fit the new curriculum. Commercial companies selling new instructional media are often pleased (indeed eager) to hold demonstration sessions and will bring in their own consultants.

Special Problem In-service

In-service programs are also organized about some identified area of special concern. There is likely to be an ad hoc committee whose purpose is to investigate the problem and make recommendations to a legislative or administrative body. An example of this could be a homework committee, organized to develop a school policy for presentation to the faculty for ratification and eventually given to the board of education for adoption. Such a group may survey homework practices within the school or district, gather homework policies from other districts, test opinions of students, faculty, and parents, and then work out an appropriate recommended guide for homework within their school or district. Other typical special study areas could be report cards, the student activity program, assembly programs, or student discipline.

Some Administrative Problems of In-service   While there are numerous items which could be considered as administrative problems of in-service work, we shall restrict ourselves to three, namely, the problem of time for in-service work, the sources of knowledge for in-service work, and problem of motivation for in-service work.

Time looms as the most pressing problem for in-service programs, especially in the secondary school. Since the typical secondary school instructional day covers a period of 7 hours, it is unrealistic to expect a great deal of teacher enthusiasm about starting an in-service meeting 8 hours after they have come to school. Yet, this is the common pattern, and it is no doubt a tribute to the willing professional dedication of a majority of teachers that it is the modal practice.

Many school districts try to hold in-service work at a time when the participants will be fresher for this demanding and creative work. There are an increasing number of districts which secure authorization from boards of education to hold early dismissals, half days, or even whole days for in-service work. Many boards of education appear to have acquired an appreciation for the significance of in-service work and recognize that it is professional work necessary for the continued advancement of a school.

A second administrative problem of in-service work is the one centering about the question of which sources of knowledge are to be tapped. Nearly all schools possess some energetic and capable staff members who can serve as resources of special knowledge; yet no school possesses all the resources of special knowledge necessary for some kinds of work. This is to suggest that both inside and outside consultants may be used. When the best use is made of local staff, not only is it indicative of a high-caliber staff, but it furnishes an excellent opportunity for individual members to develop special skills and knowledge and thereby enhance their professional status. In fact, active involvement in in-service work is one of the best routes to promotion for teachers seeking advancement within the system. At the same time, the use of outside consultants can be highly beneficial. The nationally known public school system of Newton, Massachusetts, has continually employed outstanding consultants from Harvard and other leading universities. Nova High School in Broward County, Florida, also recognized as an exciting new venture in secondary education, has continuing consultative arrangements with subject-matter specialists. The use of outside consultants representing commercial companies is another source of knowledge for in-service programs. While the latter freely admit they have a product to sell, many nonetheless do make genuine noncommercial presentations.

The third general problem of in-service education is that of adequate motivation by the participants. In districts where in-service education is held in low esteem by the faculty, there is noticeable lack of motivation for programs. The problem is difficult for an administrator who is anxious to act as a change agent in his school when he finds that his efforts to generate enthusiasm for the in-service program are regarded with polite apathy (and sometimes impolite hostility). The solution to this one is bound up in the complexities of the whole in-service movement, many of which have already been listed. Assuming that the time problem can be overcome, administrators can more likely expect teachers to be moderately motivated when the following conditions are met: (1) that teachers have had a share in the determination of the content of the in-service program; (2) that teachers perceive that the program will be oriented toward the solution of practical classroom problems; (3) that teachers have had prior experiences with in-service work which led to meaningful changes which they could witness either within the school district at large or in their own school; (4) that teachers expect the meeting or program will not extend significantly beyond the stated termination time; and (5) that the program is held, at least some of the time, during regular in-school time.

SUMMARY

The modern secondary school principal believes that the instructional program within his school can be improved. The modern secondary school principal accepts the belief in improvability as a high challenge to his job. Thus he strives unceasingly to reach greater heights of excellence.

Other coworkers share this responsibility with the principal. The central office staff, department heads, and teachers—all must accept responsibility for the improvement of instruction.

Supervision is seen as a subfunction of administration whose purpose is to help those who are working at the classroom level, that is, the teachers. Supervision is seen as another dimension of educational leadership.

A good supervision program is one which is planned and organized rather than haphazard and incidental. While it keeps its central focus on the improvement of teaching, it maintains a close sensitivity to the necessity for good human relations.

Classroom observation is an important working tool as a supervision technique. It was suggested that there are five elements capable of being observed in any classroom. Formal conferences, informal conferences, the solicitation of student opinions, attendance at educational conferences, and faculty meetings are all part of a well-designed supervisory program. The in-service program also contributes to the improvement of instruction.

SUGGESTED EXERCISES

1. The authors have indicated that the principal's responsibility for program improvement varies considerably with the organizational structure of the school district. Secure an organization chart from three different sized districts: large city, small city, and small central or rural district; and seek to determine what differences there are in role expectations for the secondary principal in each.

2. Secure the NEA Project on Instruction publication, *From Bookshelves to Action: A Guide to Using the Recommendations of the NEA Project on Instruction*. Make a definite plan to implement a number of these recommendations within a school that you know. Ask class members to evaluate your plan.

3. Assume that a secondary principal feels that he can afford to spend $60 annually for professional memberships. Give your recommendation for the best investment of his $60.

4. Develop an observational checklist for use in classroom observations.

5. Plan a role-playing conference where one class member plays the role of principal and one the role of a teacher who has been observed by the principal that day.

6. Survey a number of school districts on the problem of time for in-service work. Catalog the variety of patterns which indicate some effort to put this work within the regular teaching day.

SELECTED REFERENCES

BLUMBERG, ARTHUR, "Supervisory Behavior and Interpersonal Relations," *Educational Administration Quarterly*, vol. iv, no. 2, pp. 34–45, Spring, 1968.

CONANT, JAMES B., *Shaping Educational Policy*, McGraw-Hill Book Company, New York, 1964.

HALPIN, ANDREW W., AND DON B. CROFT, *The Organizational Climate of Schools*, Midwest Administration Center, University of Chicago, 1963.

HARRIS, BEN M., *Supervisory Behavior in Education*, Prentice-Hall, Inc., Englewood Cliffs, N.J., 1963, chap. 5.

MASTERS, NICHOLAS, AND LAWRENCE K. PETTIT, "Some Changing Patterns in Educational Policy-making," *Educational Administration Quarterly*, vol. ii, no. 2, pp. 81–100, Spring, 1966.

MCCLEARY, LLOYD, AND STEPHEN P. HENCLEY, *Secondary School Administration*, Dodd, Mead & Company, Inc., New York, 1965, chaps. 11 and 12.

Role of the Supervisor and Curriculum Director in a Climate of Change, 1965, Association for Supervision and Curriculum Development Yearbook, Washington, D.C., 1965, 170 pp.

SEC-TION 4

supporting school services

INTRODUCTION   This section of the book has to do with the supporting school services. Chapter 17 deals with staff personnel and gives detailed information about certified personnel and principles relating to staffing the school. This chapter also covers the maintaining of good teachers and the developing and maintaining of good morale. Chapter 18 reviews the area of guidance and pupil personnel services from the standpoint of the principal and guidance personnel needed to implement such a program in the secondary school. The organizational plans and techniques of guidance along with records are presented in this chapter. Chapter 19 treats management of the principal's office. It considers such factors as the facilities, the duties of the principal, the administrative organization, records and reports, and the opening and closing of the school year. Chapter 20 has to do with the management services of the school. These services include school facilities, the use of space, operation, and maintenance, and the planning of new facilities. In addition, this chapter deals with supplies and equipment, the cafeteria, and transportation. Public relations is an important responsibility of the principal, and this position is supported in Chapter 21. Objectives of the public relations program, methods of organization and administering the program along with determining the avenues, agencies, and media of public relations are reviewed. Public relations and its relationship to groups and methods of evaluating public relations are also presented. The last chapter in this section and in the book deals with research and development. It reviews methods of initiating change in school practices and ways of improving the analysis of group pressures. Further, this chapter discusses research policies and the principal and his relationship to research.

CHAPTER 17

STAFF
PERSONNEL
The history of the growth and development of almost any worthwhile institution is of interest to those who are affected by it and especially to those with a vested interest in its growth and operation. The value of this history lies in its use to refine the function and the planning of the direction of the institution. An institution may express its purposes through its philosophy and its function. So it is with the secondary school.

The area of personnel administration may be defined as the complex of specific activities engaged in by the school district to make a pointed effort to secure the greatest possible worker effectiveness consistent with the school's objectives.[1] Getzels and Guba say that the purpose of staff relations is to integrate the demands of staff members in a way that is organizationally productive and individually fulfilling.[2] This does not necessarily imply that organizational demands and individual needs are

[1] James A. Van Zwoll, *School Personnel Administration*, Appleton-Century-Crofts, Inc., New York, 1964, p. 3.
[2] J. W. Getzels and E. G. Guba, "Social Behavior and the Administrative Process," *The School Review*, vol. 65, no. 4, p. 430, Winter, 1957.

always compatible. Reasons for this obvious disparity may be found both in the individual and in the institution.

In a real sense personnel administration concerns itself with providing or arranging conditions which will make possible greater self-direction by personnel in the performance of their work. This concept implies that the administration has placed a trust in its personnel. Further it indicates that the end product of the educational process is determined by the effectiveness of staff personnel.

The purpose of this chapter is to discuss certification, staffing the schools, and maintaining an effective staff. Further, treatment will be given to developing morale and improving the competency of the staff.

CERTIFICATION OF PERSONNEL

Purposes of Certification

An often used expression is, "A school is only as effective as its staff." Although this statement is only a partial truth, it signifies a principle that needs elaboration. First, it is incumbent to point out that the primary purpose of teacher certification is to improve education for the children of the nation. The competence and the character of those who teach our youth affect the quality of educational programs. A secondary purpose of teacher certification is to protect the teacher and the profession. If unqualified and unethical persons are to be kept out of teaching, some manner of protection is needed for those who are qualified. In one sense the standards of a state's educational program are reflected in its certification requirements. Likewise, there is often a positive relationship between certification requirements, salary schedules, and teaching effectiveness.

Although certification requirements are handled through state departments of education in most states, there have been occasions when these requirements have been used improperly. During the depression days of the thirties certification was used to limit or restrict teachers from a particular geographic region. Married women were not permitted to teach in some districts. Teachers often were forced to live in the district in which they taught. In some instances teachers were expected to spend their salaries in the communities where the salaries were paid.

Certified Personnel

In order to become eligible to teach in public schools of the various states, it is necessary for teachers to qualify for a teacher's certificate. These certificates are issued by the state department of education in accordance with state laws and with the rules and regulations of the state board of education. The requirements within an individual state usually reflect the thinking of the leaders in education as revealed by the state education association, the state department, and the colleges and universities that prepare teachers.

Among the persons who should be licensed in addition to teachers are the school psychologist, the school social workers, school nurses, and all administrative and supervisory personnel. It is becoming more common for certification to apply also to selected persons in the nonprofessional personnel. This may be the engineer, the chief of custodial personnel, and others. Again, certification holds no guarantee of success for personnel but does tend to eliminate those persons who fail to meet minimum qualifications for a respective position.

Trends in Certification

A close look at certification requirements for teachers over the past two decades indicates three major trends. First, there is a growing trend toward the raising of certification standards in general. Although certification requirements reflect only the minimum standards of a particular state, an upward trend in these requirements is in order if the teaching profession is to be viewed with any degree of stature.

Second, there is a trend toward closer cooperation between state authorities and professional educators in the formulation of policy concerning certification. Although the profession itself has to assume much of the responsibility for improving certification requirements, there is a general feeling that these requirements should be formulated under the leadership of professional personnel composed of members of the teaching profession, professional educators, and members of the state department of education.

Third, a trend that is developing at a much slower pace than the two previously mentioned is toward more reciprocity compacts among the various states. As the mobility of our population increases, the more important this trend becomes. Additional institutional accreditation policies need to be developed and implemented to expedite this healthy trend.

It is recommended that groups whose purpose is to help formulate certification policy, whether they be state advisory councils or state commissions, assist their members in preparing adequately for active participation. This means a high level of professional competence, keeping abreast of educational research findings, and an acute awareness of the many problems and issues associated with certification.

STAFFING THE SCHOOL

Supplying the schools with competent teachers is one of the most formidable tasks facing the American people today. This challenge becomes even more bold when one considers that it contains at least four facets. First, an adequate supply of qualified personnel must be found to staff the schools. Second, these people must be recruited and some distinction made between effective and ineffective teachers during the selection process. Third, teachers must be appropriately assigned in terms of their potential contributions. Fourth, teachers need orientation to the school and the school system.

Recruitment and Sources of Supply

The supply of teachers is affected by the general economic situation. In times of depression, more teachers are available than positions, and the reverse tends to be true in periods of inflation. These generalizations are based upon past experiences and may not hold for the future. When one considers the many problems confronting those whose task it is to secure teachers, the evidence of difficulty of providing the secondary schools with an adequate supply of efficient teachers is almost overwhelming. Consider for a moment that the secondary pupil enrollment increased about 5 million during the decade 1955–1965. Also the current annual production of new teachers nowhere near approaches the number of teachers needed to provide for this increase in enrollment. Additional needs for secondary teachers are being brought about yearly by the continuous demand for increased school services.

Another factor which contributes to the overall problem of teacher supply is that only approximately 6 percent of our high school graduates contemplate teaching as a profession.[3] It has been suggested by Hall and Vincent that if 8 percent of all the high school graduates in the United States were to enter teaching, they would fill only the places made vacant by the teachers who leave the profession each year.[4]

Although the competition for special talent has been increasing, the probability that education will succeed in obtaining its share of potential leaders has been decreasing. One of the contributing factors has been teachers themselves who do not help the recruitment cause. Lonsdale reports an Oregon study which showed that sixth-grade pupils do not have the negative attitude toward teaching that is revealed among high school students.[5] Another study of 1,556 teachers revealed that 24 percent said they would not reenter teaching if they had their lives to live over.[6] These data indicate that pupils develop some of the attitudes held by teachers toward teaching, especially those that are negative. Since there

[3] Curtis H. Trelkeld, "Problems in the Recruitment and Adjustment of Teachers," *NASSP Bulletin,* vol. 32, pp. 169–175, March, 1948.
[4] Roy M. Hall and Antonio M. Vincent, "Staff: Selection and Appointment," *Encyclopedia of Educational Research,* The Macmillan Company, New York, 1960, pp. 1375–1377.
[5] Richard C. Lonsdale, "Recruiting Young People for Teaching," *School Executive,* vol. 75, pp. 19–21, 1955.
[6] Trelkeld, *op. cit.,* pp. 170–175.

are indications that this is more true at the secondary level, the problem of recruiting becomes more complex.

One of the offsetting factors about pupils deciding to enter the teaching profession is the indices that parents in large numbers approve of their sons and daughters choosing teaching as a profession. One survey of parental attitudes revealed that 52 percent of the parents wanted their children to become teachers, 29 percent were neutral, and 19 percent would be displeased if their children went into teaching as a profession.[7] Despite the fact that this survey produces good evidence concerning parents and their interest in the teaching profession, one cannot generalize for the total population.

Uneven Distribution of Teacher Shortage

There is an imbalance in the number of teachers for certain secondary school areas. There is an underproduction in science, mathematics, girls' physical education, home economics, music, and art. There is an overproduction in men's physical education, social studies and in some locations, English and business education. Also related to the supply of teachers is a geographical factor. Some states have had severe population losses while others have had more than 100 percent increases. Among the rapid growth group would be Alaska, Arizona, Florida, Nevada, and California.

There is a definite shortage of men teachers in the teaching profession. Many factors are militating against securing and keeping men teachers in the secondary schools. First, teaching has become thought of as a feminine profession by many people. Second, some districts do not advance women in the profession at the same rate as men because they are not looked upon as the official "breadwinner" of a family. Of course men also leave teaching more often than women to enter other occupations or businesses in order to provide for growing families. Also some men leave the profession because they are unable to advance at a rate which they feel is essential to their own morale and satisfaction.

Selection Procedures

Before teachers are employed by school boards, their qualifications for the vacancy are examined by representatives of the school system. Included in the school's representatives will likely be the chief administrator or his assistant, the principal, and other designated faculty members. Where the principal uses a team of teachers to assist in the selection, they will help in evaluating data about prospective employees and in the interviews. Generally, the principal with the aid of selected faculty members nominates, the superintendent recommends, and the board of education appoints employees.

[7] *Ibid.*, pp. 173–175.

There are at least four administrative policies which are dependent upon the organization of the personnel department of a school district. These are: geographical limitations, position descriptions, examination for selection, and qualifications.[8]

Some school authorities look upon the local community and its adjoining neighborhoods as a source of teacher supply and thus giving an element of stability to the staff. Often this type of policy limits recruitment outside the area to those individuals who initiate the action concerning potential employment. Of course this type of policy presupposes that the district has many favorable factors such as a quality program, high salary level, desirable geographical location, pleasant climate, and is near teacher training institutions. This type of choice places too great an emphasis upon the initiative of potential candidates to make application and often restricts selection to such candidates. A better alternative in the eyes of the authors is to assume, regardless of the quality and number of applications received, that only an active vigorous recruiting campaign will meet the competition for the most capable teaching faculty which the district can attract.

Due to the more specialized positions within the instructional program today, it is important to develop position descriptions. These descriptions should be developed in terms of the requirements and responsibilities of the position rather than a mere description of the individual sought to occupy the position. Certification requirements do this to some extent, but such operations as team teaching, departmentalization, and specialists in various teaching areas create a larger demand for position descriptions.

The main arguments for examination and selection are based upon two factors. First, examination results add further evidence to the data considered in the selection process. Second, they are helpful when recruitment is done on a wide range of several states and when the various teacher training institutions are not well known to the local school people. When and how to use examinations in teacher selection is still open to discussion since many local school systems are not convinced of their value. One of the most frequently used examinations is the National Teachers Examination. It is designed to measure knowledge, ability, and qualities expected in a teacher. Personality testing is not used very widely for teacher selection or for screening for promotion. Lipsett states: "The most sophisticated body of thinking in the profession of testing today would probably hold that testing for personality factors cannot be done effectively without projective tests, and there is insufficient evidence that it can be done with tests." [9]

[8] James P. Steffensen, *Staff Personnel Administration*, U.S. Department of Health, Education and Welfare, Office of Education, 1963, pp. 14–18.
[9] Lawrence Lipsett, "Guideposts for Personnel Testing," *Personnel Journal*, vol. 40, p. 264, November, 1961.

In a study of recruitment practices in Pennsylvania, Rudisill found the most important factors considered in the selection to be in rank order were: interviews, previous employer's statement, student teacher's statement, classroom observation, application data, college academic record, and references named by teachers.[10] In far too many instances the most attention is found to focus upon the interview. Although the interview is all important, perhaps more concentration and planning could be devoted to observing teachers in teaching situations prior to the interview or employment.

In selecting teachers, representatives of school systems tend to seek candidates whose qualities include a positive attitude toward their work, emotional stability, knowledge of subject matter, ability to plan and organize, logical thought, a positive personality, speech, poise, and tact, a well thought out philosophy of education, and a pleasant speaking voice. Despite limited general agreement upon qualities expected in applicants, there is an equal degree of disagreement.

Again, Lipsett examined forms used for employment applications and found many differences.[11] Some forms are limited to qualifications which are related only to a prediction of probable success in terms of pupil-teacher interaction in the classroom; others attempt to assess the teacher's probable acceptance within and contribution to community life. The latter area sought to determine the number of noneducational organizations to which the prospective teacher belongs. Most of the variations that applied to the selection process likewise applied to evaluation for promotion process too.

Teacher Assignment

If, when vacancies occur in teaching positions, replacements are sought for specific teaching positions, then assignment of teachers becomes a matter of follow-up in the total process. The administration should seek a teacher to fit a position rather than attempt to make the position fit the teacher. Positions have their peculiarities just as teachers have theirs. A prospective teacher ought to be placed in the school and in the position for which he has the most depth of training and in which he feels most secure. It is not always possible to consider how the teacher fits into the total faculty of a particular school, but when it can be done, it should be taken into account.

Teacher assignment must take into consideration such things as number of different class preparations, size of classes, and out-of-class and special activities. Of course interest and motivation in a particular subject

[10] Mervin D. Rudisill, "A Study of Practices and Procedures Used by Public Schools in Pennsylvania to Recruit and Employ Teachers," unpublished doctoral dissertation, Temple University, Philadelphia, 1965.
[11] Lipsett, *op. cit.*, p. 264.

are of prime importance in placing a teacher where he has the best opportunity for success.

Although each new teacher should be employed for a specific position in the school system, it is occasionally necessary to revise the original assignment of teachers. As a matter of administrative expediency, therefore, it is advisable, particularly in the larger school systems, to employ teachers for a position in the school system rather than for a specific position or school.

At the time of appointment newly selected staff members should be informed, insofar as possible, about what their duties will be. This enables them to make preparation for their future work and tends to prevent misunderstandings later about a given assignment within their school.

Orientation Procedures

The orientation period for new teachers, including those new to the system and new to the profession, may be considered as the beginning of an in-service training program. The basic purpose of such a period is to introduce the new staff member to the school district, the school, and the community. It is best not to restrict the program to the welcoming aspect but to include the development of both attitudes and information about the entire school.[12] New teachers as well as those already in the system need to understand the problems and policies of the system as a whole as well as those that relate to their own individual school.

If properly handled, the orientation period is welcomed by new teachers; they see it as an opportunity to learn about the system and its working conditions. Teachers may be helped to recognize that teaching children in a particular school system is a team effort and that the schools operate to provide benefits for children. Administrative employees and teachers can be of assistance to new teachers by helping them become acquainted with their colleagues, pupils, parents, and other people of the community. A second way to assist new teachers is by familiarizing them with the special requirements and administrative machinery of the school system in which they are to work and with any special community characteristics or expected modes of behavior.

Teachers new to the system need information about their own school in areas such as marking and examination procedures, how pupils are classified, how to obtain supplies and equipment, school reports, local school policies, and sources of information for specific questions that may arise which are not covered in faculty handbooks, school district policies, or other data given the teachers at the time of signing the contract. The orientation period should not be one of indoctrination but a learning experience which helps teachers see the framework within which they are

[12] *Ibid.*, p. 20.

expected to work and a period of identification of sources of help to make their work satisfactory and pleasant. It should be the beginning of their in-service education in the school system.

One such orientation program is reported by Smith as being carried on in the school district of the District of Columbia.[13] It is thought that the program described briefly here is effective in helping new teachers form attitudes toward the school and the district as well as learn about the system.

The superintendent and other administrative officials set aside 4 days prior to the opening of school for the initial orientation of new teachers. During the first 3 days, the newcomers meet with administrators, teachers, and supervisors; the fourth day they report to their assigned schools to become acquainted with the principal, faculty, school building, and school community.

The District of Columbia Education Association is included in the overall planning and presentation. A part of the session is also used to publicize projects specially designed for new teachers.

The planning that goes into the orientation sessions consumes a great deal more time than the 4 days it takes to carry out the program. Indeed, the planning for the next year's orientation begins immediately after the September orientation, when supervisors evaluate and make tentative plans.

Long after the 4-day intensive sessions have been completed, in-service demonstrations and meetings are continued as a part of the orientation program. The first involves formation of a systemwide planning committee to determine an overall strategy for the orientation.

The widespread interest in beginning teachers is evident from the makeup of the planning group. The inclusion of persons from the various departments not only ensures comprehensive coverage of details but also avoids unnecessary duplication of effort.

An outstanding feature of this program is that during the orientation period the presentation techniques are varied in order to hold the attention of the audience. For example, demonstration lessons, group discussions, question and answer periods, and various kinds of educational media are utilized to prevent boredom and monotony.

As in all good orientation programs, there is the evaluation. At the end of the final session teachers write their opinions of the orientation program and give general and specific impressions of its value. Evaluation must be frequent and carried on over a period of time.

An effective orientation program involves a great deal of time, effort, and thought. The end result of such a program can prove to be satisfying and rewarding not only to the new teacher but also to the persons who

13 Grace H. Smith, "An Effective Orientation Program," *NEA Journal*, vol. 54, pp. 47–48, May, 1965.

plan and help present it as well as to the pupils who really are its benefactors.

KEEPING GOOD TEACHERS

After teachers have been located, employed, and deemed competent, the administrator then has to think in terms of striving to retain them in the school system. Numerous methods and practices have been employed by school administrators and boards of education to induce teachers of high quality to remain in the system. Among the more significant areas of concern are teaching loads and teacher load, adequate salaries and promotional machinery, broad welfare benefits, and evaluation of teachers.

Teaching Load and Teacher Load

First it is important to define exactly what one is talking about. For the purpose of this discussion *teaching load* will be used to include the actual teaching assignment and those out-of-class activities which are directly related to the classes taught. These duties would include such things as the marking and grading of papers, reading themes, and preparation of future class materials and assignments. *Teacher load* may be used to refer to the total job assignment given to an individual teacher. Although it is possible for an excellent teacher to be given a teaching load that is too heavy, it is much more likely that it is the total teacher load that becomes unreasonable and discouraging. As in most organizations, there are within the public school system jobs to be done that require special skills. The better teachers are in demand for research projects, for experimentation, to serve on committees, to participate in curricular development, and to aid in the formulation of local administrative policy. Most professionally minded teachers prefer to work in a dynamic and stimulating environment if the teacher load is reasonable and just. Part of the leadership role of the secondary principal involves planning ways to make wise use of the teacher's time and talents. Hedges refers to this type of planning as "the organization of the teacher's working day." [14] He deplores the idea that secondary teachers are given five solid subjects to teach daily plus additional duties such as study hall, hall duty, and extracurricular activities, along with some school-connected work at home. This enormous teacher load may result in a teacher's not having time to make adequate class preparation, to read professionally, to secure adequate physical rest, or to think clearly about his work. Often associated with overwork is a deep feeling of frustration

[14] William D. Hedges, "A Straightforward Plan to Reduce the Teacher's Load," *The Clearing House*, vol. 38, pp. 342–345, February, 1964.

and dissatisfaction. When this feeling becomes intense, teachers may look for another position, retreat somewhat in their planning, or resort to other forms of adjustment that enable them to cope with local conditions. First and foremost, the students are the unfortunate recipients of this type of teacher behavior.

It is the responsibility of the school board and the administrators to provide time for teacher planning. This can be done by removing as many clerical duties as possible from teachers. The teacher ought to be given adequate time for planning but not necessarily a shorter day. Most of the school planning should be done at school and on school time. The professional materials available at school should be of great help to the teacher.

Adequate Salaries and Promotional Machinery

In order to maintain a strong and competent faculty, it is imperative to have an adequate salary schedule and one that can be modified in terms of costs of living or in some way be related to the economic conditions that prevail. Teachers ought to be able to make a living at their profession without having to moonlight at part-time jobs. In a rather real sense the salary schedule reflects the philosophy of the district and the thinking of the community. Of course this type of reasoning must be based upon the financial resources of the district and its ability to pay for high-level instruction. In order to prevent a widespread practice of teacher turnover, salaries have to be equivalent to or better than those of the surrounding districts. This may sound like an impossible situation, but it has merit in that teachers who want to advance can see opportunities for advancing within their own district.

Many districts reward career teachers or those teachers who have been properly qualified and have taught in the district or state for 10 or more years. These people may be distinguished for their experience and demonstrated competence rather than for teaching for a short period in order to pay for a trip to Europe or for the purchase of a new car. They are dedicated and plan to remain in the profession. It is the opinion of the authors that such teachers should receive financial rewards above the normal salary schedules. This additional reward can go as high as $1,000 to $2,000 above the regular salary scale, depending upon the money available for instruction. Likewise, districts should be able to employ teachers from other districts and give them credit on the salary scale for their total years of experience.

Within most school systems there should be some type of arrangement whereby an outstanding teacher may advance himself. A large part of the problem of keeping competent teachers is to make such opportunities available. It does not necessarily stand that all teachers desire to be administrators, but many may wish to be promoted to department head-ships, to assistant principalships, or other administrative positions. Some teachers desire only to receive more income for what they are doing and learning to do better. Certainly the least a district can hope to do is to make known to all faculty members when vacancies occur and to provide them with the same data and opportunity for advancement that are given to persons from outside the district.

The need for organized recruitment of talented candidates for school leadership positions is so great and urgent that promotional machinery for teachers is urgently needed to help fulfill this need.[15] An incentive any district may use to keep teachers is to pay them what they are worth and to help them work in areas of interest.

Broad Welfare Benefits

Like any other professional, the teacher has a strong interest in his own contentment and prosperity. Although the body of research concerning the relationship between welfare benefits and faculty effectiveness is al-most nonexistent, administrators have generalized from experience that adequate welfare benefits aid both the teachers and the school system. It is implied by administrators that (1) recruitment is easier, (2) teacher turnover is less, and (3) teacher effectiveness is higher where broad welfare benefits exist. Kindred and Woodard reviewed the personnel policies and practices of 300 school systems in the United States and found that, in addition to salary, tenure, and retirement, other practices that should receive careful attention are: health and recreation, working conditions and environment, leaves of absence, insurance policies, and benefit asso-ciations and services.[16] Again, this analysis of personnel policies indicated that teachers look for more than money, tenure, and retirement. The entire package of staff welfare benefits is needed if school systems are to keep effective teachers. Teachers need to feel that their work is important and that they have a professional service to sell. The school system that responds with the idea that it is searching for teachers who wish to become career teachers will attempt in every way to keep these same teachers and is likely to provide broad welfare benefits.

DEVELOPING AND MAINTAINING MORALE

Staff morale is a significant responsibility that rests mainly in the hands of the principal. It depends on the democratic relationships developed cooperatively by the principal and his staff. The word "morale" is used

[15] Jack Culbertson, *The Selective Recruitment of Educational Leaders,* The University Council for Educational Administration, Columbus, Ohio, January, 1966, p. 20.
[16] Leslie W. Kindred and Prince B. Woodard, *Staff Welfare Practices in the Public Schools,* The Center for Applied Research in Education, Inc., New York, 1963, p. 105.

here to refer to the capacity of a group to work closely in a cooperative, lasting, and stable manner in the seeking for or carrying out of common goals. A discussion of the five factors that follow provides some insight into morale.

Stimulating Environment

Staff members need an environment that is exciting and stimulating and one in which they are made to realize that they have opportunities for professional growth and advancement. Staff members need to feel that they are a part of a team and need to have respect for the administration. Likewise, teachers need to provide a warm and friendly atmosphere and to understand the point of view of the administration, and the administration needs to understand the point of view of the staff. Principals ought to be reminded that confidence in others should begin with the principals' having confidence in teachers and then encouraging teachers to confide in them. When principals fail to support teachers, the staff tends to view this as a type of weakness; however, there may be instances where it is not wise to support the teacher. An atmosphere of mutual confidence between principal and teachers is of paramount importance. Individual teachers need to share the feelings of oneness and of operating as a unit.

Definite Responsibilities

Staff members need to know the activities for which they are responsible. Lines of communication should always be open to teachers, and they should be encouraged to ask questions relative to their responsibilities and duties. Principals can often ease the tension of teachers by consulting them before decisions that affect their working conditions are made. For example, suppose that it becomes necessary for the principal to assign a section of general mathematics to a science teacher because of the way in which scheduling has developed. It would be a wise principal who would call the teacher in and request his help in a rather unusual situation rather than make the assignment and let the teacher learn about the change in teaching assignment by reading it on the printed schedule.

Teachers need to know that their teaching loads are reasonable and fair in comparison to those of teachers in the system. In addition, staff members should not feel that they are restricted by school policy to the extent that creativity in teaching is hindered. Freedom to experiment and to create is necessary for the self-satisfaction of teachers.

Grievance Machinery

In almost any large school system one may find annoyances or grievances. Where obvious inequities exist, teachers will become vexed. At times the fault lies with the teacher, and at other times the fault may rest with his immediate superior, or there may be instances where they share the blame. Typical examples of grievances of school employees include objections to a particular principal or supervisor, objections to methods of rating teachers, dissatisfaction with the salary schedule, duties other than teaching, and staff meetings. Of course administrative staff members also have grievances that deserve attention.

If teachers or administrators, as the case may be, are provided the opportunity to have a fair and just hearing, the effect on morale is apt to be favorable. If grievances are suppressed or ignored, they can lead to great dissatisfaction among those who deserve to be heard. The principal, as well as all those concerned with handling teacher complaints, must assume a positive and professional attitude.

Academic and Personal Freedom

To the extent that teachers are capable and willing, they should have the right and opportunity to contribute ideas and suggestions to the principal. Faculty members need the right and freedom to exchange information and ideas in open seminars if the principal desires high morale. Sometimes particular conditions in the working environment have to be changed to prevent teacher frustration and to promote a healthier place to work. Teachers want to feel that they will be supported by the principal in their efforts, but they do not like to have someone breathing down their necks. They desire freedom to exercise creative efforts which may not always come out successfully.

A modern secondary school principal will make it possible for teachers to discuss and to participate in policy making where needed. Any major participation by the staff in policy making requires more time than routine administration but may in the long run save time as a result of increased understanding and efficiency. The way one feels about his position is influenced by his participation and his involvement.

Usually a direct relationship exists between human efficiency and high morale. The way in which teachers perceive the community in which they work and the way in which the community perceives the teachers is important in understanding teacher morale. Most teachers desire to live their own lives and not be restricted by the community, yet at the same time, they feel obligations to perform as professionals in their personal lives. The principal must recognize that an environment conducive to high morale is not to be achieved by chance, and he should accept a major responsibility for planning and advancing it.

STAFF IMPROVEMENT

One of the greatest tests of an administrator's ability is the leadership he provides in initiating and following through on a program for staff improvement. The secondary principal must assume an active role in promoting self-improvement among his staff members. Among the areas of concern he will include: (1) discovering the needs, (2) developing the purposes, and (3) providing activities for staff improvement.

Discovering Needs

The secondary principal of today cannot afford to have a program for staff improvement based upon what he and other administrators think might be teacher problems. He must go further and discover what type of needs for staff improvement exist. The principal may discover needs for in-service education through the types of questions raised by staff members at faculty meetings. He may gather certain information about teachers based upon the type of problems which they bring to him or discuss with him. There is much to be gained from a study of the teachers and their personnel records and from studying the children. The principal should understand the perceptions of teachers about themselves, about the school in which they work, and about the principal. He ought to be familiar with the questions and problems raised most frequently by parents about the school. The principal may use a questionnaire or some type of opinion poll to secure teacher ideas about areas of their work in which they wish help.

Developing Motives and Purposes

In any program of in-service improvement the motives and purposes should be clear to all participants. Approaches based upon superficial purposes are doomed to failure. Teachers' concerns and interests should be given a high priority. Much of what is known about in-service education indicates that individuals tend to improve when they themselves are engaged in trying to improve a program. When teachers have a voice in the selection of problems for study, there is a greater likelihood that they will gain from the experience than when problems are selected by the administrators and supervisors alone. For certain types of in-service education, some school systems make it possible for the teacher to receive credit on the salary schedule. In some instances, in-service education is conducted in cooperation with a university, and teachers have the opportunity for university credit. Other types of motivation include praise and encouragement to attend leadership seminars from which recruits may be taken to fill administrative or supervisory positions at a later date.

Providing Activities

A third factor and one that is vital is the variety of activities used in meeting the in-service education needs of teachers. Elsbree and Reutter support and discuss the following five activities: workshops, faculty meetings, classroom supervision, teacher rating, and individual-growth situations.[17] Although these five factors seem to stand out, there are many others that are helpful. For example, the way in which the secondary principal seeks to effect change will be significant in relationship to the activities he and the staff use. McLeary and Hencley list the following eight generalizations as being important in the initiation and control of change processes within school organizations: [18]

1. Group membership exerts strong influence upon members behavior— either toward change or toward maintenance of the status quo.
2. In working toward permanent change, the expectations of formal leaders must be both supportive and widely known.
3. Change is costly in terms of time, risk, and demands upon leadership.
4. The prestige of organizational effectiveness resulting from change may accrue to all members of the institution.
5. Communication is the major vehicle for promoting change.
6. Although change may be engineered through force, lasting change is built upon a foundation of consent.
7. Change requires the acquisition of new skills.
8. Effective measuring and feedback devices are essential to the change process.

It is a major goal of the secondary principal to effect change in the administrative structure and environment of the teachers in such a way as to improve both the program and the professional competency of the teachers. The attempt to acquire new skills on the part of personnel often creates fear. A large part of the principal's job should be to help teachers dispel fear and to assist them, through improved communication, to feel secure as changes take place.

SUMMARY

Personnel administration is concerned with arranging conditions in such a manner as to make possible greater self-direction by personnel in the performance of their work. Implicit in this belief is the idea that the administration has confidence in its personnel. The end product of the educational process is determined to a large extent by the effectiveness of the staff personnel. In order to work toward this efficient level of person-

17 Willard S. Elsbree and E. Edmund Reutter, Jr., *Staff Personnel in the Public Schools*, Prentice-Hall, Inc., Englewood Cliffs, N.J., 1958, p. 225.
18 Lloyd E. McCleary and Stephen P. Hencley, *Secondary School Administration*, Dodd, Mead & Company, Inc., New York, 1965, pp. 293–298.

nel administration, it is essential to have properly certified and qualified personnel. A sustained and vigorous recruiting program must be maintained. Selection procedures should be kept up-to-date, and where possible, faculty members should participate in the selection process.

Once effective teachers have been employed and judged to be competent, the administrator needs to plan ways to retain them in the school system. Included in these plans should be a reasonable teacher load, adequate salaries and promotional machinery, broad welfare benefits, and effective evaluation of teachers.

Developing and maintaining staff morale is one of the major responsibilities of the principal. Five factors are discussed in this regard: providing a stimulating environment, defining staff responsibilities, having grievance machinery, and providing academic and personal freedom for the staff.

A real test of the principal's ability is the type of leadership he gives to staff improvement. It is desirable to have the principal bring about change in administrative structure and the environment of teachers in a manner that improves both the program and the professional competency of teachers.

SUGGESTED EXERCISES

1. What does "personnel administration" mean to you?

2. Do the purposes of certification justify the end results?

3. Are the trends in certification placing more or less responsibility upon the individual teacher? Why?

4. How would you go about meeting the shortage of well-qualified teachers if you were a principal?

5. How may our recruitment procedures be improved?

6. Why is teacher assignment important?

7. Describe the best teacher orientation program you know? How could it be improved?

8. Once a school district has obtained effective teachers, what can it do to maintain them?

9. What is the role of the principal in developing staff morale?

10. What are some ways that might be used to discover teacher needs in terms of in-service education other than those mentioned in this chapter?

11. How does one know when an in-service program is effective?

12. In addition to the activities mentioned in this chapter, suggest others which you feel would be helpful for in-service education.

13. Should the principal's nominations for teaching positions ever be vetoed by the superintendent? Why?

14. How would you approach motivating a faculty for an in-service education program? Exactly what would you, as principal, do?

SELECTED REFERENCES

CULBERTSON, JACK, *The Selective Recruitment of Educational Leaders,* The University Council for Educational Administration, Columbus, Ohio, January, 1966.

DAVIS, HAZEL, "Economic, Legal, and Social Status of Teachers: Certification, Tenure, and Autonomy," *Review of Educational Research,* vol. 33, pp. 402–403, October, 1963.

Editorial, "Conditions of Work for Quality Teaching," *NEA Journal,* vol. 54, pp. 33–44, March, 1965.

Editorial, "Evaluation of Classroom Teachers: Summary," *NEA Research Bulletin,* vol. 42, pp. 83–88, 108–111, October, 1964; vol. 43, pp. 12–18, February, 1965.

Editorial, "Few Teachers Get Top Salaries," *NEA Research Bulletin,* no. 43, p. 9, February, 1965.

Editorial, "Retirement Statistics, 1964: Summary of School Law Summaries: Retirement," *NEA Research Bulletin,* vol. 42, pp. 99–107, December, 1964.

GIBSON, R. OLIVER, AND HEROLD C. HUNT, *The School Personnel Administrator,* Houghton Mifflin Company, Boston, 1965.

GROSSBACH, WILMAR, AND ROBERT L. REEVES, "Recommend Your Teachers More Accurately," *The American School Board Journal,* vol. 150, p. 64, April, 1965.

HALL, ROY M., AND ANTONIO M. VINCENT, "Staff: Selection and Appointment," *Encyclopedia of Educational Research,* The Macmillan Company, New York, 1960.

KINDRED, LESLIE W., AND PRINCE B. WOODARD, *Staff Welfare Practices in the Public Schools,* The Center for Applied Research in Education, Inc., New York, 1963.

MOFFITT, JOHN C., *In-service Education for Teachers,* The Center for Applied Research in Education, Inc., New York, 1963.

MOORE, HAROLD E., *The Administration of Public School Personnel,* The Center for Applied Research in Education, Inc., New York, 1966.

NOLTE, M. CHESTER, "Extra Class Assignments for Teachers Must Bear Reasonable Relationships to the School Program," *The American School Board Journal,* vol. 149, pp. 17–18, October, 1964.

SEBOLD, HAROLD, AND GEORGE B. REDFERN, "Roadblocks to Recruitment," *Ohio Schools,* vol. 42, pp. 18–19, November, 1964.

SMITH, GRACE H., "An Effective Orientation Program," *NEA Journal,* vol. 54, pp. 47–48, May, 1965.

STEFFENSEN, JAMES P., *Staff Personnel Administration,* U.S. Department of Health, Education, and Welfare, Office of Education, Washington, D.C., 1965.

VAN ZWOLL, JAMES A., *School Personnel Administration,* Appleton-Century-Crofts, Inc., New York, 1964.

WOLFFER, WILFRED C., "Improved Techniques for the Recruitment and Selection of Qualified Non-instructional Employees," *The American School Board Journal,* vol. 146, pp. 37–38, June, 1963.

CHAPTER 18

GUIDANCE
SERVICES

The term "guidance" is similar to the term "curriculum" in that many people have only a hazy idea of what it is. For that reason it would be well to start out with definitions and the point of view held by the authors about guidance and pupil personnel services.

Like a balanced diet and motherhood the value of guidance and its supporting services seems to be firmly established in the minds of professional educators, legislators, and the general public. Whether the reasons for the support of these diverse groups are the same is rather doubtful.

The purpose of the authors in this chapter is not to present an exhaustive treatise on guidance, but rather to present an overview of the field and the role of the secondary school principal in organizing and administering guidance and pupil personnel services.

THE PURPOSES AND DEFINITIONS OF GUIDANCE

The theme of Chapter 5, and indeed of the entire book, is that the modern secondary school must assist young people to become adaptable. If adaptability is to be a characteristic of our youth they must be made aware of the factors affecting their environment and knowledgeable about themselves.

Guidance is that term applied to the activities carried on in a school which attempt to assist the individual youth to know himself and his environment, to recognize his problems, and to be able to deal with them effectively. To know oneself, it is necessary to understand and accept one's abilities and limitations and to set goals commensurate with one's abilities. Guidance is an integral part of the total educational process and as such is performed by a number of persons. Teachers, administrators and specialized personnel with training in guidance all have a responsibility to help youth develop adaptability. Therefore, all school personnel are members of the guidance team of the school. Good teaching itself contains elements of guidance.

NEED FOR GUIDANCE

The young person in tomorrow's world will have to be trained in today's schools. In addition to knowing himself, he must comprehend the school's curriculum and how it can relate to his own occupational and life goals. The more complex our economic system becomes, the more complex will be the training required to compete effectively as a contributor to that system.

The goals of the guidance program in a school must be to deal with the total needs of the individual. These needs would include "emotional, social, moral, health, avocational, and leisure time needs." [1] In seeking fulfillment of any need which a person has, he is confronted by problems to solve and decisions to make.

One of the major purposes of the guidance program is to assist young people to assess the dimensions of their problems, to bring to bear available resources in the solving of problems, and to make wise decisions.

Feedback to Faculty

If the school is to meet the changing needs of the young people entrusted to it, then the faculty must have the best information it is possible to obtain about students, the curriculum, the community, and so forth. Thus guidance counselors need to spend considerable time in local research, i.e., "research to determine pupil needs and determine how well the school's program and services meet these needs." [2] Studies of the characteristics of students and a follow-up of their later lives and job success can be utilized to secure information helpful to teachers, counselors, and

[1] Robert H. Knapp, *Practical Guidance Methods for Counselors, Teachers, and Administrators,* McGraw-Hill Book Company, New York, 1953, p. 1.
[2] Gordon Cawelti, "The Counselor's Role: Real and Ideal," *NASSP Bulletin,* vol. 51, no. 320, p. 68, September, 1967.

administrators. This feedback is an essential responsibility of the guidance and counseling team of the school. Because the team is comprised of teachers as well as counselors and administrators, they can make known the areas of inquiry from which they need information.

Disciplinary Problems

One of the problems facing young people is coming to terms with their need for independence which may conflict with the need of the school to ensure acceptable patterns of behavior.

It is the contention of the authors that guidance personnel should not be expected to mete out punishment for infractions of school rules. To use them in this role is to deprive them of means for establishing rapport with students. While it may be necessary to have someone in charge of enforcing rules and meting out punishment, it should not be the guidance personnel. This is a responsibility of the principal or one of his aides.[3]

The function which guidance personnel can perform in relation to disciplinary problems is to act as a bridge between administration and students. They can assist in bringing about the cooperative development of standards of behavior for young people which all can accept. The process of developing such standards calls for frank and honest discussion of the viewpoints and purposes for all.

If persons of the requisite personal characteristics and professional training are put into guidance positions, they can be of inestimable value in accomplishing the purposes of the school.

Other Needs

All purposes of guidance programs are not fully agreed upon even by professional guidance counselors, let alone by teachers, administrators, and parents. It would seem to be consistent with one of the major themes of this book that if one purpose of the school is to help students adapt to change, then the programs and personnel of the school must also be adaptable.

The organizational plan for guidance need not be the same in every school, nor should the purposes necessarily be identical. While admittedly there will probably be more similarities than differences, there is a need for guidance plans to be fitted uniquely for the individual school and its students.

The guidance program may contribute in different and unique ways to student government, clubs, and activities and other citizenship development functions of the school.

[3] Merle M. Ohlsen, *Guidance Services in the Modern School*, Harcourt, Brace & World, Inc., New York, 1964, p. 405.

TYPES OF GUIDANCE

While guidance has undoubtedly been carried on in schools in an informal sense since schools began, the development of the modern guidance movement is a comparatively recent phenomenon.

Vocational Guidance

Historically speaking, the first formalized attempts to give guidance were connected with selecting one's vocation. By 1910 all high schools in the city of Boston, Massachusetts, had vocational counselors. "Vocational guidance is the assistance given in choosing, preparing for, entering upon, and making progress in an occupation." [4] In its broadest sense all guidance is still vocational to a certain degree because it is difficult to separate kinds of guidance into discrete categories.

Program Guidance

Much of the guidance that is done in schools is related to the selection of goals for the future and the proper course of study in the junior and senior high schools to accomplish those goals. It can be seen that there is a close relationship to vocational guidance mentioned above.

Guidance personnel have several responsibilities in connection with college admission and relations with colleges and universities. There is a very real danger, however, that program guidance will become narrowly conceived as guidance for college admission. This it should not become because proper placement in programs should be a service to all pupils in the school, not just to those going on for higher education. It is still a fact that in certain rural areas of the country and in the ghetto schools of many large cities that most students will not go on for any education beyond the high school.

Teachers, guidance personnel, and administrators are themselves products of a college and university background and must be aware that this may cause them to be biased and may make it difficult for them to understand the needs of students not headed in this direction. The emphasis placed on academic training and the increased number and proportion of high school youth going on for some form of higher education must not be allowed to prevent the best guidance from being furnished to all students.

Developmental Guidance

Developmental guidance should help the individual in his physical, emotional, and social development. Many of the needs in these areas arise because society has assigned youth certain developmental tasks which he

4 Arthur J. Jones, *Principles of Guidance*, 5th ed., McGraw-Hill Book Company, 1962.

must be able to perform sooner or later. His performance of these tasks may be retarded because of certain factors in his personal makeup and/or in his environment. His needs for status and security may place him at odds with the expectations which the school has for his orderly progress. His membership in a minority group or race may make it difficult for him to accept either the means or the goals of others.

The mobility of the population in recent times has meant that many youth must adjust to a new school situation from time to time. In a recent study, it was shown that one out of five high school students move from one high school to another. Guidance for these pupils must be directed toward helping them adjust to their new situation, and to achieve a feeling of security and acceptance.

PROFESSIONAL GUIDANCE PERSONNEL

Although the need for guidance in the high school has become rather widely accepted, the proportion of professionally trained guidance personnel available to students has not increased as rapidly as needed. Conant in *The American High School Today,* published in 1959, recommended that there should be one full-time counselor for every 250 to 300 students.[5] That this goal is far from achievement is evident from the results found in his second report almost 10 years later. In *The Comprehensive High School* he revealed that in only 13.9 percent of the two thousand high schools studied was the ratio of counselor (or guidance person) 1 to 299 pupils or less.[6]

The supply of trained guidance personnel is not able to meet the ever-increasing demand for guidance services.

Full-time versus Part-time Personnel

Whereas Conant's recommendation is couched in terms of full-time counselors, in practice many school systems use the part-time counselor approach. This means that some or all of the personnel assigned to the guidance function have other duties such as teaching, supervisory, or administrative. In fact some state standards are expressed in terms of counseling periods per day per 100 pupils, which seems more realistic in terms of actual practice.

Some schools use the "every teacher a counselor" approach or the "every social studies teacher a counselor" approach. In most such cases this indicates that students are assigned a homeroom and that certain guidance activities are carried on by the homeroom teacher. If the home-

[5] James B. Conant, *The American High School Today,* McGraw-Hill Book Company, New York, 1959, p. 44.
[6] James B. Conant, *The Comprehensive High School,* McGraw-Hill Book Company, New York, 1967, p. 26.

room teacher is given a period in his teaching day for student conferences in connection with his responsibilities, this is charged toward the counselor/pupil ratio. The authors contend that all teachers need to be involved in the guidance of the youth of the school but that trained guidance personnel are also needed.

Adequate Training

Guidance and counseling positions should be filled *only* with persons who have had substantial graduate preparation in guidance and related fields. Most states have set minimum standards for certification of guidance counselors and directors of guidance. While there is still considerable discrepancy between standards of the various states, improvement can be seen over a period of years.

At the American Personnel and Guidance Association convention in 1962, Walter F. Johnson suggested the following courses and experiences as being valuable in the development of good counselors.[7]

1. Psychological foundations of human behavior.
2. Biological basis of development and behavior.
3. Sociology, anthropology, economics, and international relations.
4. Humanities.
5. Professional studies in counseling.
6. Supervised practice in counseling.
7. Opportunity for self-evaluation and developing better self-understanding.

While the authors would accept all items on the list, they would like to be certain that professional studies in counseling would provide an opportunity to develop competency in tests and measurements and in the interpretation of test results.

Of equal importance in selecting persons to fill guidance and counseling positions is the criterion of desirable personal qualifications. A master's degree in guidance and/or counseling is important, but so is a personality which is attractive to young people. Both aspects should be considered in selecting personnel. Since it is rather difficult to give people new personalities, one may have to pick teachers with the desirable personal qualifications and encourage them to get their master's degree in guidance and counseling. The granting of leave for that purpose and even board subsidization of the program is a good investment for a school system to make in order to build a strong guidance and counseling program.

The Guidance Team

The guidance team in the secondary school should include anyone whose duties and responsibilities cause them to have contact with stu-

---

[7] Joseph Hollis and Lucille Hollis, *Organizing for Efficient Guidance*, Science Research Associates, Inc., Chicago, 1965, p. 18.

dents. Thus teachers, teachers aides, counselors, physicians, dentists, school nurses, psychologists, psychometrist, librarians, social workers, cafeteria helpers, secretaries, custodians, bus drivers, and administrators are members of the school guidance team. Certain central office staff members are associate or ex officio members.

Director of Guidance

This title may be given to the person responsible for coordinating the entire school system guidance and counseling program, or it may be given to that individual who heads the program in one secondary school. In some secondary schools he may be called dean of students.

If he is a systemwide director, he probably reports to the superintendent or an assistant superintendent, and if responsible for one secondary school, he probably reports directly to the principal or through an assistant principal.

As a specialist in guidance and counseling, he provides the professional expertise for the initiation and maintenance of the school or system guidance program. He has responsibility for recruitment, selection, and orientation of staff. He clarifies the roles of specialists and makes, in conjunction with the line administrator to whom he reports, time and facility assignments. He also leads in the evaluation of the program. He should have line authority over the other professional guidance personnel and clerical personnel for whom he is responsible, but staff relationships with all others, including the other pupil personnel services professionals.

Role of the Principal

If the school director of guidance can be looked upon as the "quarterback" of the guidance team, then the principal is the coach of the team. He doesn't play all the positions, but his is the ultimate responsibility if the team fails. He, therefore, oversees the performance of each team member and leads for improvement in the total team effort.

Reitan and McDougall stated their belief that in order to make a counseling program work, the administrator must consider himself the "counselor's counselor." They assign him a large share of the responsibility for the success of the counseling program.[8] The administrator must provide the leadership for developing:

1. A written statement of the goals and purposes of the guidance program and its relationship to the total school program
2. An organizational plan for guidance that is consistent with its goals
3. A job description for guidance positions
4. Policy statements about the program

[8] Henry M. Reitan and William P. McDougall, "How to Make a Counseling Program Work," *The Nation's Schools*, vol. 77, pp. 65–67, April, 1966.

He must also interpret the program to others, see that qualified personnel are selected, and provide for the evaluation of the program at regular intervals.[9] He must lead in making known staff and facilities needs for the guidance program.

As needs change, the program may also need to change. This may mean changing the roles and functions of members of the guidance team. Evaluation should point the way for whatever adjustments are needed. Such evaluation could indicate need for in-service education of members of the guidance team and new orientation for students.

ORGANIZATIONAL PLANS

Plans for the organization of guidance services usually include provisions for group guidance and for individual counseling. Orientation programs and use of the schools-within-a-school are other means to accomplish the guidance function.

Group Guidance

When there are groups of students with the same problem and the nature of the problem is such that individual conferences are not required, it is only economical of everyone's time to handle the problem on a group basis.

Most problems of an academic or educational programming nature can be dealt with in groups. The group may be composed of all college preparatory students or all college preparatory students who are sophomores, all majors in foreign languages, junior distributive education students, all senior students, etc.

Much group guidance may take place on a homeroom basis, especially if homeroom assignments are made on a class in school basis, i.e., freshmen, sophomores, juniors, and seniors. Certain school business such as fund drives and student government representation can take place on a homeroom basis even if all first-period classes are designated as homerooms, regardless of the class standing of their members.

Orientation Programs

One of the responsibilities which may be assigned to guidance personnel is to orient young people newly come to the school or who soon will come to the school.

Senior highs, junior highs, and middle schools must work closely with their feeder schools to prepare the top grade of the lower school for the impending move to the next higher school. Guidance personnel and the

9 *Ibid.*

administrators need to conduct informational sessions for faculty, students, and even parents of the next lower school. Course and subject selection for the following year must be carried out, so that preliminary registration data necessary for scheduling for next year can proceed. This aspect of orientation was covered more fully in Chapter 15.

Students of any grade who come new to the school at any time of the year must be oriented to the school and to the community. This task is quite frequently assigned to the counseling staff. Whether they choose to use a group or an individual approach will, of course, depend on the situation, the numbers involved, and the job to be done.

Schools-within-a-School

To give students a feeling of being more than a face in a crowd or just a lost sheep among thousands of students, administrators have attempted to create organizational plans which would give students identity with smaller groups. One way to do this has been through the "house plan" or "schools-within-a-school" plan.

A 3,500-student high school could be divided into four "halls" or "houses." Each hall would have about 900 students with some from each grade housed in the school. The plan would call for the student to remain a member of his hall or house until graduation from school. Student records could be kept in the hall office, and the guidance function of the hall would predominate. Each hall could have its own student activities to supplement schoolwide activities.

The staff for each hall could be similar to that observed in Evanston Township High School halls by one of the authors as early as 1960. At that time each hall had:

1 principal (coordinates guidance function) (he might be called dean, or house master, etc.)
1 full-time clerk
4 full-time counselors
4 homeroom directors
8 homeroom assistants
3 activity directors (who teach also)
1 full-time social worker

Teachers in such a school would teach students from all halls. In the high school central office a principal and two assistant principals with several specialists and an adequate clerical staff would take care of schoolwide administration and services. The hall plan described above can provide an excellent focus for guidance and counseling.

Each hall could be located in a separate building of a campus-type school such as the Patrick Henry High School in Roanoke, Virginia, on one floor of a multistory building, or in a wing of a traditionally constructed building.

The School Guidance Committee

The roles of guidance personnel, the principal and other administrators, and of teachers have been mentioned earlier in this chapter. A device for organizing and coordinating the efforts of all persons connected with the guidance function is the school guidance committee. While there are different ways in which this committee could be used, the authors present one which they have seen work successfully.

The committee is composed of the principal (and/or an assistant principal), the director of guidance for the school, a representative of each instructional department, the school nurse, the school psychologist, and other specialized pupil services personnel as may seem appropriate. Other school personnel may be invited in for special purposes or when problems concerning their particular area of school operation are being considered. Student and parent representatives may be needed also.

Teachers frequently complain that they are ignored or overlooked in the organizing, planning, and evaluating of the guidance and counseling program in the school. Vocational and industrial arts teachers often feel that professional guidance personnel are heavily biased in favor of the college-bound students. If each instructional department is represented on the school guidance committee, policies and procedures developed can reflect the multitude of concerns of all.

TECHNIQUES AND TOOLS OF GUIDANCE

Possible techniques and tools of guidance should be understood by all guidance personnel and by administrators as well. The secondary school administrator must keep in mind that all guidance tools and techniques used must be compatible with the purposes of the guidance program and of the total educational program of that school.

Counseling

Earlier in this chapter group guidance was described as a useful method of conveying information to students and of dealing with problems not requiring an individual face-to-face conference between counselor and counselee. Moser and Moser stated that: "Counseling may be thought of as the core of the helping process, essential for the proper administration of assistance to students as they attempt to solve their problems." [10]

[10] Leslie E. Moser and Ruth S. Moser, *Counseling and Guidance: An Exploration*, Prentice-Hall, Inc., Englewood Cliffs, N.J., 1963, p. 12.

Facilities for Guidance

The counseling situation described above indicates a need for privacy. Thus guidance and counseling personnel must be provided with offices that guarantee audio and visual privacy. Counselor cubicles with walls that do not go all the way to the ceiling are unacceptable. Counselor stations in areaways, waiting rooms, closets, etc., are also not acceptable. Facilities provided often indicate to students and to others the importance attached to a function by the administration of the school.

The Testing Program

The importance of the school testing program to the overall guidance and counseling capabilities of the modern secondary school should not be slighted, nor should it be overemphasized to the detriment of other diagnostic tools available.

Career Events

To help young people make an intelligent selection of their life's occupational goals, information about the requirements and rewards of the various occupations and professions must be provided. One way to provide this information is by maintaining occupational information files and a library in the guidance office. This is a standard resource in many modern secondary schools.

Another method found with increasing frequency, especially in urban and suburban situations, is the use of a career day or career night. Interested persons who are successful members of their profession or occupational group are invited to come to the school and meet with students and parents who have indicated an interest in certain of these careers. Done on a planned basis and after careful screening and selection of the persons who will meet with students and parents, a worthwhile experience can be engendered. Attorneys, airline pilots and hostesses, businessmen, engineers, newspapermen, physicians, physicists, realtors, teachers, theatrical professionals, etc., can bring the breath of reality into the occupational or vocational guidance program of the school. Utilizing these community resources is also a technique in establishing and maintaining good community relations.

A second phase of the career experience would be student visitation to the office, factory, or business of the occupations or professions in which they were interested.

Junior high students can also be invited to senior high career events. All that is needed is good communications and broader planning. If career events similar to that described above are provided each semester, by the time a junior high student is a senior, he can, through careful selection and guidance, have had the opportunity to find out about a number of careers in which he might be interested and have some chance of succeeding in.

Follow-up Studies

By following up the careers of graduates, transfers, and dropouts from the school, much valuable information can be obtained to help in evaluating the job the school is doing. Most of such studies are done by mailing · questionnaires to graduates, transfers, and dropouts for whom addresses are known. In some cases the questionnaire is followed up by scheduled interviews with a sample of those returning the questionnaire.

Questions relating to the effectiveness and comparative value of course offerings, curriculums available, services provided, teaching methods, facilities, etc., can elicit feedback which can be useful in adapting and changing the offerings of the school. Feedback can also be valuable in showing what the strengths are in the total school program.

Placement Services

A guidance service not found in enough secondary schools is that of placement of students in summertime, after school, or after graduation jobs. More and more, however, school administrators and guidance personnel are recognizing the value of placement services to the effectiveness of the guidance program and to the holding power of the school.

The stated reason for leaving school of many dropouts is an economic one whether the economy is up or down. It seems appropriate for guidance personnel to assist such young persons to remain in school by helping them find part-time employment. In those states which require the schools to issue *work permits* for youth of certain ages, the arguments for placement service seem even more convincing.

While it is true that state and federal agencies do offer placement services to graduates of the high school, there is still need for cooperative associations between the schools and these agencies. Another aspect of the placement function is its relation to follow-up on the job to find out what and how the student is doing.[11] By maintaining relations with the business and industrial firms who hire the graduates of the high schools, follow-up study, placement, and feedback are all facilitated. It is a sobering fact that while most schools follow up their graduates who go on to higher education, not enough is done for the others. In some communities more of the others tend to remain in that community than do those who go on for higher education.

Placement services and follow-up of graduates can also have a direct

11 Glen Ovard, *Administration of the Changing Secondary School*, The Macmillan Company, New York, 1966, p. 289.

bearing on discovering continuing and adult education needs for the community.

Close Parental Relationships

Parents of the youth in our schools are usually willing and even eager to help in accomplishing the aims of the total school program. Because the school has custody of students for only a part of the day, it is only prudent that parents be aware of and subscribe to what the school is trying to do. Parents can reinforce and supplement if they are party to what is going on for their children. To be willing to do so, they should participate in discovering needs and ways to meet them.

In individual problem cases it is wise to involve the parents as soon as it becomes apparent to the guidance team that it is necessary to utilize home resources. In cases where the home environment is undesirable, other steps may need to be taken involving social workers and even juvenile court authorities. The latter should be utilized, however, only in the most extreme cases.

UTILIZATION OF RESOURCES

In an era when social protest movements, race riots, and gang warfare have even invaded the schools, school administrators and guidance personnel must utilize all the school and community resources available. The nation must be willing to provide the means for education, guidance, and other services to ameliorate the conditions which cause poverty and civil unrest, or they must face the possibility of continuing to station uniformed police on each floor of secondary schools, as is now done in certain urban school systems.

The total resources of the local community, the state, and the nation need to be brought to bear on the persistent life problems of youth and indeed of all citizens.

Facilities and Clerical Assistance

The guidance program must have adequate quarters to include easy access to student records, display of guidance materials, shelving of college catalogs and occupational materials, office space for professional and clerical guidance personnel, and waiting-room area for students and patrons.

One of the most flagrant violations of good business procedure is to have high-priced professional persons doing clerical tasks which could be done more economically by clerks and secretaries. It is only good business to free the time of the professional to do what he is trained to do. It seems to be a rather widely understood fact that it is easier to gain board approval for another teacher or counselor than for obtaining a clerk or secretary.

Health and Medical Services

Other resource personnel who have much to contribute to the guidance function are those engaged in giving health and medical services to the schools and the community. Nurses, dentists, physicians, psychiatrists, etc., in an increasing number of school systems are being retained either as full- or part-time employees. In other situations the local, county, or state health departments may furnish all or part of such services. In Pennsylvania the law requires local school districts to furnish certain health services not only to public school pupils but also to those in private schools.

The information from periodic physical examinations performed by competent medical personnel can be useful not only to inform parents as to corrective measures needed for hearing, dental, sight, and other physical disabilities,[12] but also as information useful to understanding academic and social disabilities.

As mentioned earlier in this chapter, health and medical personnel should be available for meeting with the school guidance committee in planning and evaluating needs relating to pupil welfare.

SUMMARY

Guidance was defined as those activities carried on in a school which attempt to assist the individual youth to know himself and his environment, to recognize his problems, and to be able to deal with them effectively. All school personnel should be considered members of the guidance team to assist him in this endeavor.

The student has need for guidance in selecting his life's goals and the curriculum which will best enable him to realize those goals. He also has needs in the areas of emotional, social, moral, and health development. The guidance and counseling program must assist students to assess their needs in these areas and to bring to bear certain resources in the solving of problems and in making wise decisions.

The guidance services of the school can also provide feedback to teachers, administrators, and others about program change and adaption needed in the curriculum and in the total school program. Sources of this feedback information are from the testing program, counseling conferences, and from follow-up studies of graduates, transfers, and dropouts.

The advisability of recruiting and selecting persons who have adequate

---

[12] Daniel Tanner, *Schools for Youth*, The Macmillan Company, New York, 1965, p. 470.

professional training and possess desirable personal characteristics was emphasized.

While the roles of all persons comprising the guidance team were described, the roles of the principal, the director of guidance, and the school guidance committee were considered crucial to a successful guidance program.

Possible organizational plans and certain techniques and tools of guidance were outlined in brief fashion. Close relationships with the home and the utilization of the total resources in the community are essential if the school guidance program is to perform its function in a satisfactory manner.

SUGGESTED EXERCISES

1. *a.* Secure four or five definitions of guidance from the literature, and see whether you can find any significant differences among them.
    b. Have class members or colleagues write out their own definitions of guidance, and compare them with each other and those in *a* above.
    c. Write your own definition of guidance which includes a description of its purposes.

2. Go to the director of guidance of a secondary school convenient to you, and ask him to describe what the guidance services currently are and what he would like them to be.

3. Devise a checklist to evaluate the guidance and counseling program in a secondary school, using the information gathered for 1 and 2 above and from any other sources you choose, e.g., the latest *Evaluative Criteria.*

4. *a.* Draw up an outline of the general areas which should be included in a follow-up study of graduates, transfers, and dropouts of a secondary school.
    b. Select two or three areas from *a* above, and develop some specific questions which would obtain the kind of information needed.
    c. Do *a* and *b* on a class assignment basis, assigning each area developed in *a,* so that the class produces a complete questionnaire.

5. Secure the cooperation of a secondary school represented by someone in the class, and offer to conduct a follow-up study for them.

6. Survey a number of schools, and discover how many use the concept of the school guidance committee described in this chapter.

7. Attend a career event such as mentioned in this chapter, and evaluate it on the basis of criteria developed by the class or by you as an individual.

8. Develop a role-playing situation involving adapting the guidance program to changing needs discovered from a follow-up study. Describe the situation, assign the roles of various persons, and carry out the production in front of the class or a faculty group in your school.

SELECTED REFERENCES

CAWELTI, GORDON, "The Counselor's Role, Real and Ideal," *NASSP Bulletin*, vol. 51, no. 320, September, 1967.

CONANT, JAMES B., *The American High School Today*, McGraw-Hill Book Company, New York, 1959.

————, *The Comprehensive High School*, McGraw-Hill Book Company, New York, 1967.

Connecticut State Department of Education, *The Guidance Program, Its Services and Place in Secondary Education*, Bulletin 45, June, 1957.

CROW, LESTER D., AND ALICE CROW, *Organization and Conduct of Guidance Services*, David McKay Company, Inc., New York, 1965.

HOLLIS, JOSEPH, AND LUCILLE HOLLIS, *Organizing for Efficient Guidance*, Science Research Associates, Inc., Chicago, 1965.

JONES, ARTHUR J., *Principles of Guidance*, 5th ed., McGraw-Hill Book Company, New York, 1962.

MILLER, LEONARD M., *Dropouts: Selected References*, U.S. Department of Health, Education and Welfare, OE-20070, Bulletin 1965, no. 7, 1964.

MOSER, LESLIE E., AND RUTH S. MOSER, *Counseling and Guidance: An Exploration*, Prentice-Hall, Inc., Englewood Cliffs, N.J., 1963.

OHLSEN, MERLE M., *Guidance Services in the Modern School*, Harcourt, Brace & World, Inc., New York, 1964.

OVARD, GLEN, *Administration of the Changing Secondary School*, The Macmillan Company, New York, 1966.

REITAN, HENRY M., AND WILLIAM P. McDOUGALL, "How to Make a Counseling Program Work," *The Nation's Schools*, vol. 77, April, 1966.

ROEBER, EDWARD C., CLIFFORD E. ERICKSON, AND GLENN E. SMITH, *Organization and Administration of Guidance Services*, 2d ed., McGraw-Hill Book Company, New York, 1955.

TANNER, DANIEL, *Schools for Youth*, The Macmillan Company, New York, 1965.

WRENN, C. GILBERT, *The Counselor in a Changing World*, American Personnel and Guidance Association, Washington, D.C., 1962.

CHAPTER 19

OFFICE
MANAGEMENT | The school office is the heart of administrative services. It lies at the center of a complex communications web. From it, messages of many types flow to and fro. The school office is not only a place; it is also a service. While most of the school's office work is done in what we customarily call "the office," the services of the office may reach into all parts of the school building.

As a communications center it coordinates messages from the inside, that is, those originating from within the building. It also handles communications from the outside. It serves to coordinate the internal workings of the school itself and also serves to help the school with its adjustments to its external environment.

The school office is also the chief workplace of the principal. It is the place where he spends at least half of his in-school time.

Purposes of the Office

By the school office, it is meant the entire administrative wing of a school building, if, indeed, a school has such a unit. In other words, the concept of office is not restricted only to that particular place where the school secretary has a desk and the inner office over which she stands guard. The office concept is extended to mean any areas and services in the school building which serve to perform office and clerical services for school personnel. This includes office work as a portion of guidance services, health services, physical education services, cafeteria services, and teacher services.

According to Roe: "Office work may be simply defined as the process of facilitating communications within and without an organization by putting into written form for use when needed the plans, ideas, agreements, accomplishments and records which, under simpler conditions would be stored in the mind of one person." [1] Under this definition of office work, almost any work directed toward the recording and storage of information classifies as office work.

The major purpose of office work is the facilitation of the central work of the school. The central work of the school is, of course, teaching and learning. As fundamental as this truth is, it is often forgotten in the press of routine work which is characteristic of office work. Office work has a tendency to acquire a virtue for its own sake. Those who perform office work need to be made aware of its purpose, otherwise they too become slaves to activity devoid of worthwhile purposes.

The work of the school is essential to the operation of the school. As Hencley points out, some boards of education, teachers, and even administrators cling to the outmoded notion of the office as overhead.[2] To the extent that this idea is held, it is a severely limiting factor on the effectiveness of a school and of the personal efficiency of a principal.

Others react similarly against office work as paper shuffling, red tape, and similar derogatory descriptive terms. While it is true that some offices revel in high piles of unnecessary paper forms, reflection will reveal that all paper work has, or at least once had, a necessary function. Perhaps the key is to keep the paper work restricted only to those items which do, in fact, perform currently necessary functions for the organization.

ORGANIZATION OF THE OFFICE

Physical Facilities

Office layout is a technical matter and will therefore be only briefly referred to here. As a rough rule of thumb, 60 square feet of area per clerical person is suggested.[3] Adequate space in front of filing cabinets is

---

[1] William H. Roe, "Operation Aspects of Office Management," Appendix I in *Guiding Principles and Practices in Office Management*, Research Bulletin no. 4, Association of School Business Officials, Chicago, 1966, p. 48.

[2] Lloyd E. McCleary and Stephen P. Hencley, *Secondary School Administration*, Dodd, Mead & Company, Inc., New York 1965, p. 312.

[3] Association of School Business Officials, *Guiding Principles and Practices in Office Management*, Research Bulletin no. 4, Chicago, 1966, p. 43.

considered the length of the drawer plus 24 inches. Unless privacy is required, one large space accommodating several office workers is preferred to smaller spaces. Principles of office layout emphasize the desirability of maintaining a feeling of spaciousness and symmetry. This not only has more aesthetic appeal, but it adds to working efficiency.

Of particular importance is the flow of traffic. If teachers, visitors, or students will need to enter portions of the office, particular care must be taken for the appropriateness of their entry. If clerks will be working on student records, it would be inappropriate for students to have close access to that point of work. If a secretary must work on matters of confidence involving teachers, this work area ought to be away from the main stream of teacher and student traffic.

Office Equipment

Fortunately most new schools are being built with adequate office space and at least a minimum of office equipment. Adequate filing cabinets, work tables as well as desks, a coordinated telephone system, sufficient typewriters (electric is preferred), electronic dictating equipment, duplicating equipment, a communications control panel, and copying equipment are considered basic to an adequate office set up to handle the office work for a school of 700 or more students.

To some boards of education unaccustomed to capital expenditures for office equipment, a list like the above may seem to represent a fortune in funds which might be spent in other places. Yet, boards which have even a rudimentary knowledge of modern business methods will recognize that in any office people are more costly than equipment. Any piece of equipment or device which increases an office worker's efficiency will pay for itself many times over. Most important of all, the equipment should enable the flow of office work to be speeded up and/or increased in accuracy. It is common knowledge that an all-too-frequent bottleneck in many offices is the delay in getting out reports, letters, and memoranda. These bottlenecks may be due to poor quality personnel, but they may also be due to good quality personnel hindered by a lack of modern equipment.

Office Relationships

Poor office relationships can create serious problems which will divert the administrator's attention away from his main work. More often than not, the poor relationships are the result of lack of role clarity rather than "hard to get along with" people. People working in organizations need to know what is expected behavior in many subtle situations. If an office staff is composed of more than one worker, there needs to be some system of relationships for determining who does what work, who decides what shall be done, whether or not the work is shared, and many other simple yet paradoxically complex questions. The simple formula "let's all work together" will be satisfactory only as long as there are few differences of opinions.

In addition to the potential problems resulting from the interrelationships among the members of the office staff itself, there is the potential for problems with the other school staff members. This potential problem area arises in schools, as well as in many formal organizations, where the office workers (and particularly private secretaries) develop a sense of loyalty and identification with the administrators. They come to share some of the normal frustrations that any superordinate experiences in dealing with his subordinates. For example, when the attendance reports from teachers fail to come in on time, the office worker who must actually work with these reports tends to feel like scolding the tardy teachers. Yet, by definition of the formal authority structure of the school, the office worker is a nonprofessional with no educational or administrative authority over teachers. Any attempt of an office worker to apply some of her administrator's reflected authority is usually poorly received by the teachers and leads to poor staff morale and less efficient working relationships. The administrator's best defense against this delicate problem is to establish clear operating guidelines for working relationships.

Another important dimension of office relationships is the way school office personnel interact with representatives from outside the school. This is an especially crucial concern since nearly all outsiders who initiate contacts with the school do so through office personnel. The initial handling of a thousand items by a school secretary or a switchboard operator or a reception clerk can set the tone for a positive or a negative attitude. The school administrator will want to make it very clear what type of attitude his office personnel are to take with all manner of outside contacts, from the typical irate parent to the urgent call from the superintendent.

The Office Manual

One of the best ways to improve office operation is through the development of an office manual. An office manual will contain job descriptions, policies, procedures, and specific instructions. It can be used to orient and train new office workers.

Another value of an office manual is achieved if the workers themselves help develop it. It then holds much greater meaning for them.

The Filing System

An efficient office is one which can quickly locate relevant information. As was noted earlier, office work is defined as the process of facilitating communications. No matter how complete the equipment, how well-designed the layout, or how skilled the office workers, if the wanted information cannot be located quickly, it loses its other advantages.

An up-to-date filing system is one safeguard against this embarrassing condition. The term "filing system" is employed to mean an organized arrangement for classifying, storing, and retrieving written data. It is usually the assistant superintendent for business who may be instrumental in ensuring that there is a uniform system throughout the school district. In New York State, for example, the state department of education has a well-developed filing system available, complete with consultant services for districts wishing to implement the system.

Too often, school district files are maintained very casually, in a most unbusinesslike manner. Not that there is necessarily educational virtue in imitation of business methods, it is rather that for effective administrative operation, the principal and his office staff require accurate information. A standard filing system greatly assists in this regard.

Standard Office Forms

It is a general principle of administration that the use of a standard form for the transmission and recording of certain recurring communications adds to overall efficiency. For example, schools continually receive requests from other schools to forward students' academic and other records. The use of a standard procedure and form for processing this routine activity makes it possible for a clerk to adequately handle this constantly recurring task. Some types of communications from the school to parents can be reduced to standard forms.

Research Bulletin Number 4 of the Association of School Business Officials suggests the following in designing forms for school office use: [4]

TITLE: For easy identification, the title should appear at the top.

CONSECUTIVE NUMBERING: Numbering of forms should not be used indiscriminately. When necessary, numbers should be placed in upper right corner.

INSTRUCTIONS: Instructions should be printed directly on the form. They should be clear, simple, specific and brief.

BODY: The form should be designed for easy entry and easy use of the information. Information should be requested in orderly sequence. Information required should be checked against the clearly defined purposes for which the form was designed. The form should request all necessary information and STOP!

AUTHORIZATION: Provision should be made for placing responsibility for all data entered.

Although the use of standard forms is encouraged as an aid to effective communication and office efficiency, a word of caution is in order. The

[4] Association of School Business Officials, *op. cit.*, p. 41.

administrator needs to exercise his professional judgment in determining when not to employ a standard form, even though the message required might be capable of being sent on a form. People often resent receiving forms. It makes them feel as if they are dealing with an impersonal bureaucracy. Although the communication may be routine to the school office, to its receiver—whether he be parent, teacher, or ordinary citizen—the message may bear a great deal of personal meaning. The principal may need to set aside his use of forms and see that some kinds of messages are given the time-consuming attention of a personal letter, a telephone call, or even a personal conference. He must make this judgment, weighing the values and costs of this action against the probable consequences of using a form.

Electronic Data Processing

The utilization of electronic data processing in education is growing so rapidly that it is nearly futile to attempt to put into book form anything which will remain timely. In a book designed primarily for potential and practicing secondary administrators, the subject of electronic data processing would be appropriate at several points. The brief discussion here relates to its potential use as a management tool as applied to the school administrator's office.

In the field of data processing, the term "systems" plays a large part. One finds the terms "systems analysis," "systems review," or "systems approach," in common usage among sophisticates in the data processing field. The term has various interpretations, but the most common meaning of *the systems concept* is that it is an intellectual method for dealing with operational problems. It emphasizes the defining of objectives and the seeking of possible alternatives with their concurrent costs. In short, it is an attempt to deal with many problems through logic and rationality.

Data processing systems contain two major classifications of parts: hardware and software. The term "hardware" refers to the electronic and mechanical elements of a data processing system. These would include the actual machines. "Software" is used in opposition to hardware to include the programming components of a data processing system. *Programming* is the process of giving proper instructions to a machine so that it will complete the desired operations. Programming requires a special language for communication with a computer. One widely known programming language is FORTRAN (a made-up word for Formula Translator).

Data processing by means of hardware requires at least three operations: (1) input, (2) processing, and (3) output. In short, information (generally on cards or magnetic tape) is collected and fed into a machine.

The information is then processed by the machine, and since the machine has been given instructions by means of a program, an output of new information is turned out.

School administrators may not need to acquire technical expertise in hardware matters, but it is quite clear that the up-to-date administrator must keep up with overall possibilities for educational use. Referring again to the definition of office work as the process of facilitating communications, data processing bears a direct implication, for data processing is, above all, a system for the facilitation of communications.

In fact, some authorities feel that today's school administrator ought to have some technical competence in understanding basic computer systems and ought to have been through at least a general course in programming. When looking at the on-the-job requirements for school administrators of the future, the case becomes even stronger. Not that administrators will necessarily operate computers (this is a job for technicians), nor will they necessarily write programs (this is the job of the programmer), but it seems clear that they will be required to participate in decisions about the kinds of use to be made of computers. When systems are installed, they must maintain administrative supervision over the installation. The least defensible position would be represented by the administrator who ignores the field of electronic data processing. Such an attitude is a short route to administrative obsolescence.

Within-school Use Electronic data processing can be employed to accomplish many clerical functions within a secondary school. Its most obvious applications are in the general area of student accounting. Efficient systems are now feasible and economical for attendance accounting, grade reporting, census recording, maintaining permanent records, student scheduling, and test scoring.

The use of these systems makes it possible to remove a great amount of the clerical work from teachers. Through the use of data processing equipment, it is done more accurately, more objectively, and with much greater efficiency of human resources.

For Educational Decision Making So far, most of the electronic data processing systems within schools have been instituted for the primary purpose of more efficient handling of the important but routine kinds of information used by schools. The greatest promise—or threat, as some see it—in the use of computers lies in the area of decision making. Some experts in the field foresee the day when many decisions now being made at middle management levels in large organizations, that is, industrial organizations, hospitals, and military organizations, as well as schools, will be made largely by a computer out of a central facility. Within the framework of the study of formal organizations, principals are considered "middle management." It may be difficult to conceive of educational decisions, as, for example, decisions about new courses or decisions about teachers to employ or decisions about teaching methods to use, ever being made by a computer. However, it must be remembered that computerization is actually a sophisticated attempt at the rationalization of decisions. As knowledge advances in the educational field, this goal may not be as distant as is commonly thought.

Work in the application of data processing for educational use is going on in many portions of the country. One notable location is the work at the Iowa Educational Information Center at the University of Iowa. As of 1966 it reported that it was currently preparing school schedules for 50,000 students in fifty different schools.[5]

The possibilities for practical applications of electronic data processing are just beginning to be realized by educational administrators. Yet, awareness is spreading. As a 1967 publication of the American Association of School Administrators states: [6]

> More schools are using electronic data processing than ever before, and the growth rate is likely to increase in the years ahead. Unfortunately, the state of the art at present must be described as rudimentary. The time is ripe for challenging the imagination of professionals of all ranks in education to do something more with EDP than simply speed up the processing of specified clerical tasks, for this alone hardly justifies the cost of a computer. What makes EDP exciting in our time is that we have only begun to sense the dramatic developments that lie ahead.

THE PRINCIPAL'S ROLE IN OFFICE MANAGEMENT

As Supervisor of the Office

Whether the office staff consists of one part-time clerk or whether it consists of several clerks, stenographers, receptionists, and an accountant, the principal of a secondary school serves as the general supervisor of the office. In the case of a larger office there may be a head secretary or an office manager who exercises on-the-job supervision over the rest of the office staff. Nevertheless, it is the principal who holds the final responsibility for office management.

In this capacity the principal needs to exercise wisdom and judgment in working with these personnel. Good human relations is particularly important. Since most school office employees' salary scales compare unfavorably with comparable jobs in the industrial world, the job must

---

[5] Robert W. Marker, "Computer-based Educational Information Systems: The Iowa Case," in Robert W. Marker, Peter P. McGraw, and Franklin D. Stone (eds.), *Computer Concepts and Educational Administration*, The Iowa Educational Information Center, The University of Iowa, Iowa City, Iowa, 1966, p. 77.

[6] *EDP and the School Administrator*, American Association of School Administrators, Washington, D.C., 1967, p. 8.

bring rewards other than money. Good human relations practices are a cornerstone of good working conditions.

In addition to good human relations, the principal in his role as supervisor of the office can work toward teaching all members of the office staff the importance of their work. As office employees come to understand the relationship of the office work to the work of the school in general, it is more likely that they will attend to their work with greater care and enthusiasm.

Another point often overlooked in the principal's role as supervisor of the office is the example which he sets for the rest of the staff. If the principal wants a staff which is warm and friendly and which enjoys working together, he can set the tone by his own example. If the principal wants a working staff which is punctual, neat, and well-groomed, he can set this example as well. An office staff or, for that matter, the entire building staff will quickly sense the standards the principal sets for working relationships.

As a Planner of His Own Work

As was said at the outset of this chapter, one purpose for the office is to provide the principal with a place for his own work. Many administrators fail to grasp the significance of this. They see the office only as a place where they go to do their work, and the work they *do* is what they *find* to do. Their failure is in sensing that the office is the place where the principal performs his planning function. Planning is one of the primary functions of any administrative position. The administrator who performs his tasks routinely lacks planning.

Especially in the principal's position, it is all too easy to ignore planning. By simply going to work and attending to whatever comes through the office, the principal may, in fact, do a poor job. What is suggested is that the principal needs to plan his own work just as he urges teachers to plan theirs. Only through systematic planning can the principal avoid spending all his time attending to the details which come through the office. Administrators who are able to avoid the debilitating perils of what is so often called "administrivia" do so by blocking out whole days or portions of days for phases of their jobs that are essential but so easy to put off in favor of some more immediate desk work. Long-range budget planning, for example, is considered fundamental to good budgeting development. To actually effect this kind of advance planning, time is required to work through many of the school's plans in advance of the next year. Many aspects of personnel administration require that the principal develop a planned program, rather than a day-to-day job approach. Other phases of the principal's job which profit from planning are curriculum development and community relations.

One simple device to assist the principal in planning his time is to keep a diary or a time log for a few days or a week. It only requires recording the time he spends on an activity. For example, a portion of a principal's diary might look like this:

Mon:	8:15–8:45	Handle mail
	9:15–10:15	Counsel three problem students referred to office
	10:15–10:30	Returned two parent phone calls
	10:30–10:50	Talked to book salesman
	etc.	

After a few days of keeping a record such as this, it is relatively simple to look at the distribution of the principal's time spent on various phases of his job. In this way he can make self-judgments on whether his distribution of time is in keeping with the way he understands his job. This simple procedure is recommended because so often school principals find themselves caught up in running from one thing to another, scrambling to stay on top of things as they come along. Often they fail to realize how they actually distribute their time. The analysis of a diary record such as this furnishes objective evidence of the way a principal spends his time. When confronting themselves with this evidence, administrators are often inclined to rationalize their present pattern of activities on the grounds of necessity. It may be true that one's customary allocation of his time is what is necessary to the job, but it is also equally true that all of us follow a strong tendency to do those things we like to do and those things we feel comfortable doing. Very often, the administrator who complains loudly that he would like to spend more of his time on instructional matters but that the paper work keeps him tied to the desk is finding security in his paper work and avoiding the other dimensions of the job. Honest self-appraisal is a valuable aid to any principal.

SUMMARY

The school office is not only a place, but it is the center of administrative services. It is the main instrument of communication for within-school and outside-of-school communication. Seen in this central focus, it shares a crucial role in the success of the school. Its constant and over-reaching purpose is facilitation of the central purpose of the school.

Physical facilities, office equipment, and the prevailing tone of human relationships, as well as technical matters like the filing system and standard forms, can go far toward enabling the office to accomplish its purposes with efficiency and effectiveness.

To the principal, the office is seen twofold; first, it and the personnel who staff it compose an area over which he exercises direct supervision;

second, it is his own chief working area. Through a careful analysis of his own working time, the principal may be able to avoid the common administrative weakness of being tied to the office doing routine tasks. Planning his own work is crucial here.

SUGGESTED EXERCISES

1. For those who are not in administrative positions, ask a principal to maintain an activity diary such as the one suggested in this chapter for one week. Analyze the results, and classify the activities according to the major components of the principal's job.

2. Make a survey of a limited number of schools to see how many have a standard filing system.

3. Collect a number of office manuals. Examine them for common and dissimilar elements.

SELECTED REFERENCES

COHEN, LOUIS, *The Administration of Non-instructional Personnel in Public Schools,* Research Bulletin no. 1, Research Corporation of the Association of School Business Officials, Chicago, 1964, 96 pp.

EDP and the School Administrator, American Association of School Administrators, Washington, D.C., 1967, 76 pp.

Guiding Principles and Practices in Office Management, Research Bulletin no. 4, Research Corporation of the Association of School Business Officials, Chicago, 1966, 72 pp.

MARKER, ROBERT W., PETER P. McGRAW, AND FRANKLIN D. STONE (eds.), *Computer Concepts and Educational Administration,* Iowa Educational Information Center, The Department of Publications, State University of Iowa, Iowa City, Iowa, 1966, 143 pp.

ROE, WILLIAM H., *School Business Management,* McGraw-Hill Book Company, New York, 1961, 313 pp.

WHITLOCK, JAMES W., *Automatic Data Processing in Education,* The Macmillan Company, New York, 1964, 144 pp.

CHAPTER **20**

MANAGEMENT
SERVICES

It is the purpose of this chapter to treat the
various aspects of management services including school facilities, supplies and equipment, cafeteria, and transportation. The type and quality
of school facilities provided for secondary schools will determine to a
large extent the quality of the program or educational opportunities provided for the students.

MANAGEMENT OF PRESENT FACILITIES

Without question, the area of management is one that needs further
study and clarification. Management problems have existed wherever
people have formed groups to fulfill objectives that could not be accomplished by individuals. Management implies dealing with both people
and things; therefore, one finds that cooperative action is often involved
rather than simple face-to-face relationships. The most challenging task
is to coordinate human beings in a manner that produces satisfaction and
efficiency.

Meaning of School Plant Management

School plant management is an area of significant responsibility in educational administration and involves all services, activities, and procedures concerned with seeing that existing school facilities are kept open and in usable condition.[1] The operation of the school plant includes those services that are maintained on a day-to-day basis which are essential to the safety, comfort, and well-being of those who occupy and use school facilities. Primarily, these services will be performed by custodial personnel as a part of the total program of school plant service.

Shared Responsibilities

As school districts have grown in size, the number of functions administered at the district level have also increased. An example of this trend is the management of custodial services on a shared basis with the local secondary principal. In districts that are large enough to employ business managers, one finds that they manage or share with the principals the responsibility for custodial operations of the school buildings. Generally, the custodial personnel are employed by the business manager, and he determines work loads, pay scales, and general conditions of employment. Yet, there are instances in which the principal is the person who works most closely with these personnel and is responsible for their supervision. In instances where the business manager selects the custodial personnel without consultation with the principal, it should be thoroughly understood by the employees that they will be under the supervision of the principal a great deal of the time. This type of shared arrangement can be a source of friction unless the lines of authority and responsibility are kept clear. It is wise to have policies that specify the respective responsibilities of the business manager, principal, and other employees.

Other Responsibilities of the Principal

In addition to sharing responsibilities with the business manager, the principal has other definite functions in which he must participate actively if proper care is to be taken of the buildings. First, the principal must see that teachers, pupils, and community members contribute to good housekeeping. Effective school plant management programs demand diligent planning; they do not just happen. A well-kept school building is a source of pride and joy to all the people who use it as well as to those who view and help pay for it. Having pride in a well-kept building will assist in preventing damage and vandalism to school equipment, furniture, and property. Another duty of the principal is to see

[1] R. N. Finchum, *School Plant Management: Administering the Custodial Program*, U.S. Department of Health, Education and Welfare, 1961, p. 1.

that the interior of the building is beautified as well as to carry on a beautification program for the exterior and grounds. Teachers and students alike can aid in keeping the grounds and hallways clean and unobstructed. Second, the principal can encourage and assist the custodian in analyzing his job and in making sure that the building has a clean and healthy appearance. Teachers can report minor needs in terms of housekeeping to the principal, who will see that these needs are met. The principal along with the head custodian and the business manager should be involved in rating and evaluating custodial personnel. This type of participation helps the custodian understand that the principal is his supervisor part of the time.

Custodial Services

The significance and problems of the work of school custodians must be fully understood and appreciated by the principal. Whether or not the school has a custodian's handbook is not as important as that there be general agreement between the custodians on their duties and responsibilities and a general acknowledgment by the school staff as to the nature and limitations of the custodians' regular responsibilities and from whom they take orders.[2] No matter how willing, custodians cannot do individual work for teachers and keep their regularly scheduled assignments. All teacher requests for custodial help should be channeled through the principal, thus permitting custodians to perform their regular duties.

The increasing emphasis on adequate school facilities, combined with newer concepts of property preservation, learning environment, safety, and a greater utilization of school facilities by the public, is helping boards of education and school administrators recognize the value of adequate custodial services and the importance of providing trained people to do the work. Accompanying these newer concepts in terms of operational school plant needs are certain well-defined purposes of custodial services. Among these purposes are (1) preserving property values, (2) protecting health and safety, (3) providing a climate for learning, (4) developing goodwill, (5) maintaining cleanliness and neatness, and (6) effecting operating economies.[3]

Members of the custodial staff must be able to work cooperatively with other employees within the school system. They ought to exercise the same discretion that professional employees do in discussing school affairs and activities. Parents often judge the school by the way in which the custodian performs his duties and the manner in which he conducts himself at public functions held at the school.[4]

[2] Ivan H. Linder and Henry M. Gunn, *Secondary School Administration: Problems and Practices,* Charles E. Merrill Books, Inc., Columbus, Ohio, 1963, p. 54.
[3] Finchum, *op. cit.,* p. 2.
[4] James J. Jones, *School Public Relations,* The Center for Applied Research in Education, New York, 1966, p. 83.

Utilization of Space

The problem of effective utilization and assignment of space in buildings is a continuous one. With the population explosion of recent years, administrators have attempted to discover every conceivable way of using space more effectively in order to limit the amount of needed construction and cost. Studies indicate that a *room* utilization of 80 to 85 percent for a general classroom is considered fairly representative.[5] Likewise, a room utilization of 70 to 75 percent for special classroom and laboratories is considered an acceptable goal. For example, if a room with a rated capacity of thirty pupils has a class of twenty, so far as the room itself is concerned, it is 100 percent utilized since it would not be feasible to have another class going on in the room at the same time. Where *pupil station* is concerned, it is only 66⅔ percent utilized. An acceptable goal for pupil-station utilization in regular classrooms is 70 percent and for special classrooms 55 percent. Of course these figures will vary with the nature of the program, the size of the school, and how well the educational space houses the particular program offered.

Newer construction tends to be planned in such a manner as to provide both better room and pupil-station utilization. This flexibility concept enables the administrator to schedule small classes in small rooms. Likewise there may be rooms where partitions may be used as dividers to create two or more small rooms and then be removed to make one large room.

The basic purpose of the school plant is to house the instructional program. It is expected to house the pupils and staff and to expedite the attainment of a desirable educational program. School buildings should be used by the community or the general public in such a way that schoolwork will not be hindered. Every school board, whether representing a large or small school system, should adopt a policy concerning the use of the school plant, grounds, and equipment by community groups. A copy of rules and regulations should be given to every group requesting use of the buildings, grounds, and equipment. These regulations should prescribe the method of obtaining permission to use the property, the time of use, conditions of use, and the fees, if any, which must be paid for their use. Likewise, all legal restrictions that govern the extended use of school properties for other than school purposes should be made known.

Within the last two decades there has been a well-defined movement toward making the school the center of community life. This return to a full-time use of school facilities has been influenced by the trend of our populace in moving away from closely packed urban areas to suburban environments, by the school's invitations to the adult population to make

---

[5] *Studies of Utilization of Staff, Buildings and Audio-visual Aids in Public Schools,* Research Division, National Education Association, 1959.

use of the buildings, and by permitting children to use the school facilities for leisure-time activities.

MAINTENANCE OF THE SCHOOL PLANT

In terms of financial accounting, *maintenance* refers to keeping the school site, the building, and the equipment in as near their original state of repair as possible.[6] Of course there is a direct relationship between how well the custodians keep the buildings and the need for repair. Most maintenance involves repairs and replacements. In far too many instances, boards of education tend to cut the budget in the area of maintenance because minor repairs can wait for another year. This is not a sound practice since some minor repairs become major ones if not made immediately.

Purposes of Maintenance

The general purpose of maintenance is to keep school facilities in such a high state of repair that they will serve the educational program with as little interruption as possible. Specific purposes of maintenance are those activities and services which (1) promote health and safety, (2) provide operating economies, (3) prevent time loss, (4) preserve property values, (5) retard deterioration, (6) prevent obsolescence, and (7) develop community pride.[7]

Early Detection

The exact role the principal should play in identifying the need for repairs and replacements and in requisitioning them will depend upon the administrative structure of the district. If the business manager of the district is in charge of maintenance, the principal and the building custodian may both request repairs from the business manager's office or through his representative. In some school systems there is a department of buildings and grounds, and maintenance is done through this department. Where these structures do not exist, the principal or the custodian under the principal's direction may contact the office of the superintendent. In all instances, requests for repairs and replacements by members of the staff should be cleared through the principal.

With the assistance of the teachers and custodians, the principal should make an annual survey of the school facilities near the end of the school year to discover repairs that need to be made during the coming summer. Since it may not be possible to make all the necessary repairs, he should submit the list of needs in terms of priority. The head cus-

---

[6] Jones, *op. cit.*, p. 84.
[7] R. N. Finchum, *School Plant Management: Organizing the Maintenance Program*, U.S. Department of Health, Education and Welfare, 1960, pp. 7–15.

todian will be of tremendous assistance in helping anticipate and prevent many maintenance problems.

Making Repairs

Although many routine repairs will be made during the school year, summer and vacation periods permit the scheduling of a large volume of work. Many jobs may be planned in 3- to 5-year cycles. An example of such a job would be painting, roofing, and weatherproofing. Maintaining the grounds is a year-long job. During the warmer months, lawns and shrubs are to be kept and fed. During the winter months, there is snow to be removed, and there are trees to be pruned. A well-planned maintenance program for most school districts will cost approximately 5 percent of the operating budget. This is a small amount to pay for keeping the district's facilities where an optimal amount of use is made of them and at the same time for protecting the district's financial investment in them.

PLANNING NEW FACILITIES

Although every secondary school principal may not become involved in planning new school buildings, most will find themselves involved in some phase of planning facilities and relating to the district office in some manner with regard to new plant needs. The tremendous population growth affecting the secondary schools makes it almost mandatory that a secondary school principal be involved in school plant planning at some point in his career.

Philosophy of the Educational Program

Planning and rehabilitating school buildings today is a very complex undertaking. No longer can a school board and local builders bring about the completion of an adequate plant within a short span of time. If one compares present-day school buildings with those of two or three decades ago, he is likely to become convinced that there is an underlying difference in philosophy as to the purpose of the school plant. Formerly, the plant was considered to be "the place where school was kept"—now it is a place for school. Some of the early American school buildings were designed to provide spaces where pupils sat to be instructed—now school plants are conceived to be activity areas where students go to participate in learning activities that can result in understandings, attitudes, skills, ideals, and appreciations, enabling them to live as intelligent and informed social beings. A high priority is given to the space relationship that exists between the school program and the physical plant.

In a very real sense a school plant is not only the largest but the most important piece of teaching equipment necessary for an efficient school. In order to secure an effective school plant, plans must be made to provide for consideration of the nature, adequacy, and arrangement of space within the building.

The best educational environment is planned around and for pupils. It must care for their psychological and physical needs. The building must be safe, healthful, comfortable, and inviting. The whole school plant should be such that it requires a minimum of energy for the child to adjust to it, thus saving a maximum of energy to apply to the learning process itself. Every activity to be carried on in the school should be thoroughly considered in the planning of that school. Since activities and learning experiences do change, school plants should be sufficiently flexible to be readily and economically adapted to changing needs.

Planning Procedures

The type of building needed in a particular community is determined by the kind of educational experiences to be provided in the educational program and by local needs. The major steps to be followed in planning new facilities may be outlined as follows: [8]

1. Analyze the educational needs of the community and determine the future school program as a basis for the evaluation of existing facilities as well as for the planning of new or remodeled ones.
2. Survey the entire school district to establish a master plan which should give consideration to the possibility of district reorganization where this is likely to occur.
3. Select and acquire any sites needed to implement the over-all approved plan resulting from the survey.
4. Develop the educational specifications for each separate project in the approved master plan.
5. Design each separate project in accordance with the approved educational specifications.
6. Secure bids, let contracts, and erect the buildings in accordance with the approved working drawing.
7. Equip the completed building and put it into use.

Discovering Needs and Translating Them into Facilities

A large part of the principal's job is to assist the central office in making the community aware of the need for a building program if one is necessary. His defense for the needed improvements must be based upon the improved learning opportunities that will result for pupils. It may well be that a comprehensive school survey will be needed to ascertain the total needs. A comprehensive study will likely include data about the

[8] *Guide for Planning School Plants,* National Council on Schoolhouse Construction, Nashville, Tenn., 1958, p. 11.

community and its growth possibilities, population predictions, building needs, programs to be housed, finances available or feasible, and the administrative structure.

Planning educational facilities should be thought of as a continuous process. Education is a continuous process, and one does not contemplate that buildings will be worn out with the end of a board member's term or the end of a particular contract with the superintendent. Once the building needs are found, it becomes imperative that they be translated into the needed facilities.

It is no longer considered sufficient for the superintendent and the board of education to be the sole judges of the architect's plans and specifications.[9] There is a marked trend toward close cooperation among the architect, board of education, administration, the faculty, and selected lay citizens. The concept of cooperative planning will improve school plant planning as well as build better school-community relations.

MANAGEMENT OF SUPPLIES AND EQUIPMENT

Operating with the concept of management as a service, the secondary administrator needs to direct his attention to organizing an effective system for the acquisition, control, and maintenance of school supplies and equipment.

The Meaning of Supplies and Equipment

In school business management terminology *supplies* are considered those items of small unit value which are either consumed through use or are considered expendable. Supplies are both instructional and non-instructional. Chalk, paste, duplicating paper, and pencils are instructional supply items. Floor wax, janitorial brushes, and boiler compounds are examples of noninstructional supplies. The distinction is important from a budget classification point of view.

Equipment includes items of greater unit value that are nonexpendable and have greater expected lifetimes. When equipment is damaged, it is generally repaired. Equipment may be either instructional, for example, overhead projectors and flying rings for gymnasiums, or noninstructional, for example, office typewriters, duplicating machines, and floor polishers. Actually, the line between supply and equipment, and between instructional and noninstructional is not particularly important from the principal's point of view except as he needs to conform to his state and local budget classification system.

The key to management of supplies and equipment is the development and maintenance of an effective system. Rather than describe a good

[9] Emery Stoops and M. L. Rafferty, Jr., *Practices and Trends in School Administration*, Ginn and Company, Boston, 1961, p. 241.

system in detail, the purpose here shall be to establish criteria of a good system. Since secondary principals will find themselves in such varying school situations, it would be difficult to describe a system suitable for all situations.

The Supply Management System Is Effective

The primary criterion of a good system is its effectiveness. Effectiveness is the measure of the extent to which the management system places the wanted items in the hands of those who require them at the appropriate time. As simple as this idea is, it affords wide latitude for things going awry. If the needed items get into the hands of one who doesn't want them, the system has failed. If the person who wants an item doesn't get it, the system has failed. If the right item gets to the right person at the wrong time—either too soon or too late—the system has failed. And if the item which is wanted gets to the right person at the right time but turns out to be an inferior or defective item, then the system has failed. And finally, if the right item, being kept by the right person, is improperly stored so that it becomes lost, stolen, or deteriorates, then the system has failed. Effectiveness requires a neat meshing of these elements.

One simple test which an administrator can apply to test the system's effectiveness is to compile a list of instances where the system partially fails. His staff can assist in this regard. Through the development of a list of system failures, the administrator can determine the point at which the breakdown occurs. Much of the system weakness may be out of his immediate control—perhaps in the business office at the district headquarters. Or, the weakness may be in his own office; for example, his clerical staff may be overburdened, making long time delays in writing orders. Analysis of system breakdown is a necessary step in testing the system's effectiveness.

The Supply Management System Is
Relatively Simple for the Users to Operate

A second criterion for a good system is that those who must use it find it relatively simple. Particularly for the users of the supplies and equipment, that is, the teachers, custodians, secretaries, and cafeteria workers, the system should seem clear-cut and uncomplicated. A system which requires a great deal of personal attention on the part of those who use it greatly increases the chance of system failure. If the system for requesting a new item of teaching equipment (assuming budget approval) requires a lot of paper work, it is likely that teachers will be less inclined to make requests. There seems to be a direct correlation between the ease of a system and the use to which it is put. Cumbersome details encourage flouting the system. When this occurs, the system has failed again.

The necessity for a simple system is no reflection upon the intelligence of its users. Highly trained teachers require a simple system as well as an unskilled cleaner-custodian.

The same principle applies to control and management of textbooks. It makes good business sense for teachers to insist that students take good care of school books. It is a matter of control and also a matter of teaching respect for loaned items. Teachers can be expected to distribute textbooks and also to inspect occasionally for excessive wear or damage. However, it would seem to go beyond the bounds of good educational and business sense to ask teachers to spend time in rigid accounting systems where they are required to make detailed records of every book, its owner, and its condition.

The Supply Management System Provides Administrative Control

An adequate system provides the unit administrator with control over the supply and equipment management process. The building principal is officially designated as the head of the school who holds responsibility for all phases of the total operation and who must be able to exercise control over supplies and equipment. Control, in this sense, means not that the administrator individually supervises each act of the supply process, but rather that he has access to complete information on its operation and can determine rather quickly whether the system is working in the prescribed manner. With a good system, well-controlled, the responsible administrator can fully account for everything should an occasion arise where this is necessary.

The Supply Management System
Operates with a Minimum of Administrator Attention

A final important criterion of a good supply and management system is that it requires little attention from the administrator. For the day-to-day operations the administrator should rarely need to become involved. Only when the system fails to handle the current operation does he need to direct his attention to it. This is what some management consultants call "management by exception." The management (administrator) directs his attention only to the exceptions. It is a sound principle of administration as applied to business management aspects of school administration because the recurring cyclic operations should be standardized and routinized so that they can be monitored by an office manager or clerk.

It simply does not make sense that any system of supply and equipment management require intensive participation of the administrator. The principal (or any of his professional assistants) should not be required to perform clerical tasks such as looking up prices in catalogs, totaling requisition sheets into combined orders, checking in school supply orders, handing out supplemental books from a central book repository, or inventorying art paper, etc. Tasks such as these do not require the talents of a professionally trained educator. (Actually, the educator is probably less exacting with these tasks than a clerk). Clerks at one-third the salary of administrators can better perform these activities.

Administrative attention is required, though, at key times, that is, whenever there is an educational decision to be made, or perhaps a problem to be straightened out, or perhaps a new system to be inaugurated.

CAFETERIA MANAGEMENT

A well-run cafeteria may be representative of the tone of a school. School cafeterias serve purposes other than food service. Although business management techniques can and should be applied to school cafeterias, their educational purposes need to be maintained.

School Cafeteria Purposes

Modern schools are built with cafeterias so that the overall educational objectives can be realized more effectively. Rather than simply to turn the students out to the nearest commercial lunchroom (if there are any nearby) or to require them to travel home for lunch or to ask them to carry lunches from home, the modern school finds it more feasible to provide a cafeteria and furnish low-cost meals.

As Roe points out, "school lunch is education" is a much discussed theme among administrators, teachers, and food-service workers.[10] Unfortunately, he goes on to state: "Yet seldom does one see an example of a serious attempt to make the lunchroom a good learning situation." [11] Roe lists a number of educational possibilities for food service within schools.[12] It can:

1. Provide opportunity for vocational training and exploration for a few students
2. Serve to assist in teaching the facts of nutrition
3. Help children learn to select the right food
4. Emphasize use of correct table manners and similar social graces
5. Encourage cleanliness and sanitation
6. Emphasize courtesy in crowds and in working and living together
7. Serve as a portion of an educational unit where eating habits and food are stressed
8. Serve as an illustration of good management practices
9. Show the coordination of agriculture and industry

[10] William H. Roe, *School Business Management*, McGraw-Hill Book Company, New York, 1961, p. 281.
[11] *Ibid.*
[12] *Ibid.*

In addition to these above listed educational possibilities, the cafeteria serves the school in other ways.

Fundamentally, it solves the daily lunch problem for everyone who happens to be at school. More than that though, through professionally planned meals, students receive a healthful, balanced, nutritious meal at least once a day. In some areas which have significant numbers of economically disadvantaged, the school cafeteria lunch is the *only* balanced nutritious meal the students get.

The well-run cafeteria provides students with a daily opportunity to meet together in a normal healthy social situation. They need this type of break from their academic routines. For this reason, the well-run cafeteria is not necessarily the one which is tightly controlled, with an extremely low noise level. By the same token, neither social nor educational objectives are furthered by the cafeteria which is wild and disorderly.

The Principal's Role in Cafeteria Operation

As in other phases of administration, the principal's role is dependent upon the organizational pattern of the school district. In larger districts, there is generally a cafeteria director, who is responsible for districtwide menu planning, supply ordering, personnel employment, and cafeteria accounting. In smaller districts, the principal may be the only administrator and must therefore become directly involved in some of the business management aspects of the school cafeteria. In these cases, it is recommended that the principal attempt to work toward the development of some specially trained person to perform these tasks.

Regardless of the district organization, the principal is responsible for seeing that the cafeteria serves the school's educational objectives. In this capacity, he must be responsible for monitoring the cafeteria schedule. In most cafeterias, the daily schedule of when students arrive is part of the administrative controlling mechanism. Students need time enough to eat in relaxed fashion, yet the cafeteria must get the necessary numbers through in time to prevent a too long lunch period.

The principal is responsible for helping establish the behavioral standards at lunch time. Not that he will personally dictate standards, but he can be the leader in building a healthy, constructive, and consistent faculty attitude toward appropriate student behavior in the cafeteria.

Since the cafeteria also serves the faculty, some arrangements for their comfort need to be taken. Teachers generally prefer to eat by themselves, in some way physically separated from students. They feel they need this time as relief from the tension of constant attention to students. Even if separate facilities are not present, it is relatively easy to provide the minimum in the form of folding screens. In this way, a harbor of refuge for harassed teachers is furnished. Of course, any teachers who are "on duty" will be with students.

TRANSPORTATION MANAGEMENT

Many American oldsters are fond of amusing their grandchildren with stories of how far they walked to school as youngsters. It has been said that the older a man gets, the farther he had to walk to school and the deeper was the snow. Although there was probably a certain hardening virtue won by those who did, in fact, slog it out through the snow to the village school from distances in the country, the disadvantages and discrimination of a system which left students to their own devices to get to school are too seldom remembered.

Purposes of School Bus Transportation

Because the transportation of youngsters by school bus has now become so well-established, it may seem almost superfluous to mention purposes. Obviously, school bus transportation is for the express purpose of bringing students to school.

Since the 1930s American public schools have been moving steadily along the road toward equalizing educational opportunity. One of the formidable barriers to this equality has been the location of a student's home in relation to the school. Students who lived in the remote, rural, and less densely populated areas could not get to school as easily or as often as those living closer. Often, there was a direct relationship between the school attendance and accessibility to the school.

To help minimize the factor of distance from the school and thereby enhance equality of opportunity, most states enacted legislation requiring school districts to furnish transportation to their students when they live beyond certain specified distances. The expenditure of public monies for pupil transportation was first legalized by Massachusetts in 1869.[13] Budget funds for transportation are now upheld in every state and are one of the major auxiliary expenses of public education. Transportation by school bus has grown to such proportion that in 1966, 270,000 vehicles carried 16,000,000 pupils daily nearly 2 billion miles.[14]

Transportation Administration

A major point in the administration of public school transportation is the local school district policy for deciding which children to transport. Most states require schools to transport children when they live beyond

[13] *Ibid.*, p. 227.
[14] Paul T. Stewart, "Types, Causes and Results of Accidents," *The American School Board Journal*, vol. 154, no. 2, pp. 30–31, February, 1967.

a certain distance from the school. For secondary students this distance is commonly 2 miles. However, school districts are usually permitted to enact local policies that are more liberal than the minimum state requirement; that is, they may adopt a policy that will pick up students who live less than 2 miles away.

Whatever the board adopts as its policy, school administrators must apply it uniformly. No matter what the pickup distance is, there will always be those who live just 0.1 mile or less beyond it and who may be quite likely to think that their children, too, ought to receive bus transportation. Unless there is some unusual hazard to be considered, the most defensible policy is an arbitrary distance administered uniformly.

Secondary school administrators are not generally involved in establishing bus routes. This is an exacting task, which requires the full time of someone other than a principal. Of course, the number of students to be transported in any school depends upon the local situation.

A school bus is considered an extension of the school. For this reason, students are under the control of the school while on buses. This is true whether school buses are district owned or privately contracted. The only exception to school control is when the school district contracts with a public utility carrier, and students therefore ride as regular public passengers. This arrangement is most common in urban districts where there are available public bus, subway, or other rapid transit facilities.

Since the school's control and responsibility for students extends to the school bus, the administrator must also include this as his area of responsibility. This is very often one of the difficult areas in which to work effectively. Students, especially early adolescents, are not the least bit reluctant to turn the bus into a place of horseplay and rowdyism. Bus drivers try to contain students under these common conditions, but they find it difficult since their first and constant concern is the operation of the bus itself. Most bus drivers lack the specialized training for student control. Therefore, it is important that the professional control exercised by teachers and administrators be felt—even at a distance—on the school bus.

Student self-discipline is the best solution. Most students learn to accept responsibility for their own reasonable behavior on the school bus. However, as every driver knows, there are usually two or three (and maybe more) who delight in attempting to thwart the rules of safe bus conduct. The school administration must be prepared to deal swiftly and surely with bus conduct cases. States and local boards have generally been supportive of the principal's efforts to maintain good bus behavior.

Bus Safety

Riding on a public school bus is probably the safest way a student can get to school. Even though the accident rate on school buses is reported rising,[15] it is still an amazingly low rate of 18 accidents per million miles. One reason why school buses are so safe is that they are subjected to rigid performance standards. Drivers are specially licensed and specially trained. School officials make constant efforts to inculcate students with habits of safe bus behavior. Apparently such efforts have paid off.

One point sometimes neglected by schools is the instruction of students who do not regularly ride school buses. Bus safety instruction should be given to all students since, from time to time, all students ride on school buses for field trips and special events.

The Principal's Role in School Bus Operation

Secondary principals become most directly involved in the management of bus transportation through solving problems arising out of incidents on school buses. The principal or one of his assistants will need to receive and process complaints made by parents or students about other students' behavior on school buses. They may also be involved in alleged incidents of improper behavior of bus drivers. Many school districts adopt some standard report form which is filed by a bus driver describing incidents. These are handled by the principal's office.

The elements of coordination and cooperation are especially important in the overall management of bus transportation. Usually buses are tied to a complex schedule which serves more than one school. The administrator has the responsibility to see that his school's students are able to meet the schedules once they are established. Cooperation with non-public schools is often necessary also since, in many states, public transportation of private school youngsters has become mandated.

School Traffic

The secondary administrator will also need to be concerned with traffic flow in and around his school. If he has a number of buses arriving or departing at specified times and within limited spaces, he will probably need to restrict other vehicular traffic at those times. If these spaces are part of a municipal area, he will need to work with local police to develop appropriate regulations. If the area is school property, these will be directly under school control.

Of critical importance in regard to bus and vehicular traffic is the pattern of student flow when entering or leaving the building. This must be worked out so that walking students are not crossing in or near buses.

[15] *Ibid.*, p. 30.

SUMMARY

This chapter has dealt with management services. It has presented the view that the school facilities (including the building itself), supplies and equipment, the cafeteria system, and the transportation system are services instituted to contribute to the betterment of the educational program.

Secondary school administrators are urged to consider various management services as important parts of their responsibility. Even though this entire book stresses the principal's emphasis upon instructional leadership, this chapter makes it clear that instructional leadership assumes efficient operation of management services. In the well-managed school building, facilities are well cared for; proper supplies are available when needed; the cafeteria is a pleasant place to eat; and the buses come and go with order and safety. When these positive conditions prevail, the school is being well managed.

The authors' recommended approach is that the secondary school administrator view management services as administrative systems. The actual daily operations of these systems are performed generally by noninstructional personnel. The principal should be required only to give his attention to the problem areas as they arise; the better his administrative organization, the less frequently they will arise. In this way, the effective principal has his management services under full control so that he can devote the major share of his time to instructional leadership.

SUGGESTED EXERCISES

1. Give your own definition of school plant management.

2. What can be done in terms of shared responsibilities in order that confusion will not result with regard to the business manager, the principal, and custodians?

3. Find out from your principal what his responsibilities are with regard to plant management, and compare them with those suggested by the authors.

4. Who should be involved in evaluating the custodians?

5. What are some novel ways of utilizing space through better plant planning?

6. What problems have you encountered in your teaching career that can be associated with maintenance of the school plant? As an administrator?

7. What part does the philosophy of the educational program play in planning new facilities?

8. Once school plant needs have been discovered, how does the principal of a given secondary school see to it that these needs are translated into the new facilities?

9. Develop a checklist to be used by a principal for an inventory of his time. Include the major categories of management services included in this chapter.

Through keeping a time log, try to determine what percentage of time an administrator spends on these management services.

10. Some educators advocate that students should be closely controlled and supervised during lunch; others take the point that supervisory controls should be minimum. Debate this issue. drawing upon available research findings.

SELECTED REFERENCES

BROCKMAN, F. H., "Unit System Tells How Many Custodians Can Do the Job," *The Nation's Schools,* vol. 78, pp. 56ff., August, 1966.

COHEN, LOUIS, *The Administration of Non-instructional Personnel in Public Schools,* Research Bulletin no. 1, Research Corporation of the Association of School Business Officials, 1964, 96 pp.

ROE, WILLIAM H., *School Business Management,* McGraw-Hill Book Company, New York, 1961, 313 pp.

SCHAUER, R. J., "Here Are 18 Short Cuts to Easier Maintenance," *The Nation's Schools,* vol. 78, p. 104, September, 1966.

"School Building Maintenance Procedures," U.S. Office of Education (OE 21027) bibliography, U.S. Office of Education Bulletin, 1964, no. 17, 175 pp.

TONIGAN, R. F., "Organizing a Plant Planning Program," *American School and University,* vol. 38, pp. 39–40, July, 1966.

"Transportation," Special Report, *The American School Board Journal,* vol. 154, no. 2, pp. 19–50, February, 1967.

CHAPTER 21

PUBLIC RELATIONS

The basic purpose of this chapter is to discuss the various aspects of public relations, including its nature and purposes, the need for and importance of public relations, responsibilities of the principal, the various media, relationships with the community, and appraisal of the program. This chapter will present those aspects of concern that deal directly with the secondary school and those for which the secondary principal will be responsible.

NATURE AND PURPOSES

Meaning of Public Relations

Many authorities in educational administration have defined public relations with some common elements of agreement. The American Association of School Administrators states that: "Public relations seek to bring about a harmony of understanding between any group and the public it serves and upon whose good will it depends." [1] Administrators

[1] *Public Relations for America's Schools,* American Association of School Administrators, Washington, D.C., 1950, p. 12.

who are willing to accept this definition should be acquainted with broad areas of knowledge and have some understanding of social and educational psychology, economics, sociology, history, and philosophy.

Carter Good, editor of *Dictionary of Education,* says that public relations is the formal activity of improving the relations of a school within a community.[2] It is an activity concerned with giving information to the public about the school and creating goodwill for the school. This definition is primarily one of interpretation.

Harry L. Stearns says: "Public relations is the opening of two-way channels of communications between the citizens of a community, who possess and support the schools, and the professional people who conduct them." [3] This meaning implies a two-way street with room for mutual interaction.

A related definition is given by Reeder, who states that public relations is the phase of educational administration that seeks to bring a harmonious working relationship between the schools and the public which the schools serve.[4] This meaning includes a working relationship that secures effective results.

The most workable definition of public relations is given by Jones, and it is the one supported by the authors in this volume.[5] As used in this book *public relations* is defined in a broad sense and designates all the functions and relationships that pertain in a two-way exchange of ideas between school and community and that establish the basis for joint understanding. "Public relations" and "school public relations" will be used interchangeably with "school-community relations." To separate public relations from other aspects of school administration is a most difficult task since every part of the work of the schools has some bearing upon the relationship between the school and the community.

Purposes of Public Relations

School public relations began with an emphasis upon selling the school to the public. Schools borrowed the idea from business during the early thirties. School people soon saw that such a limited purpose did not fulfill the needs of the schools.

School public relations has become a much broader concept than mere publicity or interpretation. It involves the way in which one relates him-

---

[2] Carter V. Good (ed.), *Dictionary of Education,* 2d ed., McGraw-Hill Book Company, New York, 1959, p. 430.

[3] Harry L. Stearns, *Community Relations and the Public Schools,* Prentice-Hall, Inc., Englewood Cliffs, N.J., 1955, p. 7.

[4] Ward G. Reeder, *The Fundamentals of Public School Administration,* The Macmillan Company, New York, 1958, p. 575.

[5] James J. Jones, *School Public Relations,* The Center for Applied Research in Education, New York, 1966, p. 2.

self to his surroundings. Since there are many publics to be satisfied, the school must keep the child's welfare as its focus along with the essential needs of society. The American Association of School Administrators was among the first professional groups to recognize the broader purposes of public relations.[6] Their purposes were:

1. To inform the public as to the work of the school.
2. To establish confidence in schools.
3. To rally support for proper maintenance of the educational program.
4. To develop awareness of the importance of education in a democracy.
5. To improve the partnership concept by uniting parents and teachers in meeting the educational needs of the children.
6. To integrate the home, school, and community in improving the educational opportunities for all children.
7. To evaluate the offering of the school in meeting the needs of the children of the community.
8. To correct misunderstandings as to the aims and activities of the school.

If a public relations program is to be successful in the secondary school, it is essential that those persons who are responsible for its origin, development, and growth understand the goals that such a program seeks to achieve. To a large extent, the purposes of a public relations program are conditioned by what the professional school people believe about education and about how public relations may become an agent of the school and community. Purposes of public relations have been reviewed by many authorities. Jones summarized the most pertinent purposes of public relations as seen by several authorities in educational administration, and these purposes are: [7]

1. To explain to the community the school system's philosophy of education, its aims, and its means of achieving these aims.
2. To interpret the educational program to the people of the community in a way that will encourage them to take pride in and support their schools.
3. To establish confidence in the ongoing institution.
4. To indicate to the public that it is receiving full value for monies expended on education.
5. To develop an understanding of what is possible in education when adequate support is provided.
6. To acquaint the public with the trends in education.
7. To correct misunderstandings or errors.
8. To help the public feel some sense of responsibility for the quality of education the school distributes.

[6] Public Relations for America's Schools, Twenty-eighth Yearbook, American Association of School Administrators, Washington, D.C., 1950, p. 14.
[7] Jones, School Public Relations, p. 8.

THE NEED FOR PUBLIC RELATIONS

If one investigates carefully, he will find many people working with the public schools such as administrators, supervisors, teachers, board members, graduate students, professors of education, and others who are engaged in studying or administering school public relations. Since public relations affects all phases of the educational program, persons who work with the program and with children can visualize the need for better understanding of the program in detail.

While there has been a vast increase in the quantity of research in school public relations, relatively few problems in the field have been completely or adequately solved. Numerous individuals doing research in educational administration have pointed out various reasons why administrators should be concerned with public relations. A review of some of the more recent needs follows.

Variation and Innovation

In the early periods of American education it was relatively easy for pupils, parents, and the general public to know and to understand most of what happened at school and in the community. Life was fairly simple, and the community and school were so interrelated that both knew what was taking place in each situation. There have been many changes and innovations in regard to purpose, content, teaching methods, and facilities, including the increasing size of secondary schools, which have tended to confuse the general public and to leave it with inadequate information. Terms such as "team teaching," "large-group instruction," "computerized learning," "track plans," and various other names by which new procedures have been developed and put into use indicate just a few examples of such changes. Today's complex and urbanized society demands that public school pupils be provided educational experiences quite different from many of those which present-day parents themselves received when they were in school. The limited and often inaccurate information possessed by citizens concerning the work of the schools further points up the need for more adequate public relations.

Potentiality for Improvement

In many instances the people who reside in a school district do not understand or conceive what is possible in the way of improvements that may be made in the public schools. As schools developed new goals in regard to educating youth, they have not always expressed them in a manner that is easily understood; therefore, this has been a source of confusion to the layman. A tendency to look with suspicion upon any contemplated school change characterizes the attitude of far too many communities. As a result, one may find a public tendency to conserve the status quo and to oppose both professionals and nonprofessionals when they attempt to lead the way toward improvement or to bring about changes. It is commonly accepted by many of our educators that the performance of the majority of schools in the United States is far below what it might be if most of the knowledge about the science or art of education were put into practice.

Professionalization of Faculty

For many years our public schools were staffed and taught by people who relieved themselves from other jobs long enough to give some time to the training of youth, although their major preparation and interests were not in the field of education. Today, education has developed and improved as a profession, and both interest and preparation have to meet higher standards of expectation than before. Accompanying this increased professionalization of the staff are many changes in planning methods, counseling, assignments, evaluation of pupils, parent conferences, disciplinary methods, etc. These changes are a result of the staffing of schools with better prepared teachers who tend to reflect their training through experimentation and advanced study. Changes need to be understood by the public in order that better school and community relations can be provided.

The Layman's Concept of the Teacher

The reluctance of the public to grant teachers freedom in the classroom and the public's lack of appreciation of the role of the teacher in community affairs is not in accord with the improved professional training required of teachers. The public may think the work of the teacher is important but not as significant as that of people in other professions or occupations. Apparently teachers occupy a secondary position in the eyes of the community despite the fact that many of them have undergone longer and more intensive periods of study and preparation than people in some other professions. In the eyes of laymen, American teachers are not free. Teachers are expected to conform to community patterns of behavior although the customs may be practiced in only the isolated and remote areas. Teachers should participate in community affairs to the same extent that members of other professions do. They should not be expected to spend as much free time in community work as they devote to teaching. Teachers need to be free to experiment in the classroom and to live a normal life in the community.

Pressure Groups

Not all pressure groups are harmful to the school; some work for goals that help advance the school. Other pressure groups work for the vocal minority and do not in any way represent the majority. Another need for public relations is indicated by the increasing number of board policies and state statutes which have been passed as an indirect result of some pressure group. Much of this legislation and many policies restrict the educational program and limit what the teacher is able to do. The real need is for the administrator to be able to identify and to analyze pressure groups and to discover their purposes and actions.

SIGNIFICANCE OF PUBLIC RELATIONS

In early American history, schools were developed as a result of the recognition by the community of the vital need for education. The school was considered by the community to be an integral part of its organization. Schools were publicly originated, controlled, and supervised. Public relations programs were not necessary because of the position of the school as a center of the community. Teachers, because of the position of the school as a center of the community, took part in community affairs to a considerable degree. There was no clear-cut division between the administrative and supervisory processes, nor in the earlier years was either process considered a professional function. There was little need for an organized program of public relations during a time when lay interest and control were so active.

Seldom, if ever, have the schools been under such critical examination by parents and the public at large as they are today. Although criticism is important in maintaining the quality and integrity of public institutions in a democracy, the great flood of critical articles, many without an adequate presentation of the facts, needs, and accomplishments of public institutions, tends to weaken or destroy the latter.[8] It is significant then that the general public know the facts about public schools and their achievements. This new concern for schools provides opportunities for school personnel to interpret the educational program and its needs.

The American public school embraces the principles of democracy. In order to fulfill the objectives of the American way of life, a large investment in public education has become essential. This investment involves supporting elementary schools, the junior and senior high schools, and in selected communities, the junior college. The public has

---

[8] Lester W. Anderson and Lauren A. Van Dyke, *Secondary School Administration*, Houghton Mifflin Company, Boston, 1963, p. 469.

made an initial investment and has added to it large annual sums for the continued support of education.

Education can meet the current needs of the public only as the great body of the common people comprehend the schools and their work and participate actively in upholding them. The development of education in the United States depends, to a large extent, upon the attitudes of the public and its willingness and ability to provide the necessary finances. As long as education justifies itself in the minds of those who are instrumental in financing it, the financing will likely continue. Most citizens are eager to take part in strengthening the school program.

Public relations seeks the support of the people in the maintenance and the direction of an institution which is really basic to popular government as we know it today. Our schools are expected to make a significant contribution to the future as children who are being educated in our schools today become the adults of tomorrow. The type of job that is needed makes public relations a necessity since education can grow and expand better as the public becomes conscious of the role that schools play in our society.

RESPONSIBILITIES OF THE PRINCIPAL

No attempt is made to present all the responsibilities of the secondary principal in public relations, but the more important aspects will be reviewed. Responsibilities for public relations in secondary schools will vary with the size, location, and personnel as well as with the administrative structure of the school and the district.

Relationships with the Central Office

Whatever the administrative structure, the principal must maintain some type of relationship with the district office and the superintendent of schools. If the organizational plan for public relations is centralized, the principal may very well be responsible to the director of public relations or some other person who is directly responsible to the superintendent. If the organizational structure for public relations is decentralized, the principal may direct his own building programs of public relations in cooperation with the superintendent. In either case, he will wish to cooperate with the districtwide elements of the public relations program.

With reference to contacts with the board of education, the superintendent of schools is the official representative of the principal and the teachers. Normally principals do not appear before the board except upon invitation by the superintendent or as a part of some cooperative plan between the superintendent and the principal.

Organize the Program

Systematized public relations programs hold an important place in the administrative phase of our public schools. To plan and to carry out such programs at the individual school level requires that someone assume the responsibility for coordinating the various elements of such programs in each school. In most secondary schools this challenge belongs to the principal.

Usually the principal and staff participate in the districtwide program and also conduct a special program of public relations for the school in which they work. It is a part of the principal's job to organize the machinery for public relations within his own school.[9] The principal is the person who keeps contacts between the school and the larger community as well as between the district office and the larger community it serves.[10] In this capacity, the principal can either make or break the relationships with the community.

Use Individual Contacts

Important also to the public relations program are the individual contacts of the principal. Each day the secondary principal meets and talks with many parents, citizens, and students. He is often under fire to explain some policy or practice of the school district or of the school. Likewise he may be called upon to explain some accident or unusual occurrence at school as well as what the school program proposes to do.

Develop a Quality Educational Program

The primary purpose of the school is to teach students those subjects and ideas that they need most for survival in a modern society. The better the educational program, the easier it is to develop a satisfactory program of public relations. No quantity of publicity can substitute for a program of *quality*. The school program must meet the needs of all pupils, not just those who are preparing for college. The attitudes of parents are conditioned by the success or failure their children's experience in school.

A major responsibility of the principal is to help raise the sights of the community in regard to education. As a community leader, he can do much to lead the community into a cooperative program of action. If the school is to do an effective job, it must indirectly contribute to improving the quality of living in the community. A satisfied parent and a happy pupil make a wonderful combination for understanding the school.

---

[9] James J. Jones, "The Principal and Public Relations," *Educational Administration and Supervision*, vol. 41, p. 313, May, 1955.
[10] Jones, *School Public Relations*, p. 50.

Provide Leadership for the School

It is the job of the principal to help familiarize the staff at every level with the general aims of the overall program and with the special techniques and procedures applicable at each level. There is a public relations responsibility for every member of the school system. This job is usually a part of his regular work. The principal and his staff by their very existence affect public relations. The secondary principal is responsible for giving leadership that will develop the program and staff to the fullest extent.

AGENCIES, AVENUES, AND MEDIA

Much research in public relations has been concerned with the various channels of communication, particularly those media that have to do with promoting and developing understanding between the school and the public. Although there have been numerous studies, unfortunately most of them have been status studies such as surveys and opinion polls. One cannot select with a high degree of definiteness the most effective techniques of public relations. Despite these limitations, there are some agencies, avenues, and media that have proved fruitful. It is the purpose of this section to review some of the most helpful media.

Students

Although not fully recognized by all educators, the pupil is one of the most significant public relations agents of the school. The pupil is a prime agent for providing information about the school to parents and others in the community. It is doubtful whether educators could keep pupils from telling about their school experiences even if they tried; however, most educators desire that pupils report accurately and often. In fact, building a foundation for worthy attainment by students is not only a privilege of the school, but also one of its duties.

Parental attitudes toward the school are often determined by the feelings which students express during the hours they spend at home. If pupils appear to be happy and in general satisfied, parents tend to feel the same way about the school. Of course the most vocal students are likely to be those who are unhappy. A part of the school's job is to help students understand the school they attend. Students have the chief qualification of effective public relations agents in that they are well informed about the school. In fact, no group, excluding school officials and employees, knows as much about the school. Students know about the program, the progress or lack of it in classes, the teaching methods, the adequacy or inadequacy of teaching material and equipment, the various personalities of teachers, the frequency of visits by the principal, and the total function of student activities. The student hears and sees much and can tell many things about the school. Therefore, it is urgent that he know and understand what takes place at his school in order that he will present the facts adequately. Jones says in this regard: "Every student carries home to his parents certain definite impressions of the school; the type of teacher employed, the fairness or unfairness of teacher and principal, the standard of conduct permitted in the schoolroom, the soundness or futility of the courses studied." [11]

Generally, any special effort made to inform students about the work of the school pays dividends in terms of public relations. The pupils of today may become parents of tomorrow's students. Their influences extend far beyond the home. They come in contact with many persons who do not themselves come into direct contact with the school.

The Teacher

The teacher most likely plays the greatest and most meaningful role of any individual in developing and maintaining efficient public relations for the schools. By the very nature of his position the teacher comes into contact with pupils, parents, and others in the community. To a large extent, a school's public relations program consists of what the people of the community think about the staff and the program that the school offers and what success their children have attained in the classes which they have attended. The attitude then of the community about the local schools, teachers, and educational achievement is vitally tied up with the by-products of teaching. Community attitudes begin to take form the day the children of the patrons of the school enter the various classrooms. Everything that takes place in the classroom, on the playground, or in any off-campus relationships colors the attitude which constitutes public relations.

The best public relations program, staffed by the ablest teachers obtainable and carried out with all the care and effectiveness of a well-run public relations organization, will prove to be no match for the stubborn, arbitrary, and often unreasonable attitudes that 12 years, or less, of public school have helped form.

Basically, then the public relations program is a problem of fundamental attitudes because public opinion is conditioned by them—by the memories which each person has of his youth of understanding and helpful teachers—and by the experiences and reactions of today's children toward the school. These attitudes reflect the action of people as something which will need to be counteracted or to be built on as something positive for the good of the school and community.

[11] *Ibid.*, p. 64.

The too often heard criticism that teachers are timid, quiet, and take too little interest in community affairs is to some extent the result of actions of legislatures, autocratic dictation of administrators, boards of education, and community groups, which, through restrictive legislation and social and economic discrimination, have forced teachers to function as second-class citizens.

All too often superintendents and principals have failed to be concerned with teachers' status and rights. As long as teachers must be tolerated as unpleasant necessities, the pattern of subservience and timidity will continue to influence those who enter into the profession. In some sections of the United States, notably in the larger centers of population, teachers have achieved a substantial degree of freedom, social acceptance, and security. In other areas, especially the more isolated areas, the fight for recognition as human beings and citizens worthy of their hire is far from being won.

The problem then is to determine what the school administrator can do in the daily conduct of the schools to build positive attitudes toward teachers and the schools. Teachers who are happy, free, and secure in their jobs are a good investment in achieving better public relations. Through the daily contact of the teachers with pupils, parents, and the public, lasting public relations are formed. Teachers who are proud of their profession and convinced of their importance to society are usually free and eager to do their best for their pupils. The removal of social restrictions gives them the opportunity to participate in the life of the community and to make their influence felt for the social good. In a like manner, adequate salaries and decent working conditions—especially fair and democratic teacher-administrator relations—will do much to attract to the teaching profession the right kind of young people we so urgently need in our public schools.

The importance of having teachers participate in the development of administrative and teaching policies is gaining headway in public schools and cannot be overemphasized. This practice dignifies the status of the teacher, gives him a sense of belonging, and humanizes the relationship between the administrator and the staff.

Since any public relations program rests fundamentally upon the competency, character, and integrity of the staff, strict adherence to professional standards in the selection of teachers is of great importance. Also it is important that the best-trained teachers be selected, for many people form their opinions of teachers from contact with a limited number of teachers. Where the staff members are being selected and promoted on the basis of political, racial, or religious considerations, one need not expect teachers to be respected within the community.

Student Activities

The types and purposes of student activities discussed in Chapter 15 tend to promote a greater understanding between the secondary school and its community. Although some educators may not be convinced of the educational value of student activities such as interscholastic athletics, many profess to see values in the student activities program equal to those found in the general program of education. Certainly the public relations values of student activities as well as their educational values help unite the school and the community through the activities program.

Since activities are considered a functional part of the life training for boys and girls, the public should be acquainted with the activities program in the school. In presenting the school to the public through the school's activities, the teacher can, not only combat the critics of the activity program, but he can also win friends for the school and influence the thinking of alert citizens to help them see the values of the extracurricular activities.

The importance of the extracurricular program as a public relations medium is obvious. In no other phase of the school's program does the school even begin to approach the large numbers of people in the community as it does through the various activities.

School Visits

Although it is not the intent of this section to criticize home visits made by school personnel, it has been demonstrated both by research and through experience that home visits are not always practicable. A public relations technique that is far more effective, due to many factors such as feeling that the school has nothing to hide, being permitted to see the school in operation, and visualizing what a school is like today, is the school visit by school patrons. One of the basic purposes of having parents visit the secondary school is to have them near the scene of action or where records and other materials concerning their sons and daughters are easily available.

One example of such successful practice is reported by Jones in which a secondary school principal invites five parents to visit the school daily.[12] The purposes of parent visits are (1) to familiarize parents with personnel, plant, and curriculum activities available, (2) to provide teachers with opportunities to discuss student problems with them, (3) to give students a chance to acquaint parents with the school environment, (4) to help parents get information about school problems, (5) to assist parents to regard school visits as part of their normal activity, and (6) to educate

---

[12] James J. Jones, "Three Technics for Bettering School-Community Relations," *The Nation's Schools*, vol. 55, p. 82, April, 1955.

students to the fact that parents should take an active part in planning school activities.[13] In the school visitation program just mentioned, parents were selected from an alphabetical list of all parents of the school, and five were invited each day to arrive at school by 10 A.M. and to stay as long as they desired. They were given a copy of their child's daily activities and a copy of the complete school schedule. The guests were encouraged to eat in the lunchroom and to visit the entire school campus. Before departing, parents were requested to visit with the principal and to discuss any part of their observations. Likewise, the principal may ask the parents for their opinions of what they observed.

The school visitation program described above has many advantages over casual visits. First, it permits parents to see any phase of the program they may desire. Second, it encourages the parents to visit at times other than Education Week. Third, it provides opportunities for visitation that many, many parents desire but for a variety of reasons may never request. Fourth, it indicates what is possible in terms of having parents visit a modern school. In this particular example, more than a majority of parents have visited annually and have given glowing reports to the principal along with minor suggestions. This is one of the most effective public relations techniques when used in a satisfactory manner.

Mass Media

The most commonly used mass media include the newspapers, radio, and television. To indicate that the research in journalism, for example, is complete is a mistaken notion. White found that for the past twenty years, communications researchers in journalism schools have been primarily concerned with developing the necessary tools for their research.[14] In many instances they merely adapted the tools of research from other disciplines. A large number of studies of public newspaper content has indicated that newspaper articles devoted to school news give most space to student activities and athletics. A minor emphasis is upon the school program and the progress of students. Yet, there is strong evidence to indicate that although the subject of extracurricular affairs is highest in amounts of newspaper space, it is lowest in terms of parental interest. A possible explanation for this wide coverage is based upon the fact that the major purpose of the newspaper is to publish information and news. Generally, newspapers donate thousands of dollars worth of space free to public schools. Yet, one should not think of the treatment of school news as charity to the schools, for school news is also included wishfully to increase circulation.

[13] *Ibid.*, p. 83.
[14] David M. White, "The Role of Journalism Education in Mass Communications Research," in *Communications Research and School Community Relations*, Cooperative Research Program of the Office of Education, and College of Education, Temple University, Philadelphia, 1965, pp. 55–56.

As a channel of communication the newspaper rates very high since it has such wide coverage and almost everyone reads at least one daily. The newspaper provides a convenient opportunity for administrators to make use of this agency to provide the public with information about schools. Working together, the newspaper and the school people have tremendous power to influence the thinking of people in a given locality.

Another technique which is very helpful in public relations is the radio. Since more than 98 percent of the American homes have at least one radio and since one or more persons in each listens to the radio 2 hours or more daily, wide coverage of school news can be expected. Up to 25 percent of the broadcasting time is spent free on "public service." These can be used to upgrade and inform the general public about school problems and issues. Schools generally get their share of this free time.

The field of television is much younger than radio or journalism, and its use is much more expensive than either. More than 85 percent of the homes have at least one television set. In the typical home the set is turned on for a total of 6 hours including day and evening. Television has the capacity to bring both programs and people into our homes. It has much to offer in public relations as well as in instruction. School personnel should work very closely with station managers to get the proper coverage for school news and programs. As a medium of communications, television has almost unlimited potential. At present we do not know enough about its effect to evaluate it properly.

RELATIONSHIPS WITH THE COMMUNITY

In order to understand the community, many factors need to be considered. The community surrounding the local secondary school has a large potential for influencing the character of education in the school. In order to understand community life, it is essential to comprehend the structure of the community. Structure is used here to mean all the necessary functions and their interrelations by which a local population maintains itself.

Community Groups

Within each community there are many groups interested in public education for various reasons. Some groups wish to study and support the school program; others seek to improve the schools or to defend them from unjustified attacks; and others seek only to find fault with the school. This latter group is more interested in lowering the tax rate, censoring the schools, and keeping the status quo, rather than in helping improve education.

Every community has organizations that are capable of giving some service in the development of school-community relations. Perhaps the smaller community may provide these groups with the opportunity for proportionally greater influence than the larger communities. In the larger areas, the great diversity and competition of outside interests tends to restrict the power of a single unit. Moehlman and Van Zwoll enumerate and describe the following organizations in terms of their interests, value, and means: [15] (1) civic, (2) cultural, (3) economic, (4) political, (5) professional, (6) social, (7) women's groups, and (8) welfare groups. Although these groups may not appear to be closely related to public schools, it is necessary for the school to study each organization and plan some way of interesting the group in public education.

Citizen's Advisory Committee

In some communities in America a rather high percentage of the total population is composed of nonparents, parents whose children have already graduated from school, or parents who send their children to private schools. Members of the latter group may even be opposed to public schools. It is obvious that a need exists for these people, as well as the parents of public school pupils, to have an understanding of the public schools and to communicate their thoughts to the local school officials. A group that seems to fulfill this need quite well is known as a "citizen's advisory committee," "lay advisory group," or other similar titles. A citizen's advisory committee is generally composed of representative citizens who are willing to give time, energy, and thought to advising the local school officials with regard to the schools. Its major functions have been defined by Sumption and Engstrom as follows: [16] (1) to aid in developing educational policy; (2) to aid in developing long-range plans; (3) to help in solving school-community problems; (4) to assist in evaluating the work of the school; and (5) to aid in maintaining two-way communication between community and school. In carrying out these functions, it should be borne in mind that this body has no legal authority to make policy, it can only make recommendations to school authorities. One of the greatest benefits that this group can make is in bringing together many nonparents and parents whose children have already completed school. Thus the administrator can obtain a view from citizens other than parents.

APPRAISING THE PROGRAM

One of the most difficult areas of the entire program is that of evaluation. The elements and activities of the public relations program should be appraised in the light of the objectives and purposes for which they

[15] Arthur B. Moehlman and James A. Van Zwoll, *School Public Relations*, Appleton-Century-Crofts, Inc., New York, 1957, pp. 416–426.
[16] Merle R. Sumption and Yvonne Engstrom, *School-Community Relations*, McGraw-Hill Book Company, New York, 1966, pp. 84–86.

were planned. Methods of evaluation include informal methods, evaluation in terms of general principles, opinion polls and surveys, checklists, and rating scales. These appraisal techniques have been used for a number of years. Yet, much research remains to be done before one is able to ascertain how effective any individual technique may be.

SUMMARY

Public relations is defined in a broad manner and includes all the functions and relationships that pertain in a two-way exchange of ideas between school and community that establish the basis for joint understanding. The purposes of public relations are conditioned by what the professional staff members think about education.

The need for public relations has been defined very clearly. Likewise, the significance of public relations is related to the fact that our schools are teaching children today who may become the adults and parents of tomorrow.

The modern principal will find that his work in the area will involve developing satisfactory relationships with the central office, organizing the program, using his individual contacts, developing a quality educational program, and providing general leadership for the school.

Among the more successful media are students, teachers, student activities, school visits, and the mass media such as newspapers, radio, and television.

The principal should understand the community groups, citizen's advisory groups, and program appraisal. He is the key figure in most of these operations.

SUGGESTED EXERCISES

1. Give five purposes of public relations that you feel would fit your own school.

2. Why should the secondary principal be concerned with public relations?

3. What can the principal do to enhance public relations?

4. Describe the principals you have known and the manner in which they met their responsibilities for public relations.

5. What new media can you think of that are helpful in telling the school story in addition to those mentioned in this chapter?

6. How do mass media differ from other media?

7. How are community groups related to public education?

8. How would you appraise your own program of public relations?

9. What implications for leadership can you see for a secondary principal in public relations?

SELECTED REFERENCES

DAPPER, GLORIA, *Public Relations for Educators,* The Macmillan Company, New York, 1964.

FOLK, CHRIS, "Interpreting the Secondary School," *The High School Journal,* vol. 58, pp. 257–261, January, 1965.

JONES, JAMES J., *School Public Relations,* The Center for Applied Research in Education, New York, 1966. '

—— AND IRVING W. STOUT, *School Public Relations: Issues and Cases,* G. P. Putnam's Sons, New York, 1960.

KINDRED, LESLIE W. (ed.), *Communications Research and School-Community Relations,* Cooperative Research Program of the Office of Education and College of Education, Temple University, Philadelphia, 1965.

SUMPTION, MERLE R., AND YVONNE ENGSTROM, *School-Community Relations: A New Approach,* McGraw-Hill Book Company, New York, 1966.

THELEN, HELEN, *Education and Human Quest,* Harper & Row, Publishers, Incorporated, New York, 1960.

CHAPTER *22*

EDUCATIONAL
RESEARCH | This chapter is addressed to the notion of
educational research and, by implication, the process of change. Anyone
who would be an educational leader must accept the responsibility for
knowledge of educational research and the related knowledge of the
process of change.

The recurring theme of leadership has pervaded this book. Alterna-
tively urging, advocating, inciting, soliciting, and exhorting secondary
administrators to accept the challenge of leadership, we have presented
many ideas which could make a real difference in the secondary classroom.

Another recurring theme is adaptability. It has been made clear that
secondary school administrators must accept the inevitability of the
change process. In many ways the modern conception of the secondary
school administrator lays a heavy stress upon his role as an agent for
change.

The contention is not that there is an inherent value in change per se,
but that the change is directed toward some improvement in the instructional program. Now the real question becomes, How do we know which

are desirable changes? Which of the many competing patterns of educational practice will furnish the greatest payoff in student learning? This is what educational research is all about, and this is what this chapter will be concerned with.

THE NATURE OF EDUCATIONAL RESEARCH

Underlying educational research, and indeed, every type of research, are three assumptions. These are the assumptions of *order, perfectability,* and *tentativeness*. Although the researcher tends to deal in matters capable of empirical testing, these assumptions remain essentially unprovable. In fact, for scientists, they become an Apostles Creed.

The Assumption of Order

The assumption of order says that phenomena are patterned. Rather than being random occurrences, the events which make up our real worlds, both physical and social, are caused by forces and events. This is similar to what Alfred North Whitehead calls "the inexpungable belief that every detailed occurrence can be correlated with its antecedents in a perfectly definite manner, exemplifying general principles." [1] The assumption of order requires believing that when Johnny refuses to do his homework in mathematics, there is some specific reason or a set of specific reasons why. This assumption requires believing that there is some general explanation for the fairly general tendency for adolescent youngsters to adopt a type of subculture of their own, complete with a particular language, a particular code of dress, and a particular code of social behavior.

One additional example of this assumption would be in the reasons why one community will give strong financial support to education while another will not. Researchers holding faith in the scientific method make the assumption that there is some systematic order and pattern to the amount of financial support a community is willing to give. To be sure, the order requires many variables to be explained, but the assumption of order claims that order is there, nonetheless.

The Assumption of Perfectability

The assumption of perfectability also lies deep in the heart of modern man. Some of its historical roots go back to the seventeenth and eighteenth centuries, and perhaps even pervade aspects of the Judaic-Christian ethic. The assumption of perfectability is what furnishes the motivation

[1] Alfred North Whitehead, *Science and the Modern World*, Mentor Books, The New American Library of World Literature, Inc., New York, 1948, p. 13.

for educational research. It assumes that things can be improved, if not perfected. It says that if only one can discover the order or pattern (assumption of order) he will be able to do something which will improve things. If one can manage to discover more about the conditions which foster academic learning, he will be able to subsequently make changes in the learning environment which make increased learning possible. It is this assumption which lies at the heart of many of the Anti-poverty Programs which were instituted with the Economic Opportunity Act of 1964 and the Elementary and Secondary Education Act of 1965. Under this assumption, poverty is not merely recognized, but it is boldly challenged as being capable of elimination.

Whether these dreams can be fulfilled remains to be seen. The point of significance here, though, is that the assumption of perfectability contends that major changes are possible. Even if this program fails in accomplishing its humanitarian objectives, the doctrine of perfectability would remain. It would only indicate that research had yet to uncover many more relevant variables.

It seems obvious that it is this great and hopeful assumption which continues to nourish the hearts of educators everywhere. There is a continuing search for better ways and means to accomplish educational goals for many reasons, not the least of which is the unyielding belief that improved ways and means can be found.

The Assumption of Tentativeness

The assumption of tentativeness holds that our present knowledge may be subject to dismissal at any time. It means that as methods are developed and proved effective, they are accepted as the best *for the time being*. Yet, there is no long-term allegiance. As long as the knowledge continues to serve adequately, it remains, but as soon as it begins to lose its effectiveness, it must give way to its younger competitor. The educational researcher accepts present knowledge as the best he has for the moment but considers it adequate only for the time being, and he goes on in his never-ending search for more and better knowledge.

The assumption of tentativeness has been a requirement in every branch of inquiry considered scientific. As fundamental as it is, it is probably the most difficult for the nonscientist to accept. Laymen understandably would choose to feel confident in their knowledge. Even scientists themselves are not exempt from the apparent human tendency to cling to the familiar, even when subsequent developments demonstrate its error. As difficult as it is, being a true researcher requires accepting the notion that, at best, present knowledge is only tentative. This is essential; otherwise the spirit of inquiry would be quenched every time some apparent answer was given to a problem.

TYPES OF RESEARCH

So far no effort has been made to define research; rather, the focus has centered on the unexpressed assumptions underlying research. Since this book is not a research treatise, an extended discussion of varying concepts of research will not be presented. What seems more important for those who administer schools is that they grasp the essential meaning of research.

Research is, pure and simple, a systematic way of securing answers to questions one is curious about. The secondary principal is curious about whether a system of electronic scheduling will really work in his school. A guidance counselor is curious about discovering predictive patterns of potential student dropouts. Research can provide answers to these and an infinite number of practical problems.

It is important to understand that although research provides useful (although tentative) answers to practical educational problems, it cannot provide answers to "should" questions. Research cannot answer whether a school should have two, three, or seven modern foreign languages in its curriculum offerings. This is a value choice. Research can provide answers to some related questions which may help make this decision. For example, survey research could determine how many and what languages are currently being offered in other schools. It could also determine which languages are being elected by what types of students. It might also be able to suggest whether all can be learned with equal difficulty, or it might be able to determine the advisability of students' learning more than one language. Therefore, research can provide important data which could be utilized in making the language decision, but it cannot make the decision itself. Research can determine what can be taught and how it can best be taught but never *whether* it should be taught.

Research is an attempt to describe reality. It does not attempt to dictate what the reality ought to be. Yet, for the educational leader, deciding what ought to be is often dependent upon knowing what is. Therefore, it is sometimes difficult to keep the division between the *is* and the *ought*.

Although research is often classified into different categories, there are two broad classifications: descriptive and experimental research. *Descriptive research is an attempt to describe accurately conditions and events.* It may focus on the past, as in the case of historical research, or it may focus on the present, and it is then called status or survey research. *Experimental research tries to determine what would or will happen if certain conditions are modified.* Suppose that a secondary principal becomes curious about the value of homework. He may devise a survey within his school to secure an accurate picture of present homework loads, types of assignments, and other important information. He may also secure comparative information from other schools concerning their policies and practices. All this would be considered descriptive research. But then, assume that he develops some idea (hypothesis) about the value of varying amounts and types of homework. He might devise an experiment in which he would set up matched groups of classes and then vary the treatment of each. That is, he may give no homework to some groups, little to others, and much more to others. He would attempt to measure factors which he considers important such as scores on achievement tests, attitude toward study, and amount of extra "free" reading done during the period of investigation. He would then test his hypotheses according to certain statistical requirements and thus be able to draw certain conclusions. These conclusions would be tentative, but at least he would have made an effort to reinforce his ideas about homework with something other than commonsense speculations.

Within these two broad categories are many kinds of research appropriate to education. A few of these will be considered below.

Survey Research

Although survey research is frequently not highly rated in research circles, it is of fundamental importance in education. Sophisticated researchers tend to pass over the value of survey research, feeling that it fails to contribute to new knowledge because it is limited to describing present or past conditions. While this is an inherent limitation of survey research, it remains the most widely used type of educational and social research. There are simply too many areas about which we do not yet have good descriptive studies.

Good provides three purposes and uses for descriptive surveys: [2]

1. To secure evidence concerning an existing situation or current condition
2. To identify standards or norms with which to compare present conditions in order to plan the next step
3. To determine how to make the next step (having determined where we are and where we wish to go)

Examples of large survey research studies are those conducted by the National Education Association. Published four times a year, these research bulletins contain summary statistical data on many facets of teaching and education. *The Bulletin of the National Association of Secondary-School Principals* often publishes reports of significant survey research. Inspection of *Dissertation Abstracts* will reveal a great number of theses which describe either past or present conditions.

[2] Carter V. Good, *Essentials of Educational Research*, Appleton-Century-Crofts, Inc., New York, 1966, p. 192.

The comprehensive school survey is an example of another kind of survey research frequently used in education. Generally conducted by a bureau of research or educational service bureau which is associated with a major university, these surveys have contributed a great deal to thousands of local school districts. Local school districts often contract with these survey research organizations in order to learn more about themselves. The researchers will determine present conditions and then, as a part of the contracted service, make recommendations for improvement.[3]

An example of well-done rigorous survey research would be Waldrip's "Image of the Spokane Teacher." [4] By means of a stratified random sample among 120 residents of greater Spokane, Washington, and utilizing an immediate-response opinionnaire with these respondents, Waldrip explored the current (at the time of the research, Spring, 1964) images held of teachers in comparison with images held of other professions. Among the several findings were that Spokane residents considered that teachers were underpaid, should be paid more, and made the greatest overall contribution to society. This type of survey research would provide valuable information for school boards and administrators in any community, particularly since several of the findings reject the commonly assumed stereotype of the American teacher.

Techniques of Survey Research

A detailed explanation of research techniques is beyond the scope of this book, but a few of the major techniques will be presented. A basic understanding of research techniques will aid the secondary school administrator in evaluating research reports. Even if he does not conduct research of his own, he will often be in the position of judging the merit of reported studies in professional journals and will often have opportunities to participate in some research projects.

The Questionnaire   The questionnaire has been the workhorse of educational and social research for many years. Teachers and administrators are frequently asked to fill out some questionnaire for somebody's research project. Questionnaires can be effective instruments for gathering certain kinds of data, or they can be so poorly constructed, administered, and analyzed that the conclusions drawn from them are worthless.

Questionnaires can be designed to gather structured information. For example, to the question of a person's marital status, the structured responses are single, married, separated, divorced, or widowed. Questionnaires can gather information which is less structured, such as the range

---

[3] The Temple University Educational Service Bureau conducted thirty school surveys during a recent 10-year period.

[4] Donald R. Waldrip, "Image of the Spokane Teacher," *Phi Delta Kappan*, vol. 47, no. 10, pp. 566–571, June, 1966.

of annual income reported. Other more open-ended responses can be secured by questions such as, "What do you think of the quality of education in this school?" or "What is the best thing about this school district?" If the respondents to these latter questions are not given definite answers to check, their answers are considered as a type of free response, requiring special treatment for analysis of data.

The development of a good questionnaire is a specialized task the complexity of which is frequently underestimated. It is most frequently underestimated by those untrained in the methodology of social science research. Errors can filter through from many sources. The reduction of the possibility of error is of prime importance in developing a good questionnaire. Anyone who has not had either suitable experience or formal training in questionnaire construction would profit from consulting a good resource book on research methodology.[5]

The Interview As with the technique of the questionnaire, there are many types of interviews. Good classifies interviews according to function, number of persons participating, length of contact, and respective roles assumed by interviewer and interviewee.[6] The interview has an advantage over the questionnaire in that the data gathering "instrument" is another human and, as such, is capable of gathering much more information than a questionnaire. This assumes that the instrument (interviewer) is capable and trained for his role. One limitation of the interview is its expense, which limits the size of the sample to be collected. The interview can be very useful for a school administrator in gathering certain types of survey data. Since the interview is a human face-to-face contact, it is a situation which school administrators are already trained to handle.

Observation A useful technique in survey research is observation. Very simply, observation consists of the systematic recording of some predetermined phenomenon. If a principal wishes to conduct a survey of the number of cars which come to school on a rainy day, he could simply assign someone the task of checking the number of cars which arrive at school between certain hours. The observation can be repeated over several times and then compared with figures obtained on fair weather days.

At a more complex level, an administrator could employ the observational technique in surveying the kinds of questions asked in class by his teachers. First, he would need to develop a question classification system. One way of classifying questions is whether they are factual, interpretative, or speculative. It would be then necessary to test the classification

---

[5] There are many good ones. One of long standing value is Claire Selltiz, Marie Jahoda, Morton Deutsch, and Stuart W. Cook, *Research Methods in Social Relations*, Holt, Rinehart and Winston, Inc., New York, 1961.
[6] Good, *op. cit.*, p. 231.

system to ensure that it is sufficiently inclusive, that is, that all possible questions can be classified according to the preestablished system. Finally, the administrator-researcher would establish definite periods for observing classes and classifying the types of questions asked. An observational record is then made from which summaries and conclusions could be drawn.

Observation is essential to all types of scientific research, from the simplest to the most complex. As a technique in educational research it has numerous uses.

Content Analysis Content analysis, as a technique of survey research, has often been applied to printed materials. It can be applied to verbal materials as well. Basically, the technique consists in counting the instances of certain types of material. Content analysis could be employed by a curriculum study group which wishes to examine sets of textbooks to determine the extent to which the illustrations portray interracial scenes, or they may wish to test the length of sentences or level of vocabulary. Content analysis can be used to investigate almost any topic or dimension contained in printed materials.

One use content analysis can be put to in educational research is to investigate editorial opinion contained in newspapers or magazines. Again, the period to be investigated would need to be defined, a system of classification of opinion developed, and the observations taken and recorded.

Content analysis would be appropriate in making a study of the types of educational items considered newsworthy by the local newspapers. This study might reveal that local papers seem to report primarily official board of education meetings and sports events to the virtual exclusion of news items relating to curriculum content and teaching itself.

Content analysis is a suitable technique to employ whenever a researcher wishes to survey some form of communication and to be able to back up his conclusions with quantitative information.

Experimental Research

Experimental research differs from survey research in that it attempts systematically to manipulate conditions of research. The researcher performs certain treatments on his subjects and then tests for observed changes in them. These changes are the presumed effects of the treatment. A teacher, for example, wants to experiment with programmed learning to see whether students will learn as well by this method as by conventional teacher presentation. His experiment may be to replace standard class instruction with programmed texts for a time, perhaps six weeks. At the conclusion of the period the teacher will test the test the students' knowledge in that subject. The test scores may be relatively high, and the researcher is delighted with his apparently successful experiment. However, such a trial could not qualify as a genuine experiment unless additional factors are taken into account. The stimulation of the novel approach of programmed learning may have spurred the students to greater than normal effort. The teacher's own enthusiasm may have been transmitted to the students (it usually is). What his trial fails to control are these and other variables which could have accounted for the high test performance. The test itself may be unreliable, or it may be simply a function of chance. In order to meet the test of experimental research, the trial must be designed in such a way as to control or hold constant these factors. Only then can valid inferences be drawn as to the probable effect of the programmed learning instruction.

Although the same measure of control of variables is rarely if ever achieved in the social sciences, the laboratory approach used so successfully in the physical sciences is the model that educational researchers emulate.

The use of the terms "dependent" and "independent" variables is universally accepted in educational research. *Independent variables* are those selected conditions, measurements, or qualities which the researcher systematically manipulates. Sometimes the independent variable is called the experimental variable since this is the item being experimentally altered. The *dependent* variable is the presumed effect of the experimental manipulation. In the programmed learning experiment above, the condition of instruction by programmed text would be the independent variable, while the test scores would be the dependent variable. As was pointed out, there needed to be recognition of several other independent variables.

The goal of experimental research is prediction. If it can be demonstrated that as the experimental variable is systematically modified, there always results a consistent change in the dependent variable, it can be concluded that there is a causal relationship between these variables. Note that we did not state that one causes the other, just that there is a relationship implying causality between them. This is an important distinction in scientific research. To cite the case in programmed learning again, even if this did enjoy a rigorous research design which attempted to account for many other possible sources of influence, a positive association between test scores and programmed learning would not *prove* that the results were caused by the use of the programmed text. Although strong inferences could be made, there is no proof. Proof generally lies beyond the capability of educational research.

Experimental research worthy of the name demands rigorous design. Research design is a special skill not ordinarily acquired by teachers in training. Training programs for the principalship usually contain only a minimum of attention to the matter of research design. An introductory course in descriptive statistics provides the starting point for research design but in itself is not sufficient. Additional work in research design is needed. For these reasons it is likely that neither teachers nor conventionally trained principals will be sufficiently trained in research design to be able to conduct experimental research which can stand the tests of rigor.

For the advancement of good educational research, it would be desirable if principals would acquire the necessary training in research methodology, statistics, and design. As more secondary principals achieve the doctorate, they will be more competent in research design. However, what is more important is that the secondary principal who lacks this competency recognize his inadequacy.

The principal who recognizes his inadequacy in research would not prohibit experiments similar to the one on programmed learning. It simply means that he realizes that what the teacher has done is a simple pragmatic trial, rather than a piece of experimental research. As long as he treats it in this fashion and resists the temptation to draw conclusions from such a study, it can be defended.

Education has a great need for more experimental research. It has an equal need for widespread recognition that much of the reported journal research does not meet the standards necessary for experimental research and that any suggested conclusions drawn on the basis of such studies must be considered highly tentative.

DIFFERENTIAL ROLES IN EDUCATIONAL RESEARCH AND CHANGE

Basic to the process of educational research and change is the notion that different roles are performed by different people. Generally those doing most of the research, that is, the university professors, are not in positions where they can apply their findings. Even if they were working directly in public school systems, it is unlikely that they would be able to apply their research findings directly. At the level of practice, teachers and administrators constantly seek improvements in present practice and answers to persistent problems. They may turn to research for answers. More often than not, they are disappointed since research rarely has answers to their questions; and when it does, more often than not, the answers are contradictory. What the teachers and principals seek is a practical (and preferably observable) demonstration that the new practice is successful. Even if the new practice is successful, the local school system will need to adapt it to fit its own situation.

Differential Roles

To implement research in education, there is a need for at least four roles. Historically the *research* role has been performed by the university. It functions to serve as the producer of new knowledge. In order that the knowledge generated by the research finds its way into classrooms, the *dissemination* process must occur. Professional journals and educational conferences are frequently devoted to this function. The third essential function is that of *consumer-evaluator*. Educational leaders become consumers of research and attempt to make their own evaluations of the findings within their own situations. The fourth role is that of *developer*. The developer actually puts an idea or technique into practice. The developer is most often the building administrator and teacher.

The Secondary Principal's Role in Educational Research and Change

Chapter 10 of this book, in outlining the principal's leadership responsibilities, called for the principal to be both a producer and a consumer of research. If a principal is to be a producer of research, he must be trained as a researcher. This type of training usually requires a doctorate. A doctorate is not necessary to enable one to cooperate with others in the school district and serve on a research team which becomes a producer of research.

The secondary administrator can also participate in the dissemination phase of research. Editors of professional journals are often eager to secure reports from practicing principals on new developments which they have tried. Professional writing requires a great deal of time, but it is one way of research dissemination and also is an excellent means to attain professional recognition.

The consumer-evaluator role is the one which the secondary administrator most easily assumes. The need for the consumer-evaluator role is critical. According to Ianni, "that there exists an information gap between researcher and schoolman is unquestionable." He calls for greater involvement by the educational practitioner.[7] The alert and professionally trained secondary principal can make a contribution by attempting to close this gap as he sees it within his own school.

The principal becomes a consumer of research by reading professional journals. Here some selectivity becomes necessary. Of the hundreds of educational journals, some are more highly research oriented than others. In order to be an intelligent consumer of research, a certain amount of technical knowledge is necessary. When the principal reads a research finding stating that differences between two groups were "significant at

[7] Francis A. J. Ianni, "Research and Experimentation in Education," *Phi Delta Kappan*, vol. 46, no. 10, p. 489, June, 1965.

the .05 level of confidence," he needs to understand that the statistical concept of significance relates to the probability of chance occurrence and has no direct relationship to "significance" as meaning "highly important." Statistically significant relationships can provide spurious linkage of unimportant events or conditions.

The evaluator portion of the consumer-evaluator role is directed toward assessing the worthwhileness of research findings as related to his own school situation. This is not to suggest that the principal can judge the quality of the research from the methodological and design point of view. The principal can and indeed should evaluate a great deal of research by testing its applicability to his school. What he really needs to do after consuming a research report is to sit back and ponder its implications for practice. If, for example, the principal reads a well-done piece of research on the relationship between grouping procedures and grading practices, it might cause him to reflect upon his own grouping and grading procedures. He may wish to summarize the report at the next faculty meeting to stimulate thinking.

In judging the worthwhileness of educational research, the administrator needs to be wary of the "Hawthorne effect." Hawthorne effect is the name given to the widely held finding that there is a stimulating effect on human subjects when they know that they are engaged in a new or experimental program. The term has been in vogue for the past few years, but its origin lies in the 1930s, with the publishing of *Management and the Worker* by F. J. Roethlisberger and W. J. Dickson.[8] This monumental work of over 600 pages detailed a series of industrial experiments carried out at the Hawthorne plant of the Western Electric Company between 1927 and 1932. The experiments were too many and varied to go into detail here, but they dealt generally with a hypothesized relationship between working conditions and productivity. After several years of experimentation which resulted in contradictory findings, the researchers finally realized that what was probably most significant among the working conditions relating to productivity was the previously unnoticed factor that the experimental group of workers were responding to the powerful stimulus of being singled out and identified as special and experimental. This seems so obvious and commonsense that one marvels that it took industrial managers and university professors much time and money to discover this basic truth. Yet the same phenomenon is often ignored in educational research. Untrained researchers, full of hope for an educational innovation, may joyously but erroneously conclude the superiority of the innovation, when a close scrutiny may reveal that the powerful Hawthorne effect has been uncontrolled.

[8] F. J. Roethlisberger and W. J. Dickson, *Management and the Worker*, Harvard University Press, Cambridge, Mass., 1939.

For the secondary administrator, the implication is not that he should refrain from soliciting the eager support of his teachers for some innovation, but that when it comes to evaluating the innovation, the administrator must not be afraid to admit that the results may be contaminated unless a possible Hawthorne effect has been accounted for in the research design.

The secondary administrator becomes involved in the developer role as he actually implements some new program or practice which has come through the research process. It could be a change of curriculum content, or it could be an alternative method of assigning lunch duty. Only as the administrator engages in the developer role does he bridge the information gap. What counts, after all, is what actually gets to the level of classroom practice.

RESEARCH ORGANIZATIONS

Educational research emanates from diverse organizations. Some organizations are exclusively research organizations, while others include research as an incidental or supplemental function. It is useful to be aware of types of organizations and the research capabilities they offer.

The Universities

Traditionally, research has been one of the major functions of the university. Educational research has sprung primarily from those colleges of education located within the structure of a major university. In order to produce any significant quantity of educational research, a college of education must offer graduate programs. While some worthwhile educational research is conducted at undergraduate teachers colleges, it is less likely to flourish at these institutions. Educational or any other type of research requires professors with time for research, adequate library resources, graduate students, and the stimulation of a research-oriented environment not often found in a college whose mission is primarily teaching.

Educational research at the university level has suffered from common maladies. Rarely are research efforts coordinated. University research is more likely to depend upon an individual professor's particular interest rather than upon any institutional efforts directed into common channels. Even at the best universities, the quality of educational research has often come under sharp attack.[9]

There is also the important problem of dissemination of the universities' research findings. Relatively few of the nation's research bureaus

9 James D. Koerner, *The Miseducation of American Teachers*, Houghton Mifflin Company, Boston, 1963, 360 pp.

which are attached to universities issue regular publications for dissemination.[10]

State Departments of Education

State departments of education generally staff a research bureau.[11] While some have made important contributions to education, most of their research efforts have gone into data collection. State education research offices collect and maintain many records on education within the state. One example of a large and well-designed research study would be the Quality Measurement Project conducted over a period of several years by the New York State Education Department. This project sampled the state, attempting to isolate factors of quality within individual school districts.

State departments, in addition to conducting research of their own, will often offer consultant services to school districts wishing to initiate studies of their own.

The U.S. Office of Education

The U.S. Office of Education, headed by a federal commissioner and operating as one arm of the Department of Health, Education and Welfare, gathers a large quantity of educational information and conducts research. The U.S. Office of Education, particularly through its Cooperative Research Program, has provided a stimulus for educational research within the universities by furnishing financial support for approved projects. An excellent example of this would be the National Principalship Study initiated by Neal Gross at Harvard University in 1958. The Cooperative Research Program made a series of grants for this nationwide study of the principalship. Data were secured from principals and teachers in forty-one large American cities.[12] These studies investigated several dimensions of the principalship; among them were staff leadership, background differences in principals, role conflict in the principalship, and career aspirations. Thus, the U.S. Office not only conducts research of its own but provides the stimulus for other research.

Professional Organizations

One of the hallmarks of a profession is that it develops a specialized literature of its own and is committed to the idea of continual advance-

---

[10] Chester W. Harris (ed.), *Encyclopedia of Educational Research*, 3d ed., The Macmillan Company, New York, 1960, p. 1157.
[11] *Ibid.*
[12] Two publications growing out of these studies are Neal Gross and Robert E. Herriott, *Staff Leadership in Public Schools*, John Wiley & Sons, Inc., New York, 1965; and Robert E. Herriott and Nancy Hoyt St. John, *Social Class and the Urban School*, John Wiley & Sons, Inc., New York, 1966.

ment of its knowledge.[13] Considering the secondary principalship as a specialized profession, there are several organizations which institute and furnish significant research reports.

Most appropriate for the secondary principal is *The Bulletin of the National Association of Secondary-School Principals.* In addition to articles of particular interest to secondary administrators, the bulletin frequently contains reports of significant research.

The *Phi Delta Kappan,* the monthly journal of the professional fraternity for men in positions of educational leadership, contains summaries of research. Since one of its purposes is the promotion of research, Phi Delta Kappa has been identified as having made consistent and signal contributions to educational research.

For research in the field of educational administration itself, the principal will find well done research reports in the *Educational Administration Quarterly.* A principal would find, for example, the report "Nonverbal Behavior" by Lipham and Francke worth his reading time.[14] This exploratory study of forty-two principals sought to observe their nonverbal behavior manifested during the investigator's interview. Later this sample was classified on the basis of those principals whom the central office considered promotable as compared with the nonpromotables. In comparison with nonpromotables the promotables were more likely to greet the interviewer with a handshake, less often conducted the interview from behind their desks, were more concerned for visitor's comfort, and were more likely to provide the interviewer with a tour of the school.

Regional Educational Laboratories

What may become the greatest breakthrough in educational research occurred in the spring of 1966, when twelve regional laboratories were funded by the U.S. Office of Education from funds from the Elementary and Secondary Education Act. Geographically dispersed throughout the United States, these regional laboratories hold the potential for overcoming some of the persistent drawbacks to education research.[15] The first of these problems is a lack of adequate financing for education research; and a second is lack of effective dissemination of existing research. The regional laboratories can make giant steps in reducing these chronic difficulties.[16]

A regional laboratory is a consortium of varying institutions. Sponsor-

13 American Association of School Administrators, "Profession Defined," in M. Chester Nolte ed.), *An Introduction to School Administration: Selected Readings,* The Macmillan Company, New York, 1966, p. 302.
14 James M. Lipham and Donald C. Francke, "Non-verbal Behavior of Administrators," *Educational Administration Quarterly,* vol. 2, no. 2, pp. 101–109, Spring, 1966.
15 As of 1968, there were twenty regional laboratories blanketing the United States.
16 Hendrik D. Gideonse, "The National Program of Educational Laboratories," *Phi Delta Kappan,* vol. 57, no. 3, pp. 130–133, November, 1965.

ing institutions may include universities, school districts, muncipalities, industrial organizations, and nonprofit foundations. Laboratories concern themselves with conducting basic research relating to the field of education, the development of applied research, and dissemination of research. A preliminary appraisal of these laboratories suggests that their establishment may turn out to be one of the greatest forward steps taken in many years.[17]

These laboratories will provide many secondary principals with increasing opportunities to participate in research which they will find directly useful to their own school situations.

SUMMARY

From the secondary administrator's vantage point, a major portion of his entire job is devoted to the process of bringing about educational change. Knowledge of how to bring about desirable changes probably constitutes, in the final analysis, one of the criteria of administrative effectiveness. Being able to know the difference between good and poor changes constitutes the subject of educational research.

The educational researcher must accept the assumptions of order, perfectability, and tentativeness. Order provides the researcher with the security of believing that there is something systematic to be discovered. Perfectability furnishes the motivation that things can be improved; and tentativeness keeps the researcher from acquiring an inflated opinion of his new-found knowledge.

Education research can only answer certain kinds of questions. It can suggest better ways of teaching subject matter, but it cannot answer the question whether certain subjects should be taught. These considerations remain outside research.

Education research has depended and still depends primarily upon survey research which seeks to furnish valid descriptions of present practice. Experimental research will become increasingly significant, particularly as more sophisticated research tools are developed and as solid educational concepts become operational.

As a special process, education research requires four roles in order to fulfill its promise of contributing to educational change. There is the producer role, the dissemination role, the evaluator role, and the developer role. During the course of his professional career the secondary administrator may find opportunities to combine several of these different research roles. It is probably as a developer, that is, one who is instrumental in implementing the results of research into classroom changes

[17] Richard I. Miller, "Regional Educational Laboratories," *Phi Delta Kappan*, vol. 58, no. 4, pp. 144–149, December, 1966.

and programs that the secondary administrator can make his most telling contribution.

SUGGESTED EXERCISES

1. Hold a class panel discussion built around the three major assumptions underlying educational research. One panelist can develop and extend the assumption of order, another, the assumption of perfectability, and a third, the assumption of tentativeness.

2. Make an inventory of research reports, classifying each by type, and noting the various data-gathering techniques employed.

3. Make a content analysis of the articles appearing in a professional journal during the course of one year.

4. Through discussion with class members or with a faculty group develop a listing of the three most significant educational questions in secondary education to which research has yet to produce a clear answer.

SELECTED REFERENCES

ABBOTT, MAX G., AND JOHN T. LOWELL (eds.), *Change Perspectives in Educational Administration,* Auburn University, Auburn, Ala., 1965, 88 pp.

BARNES, FRED P., *Research for the Practitioner in Education: The National Elementary Principal,* National Education Association, Washington, D.C., 1964, 141 pp.

BRICKELL, HENRY M., *Organizing New York State for Educational Change,* New York State Education Department, Albany, N.Y., 1961, 107 pp.

CARLSON, RICHARD O., *Adoption of Educational Innovations,* Center for the Advanced Study of Educational Administration, Eugene, Oreg., 1965, 84 pp.

———, ART GALLAHER, JR., MATTHEW B. MILES, ROLAND J. PELLEGRIN, AND EVERETT M. ROGERS, *Change Processes in the Public Schools,* Center for the Advanced Study of Educational Administration, Eugene, Oreg., 1965, 92 pp.

CULBERTSON, JACK A., AND STEPHEN P. HENCLEY (eds.), *Educational Research: New Perspectives,* The Interstate Printers and Publishers, Danville, Ill., 1963, 374 pp.

GOOD, CARTER V., *Essentials of Educational Research,* Appleton-Century-Crofts, Inc., New York, 1966, 429 pp.

HALPIN, ANDREW W., *Theory and Research in Administration,* The Macmillan Company, New York, 1966, 352 pp.

Research Studies in Education 1965, Phi Delta Kappa, Bloomington, Ind., 1966, 217 pp.

SELLTIZ, CLAIRE, MARIE JAHODA, MORTON DEUTSCH, AND STUART W. COOK, *Research Methods in Social Relations,* rev., 1-vol. ed. Holt, Rinehart and Winston, Inc., New York, 1961, 622 pp.

WHITEHEAD, ALFRED NORTH, *Science and the Modern World,* Mentor Books, New American Library of World Literature, New York, 1948, 212 pp.

WOODS, THOMAS E., *The Administration of Educational Innovation,* Bureau of Educational Research, University of Oregon, Eugene, Oreg., 1967, 61 pp.

INDEX